HORA

Satires II

with an Introduction, Translation and Commentary

by

Frances Muecke

Aris & Phillips - Warminster - England

British Library Cataloguing in Publication Data
A catalogue entry for this book is available from the
British Library

ISBNs   *cloth 0 85668 531 3*
         limp 0 85668 532 1
ISSN   *0953 7961*

reprinted with corrections 1997

TO MARGARET HUBBARD

TEACHER

Printed and published in England by Aris & Phillips Ltd, Teddington House, Warminster, Wiltshire, BA12 8PQ

Contents

Preface

Though still not as well-known as his first book, the second book of Horace's Satires is beginning to emerge from a period of comparative neglect. How influential, or representative, was Fraenkel's lack of enthusiasm for most of the book it is difficult to say. L.P. Wilkinson honestly confessed the barriers which he felt prevent us from enjoying the Satires as a whole: their difficulty, their moralising character, the width of their vocabulary ("unfamiliar words"), and the extent to which reading them with understanding depends upon a detailed knowledge of Roman social life and values.

It was these very aspects that attracted me to the Satires. Recently we have been reminded of the finesse and irony of Horace's handling of manners and morals. The variety of vocabulary and linguistic expression may be regarded as the key to the world of the Satires. A new wave of social historians is ready to do more than collect evidence of every-day life. My aim was to make the Satires available to readers with interests in such matters, while setting them in the contexts of Roman thought, the history of satire and the contemporary literary milieu.

A full synthesis was beyond the scope of this edition, as was meeting the challenge of writing a commentary less influenced by the agendas set by Lejay and Kiessling-Heinze. In seeking to respond to some extent to the scholar's need for an *aggiornamento*, I fear I have overburdened the student reader. On the other hand, one cannot easily predict what uses the many different kinds of modern student will have for an edition such as this.

A word on the translation. I side with the literalists, and have tried to produce a close, but intelligible version, representing, as far as was possible, Horace's supreme control of linguistic effect.

Two periods of study leave from University of Sydney, the first of which was spent in the congenial environment of Clare Hall, Cambridge, helped me to begin and complete this work. An emergency research grant enabled me to employ Yasmin Haskell and Nathan Bottomley as cheerful and patient research assistants. It is a pleasure to thank those who have given so generously of their time and knowledge and without whose contributions the completed work would have been infinitely poorer. Margaret Hubbard, Robin Nisbet and Nicholas Horsfall read the whole commentary, as did my father, Douglas Muecke. I have also received help and encouragement from Robin Bond, Peter G.McC. Brown, P. Michael Brown, Kathleen Coleman, Anne Freadman, David Konstan, Kevin Lee, and John Vallance. For many years my life has been enriched by the generous friendship and hospitality of Margaret Hubbard, and Gwynneth Matthews.

Frances Muecke   Sydney, March 1993

Bibliography

J.N. Adams, *The Latin Sexual Vocabulary* (London, 1982)

M. von Albrecht, *Römische Poesie* (Heidelberg, 1977)

W.S. Anderson, 'Horace's Siren (*Serm.* 2.3.14)', *CPh* 56 (1961), 105-8

    'Recent Work in Roman Satire (1962-68)', *CW* 63 (1970), 181-94; 199; 217-22

    Essays on Roman Satire (Princeton, 1982)

    'Ironic Preambles and Satiric Self-definition in Horace *Satire* 2.1', *PCP* 19 (1984), 35-42

J. André, *Apicius: L'art culinaire* (Paris, 1965)

    L'alimentation et la cuisine à Rome[2] (Paris, 1981)

J. Andreau, *La vie financière dans le monde romain: les métiers de manieurs d'argent* (BEFAR 265, Rome, 1987)

D. Armstrong, *Horace* (New Haven and London, 1989)

    '*Horatius Eques et Scriba*: Satires 1.6 and 2.7', *TAPhA* 116 (1986), 255-88

G. Arrighetti, *Epicuro Opere*[2] (Torino, 1973)

A.E. Astin, *Scipio Aemilianus* (Oxford, 1967)

R. Astbury, *M. Terentii Varronis Saturarum Menippearum fragmenta* (Leipzig, 1985)

B. Axelson, *Unpoetische Wörter: Ein Beitrag zur Kenntnis des lateinische Dichtersprache* (Lund, 1945)

R. J. Baker, 'Maecenas and Horace *Satires* II.8', *CJ* 83 (1988), 212-32

J.P.V.D. Balsdon, *Life and Leisure in Ancient Rome* (London, 1969)

A. Barbieri, 'A proposito della satira II, 6 di Orazio', *RAL* 31 (1976), 479-507

R.A. Bauman, *Lawyers in Roman Transitional Politics* (Munich, 1985)

C. Becker, *Das Spätwerk des Horaz* (Göttingen, 1963)

R. Bentley, *Q. Horatius Flaccus*[3] I, II (Berlin, 1869)

M.A. Bernstein, ' "O totiens servus": Saturnalia and Servitude in Augustan Rome', *Critical Inquiry* 13 (1987), 450-74

D. Bo, *Lexicon Horatianum* I, II (Hildesheim, 1965, 1966)

R.P. Bond, 'A discussion of various tensions in Horace, Satires 2.7', *Prudentia* 10 (1978), 85-98

    'The Characterization of Ofellus in Horace, *Satires* 2.2 and a Note on v.123', *Antichthon* 14 (1980), 112-126

    'The Characterisation of the Interlocutors in Horace *Satires* 2.3', *Prudentia* 19 (1987), 1-21

    'Dialectic, Eclectic and Myth (?) in Horace, *Satires* 2.6', *Antichthon* 19 (1985), 68-86

Smith Palmer Bovie *The Satires and Epistles of Horace* (Chicago, 1959)

K.R. Bradley, *Slaves and Masters in the Roman Empire. A Study in Social Control* (Oxford, 1987)

A. Bradshaw, 'Horace *in Sabinis*', in *Studies in Latin Literature and Roman History* V 1989 (Collection Latomus 206), 160-86

J.C. Bramble, *Persius and the Programmatic Satire* (Cambridge, 1974)

S.H. Braund, *Beyond Anger: A Study of Juvenal's Third Book of Satires* (Cambridge, 1988)

(ed.), *Satire and Society in Ancient Rome* (Exeter, 1989)

Roman Verse Satire Greece and Rome New Surveys in the Classics No. 23 (1992)

J.N. Bremmer and N.M. Horsfall, *Roman Myth and Mythography* (BICS Suppl. 52, London, 1987)

C.O. Brink, *Horace on Poetry: Prolegomena to the Literary Epistles* (Cambridge, 1963)

The 'Ars Poetica' (Cambridge, 1971)

Epistles Book II (Cambridge, 1982)

'On Reading a Horatian Satire: an interpretation of *Sermones* II 6', The Sixth Todd Memorial Lecture (Sydney, 1965), 3-19 = A.J. Dunston (ed.), *Essays on Roman Culture* (Toronto & Sarasota, 1976), 75-94

R.A. Brouwer, *Alexander Pope, The Poetry of Allusion* (Oxford, 1959)

R.P. Brown, *Lucretius on Love and Sex: DRN IV. 1030-1247* (Leiden, 1987)

P.A. Brunt, *Italian Manpower, 225 B.C. - A.D.14* (Oxford, 1971)

' "Amicitia" in the Late Roman Republic,' *PCPhS* N.S. 11 (1965), 1-20 = *The Crisis of the Roman Republic*, ed. R. Seager (Cambridge, 1969), 199-218, *The Fall of the Roman Republic and Related Essays* (Oxford, 1988), 351-81.

W.W. Buckland, *Slavery in Roman Law* (Cambridge, 1908)

J.-P. Cèbe, *La Caricature et la Parodie dans le monde romain antique des origines à Juvénal* (Paris, 1966)

Varron, Satires ménipées (Rome, 1972-)

E. Champlin, 'Creditur vulgo testamenta hominum speculum esse morum. Why the Romans made wills', *CPh* 84 (1989), 198-215

Final Judgments. Duty and Emotion in Roman Wills 200 B.C. - A.D. 250 (Berkeley, Los Angeles, Oxford, 1991)

F. Charpin, *Lucilius Satires I, II* (Paris, 1978, 1979)

R. Chevallier, *L'artiste, le collectionneur et le faussaire. Pour une sociologie de l'art romain* (Paris, 1991)

J. Christes, *Der frühe Lucilius* (Heidelberg, 1971)

C.J. Classen, 'Horace — a Cook?', *CQ* 28 (1978), 333-48

J.J. Clauss, 'Allusion and Structure in Horace *Satire* 2.1: The Callimachean Response', *TAPhA* 115 (1985), 197-206

J.V. Cody, *Horace and Callimachean Aesthetics* Collection Latomus 147 (Brussels, 1976)

M. Coffey, *Roman Satire²* (Bristol, 1989)

K.M. Coleman, *Statius Silvae IV* (Oxford, 1988)

M. Corbier, 'Idéologie et pratique de l'héritage (Ier s. av. J.-C. - IIe s. ap. J.-C.,' *Index Quaderni Camerti di Studi Romanistici* 13 (1988), 501-28.

E. Courtney, *A Commentary on the Satires of Juvenal* (London, 1980)

J.A. Crook, *The Law and Life of Rome* (London, 1967)

R.I. Curtis, *Garum and Salsamenta: Production and Commerce in Materia Medica* (Leiden, 1991)

A. Davidson, *Mediterranean Seafood²* (Harmondsworth, 1987)

J.H. D'Arms, *Commerce and Social Standing in Ancient Rome* (Cambr. Mass., 1981)

J. Diggle and F.R.D. Goodyear, *The Classical Papers of A.E. Housman*, 3 Vols. (Cambridge, 1972)

E. Doblhofer, *Die Augustuspanegyrik des Horaz in formalhistorischer Sicht* (Heidelberg, 1966)

K.J. Dover, *Greek Popular Morality in the time of Plato and Aristotle* (Oxford, 1974)

D.R. Dudley, *A History of Cynicism. From Diogenes to the 6th Century A.D.* (London, 1937)

I.M.Le M. DuQuesnay, 'Horace and Maecenas: The propaganda value of *Sermones* I', in T. Woodman and D. West (edd.), *Poetry and politics in the age of Augustus* (Cambridge, 1984), 19-58

A. Ernout - F. Thomas, *Syntaxe Latine*² (Paris, 1972)

H.B. Evans, 'Horace, *Satires* 2.7: Saturnalia and Satire', *CJ* 73 (1978), 307-12

E. Fantham, *Comparative Studies in Republican Latin Imagery* (Toronto and Buffalo, 1972)

M. I. Finley, *The Ancient Economy*² (London, 1985)

S. Fischer, '*Avaritia, luxuria* und *ambitio* in der Satire II.3 des Horaz', *Philologus* 127 (1983), 72-79.

G.C. Fiske, *Lucilius and Horace: a Study in the Classical Theory of Imitation* (Madison, 1920, reprinted Hildesheim, 1966)

T.E.S. Flintoff, 'Juvenal's Fourth Satire', *Papers of the Leeds International Latin Seminar* 6 (1990), 121-137

B. Flower, and E. Rosenbaum, *Apicius: The Roman Cookery Book* (London, 1958, reprinted 1974)

E. Fraenkel and others, *Festschrift Richard Reitzenstein* (Leipzig and Berlin, 1931)

E. Fraenkel, *Horace* (Oxford, 1957)
    Kleine Beiträge zur klassischen Philologie II (Rome, 1964)

K. Freudenburg, 'Horace's Satiric Program and the Language of Contemporary Theory in *Satires* 2.1', *AJPh* 111 (1990), 187-203

L. Friedländer, *Roman Life and Manners under the Early Empire*, English trans. of 7th ed. (London, 1908-13)

B. Frischer, *Shifting Paradigms. New Approaches to Horace's* Ars Poetica (Atlanta, Georgia, 1991)

E.N. Gardiner, *Athletics of the Ancient World* (Oxford, 1930, reprinted 1960)

P. Garnsey (ed.), *Non-Slave Labour in the Greco-Roman World* (Camb. Phil. Soc. Suppl. 6, 1980)

J. Glazewski, '*Plenus Vitae Conviva*: A Lucretian Concept in Horace's *Satires*', *CB* 47 (1971), 85-88

J.B. Gould, *The Philosophy of Chrysippus* (Leiden, 1970)

J. Gow, *Q. Horati Flacci Saturarum Liber I* (Cambridge, 1932), *Liber II* (Cambridge, 1926)

A.S. Gratwick, 'The satires of Ennius and Lucilius', in E.J. Kenney and W.V. Clausen (edd.), *The Cambridge History of Classical Literature II, Latin Literature* (Cambridge, 1982), 156-71

J. Griffin, *Latin Poets and Roman Life* (London, 1985)

J.G. Griffith, 'The Ending of Juvenal's first Satire and Lucilius, Book xxx', *Hermes* 98 (1970), 56-72

P. Grimal, *Les Jardins Romains*[2] (Paris, 1969)

A.R. Hands, *Charities and Social Aid in Greece and Rome* (London, 1968)

Jens S. Th. Hanssen, *Latin Diminutives: A Semantic Study* (Bergen, 1951)

R.A. Harvey, *A Commentary on Persius* (Leiden, 1981)

H.A. Harris, *Sport in Greece and Rome* (London, 1972)

G. Harrison, 'The Confessions of Lucilius (Horace *Sat.* 2.1.30-34): A Defense of Autobiographical Satire?', *CA* 6 (1987), 38-52

G. Hilgers, *Lateinische Gefässnamen* (Düsseldorf, 1969)

J.B. Hofmann, *Lateinische Umgangssprache*[3] (Heidelberg, 1951)

A. Holder, *Pomponi Porfyrionis Commentum in Q. Horatium Flaccum* (Innsbruck 1894, reprinted Hildesheim, 1967)

K. Hopkins, *Death and Renewal* (Cambridge, 1983)

N. Horsfall, *Cornelius Nepos: A selection, including the lives of Cato and Atticus* (Oxford, 1989)

M. Jeanneret, *A Feast of Words: Banquets and Table Talk in the Renaissance* Trans. J. Whiteley and E. Hughes (Cambridge, 1991)

H.D. Jocelyn, *The Tragedies of Ennius* (Cambridge, 1969)

H.R. Jolliffe, *The Critical Methods and Influence of Bentley's Horace* (Chicago, Illinois, 1939)

H.F. Jolowicz and B. Nicholas, *Historical Introduction to the Study of Roman Law*[3] (Cambridge, 1972)

O. Keller, *Pseudacron Scholia in Horatium Vetustiora* I, II (1902, 1904, reprinted Stuttgart, 1967)

E.J. Kenney, *The Ploughman's Lunch. Moretum: a Poem ascribed to Virgil* (Bristol, 1984)

J.F. Kindstrand, *Bion of Borysthenes* (Uppsala, 1976)

W. Kissell, 'Horaz 1936-1975: Eine Gesamtbibliographie', *ANRW* II 31.3 (Berlin/New York, 1981), 1403-1558

T. Kleberg, *Hôtels, restaurants et cabarets dans l'antiquité romaine* (Uppsala, 1957)

F. Klingner, *Horatius Opera*[3] (Leipzig, 1959)

U. Knoche, *Roman Satire* Trans. E.S. Ramage (Bloomington and London, 1975)

M. Labate, 'La satira di Orazio: morfologia di un genere irrequieto', in *Orazio, Satire* (Milan, 1981), 5-45

R. LaFleur, 'Horace and *Onomasti Komodein*: The Law of Satire', *ANRW* II 31.3 (Berlin/New York, 1981), 1790-1826

Paul B. Langford, *Horace's protean satire: Public life, ethics and literature in "Satires II"* (Diss. Princeton, 1988)

A. La Penna, *Orazio e la morale mondana europea* (Florence, 1969)

G. Lee and W. Barr, *The Satires of Persius* (Liverpool/New Hampshire, 1987)

A.D. Leeman, 'Rhetorical Status in Horace, *Serm.* 2,1', in B. Vickers (ed.), *Rhetoric Revalued* (Binghamton, N.Y., 1982), 159-63

W. Leich, *De Horatii in saturis sermone ludibundo* (Diss. Jena, 1910)

P. Lejay, *Oeuvres d'Horace: Satires* (Paris, 1911, reprinted Hildesheim, 1966)

S. Lilja, *The Treatment of Odours in the Poetry of Antiquity* (Helsinki-Helsingfors, 1972)

R.O.A.M. Lyne, *Ciris: A Poem attributed to Vergil* (Cambridge, 1978)

Words and the Poet. Characteristic Techniques of Style in Vergil's **Aeneid** (Oxford, 1989)

L'urbs: espace urbain et histoire (Ier s. ap. J.C.). Collection de l'Ecole française de Rome XVIII (Rome and Paris, 1987)

C.W. Macleod, Review of Michael Coffey, *Roman Satire, TLS* November 11, 1977, 1333
    Collected Essays (Oxford, 1982)
    Horace: The Epistles (Rome, 1986)

A. Maisack, *Das dialogische Element in der römische Satire* (Diss. Tübingen, 1949)

A.R. Mansbach, *'Captatio': Myth and Reality* (Diss. Princeton, 1982)

J. Marquardt, *Das Privatleben der Römer²* I, II (Leipzig, 1886)

J. Martin, *Symposion. Die Geschichte einer literarischen Form* (Paderborn, 1931, reprinted New York, 1968)

F. Marx, *C. Lucilii Carminum Reliquiae* I, II (Leipzig, 1902-5, reprinted Amsterdam, 1963)

R. Meiggs, *Trees and Timber in the Ancient Mediterranean World* (Oxford, 1982)

M.J. McGann, *Some Structural Devices in the Satires and Epistles of Horace* (B. Litt. thesis Oxford, 1954)
    Studies in Horace's First Book of Epistles Collection Latomus 100 (Brussels, 1969)
    "The Three Worlds of Horace's *Satires*', in C.D.N. Costa (ed.), *Horace* (London, 1973), 72-81.

J. Moles, 'Cynicism in Horace Epistles I', *Papers of the Liverpool Latin Seminar* 5 (1985), 33-60

O. Murray (ed.), *Sympotica* (Oxford, 1990)

J.-P. Néraudau, *Etre enfant à Rome* (Paris, 1984)

N.-O. Nilsson, *Metrische Stildifferenzen in den Satiren des Horaz* (Uppsala, 1952)

R.G.M. Nisbet, 'Horace's *Epodes* and History', in T. Woodman and D. West (edd.), *Poetry and politics in the age of Augustus* (Cambridge, 1984), 1-18

E. Norden, *Agnostos Theos: Untersuchungen zur Formgeschichte religiöser Rede* (Berlin, 1913, reprinted Stuttgart, 1956)

J.F. O'Connor, 'Horace's Cena Nasidieni and poetry's feast', *CJ* 86 (1990-1991), 23-34

M. O'Loughlin, *The Garlands of Repose* (Chicago and London, 1978)

A. Oltramare, *Les origines de la diatribe romaine* (Geneva, 1926)

G. Orelli - O. Baiter - W. Mewes, *Q. Horatius Flaccus⁴* II (Berlin, 1892)

A. Otto, *Die Sprichwörter und sprichwörtlichen Redensarten der Römer* (Leipzig, 1890)

W. Pabst, 'Zur Satire vom lächerlichen Mahl. Konstanz eines antiken Schemas durch Perspektiven Wechsel', *A&A* 32 (1986), 136-58

A. Palmer, *The Satires of Horace⁴* (London, 1891, reprinted 1964)

J. Perret, *Horace* (Trans. B. Humez) (New York University, 1964)

B.E. Perry, *Aesopica* (Urbana, 1952)
    Babrius and Phaedrus (London, Camb. Mass, 1965)

E.P. Phillips, *Greek Medicine* (London, 1973)

J. Pigeaud, *Folie et cures de la folie chez les médecins de l'antiquité gréco-romaine, la manie* (Paris, 1987)

S.B. Platner - T. Ashby, *A Topographical Dictionary of Ancient Rome* (London, 1929)

G. Pont, 'The Traditions of Classical Gastronomy', *Classicum* 17.1 (1991), 3-12

J.G.F. Powell, *Cicero: Cato Maior De Senectute* (Cambridge, 1988)

N. Purcell, 'Town in Country and Country in Town', in E.B. MacDougall, *Ancient Roman Villa Gardens* (Dumbarton Oaks Colloquia 10, 1987), 185-203
'Wine and Wealth in Ancient Italy', *JRS* 75 (1985), 1-19

K.A. Raaflaub and M. Toher (edd.), *Between Republic and Empire: Interpretations of Augustus and His Principate* (Berkeley, Los Angeles, Oxford, 1990)

E.S. Ramage, *Urbanitas: ancient sophistication and refinement* (Norman, Oklahoma, 1973)

E. Rawson, *Intellectual Life in the Late Roman Republic* (London, 1985)
Roman Culture and Society: Collected Essays (Oxford, 1991)

K.J. Reckford, 'Horace and Maecenas', *TAPhA* 90 (1959), 195-208

U. Reinelt, *Zur Kompositionseinheit des zweiten Satirenbuches des Horaz* (Diss. München, 1969)

M. Reinhold, *Marcus Agrippa, a biography* (Geneva/New York, 1933, reprinted 1965)
From Republic to Principate. An Historical Commentary on Cassius Dio's Roman History Books 49-52 (36-29 B.C.) (Atlanta, Georgia, 1988)

O. Ribbeck, *Kolax. Eine ethologische Studie* (Abh. der Königl. Sächs. Ges. d. Wiss. Phil.-Hist. Klasse 9 [Leipzig, 1884])

J.M. Rist, *Stoic Philosophy* (Cambridge, 1969)

M. Roberts, 'Horace *Satires* 2.5: Restrained Indignation', *AJPh* 105 (1984), 426-33

E. Roos, 'Die Person des Nasidienus bei Horatius', *Scripta minora Soc. Hum. Litt. Lundensis* 1958-1959, 3 (Lund, 1959), 3-16

H.J. Rose, *A Handbook of Greek Mythology*[6] (London 1928, reprinted 1972)

D.O. Ross, *Style and Tradition in Catullus* (Camb. Mass., 1969)

F. Ruckdeschel, *Archaismen und Vulgarismen in der Sprache des Horaz* (Erlangen, 1911, reprinted Hildesheim, 1972)

N. Rudd, 'Horace, *Sermones* II, I. A Poem of Transition', *Hermathena* 90 (1957), 47-53
The Satires of Horace (Cambridge, 1966)
The Satires of Horace and Persius (Harmondsworth, 1973)
Themes in Roman Satire (London, 1986)
Horace: Epistles Book II and Epistle to the Pisones ('Ars Poetica') (Cambridge, 1989)

R.P. Saller, *Personal Patronage under the Early Empire* (Cambridge, 1982)

K. Sallmann, 'Satirische Technik in Horaz' Erbschleichersatire (s. 2, 5)', *Hermes* 98 (1970), 178-203

E.T. Salmon, *Samnium and the Samnites* (Cambridge, 1967)

F.H. Sandbach, *The Stoics* (London, 1975)

J.E. Sandys, *A Companion to Latin Studies*[3] (Cambridge, 1925)

G. Scarpat, *Satira settima del libro secundo. Testo, Introduzione, Versione e Commento* (Brescia, 1969)

W. Schulze, *Zur Geschichte lateinischer Eigennamen* (Berlin, 1904)

H.H. Scullard, *Festivals and Ceremonies of the Roman Republic* (London, 1981)

O. Seel, 'Bemerkungen zu Horaz *sat.* 2,6', in *Verschlüsselte Gegenwart* (Stuttgart, 1972), 13-93

D.R. Shackleton Bailey, *Profile of Horace* (London, 1982)

L. R. Shero, 'The *Cena* in Roman Satire', *CPh* 18 (1923), 126-43

O. Skutsch, *The Annals of Quintus Ennius* (Oxford, 1985)

W.J. Slater (ed.), *Dining in a Classical Context* (Ann Arbor, 1991)

M.S. Smith, *Petronius Cena Trimalchionis* (Oxford, 1975)

F. Stack, *Pope and Horace: Studies in Imitation* (Cambridge, 1985)

H.-P. Stahl, 'Peinliche Erfahrung eines kleines Gottes: Horaz in seinen Satiren', *A&A* 20 (1974), 42-53

G. Stampacchia, 'Schiavitù e libertà nelle Satire di Orazio', *Index* 11 (1982), 193-219

H.P. Syndikus, *Die Lyrik des Horaz. Eine Interpretation der Oden* I, II (Darmstadt, 1972, 1973)

R. Tannahill, *Food in History* (Harmondsworth, 1988)

A. Tchernia, *Le vin de l'Italie romaine* (BEFAR 261, Rome, 1986)

A. Thill, *Alter ab illo: Recherches sur l'imitation dans la poésie personnelle à l'époque Augustéene* (Paris, 1979)

D'Arcy Wentworth Thompson, *A Glossary of Greek Fishes* (London, 1947)
 A Glossary of Greek Birds (London, 1936)

V.A. Tracy, '*Aut captantur aut captant'*, *Latomus* 39 (1980), 339-402

H. Tränkle, *Die Sprachkunst des Properz und die Tradition der lateinischen Dichtersprache* (*Hermes* Einzelschriften 15, Wiesbaden, 1960)

S. Treggiari, 'Sentiment and Property: Some Roman attitudes', in A. Parel and T. Flanagan (edd.) *Theories of Property Aristotle to the Present* (Waterloo, Ontario, 1979), 53-85

C.A. van Rooy, *Studies in Classical Satire and Related Literary Theory* (Leiden, 1966)

J. Väterlein, *Roma Ludens: Kinder und Erwachsene beim Speil im antiken Rom* (Amsterdam, 1976)

P. Veyne, *Le pain et le cirque. Sociologie historique d'un pluralisme politique* (Paris, 1976)

G. Ville, *La gladiature en Occident des origines à la mort de Domitien* (Rome, 1981)

F. Villeneuve, *Horace Satires* (Paris, 1951)

R. Vischer, *Das einfache Leben* (Göttingen, 1965)

A.Watson, *The Law of Persons in the later Roman Republic* (Oxford, 1967)
 The Law of Property in the later Roman Republic (Oxford, 1968)
 The Law of Succession in the later Roman Republic (Oxford, 1971)

D. West, *The Imagery and Poetry of Lucretius* (Edinburgh, 1969)
 'Of mice and men: Horace, *Satires* 2.6.77-117', in T. Woodman and D. West (edd.) *Quality and Pleasure in Latin Poetry* (Cambridge, 1974), 67-80.

E.C. Wickham, *The Works of Horace* I³, II (Oxford, 1896, 1891)

W. Wili, *Horaz und die augusteische Kultur* (Basel, 1948)

L.P. Wilkinson, *Horace and his Lyric Poetry*² (Cambridge, 1968)
 Golden Latin Artistry (Cambridge, 1963, reprinted 1985)

G. Williams, *Horace* Greece and Rome New Surveys in the Classics No. 6 (Oxford, 1972)
 Tradition and Originality (Oxford, 1968)

W. Wimmel, *Kallimachos in Rom* (*Hermes* Einzelschriften 16, Weisbaden, 1960)
 Zur Form der horazischen Diatribensatire (Frankfurt, 1962)

R. Winkes, *The Age of Augustus. The Rise of Imperial Ideology.* Archaeologia Transatlantica 5 (Louvain-la-Neuve, 1985)

C. Witke, *Latin Satire. The Structure of Persuasion* (Leiden, 1970)

T.P. Wiseman, *New Men in the Roman Senate 139 B.C. - A.D. 14* (Oxford, 1971)
   Roman Studies Literary and Historical (Liverpool/New Hampshire, 1987)

E.C. Woodcock, *A New Latin Syntax* (London, 1959, reprinted 1962)

T. Zielinski, *Horace et la société romain du temps d'Auguste* (Paris, 1938)

F. Zoccali, 'Parodia e Moralismo nella Satira II, 5 di Orazio', *Atti della Accademia Peloritani dei Pericolanti, Classe di Lettere Filosofia e Belle Arti* 55 (1979), 303-321

Introduction

1. HORACE IN THE LATE 30s B.C.

Horace's satires were composed in the politically uncertain and socially traumatic period between Philippi and the aftermath of the battle of Actium (41-29 B.C.). In 42 B.C. in the Philippi campaign Horace served as military tribune under Brutus against Antony and Caesar's heir, the young Octavian. In 31 B.C. he supported, with his words if not also with his presence, Octavian's victorious campaign against Antony. This is also the span of the *Epodes* (published about 30 B.C.). Actium, the great turning point, is given pride of place in the first *Epode*, a poem on Horace's commitment to Maecenas and his cause. If the political context of *Satires* Book 1 (published about 35 B.C.) is Octavian's consolidation of power in Italy and the war against Sextus Pompeius (defeated 36 B.C.), in Book 2 the battle of Actium has been won and Octavian's power is acknowledged as supreme (*Sat.* 2.1.11, *Caesaris invicti res*). Of references which can date the period of composition the latest is to 30 B.C. (*Sat.* 2.6.55f.), the earliest to 33 (*Sat.* 2.3.185, the aedileship of Agrippa).

The first half of the thirties saw Horace establishing himself, though not perhaps in the career for which his education had been preparing him. Pardoned after Philippi, he returned to Rome, and, though his father's lands at Venusia had been confiscated, he was able to purchase the not unimportant position of a treasury official (*scriba quaestorius*). The income from this would have enabled him to live comfortably and, if he could meet the required financial status, he would have been eligible for entry to the equestrian order. At the same time he was becoming recognised as a poet. Close friendships with Virgil and Varius developed, and these led, in 38 B.C., to an introduction to Maecenas, Octavian's influential organiser of public opinion.

Between Books 1 and 2 of the *Satires* the circumstances of Horace's life appear to change. In Book 1 friendship with Maecenas went hand in hand with involvement with a wider circle of literary friends (*Sat.* 1.10.81ff.), of whom only Fundanius, Varius and Viscus Thurinus are mentioned in the later collection (all in *Sat.* 2.8). 'Closer to the gods', Horace now seems a more confident, but more isolated figure. This may just be a function of his new *persona*, that of the detached observer, or the result of his giving less attention (for whatever reason) to the topic of his standing as a poet (but see *Sat.* 2.1). The purchase (with Maecenas's help) of the Sabine estate also makes a difference to the ethos of Book 2. The counterpoint of country and city life dominates two satires (2 and 6) and surfaces in two others (3 and 7). In *Sat.* 2.6 the villa and its landscape begin to take on their emblematic significance for Horace's conception of his life.

In spite of the political turmoil the early thirties were a period of extraordinary literary creativity. Of the works referred to in the list of approved contemporaries at *Sat.* 1.10.40ff., Virgil's *Eclogues* (dating from 42 B.C.) is the only one that has survived. In the exquisiteness of their artistry and their mastery of the principles of Hellenistic poetry these poems set a new agenda for Latin poetry. In Virgil's *Georgics* (completed 29 B.C.?) Callimacheanism is combined with a complex moral response to the contemporary world. However different in scope and focus were Horace's *Satires* he shared Virgil's poetic ideals.

Horace's life: for a brief summary N-H 1970, xxvii, discussed more fully by Fraenkel 1957, 1-23; in the period of the satires, Armstrong 1989, 26-67; his status at the time of the satires, Armstrong 1986, 255-88; the political itinerary of the *Epodes*, Nisbet, of *Satires* 1, DuQuesnay; friendship with Maecenas, Reckford, E. Lefèvre, 'Horaz und Maecenas', *ANRW* II.31.3 (1981), 1987-2029, DuQuesnay, 24-7; Virgil's Callimacheanism, W.V. Clausen, 'Callimachus and Latin Poetry', *GRBS* 5 (1964), 181-96; influence of *Eclogues*, C.A. van Rooy, '*Imitatio* of Vergil, *Eclogues* in Horace, *Satires* book I', *AClass* 16 (1973), 69-88.

2. SATIRE—AN ANTI-GENRE?

Modern theorists do not regard satire as a genre, but as a mode not confined to any one generic form. But in Roman literature verse satire had a fixed form, arrived at after some early experiments, collections in diverse metres dealing with a variety of subjects (e.g. Ennius's *Saturae*). From Lucilius on (Books 30, 1-21), verse satire used the hexameter, originally the metre of epic.

For this fixing of the metrical form and for his aggressive criticism of individuals, Lucilius was regarded by his followers as the inventor of the genre. His thirty books of satires were composed from about 130 B.C. and demonstrate an intense engagement with the politics and culture of his period. Given his social standing, there is nothing surprising about such an involvement. He was an *eques* ('knight') from an aristocratic and wealthy Campanian family, and he became the friend of Scipio Aemilianus (185/4-129 B.C.), a leading general and politician, as well as patron of literature with his own intellectual interests. What was original about Lucilius was his choice of an informal way of writing largely built upon his and his contemporaries' conversations.

In the generation before Horace's the polymath M. Terentius Varro introduced another kind of satiric writing to Rome. His *Menippean Satires*, imitations of the work of the Cynic philosopher Menippus of Gadara (first half of the third century B.C.), were in prose, with the occasional insertion of verse passages in diverse metres. Of the 150 books he is recorded as having written, only titles and small fragments survive. Though Horace does not refer to Varro as a predecessor, they have a great deal in common, especially their use of the different forms of dialogue, their interest in food and the symposiac setting, and the ethical criticism of current social practices. Seneca's *Apocolocyntosis* is a later Menippean satire in Varro's manner, a kind which may also have contributed to Petronius's *Satyricon*. In the second century A.D. Lucian revived Menippus in Greek.

The history of satire at Rome illustrates the diversity which still characterises this kind of writing. The word *satura* itself initially pointed to this diversity, according to the etymological explanations preserved by Diomedes, a late grammarian (*GLK* I 485). The derivations he gives are: 1) from the (Greek) satyrs, 2) from (*lanx*) *satura*, a dish full of many different first-fruits offered to the gods, 3) from a kind of sausage called *satura*, stuffed with many ingredients, and 4) from the legal term *per saturam*, of a law containing mixed provisions. Of these, the second seems most likely to be the oldest, the first being etymologically impossible and the last an extension of the meaning 'medley'. In spite of the later shift in meaning to 'abusive verse' (see *Sat.* 2.1.1), the notion of mixture or medley is one of the keys to an understanding of the genre, which combines a wide variety of subjects with a range of styles and types of language.

Another important aspect of Roman verse satire is captured by the term *Sermones* ('conversations', 'chats'), Horace's title for his satires, following Lucilius (e.g. 1039W). Satire is talk in verse, Horace's word for their style being *pedester* ('walking'). They go on foot, on the ground, in contrast to the poetic flight of the higher genres (see *Sat.* 1.4.39-62). Much follows from this conception of satire.

Satire, like conversation, is informal and loosely structured. It moves easily from one topic to another. It can be prolix, as was Lucilius (called 'loquacious', *Sat.* 1.4.12). It is talk to someone, either to an addressee imagined as present and able to respond, or between partners in a staged dialogue. It aims to entertain and amuse as well as to inform and reform. The topics of the talk are various as are the forms they take (monologue, dialogue, lecture, letter). Like gossip, satire is interested in what is happening in the streets, market-places, courtrooms, theatres, arcades, dining-rooms and bedrooms of the city. Against such back-drops, as if on a stage, people act out their lives, observed and recorded by the satirist.

It is not possible for the satirist just to record, however, and here his trouble starts. Mentioning a name, singling someone out, depicting a character — all this is inevitably read as meaning something. The point will be assumed to be a critical point. Hence arise both the traditional definition of satire as 'a poem composed to censure people's vices' (Diomedes *GLK* I 485) and the traditional defence on the grounds that the victims deserve exposure. However one-sided in relation to the actual practices of the Roman satirists it may be, this notion of satire is the one that links subsequent writers to the inventor of the genre, Lucilius, who 'scoured the city with plenty of salt' (*Sat.* 1.10.4f.) and 'arraigned the people's leaders and the people tribe by tribe' (*Sat.* 2.1.69).

The analogy with conversation illuminates only one facet of the satiric style, privileging the illusion of informality and immediacy at the expense of the range and variety of linguistic material drawn upon. The distinctive conversational approach of Horace's satires is an effect produced by considerable artistic skill, as the poet himself indicates. Though at times he may deny that satire is 'poetry', at others he criticises Lucilius for not working at his writing (*Sat.* 1.4.12f.) and he selects 'writing' as the way he himself can improve the genre (*Sat.* 1.10.47), setting out his stylistic requirements of it: readability, control and variety of tone and subtlety of approach (*Sat.* 1.10.9ff.). While preserving the Lucilian sense of casual organisation, Horace unifies his themes and underpins the connections of thought by verbal repetition and patterns of formal symmetry.

If the satires of Book 2 differ from some of those of Book 1 in having a more obvious unity of theme they still combine within them a diverse range of anecdotes and examples (e.g. *Sat.* 2.3). These bring with them linguistic difference since they provide the opportunity to incorporate and exploit pre-formed literary and non-literary material. Horace's satires abound in quotations, imitations and parodies of other poets and literary genres. Linguistic formulae from other sources — the professions, popular language with its sayings and proverbs — are also deployed with wit to add precision or colour to a context. The right word, be it technical, colloquial or metaphorical, brings a subject into sharp focus and makes for particularity.

Various factors combine to put satire at the bottom of the hierarchy of genres: its affiliations with prose, the every-day material it treats, its use of obscene, colloquial and technical words, its comic qualities of irony, wit and irreverence. Its practitioners exploited this position as its strength. The rules of the genre were not of exclusion but of inclusion. As it claimed the freedom critically to depict the varieties of human behaviour, so it could, indeed had to, draw parasitically or parodically on the full range of genres and discourses to construct its own vision of the world.

Lucilius (180 or 168/7-102/1 B.C.), see Braund 1992, 10-15, Coffey, 35-62, Rudd 1966, 86-131, Gratwick, 160-171, Henderson in Braund 1989, 99-102; Varro see Coffey, 149-64; etymology of *satura*, see Braund 1992, 6-7, Coffey, 3-23; variety, C.J. Classen, 'Satire — The Elusive Genre', *SO* 63 (1988), 95-121; urban genre, M. Hodgart, *Satire* (London, 1969), 129, A. Kernan, *The Cankered Muse: Satire of the English Renaissance* (New Haven, 1959), 7-14; "unity in diversity", Brink 1982, 488-95, 513-22, description and wit, 460-61, associative techniques of conversation, Williams 1972, 17-18, unifying structures, D. Armstrong, 'Horace, *Satires* I, 1-3: A Structural Study', *Arion* 3 (1964), 86-96; anecdotes, Fraenkel 1957, 143 n.1, McGann 1954; linguistic and metrical virtuosity, Coffey, 93-96; generic inclusiveness, Braund 1992, 3-4.

3. THE SATIRIC SELF-PORTRAIT

Lucilius's copious works filled thirty books of which about 1300 lines survive in extracts rarely exceeding two or three lines. From these we can get an idea of the range of his interests. But in attempting to reconstruct Lucilius we must remember that we lack the discursive context of these fragments and that we know relatively little about the poet's socio-cultural milieu.

The subjects of his satires range from poetry, grammar and spelling to politics, military life, a journey, a gladiators' fight, dinner-parties, food and sex. Our fragments reflect the later grammarians' interest in linguistic oddities and so convey at least the lively, if inelegant, particularity of his vocabulary.

Besides the freedom of speech for which he praised Lucilius, Horace singles out the autobiographical approach as a significant feature of his predecessor:

> In the old days, he entrusted his secrets to his books, as though to faithful friends, having no other outlet whether things had gone well or ill. The result is that the old man's whole life is open to view as if sketched on a votive tablet. (*Sat.* 2.1.30-34)

Lucilius is always a presence in his satire, relating his experiences, expressing his reactions and prejudices, and advocating his hobby-horses. He depicts himself and others in ordinary scenes and settings, in a kind of writing in which the poet and his readers connect with each other within the work. For this type of autobiographical approach

Horace uses an image drawn from painting to make us aware that the expression of the man's natural authenticity in his writing is a matter of art. The self is revealed in a self-portrait, shaped more or less well, and for a rhetorical purpose. Lucilius's *persona* (mask) was not simple, however. As speaker, he assumes different roles for different purposes, appearing not only as himself, but as teacher and preacher, clown, or urbane raconteur. This versatility in self-presentation was as important an influence on Horace as the impression of candour.

In Horace's satires there is a fascinating interplay between the different roles the poet assumes. The satiric 'speaker', especially the speaker of the monologues in Book 1, is not to be identified with the author. This is a voice constructed from the didactic-philosophical tradition, though not simply a reproduction of it. At the same time in examples, anecdotes and 'autobiographical' episodes, the satires present fragmentary visions of 'Horace' the man, as he shows himself or is seen by others to behave. This 'Horace' has a recognisable identity but is a bundle of contradictions, who nevertheless aspires to a consistent moral ideal, from which he reveals himself occasionally falling short. His failure to practise what he preaches does not necessarily devalue his ethical vision.

Modern scholars' disagreements on what the satires are about spring from the ways they understand this ironic, mock-humble self-presentation. Is Horace's irony a sign of intellectual freedom or is his wit merely harmless, a disguise of temporising servility? Do we share his vision of civilised urbanity or do we regard it as an insidious tranquilliser? For some, Horace is 'above all a poet of personal ethos and ethics' (Brink 1982, 539), concerned to fashion a way of writing that bears on his own and his fellows' problems of living; for others, his story 'reinforces the values and exclusivity' (Braund 1992, 22) of Maecenas's circle, an élite group. However apolitical they seem, it is argued, the satires are at the service of partisan politics and a particular political programme. However, the real question is not whether the satires are ethical or political (for all texts can be seen as both political and ethical in some way), but how? What kind of community do they constitute, with what values, and do those values indeed correspond to an Augustan political programme?

Horace *Sat.* 2.1.30-34: simile involves hint of naive artistry, Anderson 1982, 30-32, Horace also claiming this low status for himself, Harrison, 38-52; autobiographical approach, Harrison, 38-40; *persona* or *personae* of Horace in the satires, K.J. Reckford, *Horace* (New York, 1969), 35, Anderson 1982, 28-30, J.F.G. Zetzel, 'Horace's *Liber Sermonum*: The Structure of Ambiguity', *Arethusa* 13 (1980), 59-77; unity of ethos, Reinelt; interesting treatment of 18th century interpretations of Horace, Stack, 3-17; assessments of Horace, Braund 1992, 22, Henderson in Braund 1989, 102-3; G. Williams, 'Augustan Literary Patronage', in Raaflaub and Toher, 258-75, draws the distinction between personal panegyric and support of a programme; ethical Horace, Brouwer, 163-187, Macleod 1983, 280-91; apolitical, Rudd 1966, 10; partisan politics, DuQuesnay with D. Kennedy, *LCM* 9 (1984), 157-60; text as constitutive of community, James Boyd White, *Justice as Translation. An Essay in Cultural and Legal Criticism* (Chicago and London, 1990); for positive assessments of Augustan humanism see Z. Yavetz, 'The Personality of Augustus', in Raaflaub and Toher, 21-41, K. Galinsky, 'Recent Trends in the Interpretation of the Augustan Age', *AugAge* 5 (1986), 22-36.

4. 'DIATRIBE', DIALOGUE AND PHILOSOPHY

In Latin literary history the word 'diatribe' has acquired a special meaning. It refers to a short ethical discourse in a particular rhetorical style. The 'diatribe-style' (which may be found in a range of genres) is characterised by concrete language and vivid imagery and the use of fables, proverbs and anecdotes. It has a quasi-dramatic element in that it is addressed directly to the listener and at times incorporates the rejoinders of an imaginary interlocutor. There are examples of this style in Cicero's *Stoic Paradoxes*, Lucretius (esp. Book 3) and Seneca's *Moral Epistles* as well as Horace's *Satires*.

The use of the word 'diatribe' for this style makes the assumption that there was a particular genre of Greek popular philosophy (associated with Bion, a Cynicising philosopher of the Hellenistic period, cf. *Epist.* 2.2.59-60) which influenced Roman satire. This theory has recently been subject to sceptical scrutiny and the argument put forward that, as the Greek term 'diatribe' did not refer to a particular literary form, we should not use the derived English word as if it had an ancient equivalent.

Other modern terms applied to Horace's 'diatribe' satires, such as 'sermons', 'homilies', 'preaching', also point to the moralising content and the direct relationship between speaker and audience. This is not technical philosophy addressed to an audience of students, but popular moralising aimed at the unconverted. If we can assume a tradition of the popular philosophical lecture in a rhetorical style the question then arises of how closely Horace's satires were connected with it and to what extent the poet is self-consciously setting himself within it and against it. He never subscribes exclusively to one philosophical system, constantly ironising the professional philosophical teachers (e.g. *Sat.* 1.3.133ff., *Sat.* 2.3), who lack the true wisdom that comes from experience of life (cf. Ofellus).

The first three satires of Horace's first book are monologues in which the satirist or 'speaker' explores a succession of moral topics. The setting may be conversational but the speaker becomes more formally didactic, adopting at times a confrontational attitude towards the fictitious representative of the audience drawn into the satire. Here already Horace displayed a certain discomfort with his dual role as satirist and moral teacher, these three poems exemplifying the kind of satire that he justifies in *Sat.* 1.4 with the argument that he was really only trying to teach himself. Still, such an apology is a rhetorical tactic, which allows the teaching to continue. In Book 2 he avoids the dilemma by placing himself in the position of someone being taught and criticised by a series of 'experts' or 'would-be-experts'.

This new role means that 'Horace' the satiric speaker completely disappears (except in *Sat.* 2.2), and dialogue becomes the dominant form. Book 1 had mainly consisted of different kinds of monologue, which might incorporate snatches of quoted direct speech. Conversation now appears in its own right as dramatic dialogue, independently, or as a frame for the set-piece lectures. At first sight the distinctions of form are more clear-cut than in the monologues where 'I' is both poet and satiric speaker, yet these structures too provide the opportunity for built-in ambivalence, through which the reader is enlisted in the unmasking of the dogmatic speakers. Parodic ambiguity arises either from an ironically incongruous content (as in *Sat.* 2.4) or from the setting of the lecture in an ironic perspective (Damasippus quotes Stertinius in *Sat.* 2.3, Davus's third-hand philosophy comes from Crispinus's door-keeper in *Sat.* 2.7).

In the individual satires the dialogue-form is deployed with considerable variety. The term 'dialogue' covers a number of practices: it implies the presence of more than one speaker, the representation through direct speech of a realistic, dramatic interaction and an affiliation to the genre of the philosophical dialogue. The playful allusions to Plato and Platonic dialogue at the beginnings of *Sat.* 2.2 and 2.4 are hints about the general ethos of the book, which is at once more dramatic and more philosophical than Book 1. The content of *Sat.* 2.8, for example, is not philosophical, yet this poem too is linked to this aspect of the book by its Platonic allusion and the bow to Plato's *Symposium*. In fact, Horace's dialogues are as close to the Aristotelian/Ciceronian form as to the Platonic, in that they mainly consist of set speeches setting out a particular point of view.

However, we should not forget that the philosophic character of the satires is always tempered by its satiric setting. Philosophical dialogue aims to expound or follow the lines of ideas and arguments; satire humorously to expose the folly of dogmatists and ideologues. For Aristotle the idea of moral virtue as the mean between two extremes implied a flexible specification of moral conduct, while for Horace it was often also a way of exploiting comically exaggerated opposites. Examples often come as opposed pairs (e.g. *Sat.* 1.1.100-7, 2.2.55-69), in congruence with the Aristotelian definition of the virtues each as a mean between a pair of opposed vices. Horace sees human behaviour as a tangle of contradictions and inconsistencies: we are all lost in the wood wandering in different directions (*Sat.* 2.3.48-51), and sometimes two directions at once! This consciousness of inconsistency contributes to the ironic ambiguity, or doubleness of vision, that characterises Horace's work. The moral dialectic has its structural analogue in the frequent use of comparison and contrast and of puns and ambiguities on the semantic and syntactic levels.

Much of the moralising content that seems to belong to popular philosophy is conventional and too typical of ancient thinking about life in general to be attributed to a particular philosophical school. The three leading moral ideas of the satires, the mean, natural limits, and self-sufficiency, cohere as a personal vision of life, in spite of their eclectic origins. On the other hand, Horace had an interest in ethical problems and a good knowledge of philosophy. It is easy to recognise in his work the influence of texts that we still possess, Lucretius and Cicero's philosophical works, for example, which were written for a non-specialist public. He appears to know Aristotle's *Ethics*, but whether at first-hand is difficult to say.

On diatribe and the 'diatribe-style', see e.g. D.A. Russell, *Plutarch* (London, 1973), 29-31, the style is well described by M.C. Randolph, 'The Structural Design of Formal Verse Satire', *PhQ* 21 (1942), 386-84; for Bion and diatribe see Kindstrand, 23-5, 97-9; the debate over the term, H.D. Jocelyn, *LCM* 7.1 (1982), 3-7, 8.6 (1983), 89-91 and H.B. Gottshalk, *LCM* 7.6 (1982), 91-9, 8.6 (1983), 91-2; Greek background to the satires, Lejay, vii-xxxvi, Witke, 21-48 etc.; on *Sat.* 1.1-3, Wimmel 1962, Rudd 1966, 1-35, D. Armstrong, 'Horace, *Satires* I, 1-3: A Structural Study', *Arion* 3 (1964), 86-96; Platonic allusions, Fraenkel 1957, 136-7; dialogue in Book 2, Maisack, E.H. Haight, 'Menander at the Sabine Farm, "Exemplar Vitae" ', *CPh* 41 (1947), 147-55, Knoche, 85-88, Williams 1972, 18-19; Socratic irony, Anderson

1982, 13-49, Braund 1988, 143-48; parody, Frischer 1991, 97-100; philosophy, a basic introduction to Hellenistic philosophy, M. Schofield, M. Burnyeat, J. Barnes (edd.), *Doubt and Dogmatism Studies in Hellenistic Philosophy* (Oxford, 1980), 1-19, further, C.W. Mendell, 'Satire as Popular Philosophy', *CPh* 15 (1920), 138-57, McGann 1969, 30-32; R. Mayer, 'Horace's *Epistles* I and Philosophy', *AJPh* 107 (1986), 55-73, is a fresh look at Horace's 'eclecticism' as an original (and Socratic) quest for independence; on Horace's knowledge of Aristotle, M. Wigodsky, 'Horace's Miser (*S*. 1 1 108) and Aristotelian Self-love', *SO* 5 (1980), 35-58.

5. THE STRUCTURAL PATTERNS OF BOOK 2

Whatever the pre-publication history of the satires, Book 2 is presented and constructed as a separate entity from Book 1. Horace rounds off his first book with a literary epilogue (*Sat.* 1.10), which he gives something of the appearance of an after-thought. Its last line self-consciously closes the book. The first lines of the new book appear to spring from the poet's reaction to the critical reception of the previous one, assuming its publication, and an ensuing gap in time.

In Book 1 Horace had put more or less similar satires together in groups (esp. *Sat.* 1.1-3). There also seems to be a concentric pattern of connections between satires (4 with 10, 5 with 9, 7 with 8). In Book 2 Horace follows a more obvious schema. The book falls into two symmetrical halves, with correspondences between the two series of satires. The simplest version of the pattern is Boll's:

1	consultations	5
2	rural simplicity	6
3	Stoic sermons	7
4	follies of gastronomy	8

Subsequent critics have wondered if the symmetry is really complete, especially as regards 1 and 5, and have also stressed the importance of variety in the patterning, taking form and setting into account as well as theme. Since the parallelisms of form support Boll's thematic connections, it may be helpful to set out the formal features of each satire:

1. Dialogue between Horace and Trebatius: longest speech 35 lines.
2. Monologue of Horace: quotes Ofellus at end (20 lines).
3. Introductory and concluding dialogue between Horace and Damasippus: Damasippus's uninterrupted speech consists mostly of a report of Stertinius's advice.
4. Introductory dialogue between Horace and Catius: Catius reports his teacher's doctrine: Horace concludes.
5. Dialogue between Ulysses and Teiresias: longest speech 35 lines.
6. Monologue of Horace: quotes Cervius at end (38 lines).
7. Introductory and concluding dialogue between Horace and Davus: Davus's uninterrupted speech claims inspiration from Crispinus's doorkeeper.

8. Short introductory dialogue between Horace and Fundanius: Fundanius's narrative relates the events of Nasidienus's dinner-party: Horace's comments interrupt the account: no formal conclusion.

Horace generally establishes setting indirectly. The following points contribute to the patterning. In 2.3 Horace is at his country villa when Damasippus interrupts, whereas the conversation with Davus in 2.7 takes place in his town-house. In 2.4 and 2.8 the conversations arise from chance encounters in the street. So both are 'promenade-dialogues' which may be set in a tradition begun by Plato's *Phaedrus*. There are no hints of setting for the dialogues of 1 and 5, though consultations perhaps entail visits. Genre is more important than setting for 2.2 and 2.6, the one identifying itself as a lecture, the other beginning as a prayer.

The latest treatment of this question (by Ludwig) overlays the clear scheme that Rudd has identified as 'architecture' with a more complex set of relations of contrast and connexion (Rudd's 'texture'). For example, 2 and 4 and 6 and 8 can be seen as contrasted pairs. Then, if we look at the satires in their numerical order, significant contrasts begin to appear. In 1 Horace defends his own life, in 2 he interprets Ofellus's. Damasippus and Ofellus are opposed in their reactions to their misfortunes. The unscrupulous attitude to enrichment through self-abasing scheming exposed in 5 is juxtaposed with the complex feelings of gratitude and independence expressed in 6, while the ideal imagined in 6 is undercut by Davus's cynical picture of the 'real' Horace in 7. The differences between the satires as we encounter them are sufficient to counter the sense of predictability that could come from the strong architectural scheme, and in spite of the repetitions of theme and form, the prevailing impression is of variety.

Williams 1972, 20 suggests that *Sat.* 1 and 2 were published together, but the *communis opinio* still prevails; arrangement of Book 1: N. Rudd, *Lines of Enquiry. Studies in Latin Poetry* (Cambridge, 1976), 119-44, at 142-3, Book 2, F. Boll, *Hermes* 48 (1913), 143-5, Fraenkel 1957, 137, Rudd 1966, 160-61, W. Ludwig, *Poetica* 2 (1968), 304-25; formal features: my list was inspired by Rudd's similar analysis of the *Eclogues* (1976, 128) — did that book's experimentation with genres of discourse influence Horace?; 'promenade-dialogues', Braund 1988, 148; 'architecture' vs. 'texture', Rudd 1976, 144; juxtapostion of 5 and 6, C. Becker, *Gnomon* 31 (1959), 600.

6. THE FOCUS ON FOOD

A striking difference between *Satires* Books 1 and 2 is the pervasive interest in food in the later book. Every satire notices it in some way (e.g. *Sat.* 2.1.74, 2.5.10-14, 80) and in four it is integral to the conception of the piece. In Book 1 the simple meal had appeared as the emblem of the Epicurean way of life (*Sat.* 1.6.111-31) and in *Sat.* 1.1 food imagery had illustrated the main (Epicurean) theme of limiting desires to what natural needs require. Such symbolism is developed at more length in Book 2, side by side with a new concern both with dietetic and culinary lore and with hospitality, that is, the consumption of food in a particular social setting. Before we condemn the dominance of this theme as a failure of imagination, let us consider its manifold attractions for the satirist and the diverse ways in which Horace exploited it.

First, though, two barriers to our appreciation of this theme must be admitted. The original impact of Horace's descriptions of the different kinds of foods is irretrievable. We have no experience of the tastes of Roman food and sometimes even the type of food cannot be securely identified. Then there were the shared cultural assumptions, the implicit meanings with which the different foodstuffs and the rituals of food were charged. These can be reconstructed only with difficulty because, within particular social groups, they are taken for granted. Horace, and the other writers who discuss food, have in mind, but do not themselves create, these shared symbolic patterns that organise the values of food.

In Horace's contemporary social environment food was the site of competing cultural values: on the one hand, the pursuit of pleasure or prestige through competitive and ostentatious extravagance, on the other, legal regulation of expenditure (the seemingly ineffective sumptuary laws) and moral condemnation prompted by the traditional association of luxury with decadence. The old Roman diet was under pressure from the fads of fashion and the authority of gastronomical experts, who sometimes succeeded in winning acceptance for their discoveries, which were disseminated and recorded. Gossip about the latest scandalous excess or new dish was a source of vicarious enjoyment, with the added spice of moral disapproval easily thrown in.

Though there was a great increase in the élite's wealth and luxury during the period of the satires (Sen. *Suas.* 6.7-9, Tac. *Ann.* 3.55, André[2], 224f.), this is not enough to explain Horace's preoccupation with this particular form of conspicuous consumption, which had been building up for some time. Unlike Juvenal he does not develop the theme's satiric potential to attack the rich man's selfishness or gourmandism's physically disgusting aspects, but gently demonstrates the folly of leaving the path of moderation (cf. Nep. *Att.* 14.2). As important as the depiction of contemporary social mores is the complex orchestration of textual interconnections.

Before Horace, much had already been written about food in non-literary texts. In their ethics philosophers made prescriptions concerning food, and regulation of diet was of great interest to medical theorists. In the Hellenistic period dinners were described and cook-books were written. An interesting off-shoot of such interests is the 'Cook's tour' of delicacies, mainly Mediterranean fish, Archestratus's *Hedypatheia*, written in hexameters and adapted by Ennius in Latin at the beginning of the second century B.C. as the *Hedyphagetica.* At the upper end of the hierarchy epic did have its hospitality scenes, with details, even homely details, of food in a heroic setting. The context may dignify or allow a comic effect. On the whole, though, the higher genres exclude details of food and eating. These belong, with other natural bodily functions (such as sex and excretion), to the realism and social criticism of comedy and satire.

Satire was the Latin literary genre which allowed all these different discourses to meet within it. So in treating food and the dinner-party Horace was taking up possibilities offered by his genre. The theme of the dinner-party was as Lucilian (in Books 5, 13, 20 and 30) as the journey (Book 3, see *Sat.* 1.5). Varro's *Menippean Satires* also dealt with food and the conduct of the dinner-party as well as using it as a setting for conversation on the model of Plato's or Xenophon's *Symposia*. It is also tempting to play with the idea of an apt metaphorical connection based on one of the suggested etymologies of the Latin word *satura* — a 'mixed-dish'. If dinners are microcosms of life, then dinner-party satires are microcosms of satire itself.

Food, already mediated through a wide range of texts, as we have seen, offers the satirist a multi-faceted perspective on human behaviour. Eating as a basic bodily function and the social elaboration of food in its preparation, presentation and contexts of consumption provide much scope for the kind of concrete detail on which satire depends for its being. Like sex, food is a site of desire subject to normative regulations of all kinds, and like sex again, it is a difficult matter to get right. We either dismiss it as trivial (and so deny its basic importance to life) or we treat it as all-important in an unbalanced way. Gastronomy, as a rival path to the good life, forms a link with, and parodic contrast to, the overall preoccupation of Horace's *Satires* with the art of living well, as is encapsulated in the pun on *sapiens*: the wise man has good taste (see Cic. *Fin.* 2.24, *Sat.* 2.4.44N).

Horace's food satires contain varying portions of the following ingredients: moral symbolism, culinary prescription and the social environment (or hospitality). In *Sat.* 2.2 food is spoken of in a very general way and there is very little in the way of practical guidance. Choice of food is a question of values and an index of a way of life. While the philosophical framework of 2.4 remains Epicurean, the food is described with a much greater particularity and the emphasis is on its culinary use. *Sat.* 2.6 foregrounds the link between food and way of life in the moment of hospitality, as does 2.8. Here Horace moves the doctrine of 2.4 from the realm of theory to that of practice, from the stage of preparation to that of meeting the food on the table. Nasidienus is largely defined by the food he serves and the way he serves it, and the guests' refusal to finish the meal is poetic justice with a vengeance.

Food symbolism in the satires, J. Glazewski, '*Plenus Vitae Conviva*: A Lucretian Concept in Horace's Satires', *CB* 47 (1971), 85-88; social background, Griffin, 11-12, 66, 81-82; literary history, Rudd 1966, 161-65, 202-23; hospitality theme, A.S. Hollis, *Callimachus Hecale* (Oxford, 1990), 341-54; food in literature, Hudson in Braund 1989, 69-87, A. Richlin, 'Systems of Food Imagery in Catullus', *CW* 81 (1988), 355-363, E. Gowers, *The Loaded Table: representations of food in Roman Literature* (Oxford, 1993) (which I have not seen), dinners as microcosms, A. Richlin, *The Garden of Priapus. Sexuality and Aggression in Roman Humor* (New Haven and London, 1983), 180-82; Lucilian background, Fiske, 399-400, 408-15, Shero; food and verbal inventiveness, M. Jeanneret, *A Feast of Words: Banquets and Table Talk in the Renaissance* Trans. J. Whiteley and E. Hughes (Cambridge, 1991); on manners and much else, M. Visser, *The Rituals of Dinner: The Origins, Evolution, Eccentricities and Meaning of Table Manners* (New York, 1991); etymology, see Introduction §2, Jeanneret, 152f.

7. TEXT AND MANUSCRIPTS

The text of this edition is based on that of D.R. Shackleton Bailey (Stuttgart, 1985) = (SB). In some places I have silently corrected slips and misprints. Where I introduce a different reading this is noted in the apparatus. The apparatus criticus has been pruned and simplified. The MSS from which the text of *Satires* II is constructed are as follows:

a = Ambrosianus O 136 sup., ninth to tenth centuries
C/E = Monacensis 14685, eleventh to twelfth centuries
K = cod. S. Eugendi (St Claude) 2, eleventh century
R = Vaticanus Reg. lat. 1703, ninth century
z = Vossianus lat. Q. 21, twelfth century
λ = Parisinus lat. 7972, ninth century
l = Leidensis B. P. L. lat. 28, ninth century
φ = Parisinus lat. 7974, tenth century
ψ= Parisinus lat. 7971, tenth century
Ψ = zφψλl
V = Blandini(an)us vetustissimus, now lost.
g = Gothanus duc. B 61, fifteenth century, cited in a few places.

ς = codd. deteriores

pr. = *prius* (reading of the first hand)

The ancient commentators appear in the apparatus as follows:
P = Porphyrionis cod. Vaticanus 3314 (Porphyrio's interpretation).
P¹ = Porphyrio's lemma, in the cases when there is no interpretation or a differing one.
σχ = scholia 'Ps.-Acrontea.'

The relationships of the MSS are complex and it is not possible to construct a stemma. For fuller descriptions of them and an analysis of their status see Brink 1971, 1-43. Recent discussion of textual points may be found in Shackleton Bailey 1982, 84-88, 'Vindiciae Horatianae', *HSPh* 89 (1985), 153-70, 'Horatian Aftermath', *Philologus* 134 (1990), 213-28, R.G.M. Nisbet, *Gnomon* 58 (1986), 611-15, *CR* 36 (1986), 227-33, J. Delz, *Gnomon* 60 (1988), 495-501. Other relevant articles are mentioned in the Commentary.

8. NOTES ON REFERENCES AND ABBREVIATIONS

References to Greek and Latin texts follow the abbreviations set out in *OCD²*, and titles of periodicals those in *L'Année philologique*. Some frequently cited works are referred to as follows:
CIL   *Corpus Inscriptionum Latinarum* (Berlin, 1862-)

D-S   C. Daremberg and E. Saglio, *Dictionnaire des Antiquités Grecques et Romaines d'après les textes et les monuments*, 5 vols. (Paris, 1877-1919)

K-H   A. Kiessling and R. Heinze, *Q. Horatius Flaccus Satiren*[10] (Dublin/Zürich, 1968)

L-H-S M. Leumann, J.B. Hofmann, and A. Szantyr, *Lateinische Syntax und Stylistik* II (Munich, 1965)

MMR   T.S.R. Broughton, *The Magistrates of the Roman Republic* 2 vols. (New York, 1951-2)

N-H   R.G.M. Nisbet and M. Hubbard, *A Commentary on Horace: Odes Book I* (Oxford, 1970), *Odes Book II* (Oxford, 1978)

OCD²   N.G.L. Hammond and H.H. Scullard (edd.), *The Oxford Classical Dictionary*² (Oxford, 1970)

OLD   P.G.W. Glare (ed.), *The Oxford Latih Dictionary* (Oxford, 1968-1982)

ORF⁴   H. Malcovati, *Oratorum Romanorum Fragmenta*⁴ I (Turin, 1953)

RAC   *Reallexikon für Antike und Christentum* (Stuttgart, 1950-)

TLL   *Thesaurus Linguae Latinae* (Leipzig, 1900-)

SVF   H. von Arnim, *Stoicorum Veterum Fragmenta* 4 vols. (Stuttgart, 1903-5, reprinted 1986)

W   E.H. Warmington, *Remains of Old Latin*, III, Lucilius, The Twelve Tables (Camb. Mass. and London, 1979)

If unacknowledged, translations of classical texts in the Commentary are either my own or the versions in the Loeb Classical Library, sometimes slightly modified.

Chronological Table

70	Birth of Virgil
65	8th December, birth of Horace at Venusia
63	Birth of C. Octavius, later to be known as Augustus
62	Birth of M. Vipsanius Agrippa
55-45	Horace in Rome, Cicero's philosophical works written
49	Outbreak of First Civil War
45	Caesar victorious. Horace in Athens
44	Caesar assassinated. Outbreak of Civil War
42	Republican army defeated at Philippi
42/1	Horace returns to Rome, loses property in confiscations. Earliest Epodes written, Virgil begins *Eclogues*
40	Pact of Brundisium re-establishes the triumvirate, giving Octavian the West, Antony the East and Lepidus Africa
42-35	Sallust's historical works published
38	Horace introduced to Maecenas
37	Treaty of Tarentum renews triumvirate, Horace travels to Brundisium with Maecenas
36	Defeat of Sextus Pompeius
?35	*Satires* Book 1 published
35	Horace begins writing Odes
33	Aedileship of Agrippa
32	War declared against Cleopatra
31	2 September, victory of Octavian at Actium
?30	*Epodes*, *Satires* Book 2 published
29	Closing of doors of Temple of Ianus signals peace, Octavian celebrates Actium in triple triumph. Virgil's *Georgics* becoming known
27	Octavian takes the name Augustus and begins to establish the Principate
23	*Odes* 1-3 published

HORACE: SATIRES II

I

'Sunt quibus in satira videar nimis acer et ultra
legem tendere opus. sine nervis altera quidquid
composui pars esse putat similisque meorum
mille die versus deduci posse. Trebati,
quid faciam? praescribe.'
                'Quiescas.'
                        'Ne faciam, inquis,   5
omnino versus?'
            'Aio.'
                'Peream male si non
optimum erat. verum nequeo dormire.'
                    'Ter uncti
transnanto Tiberim somno quibus est opus alto
irriguumque mero sub noctem corpus habento.
aut, si tantus amor scribendi te rapit, aude   10
Caesaris invicti res dicere, multa laborum
praemia laturus.'

                  'Cupidum, pater optime, vires
deficiunt. neque enim quivis horrentia pilis
agmina nec fracta pereuntis cuspide Gallos
aut labentis equo describit vulnera Parthi.'   15

'Attamen et iustum poteras et scribere fortem,
Scipiadam ut sapiens Lucilius.'

                    'Haud mihi deero,
cum res ipsa feret. nisi dextro tempore Flacci
verba per attentam non ibunt Caesaris aurem,
cui male si palpere, recalcitret undique tutus.'   20

---

aEKRΨ(=zφψλl)

1. **10** capit ς   **15** describit R Ψ : -bet K g : -bat a E : descripsit *sch. Pers. 5.4*   **20** recalcitret ς:
-rat *codd.* σχ

ONE

HOR.   'There are some to whom I seem too ferocious in my satire and to be straining my work beyond what is legitimate. The other side reckons my compositions slack and that a thousand verses like mine can be spun in a day. Trebatius, what am I to do? Give a ruling.'

TREB.   'Take a rest.'

5   HOR.   'Not write verses at all, you mean?'

TREB.   'That is my opinion.'

HOR.   'The perfect solution. I'm damned if it were not. But I can't sleep.'

TREB.   'Let those in need of deep slumber rub themselves with oil. Thrice let them swim across the Tiber and let their body be soaked with unwatered wine before nightfall. Or, if your passion

10   for writing is irresistible, dare to tell of invincible Caesar's deeds; your efforts will be amply rewarded.'

HOR.   'That's what I'd like to do, revered sir, but the strength fails me. For it's not anyone can describe the columns bristling with javelins and Gauls dying with shattered lance or the wounds

15   of the Parthian slipping from his horse.'

TREB.   'Still you could write of his justice and magnanimity, as wise Lucilius did of the scion of Scipio.'

HOR.   'I shall do myself justice, when the occasion presents itself. Unless the time is right and Caesar's ear attentive Floppy's words will not pass into it, and if you flatter him the wrong way,

20   he will kick out to protect himself all round.'

'Quanto rectius hoc quam tristi laedere versu
Pantolabum scurram Nomentanumve nepotem,
cum sibi quisque timet, quamquam est intactus, et odit!'

'Quid faciam? saltat Milonius, ut semel icto
accessit fervor capiti numerusque lucernis;   25
Castor gaudet equis, ovo prognatus eodem
pugnis; quot capitum vivunt, totidem studiorum
milia: me pedibus delectat claudere verba
Lucili ritu, nostrum melioris utroque.
ille velut fidis arcana sodalibus olim   30
credebat libris neque, si male cesserat, usquam
decurrens alio neque si bene; quo fit ut omnis
votiva pateat veluti descripta tabella
vita senis. sequor hunc, Lucanus an Apulus anceps;
nam Venusinus arat finem sub utrumque colonus,   35
missus ad hoc pulsis, vetus est ut fama, Sabellis,
quo ne per vacuum Romano incurreret hostis,
sive quod Apula gens seu quod Lucania bellum
incuteret violenta. sed hic stilus haud petet ultro
quemquam animantem et me veluti custodiet ensis   40
vagina tectus; quem cur destringere coner
tutus ab infestis latronibus? o pater et rex
Iuppiter, ut pereat positum robigine telum
nec quisquam noceat cupido mihi pacis! at ille
qui me commorit (melius non tangere, clamo)   45
flebit et insignis tota cantabitur urbe.
Cervius iratus leges minitatur et urnam,
Canidia Albuci quibus est inimica venenum,
grande malum Turius, si quid se iudice certes.
ut quo quisque valet suspectos terreat utque   50
imperet hoc Natura potens, sic collige mecum:
dente lupus, cornu taurus petit. unde, nisi intus

---

aEKRΨ(=zφψλl)

22 ve R Ψ *P¹* (*cf. 1.8.11*) : que a E K   **31** cesserat K R *pr.* : ge- *cett.* V   usquam (V)] umq-
(unq-) K R z φ *var.* ψ *var.*   **37** quo ne (σχ)] ne quo *Doederlein*   **38** sive quid...seu quid Lucana
duelli *coni. Bentley*   **48** *et* **49** (*ita etiam P*) *inter se mutat L. Müller*   **49** quid...certes a E *P¹* :
quis (R *post ras.*)...certet K R Ψ

TREB.   'How much better that would be than abusing "Grab-all
the scrounger or Nomentanus the wastrel" with acid verse, when
every man fears for himself, and hates you, although he has not
been injured.'

HOR.   'I can't help it. Milonius dances as soon as his wine-struck
25   head has grown hotter and the number of the lighted lamps
doubled. Castor takes delight in horses, his twin born from the
same egg in boxing. For as many thousands of people as exist,
there are so many thousands of passions: my pleasure is enclosing
words in feet, in the manner of Lucilius, a better man than either
30   of us. In the old days, he entrusted his secrets to his books, as
though to faithful friends, having no other outlet whether things
had gone well or ill. The result is that the old man's whole life is
open to view as if sketched on a votive tablet. I follow him, but
whether as a Lucanian or Apulian it's hard to say. For the
35   Venusine colonist ploughs close to both their borders. As the old
report tells, he was sent for this purpose, after the Samnites had
been driven out, to prevent enemy incursions against the Romans
through the unoccupied land, whether the threat of war came from
40   the Apulian folk's violence or the Lucanians'. But this pen will not
attack any living being without cause and it will protect me like a
sword hidden in the scabbard. Why should I try to draw it so long
as I am safe from dangerous thugs? O Jupiter, Father and King,
may my weapon be laid aside and destroyed by rust and may no one
injure me, who want peace. But he who rouses me will be sorry
45   (leave well alone, I'm warning you) and will be talked about all
over the city, a marked man. When roused to anger, Cervius
threatens the law and the voting urn, Canidia threatens Albucius's
poison to her enemies, Turius's threat is "big trouble", if you were
50   to contest a case with him as judge. That everyone uses his
particular strength to scare those whom he mistrusts, and that this
is the rule of all-powerful Nature, join with me in thus inferring:
the wolf attacks with his tooth, the bull butts with his horn. From

monstratum? Scaevae vivacem crede nepoti
matrem: nil faciet sceleris pia dextera (mirum
ut neque calce lupus quemquam neque dente petit bos!),   55
sed mala tollet anum vitiato melle cicuta.
ne longum faciam: seu me tranquilla senectus
exspectat seu Mors atris circumvolat alis,
dives, inops, Romae, seu fors ita iusserit, exsul,
quisquis erit vitae, scribam, color.'
                                                    'O puer, ut sis   60
vitalis metuo et maiorum ne quis amicus
frigore te feriat.'

                    'Quid? cum est Lucilius ausus
primus in hunc operis componere carmina morem
detrahere et pellem, nitidus qua quisque per ora
cederet, introrsum turpis, num Laelius aut qui   65
duxit ab oppressa meritum Carthagine nomen
ingenio offensi aut laeso doluere Metello
famosisve Lupo cooperto versibus? atqui
primores populi arripuit populumque tributim,
scilicet uni aequus Virtuti atque eius amicis.   70
quin ubi se a vulgo et scaena in secreta remorant
virtus Scipiadae et mitis sapientia Laeli,
nugari cum illo et discincti ludere, donec
decoqueretur holus, soliti. quidquid sum ego, quamvis
infra Lucili censum ingeniumque, tamen me   75
cum magnis vixisse invita fatebitur usque
Invidia et fragili quaerens illidere dentem
offendet solido — nisi quid tu, docte Trebati,
dissentis.'

                    'Equidem nihil hic diffindere possum;
sed tamen ut monitus caveas, ne forte negoti   80

---

aEKRΨ(=zφψλl)

55 ut] ni *vel si coni. Bentley* (quod *potuit*)   petat l φ ψ   **56** mala (*Pᵇ*)] *male* E R   **65** aut a E Ψ
(*exc.* z) : et K R z   **67** aut *del. voluit L. Müller* **68** ve *Cunningham* : que *codd. Pl*   **79** hic ς :
hinc *codd. Pl*   diffindere V σχ: diffund- E : diffid- Ψ (*exc.* z) *Pᵗ P var.* : diffingere a K R z P (*cf.*
1.10.37, Carm. 1.35.39)

where did they learn, if not from instinct? Entrust his long-lived
mother to the spendthrift Lefthand: his dutiful right hand will do
nothing criminal (hardly surprising that the wolf doesn't attack
55   anyone with a hoof or the ox with a fang!), but dangerous
hemlock, in poisoned honey, will do away with the old woman. To
make a long story short: whether peaceful old age awaits me or
whether Death is hovering around me on sable wings, rich, poor,
at Rome, or if chance has so decreed it, in exile, I will write,
whatever shade my life takes on.'

60   TREB.   'Young man, I'm afraid you may not be long for this
world and that one of your great friends may strike you with a
chill.'

HOR.   'What? When Lucilius dared first to compose poems of
this kind, and to strip off the skin, in which each went sleekly
65   groomed in public, while inwardly foul, were Laelius or he who
took his well-deserved name from the crushing of Carthage
offended by his natural bent? Were they sorry because Metellus
was injured or Lupus overwhelmed by slanderous verses? And yet
70   he arraigned the people's leaders and the people tribe by tribe,
well-disposed to Virtue alone, of course, and her friends. In fact
when the brave scion of Scipio and gentle, wise Laelius had
withdrawn from the crowd, leaving the public stage for a private
place, they used to fool around with him and play in casual clothes
while waiting until the vegetables cooked.   Whatever I am,
75   although I fall short of Lucilius's fortune and natural talent, still
Envy will grudgingly admit at any rate that I have lived with the
great and seeking to drive her tooth into something brittle will
strike against something solid—unless you, my learned Trebatius,
have a dissenting opinion.'

TREB.   'Indeed I find your opinion irrefragable.   But still
80   you've been warned, so take care, for fear incompetence in the

incutiat tibi quid sanctarum inscitia legum.
si mala condiderit in quem quis carmina, ius est
iudiciumque.'
          'Esto, si quis mala; sed bona si quis
iudice condiderit laudatus Caesare? si quis
opprobriis dignum latraverit integer ipse?'   85

'Solventur risu tabulae, tu missus abibis.'

---

aEKRΨ(=zφψλl)

85 laceraverit ϛ   86 risu (P)] bis sex *Bergk (Philologus, 32, 1873, 566)*

inviolable laws occasion you some trouble with the law. If a party shall have composed harmful verses against anyone, there are the law and the courts.'

HOR.   'So be it, if the verses are bad. But if a party composes good verses and earns the praise of Caesar as judge? If he barks at someone deserving reproof, while free from blame himself?'

TREB.   'The tablets will be cancelled amid laughter, and you will go away let off.'

II

Quae virtus et quanta, boni, sit vivere parvo
(nec meus hic sermo est, sed quae praecepit Ofellus
rusticus, abnormis sapiens crassaque Minerva),
discite, non inter lances mensasque nitentis,
cum stupet insanis acies fulgoribus et cum   5
acclinis falsis animus meliora recusat,
verum hic impransi mecum disquirite. 'cur hoc?'
dicam, si potero.

          Male verum examinat omnis
corruptus iudex. leporem sectatus equove
lassus ab indomito vel, si Romana fatigat   10
militia assuetum graecari, seu pila velox
molliter austerum studio fallente laborem
seu te discus agit, pete cedentem aera disco —
cum labor extuderit fastidia, siccus, inanis
sperne cibum vilem; nisi Hymettia mella Falerno   15
ne biberis diluta. foris est promus et atrum
defendens piscis hiemat mare: cum sale panis
latrantem stomachum bene leniet. unde putas aut
qui partum? non in caro nidore voluptas
summa, sed in te ipso est. tu pulmentaria quaere   20
sudando: pinguem vitiis albumque neque ostrea
nec scarus aut poterit peregrina iuvare lagois.

Vix tamen eripiam posito pavone velis quin
hoc potius quam gallina tergere palatum,
corruptus vanis rerum, quia veneat auro   25
rara avis et picta pandat spectacula cauda,
tamquam ad rem attineat quicquam. num vesceris ista

---

aEKRΨ(=zφψλl)

2. **1** boni (V)] bonis R l *P¹* **3** abnormis Ψ *(exc.* λ) σχ : abnormi *cett.* V **5** in vanis
Peerlkamp SB   **25** - *Epist. 2.2.216 deest* K

TWO

What a virtue and how great a virtue there is, good sirs, in
living on little — this talk isn't mine, but what the countryman
Ofellus taught, he being an irregular philosopher, of homespun
wisdom — learn, not among shining dishes and tables, when the
5   vision is dazed by crazy glitterings and when the mind is inclined
to false appearances and rejects better things, but here and now,
unlunched, join me in an investigation. 'Why so?' I'll tell you, if
I can.

Every corrupt judge weighs truth badly. After chasing the
hare, or coming away tired from a horse that is hard to control, or
10   (if you're used to playing the Greek and Roman military drill tires
you) if either the swift ball, enthusiasm softly beguiling the harsh
work, or the discus makes you move, go for the yielding air with
your discus — when work has hammered the choosiness out of
you, when you're thirsty and hungry, go on, reject cheap food;
15   don't drink anything but that drink made of honey from Mt.
Hymettus diluted with Falernian wine. The butler is out and the
sea storms blackly keeping the fish safe: bread and salt will calm
down your growling stomach perfectly well. Where do you think
this satisfaction comes from or how was it won? The supreme
pleasure is not to be found in costly aroma, but in you yourself.
20   Earn your sauce through your sweat; the man whom excess has
made bloated and pale will not be capable of enjoying oysters and
parrotfish or the exotic ptarmigan.

All the same, when a peacock has been put before you, I
will not find it easy to eradicate your desire to brush your palate
with this rather than with a chicken, for you have been corrupted
25   by vanities, because it sells for gold, this rare bird, and puts on a
fine show with its colourful tail spread out, as if that had any

quam laudas pluma? cocto num adest honor idem?
carne tamen quamvis distat nihil, hanc magis illa
imparibus formis deceptum te petere! esto: 30
unde datum sentis lupus hic Tiberinus an alto
captus hiet, pontisne inter iactatus an amnis
ostia sub Tusci? laudas, insane, trilibrem
mullum in singula quem minuas pulmenta necesse est.
ducit te species, video; quo pertinet ergo   35
proceros odisse lupos? quia scilicet illis
maiorem Natura modum dedit, his breve pondus.
[ieiunus raro stomachus vulgaria temnit.]
'porrectum magno magnum spectare catino
vellem' ait Harpyiis gula digna rapacibus. at vos,   40
praesentes Austri, coquite horum obsonia! quamquam
putet aper rhombusque recens, mala copia quando
aegrum sollicitat stomachum, cum rapula plenus
atque acidas mavult inulas. necdum omnis abacta
pauperies epulis regum; nam vilibus ovis   45
nigrisque est oleis hodie locus. haud ita pridem
Galloni praeconis erat acipensere mensa
infamis. quid? tunc rhombos minus aequor alebat?
tutus erat rhombus tutoque ciconia nido,
donec vos auctor docuit praetorius. ergo,   50
si quis nunc mergos suavis edixerit assos,
parebit pravi docilis Romana iuventus.

Sordidus a tenui victu distabit Ofello
iudice. nam frustra vitium vitaveris illud,
si te alio pravum detorseris. Avidienus,   55
cui 'Canis' ex vero ductum cognomen adhaeret,
quinquennis oleas est et silvestria corna

---

aERΨ(=zɸψλl)

29 hanc *L. Müller* : hac *codd.*   illa a Ψ : illam E R *(?)* ψ *var. P*   **30** te petere a R *pr.* (?) ψ
var. P : deperere E : te patet R *corr.* Ψ *SB*   **38** *damnat Bentley ad A. P. 337. aut post 22*
ponendum susp. SB   **48** tunc a E V : cum R Ψ *P¹*   (a)equor alebat a R Ψ V : aequora -ant E
53 distabit ς : distabat *codd.* V   **55** pravus ς   avidienus *codd.* Pl σχ : aufidienus ς *SB*
56 ductum V : dictum *codd*

bearing on the matter. Surely you don't feed on these feathers that
you praise? Cooked, does it keep its beauty? Yet, although there
is no difference in the flesh, to think that, deceived by unequal
30   appearances, you have an appetite for this rather than the chicken!
So be it. From what evidence can you tell whether this gaping bass
here was caught in the Tiber or in the open sea, whether it was
tossed about between the bridges or just inside the Etruscan river's
mouth? You praise a three-pound mullet, you lunatic, which you
must cut down into single servings. It's just the look that attracts
35   you, I see: what is the point then of rejecting lengthy bass? To be
sure it's because Nature has given them a greater length, mullets
a short weight. [The empty stomach rarely despises what is
commonly available.] 'The sight I'd like to see is a big fish
stretched out on a big dish,' says the gullet fit for the snatching
40   Harpies. But come, favouring South Winds, and warm up their
side-dishes! Though in fact there's a stink from boar and turbot
absolutely fresh, seeing that a surfeit makes the sick stomach
uneasy, when, full up, it prefers radishes and tart elecampane. All
poor-man's fare has not yet been removed from the feasts of the
45   wealthy: for there's still a place today for cheap eggs and black
olives. Not so long ago the auctioneer Gallonius's table was
notorious for sturgeon. Why? Did the sea raise fewer turbot then?
The turbot was safe, and the stork's nestlings safe, until an
50   authority of praetorian status enlightened you. So, if someone
were now to decree roast sea gull delicious, the youth of Rome,
quick in learning wrong, will obey.

The stingy diet and the simple one will be found distinct,
in the judgement of Ofellus. For it will be pointless for you to avoid
the former fault, if you set off going askew in the other direction.
55   Avidienus, stuck with the nickname 'Dog' derived from the facts,
eats five-year-old olives and wild cornel-berries and can't bring

ac nisi mutatum parcit defundere vinum et,
cuius odorem olei nequeas perferre, licebit
ille repotia, natalis aliosve dierum   60
festos albatus celebret, cornu ipse bilibri
caulibus instillat, veteris non parcus aceti.
quali igitur victu sapiens utetur, et horum
utrum imitabitur? hac urget lupus, hac canis, aiunt.
mundus erit qua non offendat sordibus atque   65
in neutram partem cultus miser. hic neque servis,
Albuci senis exemplo, dum munia didit,
saevus erit nec sic ut simplex Naevius unctam
convivis praebebit aquam; vitium hoc quoque magnum.

Accipe nunc victus tenuis quae quantaque secum   70
afferat. imprimis valeas bene. nam variae res
ut noceant homini credas memor illius escae,
quae simplex olim tibi sederit. at simul assis
miscueris elixa, simul conchylia turdis,
dulcia se in bilem vertent stomachoque tumultum   75
lenta feret pituita. vides ut pallidus omnis
cena desurgat dubia? quin corpus onustum
hesternis vitiis animum quoque praegravat una
atque affigit humo divinae particulam aurae.
alter ubi dicto citius curata sopori   80
membra dedit, vegetus praescripta ad munia surgit.
hic tamen ad melius poterit transcurrere quondam,
sive diem festum rediens advexerit annus
seu recreare volet tenuatum corpus ubique
accedent anni et tractari mollius aetas   85
imbecilla volet: tibi quidnam accedet ad istam
quam puer et validus praesumis mollitiem, seu
dura valetudo inciderit seu tarda senectus?
rancidum aprum antiqui laudabant, non quia nasus
illis nullus erat, sed, credo, hac mente, quod hospes   90

---

aERΨ(=zψφλl)

84 ubive *Bentley*   **85** et *add.* ς

himself to open his wine until it's turned. As for his oil, the smell
of it beyond your bearing, even though, dressed in white, he might
60   be celebrating a wedding or birthday or some other festal occasion,
he himself pours it out drop by drop from a two-gallon jar onto
the cabbage, not economical of the aged vinegar. Which style of
life, then, will the man of sense adopt, and which of these two will
he copy? 'Caught between the wolf and the dog,' as they say.
65   He will be refined enough not to give offence through squalor, and
not in either direction follow a wretched mode of life. He will not,
on old Albucius's model, be cruel to his slaves when he hands them
out their work, nor like easy-going Naevius will he offer greasy
water to his guests: this too is a great fault.
70   Now listen to what advantages and what great advantages
the simple diet brings with it. First of all, one is in good health.
For it should become obvious how harmful to man is a mix of
things when you remember that simple food which long ago sat
75   well on your stomach. But as soon as you have mixed boiled with
roasted, shellfish with thrushes, the sweet things will turn to bitter
bile, and clogging phlegm will cause the stomach to revolt. Do you
see how everyone gets up pale from a perplexing dinner? More-
over the body laden with yesterday's excesses weighs down the
soul too together with it and nails to the ground that particle of
80   divine breath. On the other hand, when a man, and sooner done
than said, has refreshed his limbs and given them over to a deep
sleep, he rises alert to his prescribed tasks. Yet he will be able to
change over to something better occasionally, if the returning year
has brought round a holiday or if his body has shrunk and he wants
85   to restore it, and when the years add up, and feeble old age requires
gentler treatment: but in your case, if harsh ill-health or dragging
old age strikes you, what on earth will be added to that softness that
you are usurping while young and strong? The men of old used to
praise rank boar, not because they had no sense of smell, but, I
90   believe, with this in mind, that if a guest arrived rather late, it was

tardius adveniens vitiatum commodius quam
integrum edax dominus consumeret. hos utinam inter
heroas natum tellus me prima tulisset!

Das aliquid famae, quae carmine gratior aurem
occupat humanam? grandes rhombi patinaeque   95
grande ferunt una cum damno dedecus. adde
iratum patruum, vicinos, te tibi iniquum
et frustra mortis cupidum, cum deerit egenti
as, laquei pretium. 'iure' inquit 'Trausius istis
iurgatur verbis. ego vectigalia magna   100
divitiasque habeo tribus amplas regibus.' ergo
quod superat non est melius quo insumere possis?
cur eget indignus quisquam te divite? quare
templa ruunt antiqua deum? cur, improbe, carae
non aliquid patriae tanto emetiris acervo?   105
uni nimirum recte tibi semper erunt res,
o magnus posthac inimicis risus! uterne
ad casus dubios fidet sibi certius? hic qui
pluribus assuerit mentem corpusque superbum,
an qui contentus parvo metuensque futuri   110
in pace, ut sapiens, aptarit idonea bello?

Quo magis his credas, puer hunc ego parvus Ofellum
integris opibus novi non latius usum
quam nunc accisis. videas metato in agello
cum pecore et gnatis fortem mercede colonum,   115
'non ego' narrantem 'temere edi luce profesta
quicquam praeter holus fumosae cum pede pernae.
ac mihi seu longum post tempus venerat hospes
sive operum vacuo gratus conviva per imbrem
vicinus, bene erat non piscibus urbe petitis,   120

---

aERΨ(=zφψλl)

91 vitiatum Ψ σχ : vitiaret a E R *(?)* σχ   **95** (h)occupat R Ψ *(exc. λ) P^l* : occupet a E λ   V
112 puer λ : puerum *cett.*   **114** metato (σχ)] metatum Ψ   **118** ac] at R ψ *SB*   **122** ficu a *V^r*
(exc. z) Charis. GL 1.96 Prisc. GL 2.340. cod. h : fico E R z *Prisc. codd. plerique*

more fitting for him to eat it tainted than for the master greedily to
eat it fresh and whole. Would that a youthful earth had given me
birth among these heroes!

Do you set any store by a good name, which, more
95   welcome than song, fills the ear of man? Big turbots on big dishes
bring big disgrace together with the financial loss. Add an angry
uncle, neighbours, you your own enemy and your longing for
death thwarted by the need of a penny, the price of a noose. 'It's
all right,' he replies ' to scold Trausius in these terms. *I* have great
100   revenues and riches more than enough for three kings.' Then
haven't you something better to spend the surplus on? Why is any
man undeservedly in need while you are rich? Why are the ancient
temples of the gods falling down? Why, you reprobate, don't you
105   dole out from so great a pile something for your beloved country?
For you alone evidently things will always be all right — a big
laugh for your enemies later on! Which of these two, facing the
vagaries of chance, will rely on himself more confidently? He who
has habituated a disdainful mind and body to abundance, or he
110   who, satisfied with little and fearful of the future, in peace, like the
wise man he is, has got ready what war requires?

To give more credence to my words, I know (from when
I was a small boy) that this Ofellus made no more use of his
unimpaired resources than he does of them now that they have
been cut back. After the surveying, you could see him in his plot
115   with his beasts and his sons, a sturdy tenant-farmer, explaining 'I
did not readily eat on a working day anything more than vegeta-
bles with a foot of smoked ham. And if after a long interval a guest
had turned up, or a neighbour, a welcome companion for me free
120   from work during the rain, we enjoyed ourselves not with fish

sed pullo atque haedo; tum pensilis uva secundas
et nux ornabat mensas cum duplice ficu.
post hoc ludus erat captu potare magistro
ac venerata Ceres, ita culmo surgeret alto,
explicuit vino contractae seria frontis.   125
saeviat atque novos moveat Fortuna tumultus:
quantum hinc imminuet? quanto aut ego parcius aut vos,
o pueri, nituistis ut huc novus incola venit?
nam propriae telluris erum Natura neque illum
nec me nec quemquam statuit. nos expulit ille,   130
illum aut nequities aut vafri inscitia iuris,
postremum expellet certe vivacior heres.
nunc ager Umbreni sub nomine, nuper Ofelli
dictus, erit nulli proprius, sed cedit in usum
nunc mihi nunc alii. quocirca vivite fortes   135
fortiaque adversis opponite pectora rebus.'

---

aERΨ(=zφψλ)

123 captu... magistro *Housman* : culpa (V)...magistra *codd. P* : cupa...magistra ς   *alii alia*
127 quantum Ψ   **132** postremum *codd.* : postremo g *SB*   **134** cedit R : cedet *cett.*

fetched from the city, but with a chicken and a kid; then the table was decked for dessert with hung-dried grapes, nuts and split figs. After this the sport was deep-drinking with capacity in charge, and Ceres, to whom we prayed, so might she rise with tall stalk,

125 smoothed away with wine the gravity of the frowning brow. Let Fortune rage and stir up fresh disorders: how much will she take away from us here? How much have I or you, my sons, looked less sleek since the new settler came here? For as owner of his own land Nature has not fixed him or me or anyone. He has expelled us, and

130 he will be expelled either by worthlessness or incompetence in the tricksy law, in the end at any rate by an heir with more life ahead of him. Now the farm goes under Umbrenus's name, a little while ago it was called Ofellus's, it will belong to no one for ever, but

135 passes now into my use, now into another's. Therefore live bravely, and confront adversity with brave hearts.'

III

'Sic raro scribis ut toto non quater anno
membranam poscas, scriptorum quaeque retexens,
iratus tibi quod vini somnique benignus
nil dignum sermone canas. quid fiet? at ipsis
Saturnalibus huc fugisti sobrius. ergo   5
dic aliquid dignum promissis: incipe. nil est.
culpantur frustra calami immeritusque laborat
iratis natus paries dis atque poetis.
atqui vultus erat multa et praeclara minantis,
si vacuum tepido cepisset villula tecto.   10
quorsum pertinuit stipare Platona Menandro,
Eupolin Archilocho, comites educere tantos?
invidiam placare paras virtute relicta?
contemnere miser. vitanda est improba Siren
Desidia, aut quidquid vita meliore parasti   15
ponendum aequo animo.'

　　　　　　　　　'Di te, Damasippe, deaeque
verum ob consilium donent — tonsore! sed unde
tam bene me nosti?'

　　　　　　　　　'Postquam omnis res mea Ianum
ad Medium fracta est, aliena negotia curo,
excussus propriis. olim nam quaerere amabam   20
quo vafer ille pedes lavisset Sisyphus aere,
quid scalptum infabre, quid fusum durius esset;
callidus huic signo ponebam milia centum;
hortos egregiasque domos mercarier unus
cum lucro noram; unde frequentia Mercuriali   25
imposuere mihi cognomen compita.'

---

aER𝚿(=z𝜙𝜓λl)

3. **1** sic] si E P^lσχ　　scribes a E R P^l　σχ ad 4　**12** archilocho z (*cf. Bentley*) : archilochum *cett.*　**22** scalptum R l 𝜙 𝜓 : sculptum *cett.* V　**23-2.6.92** *deest* z　**25** Mercuriali *Gryphius*: Mercuriale *codd.* P^l: Mercurialem ς (*cf. P*)

THREE

DAM. 'You write so infrequently that in a whole year you don't call for parchment four times, unweaving everything you have written, angry with yourself because, lavish with wine and sleep, you compose nothing worthy of talk. What will become of this? But (you say) right at the time of the Saturnalia you have got away to here and stayed sober. In that case recite something worthy of what you've promised: begin. It's no use. It's no good putting the blame on your reed-pens and giving a hard time to the innocent wall which was born under the wrath of gods — and poets. And yet your look was of one threatening much brilliant stuff once you had some free time and the little farmstead had welcomed you under its warm shelter. What aim did it serve, then, to pack in Plato with Menander, Eupolis with Archilochus, to take such mighty companions away with you? Do you intend to pacify envy by abandoning what you excel in? You'll be despised now, poor fellow. You must avoid the presumptuous Siren Sloth or give up with equanimity whatever you've achieved in a more productive time of life.'

HOR. 'May the gods and goddesses, Damasippus, for this true advice, bestow on you — a barber! But how come you know me so well?'

DAM. 'Ever since all my wealth was shipwrecked at the central Ianus, I've been looking after the affairs of others, now I'm tossed out from my own. Once, you see, I used to love to try to discover in what bronze piece the wily Sisyphus had washed his feet, to go into what had been carved unskilfully, what cast too stiffly. As an expert I used to invest a hundred thousand in a given statue; I was without equal in knowing how to deal profitably in gardens and fine houses; whence the crowds at the street corners gave me the nickname "Mercury's man".'

'Novi
et miror morbi purgatum te illius. atqui
emovit veterem mire novus, ut solet, in cor
traiecto lateris miseri capitisve dolore,
ut lethargicus hic cum fit pugil et medicum urget.   30
dum ne quid simile huic, esto ut libet.'

'O bone, ne te
frustrere, insanis et tu stultique prope omnes,
si quid Stertinius veri crepat, unde ego mira
descripsi docilis praecepta haec, tempore quo me
solatus iussit sapientem pascere barbam   35
atque a Fabricio non tristem Ponte reverti.
nam male re gesta cum vellem mittere operto
me capite in flumen, dexter stetit et "cave faxis
te quicquam indignum. pudor" inquit "te malus angit,
insanos qui inter vereare insanus haberi.   40
primum nam inquiram quid sit furere: hoc si erit in t͡
solo, nil verbi, pereas quin fortiter, addam.
quem mala stultitia et quemcumque inscitia veri
caecum agit, insanum Chrysippi porticus et grex
autumat. haec populos, haec magnos formula reges,   45
excepto sapiente, tenet." '

' "Nunc accipe quare
desipiant omnes aeque ac tu, qui tibi nomen
insano posuere. velut silvis, ubi passim
palantis error certo de tramite pellit,
ille sinistrorsum, hic dextrorsum abit, unus utrique   50
error, sed variis illudit partibus; hoc te
crede modo insanum, nihilo ut sapientior ille,
qui te deridet, caudam trahat." '

---

aERΨ(=ϕψλl)

28 mire] morbus *Peerlkamp* : maior *Horkel*   'Atqui...urget' *sic dist. SB*   **29** ve E : que *cett.*
50 utrique Ψ V *Prisc. GL 3.75* : utrisque E R (*de a n.l.*): utrimque ϛ   **51** varis *SB* (cf. 56)

HOR. 'I know and I'm amazed you've been cleared of that
illness. Or rather what is amazing is that a new illness has
displaced the old, as is the usual way, when the pain in the aching
chest or head has transferred itself to the stomach, just as when
30 your lethargic becomes a boxer and beats up his doctor. Provided
you don't do anything like that, let it be as you please.'
DAM. 'My dear fellow, don't deceive yourself: you are insane
and so are pretty well all foolish people, if there is any truth in what
Stertinius rattles off. From him I myself, being eager to learn, took
down these marvellous precepts, at the time when, by way of
35 consolation, he told me to nurture a philosophic beard and to go
home from the Fabrician bridge in good cheer. For when, after my
financial failure, I'd covered my head and was intending to hurl
myself into the river, he stood at my right hand and said "Watch
you don't do something unworthy of you. A false sense of shame
40 tortures you in that you're afraid to be thought mad among the
mad. Now, first I will look further into just what it is to be mad.
If this turns out to be in you alone I'll not add a word to stop you
dying bravely. Whomever dangerous folly and ignorance of the
truth drive blindly on, him the portico and flock of Chrysippus
45 maintain to be mad. This general rule holds for the masses, applies
to great kings, with the wise man only excepted.

' "Now learn why all who have given you the name of
madman are as much lacking in sense as you. Just as in the woods,
where a mistake drives men off the sure track to wander here and
50 there (that one going off to the left, this one to the right), each
makes the same mistake, but it leads them astray in different
directions; to this extent believe yourself mad, that he who mocks
you, no wiser, drags along a tail behind him.

                                          ' "Est genus unum
stultitiae nihilum metuenda timentis, ut ignis,
ut rupes fluviosque in campo obstare queratur;   55
alterum, et huic varum et nihilo sapientius, ignis
per medios fluviosque ruentis. clamet amica
mater, honesta soror, cum cognatis pater, uxor:
'hic fossa est ingens, hic rupes maxima, serva!'
non magis audierit quam Fufius ebrius olim,   60
cum Ilionam edormit, Catienis mille ducentis
'mater, te appello' clamantibus." '

                                        ' "Huic ego vulgus
errori similem cunctum insanire docebo.
insanit veteres statuas Damasippus emendo,
integer est mentis Damasippi creditor. esto.   65
'accipe quod numquam reddas mihi,' si tibi dicam,
tune insanus eris si acceperis? an magis excors
reiecta praeda quam praesens Mercurius fert?
scribe decem a Nerio. non est satis, adde Cicutae
nodosi tabulas; centum, mille adde catenas: 70
effugiet tamen haec sceleratus vincula Proteus.
cum rapies in ius malis ridentem alienis,
fiet aper, modo avis, modo saxum et, cum volet, arbor.
si male rem gerere insani est, contra bene sani,
putidius multo cerebrum est, mihi crede, Perelli   75
dictantis quod tu numquam rescribere possis." '

' "Audire atque togam iubeo componere, quisquis
ambitione mala aut argenti pallet amore,
quisquis luxuria tristive superstitione
aut alio mentis morbo calet; huc propius me,   80
dum doceo insanire omnis vos ordine, adite." '

---

aERΨ(=φψλl)

63 errori a R *post ras.* λ : -ore l φ ψ :-em E : -or g   similem a E λl : similis R φ ψ (*cf.*
Heyworth Mnem. 48, 1995, 574.6)   **81** *post* omnis *dist. SB*

' "One kind of folly is that of the man who fears things that
he need not fear at all, so that he complains that fires, precipices
and rivers block the way in an open plain; the other kind, divergent
from this and no wiser, is that of the man who rushes through fires
and rivers right in his way. Though his dear mother, respected
sister, father and relatives, wife, may shout: 'There's a huge ditch
here, there's a massive precipice here, look out!' he will hear no
more than did drunken Fufius when he was sleeping through the
part of Iliona, though twelve hundred Catienuses were shouting
'Mother, I beseech you.'

' "I will demonstrate that the whole crowd's madness is
similar to this derangement. Damasippus's madness is in buying
old statues; Damasippus's creditor is of sound mind. So be it. If
I say to you 'Take a loan never to be repaid me,' will you be mad
if you accept? Or are you more out of your mind, if you reject the
profit which propitious Mercury brings. Record ten thousand
sesterces as lent through Nerius. That is not enough security, add
Cicuta's knotty contract; add a hundred, a thousand chains. None-
theless the blasted fellow will escape these fetters, a very Proteus.
When you hale him to court as he laughs with jaws not his own, he
will become a boar, now a bird, now a rock, and, when he wishes,
a tree. If managing affairs badly means being mad, and, contrari-
wise, managing well means being sane, much more addled,
believe me, is Perellius's brain when he dictates what you are able
never to pay back.

' "I invite to listen and arrange his toga, whoever is pale
with nasty ambition or with love of silver, whoever is feverish with
lust for pleasure or gloomy superstition or any other sickness of the
mind. Come here nearer to me, while I teach in due order that you
are all mad.

' "Danda est ellebori multo pars maxima avaris.
nescio an Anticyram ratio illis destinet omnem.
heredes Staberi summam incidere sepulcro,
ni sic fecissent, gladiatorum dare centum   85
damnati populo paria atque epulum arbitrio Arri,
frumenti quantum metit Africa. 'sive ego prave
seu recte hoc volui, ne sis patruus mihi.' credo
hoc Staberi prudentem animum vidisse. quid ergo
sensit cum summam patrimoni insculpere saxo   90
heredes voluit? quoad vixit, credidit ingens
pauperiem vitium et cavit nihil acrius, ut, si
forte minus locuples uno quadrante perisset,
ipse videretur sibi nequior: 'omnis enim res,
virtus, fama, decus, divina humanaque pulchris   95
divitiis parent; quas qui construxerit, ille
clarus erit, fortis, iustus sapiensque etiam et rex
et quidquid volet.' hoc veluti virtute paratum
speravit magnae laudi fore." '

                        ' "Quid simile isti
Graecus Aristippus? qui servos proicere aurum   100
in media iussit Libya, quia tardius irent
propter onus segnes. uter est insanior horum?
nil agit exemplum litem quod lite resolvit." '

' "Si quis emat citharas, emptas comportet in unum,
nec studio citharae nec Musae deditus ulli,   105
si scalpra et formas non sutor, nautica vela
aversus mercaturis, delirus et amens
undique dicatur merito. qui discrepat istis
qui nummos aurumque recondit, nescius uti

---

aERΨ(=φψλl)

86 Arri et ς   **87** et quantum *Heindorf* **89** iussisse *sive* voluisse *Lambinus* : cavisse *Peerlkamp*
93 perisset Ψ : periret a E R **96** construxerit a E : contraxerit R Ψ V (?) **97** que E l *var.* ψ
var. : ne *cett.* (*om.* λ φ *corr.*) *Prisc. GL 3.101, quo recepto interrogatio* sapiensne? *uarie
assignatur* **99** quid sim- i- *codd.* σχ : dissimile isti *SB* : dissimilisne *coni. Peerlkamp* **108**
istis a E σχ : iste R

' "By far the largest dose of hellebore must be given to the lovers of wealth. Perhaps Reason would put all Anticyra down for them. Staberius's heirs engraved on his tomb the sum total he had bequeathed, since, if they had not done so, they would have been

85 obliged to entertain the people with a hundred pairs of gladiators together with a public banquet to be at Arrius's discretion, as much as the whole of Africa's harvest of corn. 'Whether I am right or wrong in wanting this, don't act the uncle with me.' This, I believe, is what Staberius, wisely, had in mind. What then did he

90 mean when he required his heirs to carve the legacy's total on the stone? As long as he lived, he believed poverty a huge fault and there was nothing he took keener precautions against, so that, if by chance he had died less rich by one farthing, he would think

95 himself so much the more worthless: 'Everything, you see, merit, renown, beauty, everything divine and human yields to beauteous riches; the man who has amassed riches will be illustrious, brave, just and wise, yes, and a king, and whatever he wishes.' This he hoped would bring him great glory, as if he had achieved it by merit.

100 ' "Did Aristippus, the Greek, do anything like him? He ordered his slaves to throw away gold in the middle of Libya, because they were going too slowly, sluggish on account of the load. Which of these two is more insane? There is no point in an example that solves one puzzle by raising another.

' "If someone were to buy lyres, and, no sooner bought, collect them all together, not devoted to love of the lyre or to any

105 Muse, if he bought cutting tools and lasts when he is not a cobbler, ships' sails when opposed to trade, he would be called on all sides deranged and demented, deservedly. In what respect is he different

compositis metuensque velut contingere sacrum?　　　　　　110
si quis ad ingentem frumenti semper acervum
porrectus vigilet cum longo fuste neque illinc
audeat esuriens dominus contingere granum
ac potius foliis parcus vescatur amaris;
si positis intus Chii veterisque Falerni　　　　　　　　　　115
mille cadis — nihil est, ter centum milibus — acre
potet acetum; age, si et stramentis incubet unde-
octoginta annos natus, cui stragula vestis,
blattarum ac tinearum epulae, putrescat in arca:
nimirum insanus paucis videatur, eo quod　　　　　　　　120
maxima pars hominum morbo iactatur eodem.
filius aut etiam haec libertus ut ebibat heres,
dis inimice senex, custodis? ne tibi desit?
quantulum enim summae curtabit quisque dierum
unguere si caulis oleo meliore caputque　　　　　　　　　125
coeperis impexa foedum porrigine? quare,
si quidvis satis est, periuras, surripis, aufers
undique? tun sanus?" '

　　　　　　　　　' "Populum si caedere saxis
incipias servosve tuos, quos aere pararis,
insanum te omnes pueri clamentque puellae:　　　　　　130
cum laqueo uxorem interimis matremque veneno,
incolumi capite es. quid enim? neque tu hoc facis Argis
nec ferro ut demens genetricem occidis Orestes
— an tu reris eum occisa insanisse parente
ac non ante malis dementem actum Furiis quam　　　　　135
in matris iugulo ferrum tepefecit acutum?
quin ex quo est habitus male tutae mentis Orestes
nil sane fecit quod tu reprehendere possis:
non Pyladen ferro violare aususve sororem
Electran; tantum maledicit utrique vocando　　　　　　140
hanc Furiam, hunc aliud iussit quod splendida bilis." '

---

aERΨ(=φψλι)

128 tun sanus a E : tunc sanus R : tu insanus Ψ　　**129** tuos] tuo R *pr.*(?) g　　**132** quid ni? neque
enim hoc ς　　**134** *sic distinxit SB*

110 from such men, the one who hides away cash and gold, not
knowing how to use what he has accumulated and fearing to touch
it as if it were sacred? If someone were to lie stretched out
continually watching over a huge heap of corn with a long stick,
and when hungry dared not touch a grain of it, even though its
owner, and were to dine rather on bitter leaves, to be economical;

115 if, with a thousand jars — that's nothing, three hundred thousand
— of Chian and Falernian stored in the cellar, he were to drink
sharp vinegar; look, if at the age of seventy nine he were to go to
bed on straw, when he had bedclothes rotting in a chest, a banquet

120 for moths and grubs, he would seem insane only to a very few of
course, for the reason that the greatest part of mankind tosses with
the same illness. Are you guarding these goods, you god-forsaken
old man, so that your son or even your freedman may drink them
up as heir? Or for fear you might run short? I mean, how very
little of the total will each day clip off, if you do begin to dress your

125 greens with a better oil, and your head, disgusting with uncombed
scurf? For what reason, if the least thing fills your needs, do you
break oaths, filch, plunder from everywhere? Call that being sane?

' "If you were to begin stoning people or your slaves,
whom you have paid cash for, the very boys and girls would call
you mad: when you hang your wife and poison your mother, your

130 head is untouched. After all, you're not doing this in Argos and
you're not killing with a sword the mother who bore you, like mad
Orestes — or do you really think that he went mad only after he had
killed his parent and that he was not driven mad by the terrible
Furies before he warmed his sharp sword in his mother's throat?

135 Quite on the contrary, from the time when Orestes was held to be
in a less than safe state of mind he in fact did nothing that you could
criticise: he did not dare to pierce with the sword Pylades or his
sister Electra; he merely insulted them both, calling her a Fury,

140 him something else commanded by the glittering black bile.

' "Pauper Opimius argenti positi intus et auri,
qui Veientanum festis potare diebus
Campana solitus trulla vappamque profestis,
quondam lethargo grandi est oppressus, ut heres 145
iam circum loculos et clavis laetus ovansque
curreret. hunc medicus multum celer atque fidelis
excitat hoc pacto: mensam poni iubet atque
effundi saccos nummorum, accedere pluris
ad numerandum; hominem sic erigit, addit et illud: 150
'ni tua custodis, avidus iam haec auferet heres.'
'men vivo?' 'ut vivas igitur, vigila: hoc age.' 'quid vis?'
'deficient inopem venae te, ni cibus atque
ingens accedit stomacho fultura ruenti.
tu cessas? agedum, sume hoc tisanarium oryzae.' 155
'quanti emptae?' 'parvo.' 'quanti ergo?' 'octussibus.' 'eheu!
quid refert morbo an furtis pereamque rapinis?" '

' "Quisnam igitur sanus? qui non stultus. quid avarus?
stultus et insanus. quid? si quis non sit avarus,
continuo sanus? minime. cur, Stoice? dicam. 160
non est cardiacus (Craterum dixisse putato)
hic aeger. recte est igitur surgetque? negabit,
quod latus aut renes morbo temptentur acuto.
non est periurus neque sordidus: immolet aequis
hic porcum Laribus. verum ambitiosus et audax: 165
naviget Anticyram." '

' "Quid enim? differt barathrone
dones quidquid habes an numquam utare paratis?
Servius Oppidius Canusi duo praedia, dives
antiquo censu, gnatis divisse duobus
fertur et hoc moriens pueris dixisse vocatis 170

aERΨ(=φψλl)

154 ingens] praesens *coni. Bentley* : ingesta *Markland* accedit] accedat λ ψ *corr.* **156** oct. assibus V : octo assibus ς **163** (*P Prisc. GL 2.221; cf. Epist. 1.6.28) secl. Haupt* temptentur *vel sim.* (*V P¹*)] temptantur g ς *Prisc.* **166** quid enim? *sqq. a superioribus diiunxit SB* barat(h)rone (-thone a) *codd. P¹ P var.* σχ : balatroni ς σχ : balatrone ς

' "Opimius, a poor man in spite of his silver and gold
stored away inside, one who on holidays used to drink a wine from
Veii out of a ladle from Capua, and sour wine on ordinary days, one
145 day was overcome by a tremendous lethargy, so that his heir was
already running around among the cash-boxes and keys, happy
and jubilant. His quick-witted and dependable doctor, brings him
to in this way: he orders a table to be set up and bags of cash to be
poured out and a number of people to come near to count it; so he
150 gets the man upright, and he adds the following: 'If you don't
protect what is yours, your greedy heir will make off with it
directly.' 'While I'm alive?' 'So to stay alive, be wide awake.
Look sharp!' 'What do you advise?' 'You are weak and your
blood-supply will fail you unless the strong buttressing of food is
applied to your stomach, which is collapsing. You hesitate? Come
155 on, down with this rice gruel.' 'How much did the rice cost?' 'Not
much.' 'How much then?' 'Eightpence.' 'Alas! What difference
if I'm destroyed by sickness or theft and pillage?'

' "Who is sane then? The man who is not a fool. What
about the lover of wealth? A fool and a madman. Tell me, if
someone is not a lover of wealth, does it follow that he is sane? By
160 no means. Why, Mr. Stoic? I will tell you. It is not heart-burn
(suppose Craterus to have been speaking) this sick man has. Is he
all right, then, and will he get up? Craterus will say no, because an
acute disease is attacking the chest or kidneys. He is not a cheat
or a miser: let him, in that case, sacrifice a pig to the well-disposed
165 Lares. But he is ambitious, and reckless: let him sail to Anticyra.

' "Tell me now. Does it make any difference whether you
consign whatever you have to a bottomless pit or never use what
is available? It is said that Servius Oppidius, a man of wealth as
it was reckoned in the old days, gave his two farms at Canusium
170 to his two sons as their share, and, as he lay dying, said this to the

ad lectum: 'postquam te talos, Aule, nucesque
ferre sinu laxo, donare et ludere vidi,
te, Tiberi, numerare, cavis abscondere tristem,
extimui ne vos ageret vesania discors,
tu Nomentanum, tu ne sequerere Cicutam.   175
quare, per divos oratus uterque Penatis,
tu cave ne minuas, tu ne maius facias id
quod satis esse putat pater et Natura coercet.
praeterea ne vos titillet gloria, iure
iurando obstringam ambo: uter aedilis fueritve   180
vestrum praetor, is intestabilis et sacer esto." '

' "In cicere atque faba bona tu perdasque lupinis,
latus ut in Circo spatiere et aeneus ut stes,
nudus agris, nudus nummis, insane, paternis;
scilicet ut plausus quos fert Agrippa feras tu,   185
astuta ingenuum vulpes imitata leonem?
ne quis humasse velit Aiacem, Atrida, vetas. cur?
'rex sum.' nil ultra quaero plebeius. 'et aequam
rem imperito; ac si cui videor non iustus, inulto
dicere quod sentit permitto.' maxime regum,   190
di tibi dent capta classem reducere Troia!
ergo consulere et mox respondere licebit?
'consule.' cur Aiax, heros ab Achille secundus,
putescit totiens servatis clarus Achivis,
gaudeat ut populus Priami Priamusque inhumato   195
per quem tot iuvenes patrio caruere sepulcro?
'mille ovium insanus morti dedit, inclutum Ulixen
et Menelaum una mecum se occidere clamans.'
tu cum pro vitula statuis dulcem Aulide gnatam
ante aras spargisque mola caput, improbe, salsa,   200

---

aERΨ(=φψλl)

172 ludere (σχ)] perdere *Bentley, alii alia*   **174** vesania Ψ : insania a E R   **183** et Ψ : aut a E
R   **187** vetas. cur?] *cf. 2.7.104*   **188** quaero (σχ] quaere V   **189** at λ V   **191** reducere ς
: reducere *codd.* : deducere ς P*SB*   **199** gnatam ς (*cf. Housman, Cl. pap. 1139 sq.*) : natam
codd.

boys called to the bed-side: 'Ever since I saw you, Aulus, carrying
your knucklebones and nuts in a loose fold of your dress, giving
them away and gambling, and you, Tiberius, anxiously counting
them and hiding them away in holes, I began to fear that you were
driven by antithetic insanities, that *you* might follow Nomentanus,
175   and *you* Cicuta. Wherefore, I entreat both of you by the household
gods, *you* take care not to diminish, *you* not to increase, what your
father reckons is enough and what Nature sets her limits to.
Furthermore, so that glory may not tickle your desires I shall bind
180   you both by an oath: whichever of you shall have become aedile
or praetor, he shall be outlawed and accursed.'

' "Do you waste your substance on chickpeas, beans and
lupins, so as to flaunt and promenade yourself in the Circus and
stand in bronze, denuded of your father's fields, denuded of your
father's cash, you lunatic; no doubt in order that you may win the
185   applause Agrippa receives, you the sly fox imitating the noble
lion?

' "Son of Atreus, you command that no-one bury Ajax.
Why? 'I am the king.' I enquire no further, a mere commoner.
'And what I command is fair, and if anyone thinks I am not just,
I allow him to say what he thinks with impunity.' Greatest of
190   kings, may the gods grant you take Troy and bring the fleet back!
So you will allow me to ask a question and you will reply in due
course? 'Ask your question.' Why does Ajax, the hero next to
Achilles, lie there and stink, a man famous for saving the Achaeans
so many times? Is it so that Priam's people and Priam himself may
195   rejoice that he is unburied through whom so many young men
have been deprived of an ancestral tomb? 'He was mad. He gave
to death a thousand sheep, shouting that he was killing renowned
Ulysses and Menelaus together with me.' And you, when you
stand your sweet daughter before the altars at Aulis, instead of a
200   heifer, and sprinkle her head with salt and grain, you shameless

rectum animi servas cursum? insanus quid enim Aiax
fecit cum stravit ferro pecus? abstinuit vim
uxore et gnato; mala multa precatus Atridis
non ille aut Teucrum aut ipsum violavit Ulixen.
'verum ego, ut haerentis adverso litore navis   205
eriperem, prudens placavi sanguine divos.'
nempe tuo, furiose. 'meo, sed non furiosus.'
qui species alias veris cerebrique tumultu
permixtas capiet, commotus habebitur atque
stultitiane erret nihilum distabit an ira.   210
Aiax immeritos cum occidit desipit agnos:
cum prudens scelus ob titulos admittis inanis,
stas animo et purum est vitio tibi, cum tumidum est, cor?
si quis lectica nitidam gestare amet agnam,
huic vestem, ut gnatae, paret ancillas, paret aurum,   215
Rufam aut Posillam appellet fortique marito
destinet uxorem, interdicto huic omne adimat ius
praetor et ad sanos abeat tutela propinquos.
quid? si quis gnatam pro muta devovet agna,
integer est animi? ne dixeris. ergo ubi prava   220
stultitia, hic summa est insania; qui sceleratus,
et furiosus erit; quem cepit vitrea fama,
hunc circumtonuit gaudens Bellona cruentis." '

' "Nunc, age, luxuriam et Nomentanum arripe mecum;
vincet enim stultos ratio insanire nepotes.   225
hic, simul accepit patrimoni mille talenta,
edicit piscator uti, pomarius, auceps,
unguentarius ac Tusci turba impia Vici,
cum scurris fartor, cum Velabro omne macellum,
mane domum veniant; qui cum venere frequentes,   230

---

aERΨ(=$\phi\psi\lambda$l)

201 cursum *Peerlkamp* : quorsum a E ϕ ⫿ ψ *var.* λ *corr.* l σχ : quorum Rλ *pr* .ψ *P* σχ
204 ulixen ϛ *P^l* : ulixem *codd.*   **207** furiosi *coni. Palmer*   **208** veris cerebri *Horkel* : veris
celeri *P^l* : veri sceleris a E R V σχ : veris celeris Ψ : veris sceleris g σχ : veris iecoris
Postgate   **211** cum immeritos V g   **212** cum *codd.* : tu ϛ *SB* admittis *codd.* : committis ϛ V
(?) : committit *P* g : cum admittis *Bentley, SB*   **216** aut] et V   posillam V *pr.* : pusillam *codd.*
225 vincet a E ψ *corr.* V : vincit R Ψ **230** qui cum ϛ : quid tum *vel sim. codd.*

man, are you keeping the mind's course straight? After all, what
did the madman Ajax do? When he laid low the flock with the
sword, he held back his violence from his wife and son; though he
heartily cursed the sons of Atreus, he did not wound Teucer, or
205   even Ulysses. 'Yes, but I, in order to tear away the ships stuck fast
on the unfriendly shore, I was reasonable when I placated the gods
with blood.' Your own, to be sure, maniac. 'Mine, but I'm no
maniac.' He whose mind grasps presentations differing from the
true and made indistinguishable by the tumult of the brain, will be
210   held deranged, and it will make no difference whether he goes
astray out of folly or rage. Ajax is out of his mind when he kills
the undeserving lambs: when you 'reasonably' commit a crime for
the sake of empty distinctions, are you in your right mind, and is
215   your heart, when swollen up, free of fault? Let's say someone
loved to carry around a sleek lamb in a litter, furnish it, like a
daughter, with clothes, with maids and gold, call it Rufa or Posilla,
and think to make it the wife of a gallant husband, the praetor
would put him under an injunction, and take away all his legal
rights and the guardianship would devolve upon his sane relations.
220   So, if someone sacrifices a daughter in place of a dumb lamb, is he
of unimpaired mind? Don't say so. Therefore, where folly is
depraved, you find the height of madness; he who is criminal will
also be a maniac; he who has been caught by glassy fame, about
225   his head thunders Bellona who rejoices in deeds of blood.
        ' "Come now, join me in hauling up self-indulgence and
Nomentanus. For Reason will prove that spendthrifts, being fools,
are mad. He, as soon as he got his inheritance of a thousand talents,
issued a public decree that the fisherman, the fruiterer, the bird-
catcher, the perfumer and the godless riff-raff of the Etruscans'
street, the poulterer along with the loungers and scroungers, the
230   whole covered market along with the Velabrum, should come to
his house early next day. When they had come in large numbers,

verba facit leno: 'quidquid mihi, quidquid et horum
cuique domi est, id crede tuum et vel nunc pete vel cras.'
accipe quid contra haec iuvenis responderit aequus:
'tu nive Lucana dormis ocreatus, ut aprum
cenem ego, tu piscis hiberno ex aequore verris.   235
segnis ego, indignus qui tantum possideam; aufer.
sume tibi decies; tibi tantundem; tibi triplex,
unde uxor media currit de nocte vocata.'
filius Aesopi detractam ex aure Metellae,
scilicet ut decies solidum absorberet, aceto   240
diluit insignem bacam: qui sanior ac si
illud idem in rapidum flumen iaceretve cloacam?
Quinti progenies Arri, par nobile fratrum,
nequitia et nugis pravorum et amore gemellum,
luscinias soliti impenso prandere coemptas;   245
quorsum abeant? sani ut creta, an carbone notati?" '

' "Aedificare casas, plostello adiungere mures,
ludere par impar, equitare in harundine longa
si quem delectet barbatum, amentia verset.
si puerilius his ratio esse evincet amare,   250
nec quicquam differre utrumne in pulvere, trimus
quale prius, ludas opus an meretricis amore
sollicitus plores, (quaero) faciasne quod olim
mutatus Polemon, ponas insignia morbı
(fasciolas, cubital, focalia), potus ut ille   255
dicitur ex collo furtim carpsisse coronas,
postquam est impransi correptus voce magistri?
porrigis irato puero cum poma, recusat:
'sume, catelle!' negat: si non des, optet. amator
exclusus qui distat, agit ubi secum eat an non   260
quo rediturus erat non arcessitus, et haeret

---

aERΨ (=φψλl)

234 tu *Th. Johnson* : in *codd.* : tu in *coni. Bentley*   **235** verris Ψ V σχ *var.* : vel(l)is a E R σχ
246 sani ut a E R l σχ: sanii ψ : sani λ φ *sch. Pers. 5.108* : insani ψ v *Pl* : sanin *Marcilius*
notati (V)] notandi ς σχ   **249** delectat Ψ   **255** cubital V *pr.* (?) ς *Pl Fronto p. 24.1 N* :
cubitale *codd.*

a pimp was spokesman: 'Whatever I or any of these people here
has at home, believe it yours and ask for it now or tomorrow, as you
please.' Hear what the tender-hearted young man replied to this:
'You sleep in the Lucanian snow wearing leggings, so that I can
235 dine on wild boar, you sweep fish from a stormy sea. I'm a lazy-
bones, unworthy to possess so much. Away with it. You take a
million; you the same again; you three times as much, from whose
house your wife comes running after midnight, when I send for
her.' Aesopus's son, no doubt in order to swallow a solid million
in one go, dissolved in vinegar a fabulous pearl unfastened from
240 Metella's ear: how is he saner than if he were to toss the same thing
into a swift-flowing river or the sewer? Quintus Arrius's progeny,
a celebrated pair of brothers, twins in dissipation and frivolity and
a passion for the perverse, were given to lunching on nightingales
245 procured for an untold sum. Where are they to go? Have they been
marked with chalk as sane, or with coal?

    ' "If a bearded man were to take delight in building toy
houses, yoking mice to a tiny cart, playing at odds and evens,
riding a hobby-horse, madness would be driving him. If Reason
250 proves convincingly that being in love is more childish than this,
and that it makes no difference whether you build in play in the
sand, as you did before, at the age of three, or weep and wail,
tormented by the love of a call-girl, would you (I ask) do what once
Polemo did, when converted? Would you lay aside the badges of
255 your illness (the leg-bands, arm-wrap, scarves), just as he, when
drunk, is said to have plucked surreptitiously the garlands from
around his neck, rebuked by what the teacher said before *he* had
had his lunch? When you offer apples to a child in a tantrum, he
rejects them; 'Take them, pet!' he says no; if you were not giving
them, he would want them. How is the locked out lover different,
260 when he argues with himself whether or not to go to the place
where he was on the point of returning, even without a summons,

invisis foribus? 'nec nunc, cum me vocet ultro,
accedam? an potius mediter finire dolores?
exclusit; revocat. redeam? non si obsecret.' ecce
servus non paulo sapientior: 'o ere, quae res   265
nec modum habet neque consilium, ratione modoque
tractari non vult. in amore haec sunt mala, bellum,
pax rursum. haec si quis tempestatis prope ritu
mobilia et caeca fluitantia sorte laboret
reddere certa sibi, nihilo plus explicet ac si   270
insanire paret certa ratione modoque.'
quid? cum Picenis excerpens semina pomis
gaudes si cameram percusti forte, penes te es?
quid? cum balba feris annoso verba palato,
aedificante casas qui sanior?" '

                                       ' "Adde cruorem   275
stultitiae atque ignem gladio scrutare. modo, inquam,
Hellade percussa Marius cum praecipitat se,
cerritus fuit. an commotae crimine mentis
absolves hominem et sceleris damnabis eundem,
ex more imponens cognata vocabula rebus?" '   280

' "Libertinus erat, qui circum compita siccus
lautis mane senex manibus currebat et 'unum'
('quid tam magnum?' addens), 'unum me surpite morti!
dis etenim facile est' orabat, sanus utrisque
auribus atque oculis; mentem, nisi litigiosus,   285
exciperet dominus, cum venderet. hoc quoque vulgus
Chrysippus ponit fecunda in gente Meneni.
'Iuppiter, ingentis qui das adimisque dolores,'
mater ait pueri mensis iam quinque cubantis,
'frigida si puerum quartana reliquerit, illo   290
mane die, quo tu indicis ieiunia, nudus

---

aERΨ(=φψλ1)

262 vocat ς   272, 274 quid *cum Klingner interrog. feci*   276-278 *sic Apitz* : *interrog. faciunt
plerique*   280 cognata *codd.* σχ : *non apta SB* : *non nata Horkel*   291 mane Ψ *P¹* magne a R
φ *var.* : magno E

and hangs about the doors he hates? 'Am I not to go even now, when she sends for me of her own accord? Or should I consider rather putting an end to my pains? She locked me out; she calls me back. Shall I return? Not if she were to beg.' Up comes the slave,

265 wiser by far: 'O sir, a matter which has in it no measure or sense, does not allow itself to be handled with reason or measure. In love these are the evils, war, then peace as before. If someone were to take these things — unstable almost in the way the weather is, drifting about by blind chance — and were to work at making them

270 stable for himself, he would clear things up no more than if he were to set about being mad with an infallible reason and method.' Tell me, when you pick out the pips from apples from Picenum and rejoice if you have happened to hit the coffered ceiling, are you really all there? Tell me, when you strike baby-talk from a grown man's palate, how are you saner than if you were to build toy houses?

275   ' "Add bloodshed to folly and poke the fire with the sword. Just now, for example, when Marius struck Hellas dead and hurled himself from a height, he was possessed. Or will you acquit the man of the charge of a disturbed mind and at the same time condemn him of crime, calling things by related names, as people

280 normally do?

              ' "There was a freedman, who in his old age in the early morning before touching breakfast would run around the shrines at the street corners, with washed hands, and would pray 'Me alone' (adding 'Is this such a big thing to ask') 'Snatch me alone from death. Truly for the gods it's easy.' He was sound in his two

285 ears and eyes, but, unless an owner were fond of litigation, he would exclude his mind from warranty, when he sold him. This crowd too Chrysippus includes in Menenius's prolific clan. 'Jupiter, you who send and take away great suffering' says the mother

290 of a boy lying ill for five months now, 'if the shivering quartan leaves my boy, early in the morning on that day on which you

in Tiberi stabit.' casus medicusve levarit
aegrum ex praecipiti, mater delira necabit
in gelida fixum ripa febrimque reducet;
quone malo mentem concussa? timore deorum." '   295

'Haec mihi Stertinius, sapientum octavus, amico
arma dedit, posthac ne compellarer inultus.
dixerit insanum qui me, totidem audiet atque
respicere ignoto discet pendentia tergo.'

'Stoice, post damnum sic vendas omnia pluris,   300
qua me stultitia, quoniam non est genus unum,
insanire putas? ego nam videor mihi sanus.'

'Quid? caput abscissum manibus cum portat Agave
gnati infelicis, sibi tunc furiosa videtur?'

'Stultum me fateor, liceat concedere veris,   305
atque etiam insanum. tantum hoc edissere, quo me
aegrotare putes animi vitio?'

                          'Accipe: primum
aedificas, hoc est, longos imitaris ab imo
ad summum totus moduli bipedalis; et idem
corpore maiorem rides Turbonis in armis   310
spiritum et incessum, qui ridiculus minus illo?
an, quodcumque facit Maecenas, te quoque verum est
tantum dissimilem et tanto certare minorem?
absentis ranae pullis vituli pede pressis
unus ubi effugit, matri denarrat, ut ingens   315
belua cognatos eliserit. illa rogare

---

aERΨ(=φψλl)

292 medicusque Ψ   293 necabit] negabit E R : locabit *coni. Palmer*   301 quam me stultitiam
ς   303 abscissum ς : abscisum *codd.*   manibus V g : demens *codd.*   cum portat] portavit V
304 tunc a : tum R Ψ : nunc E   305 liceat] lex est *Horkel, alii alia*   313 tantum (*pr.*) V : tanto
codd.

proclaim fasting, he will stand in the Tiber naked.' Should chance
or the doctor rescue the sick boy from the point of danger, his crazy
mother will kill him, stationing him on the freezing river's edge
and bringing back the fever; by what evil has her mind been
295 shaken? By fear of the gods."
　　　　　'These weapons Stertinius, the Eighth Sage, gave me as
his friend, so that in future I should not be called names without
taking my revenge. If anyone calls me mad, he will hear as much
said about him, and learn to look round at what hangs, unawares,
behind his own back.'
300 HOR. 'My Stoic friend, as you hope to sell everything at a profit
after your loss, with what folly, since there is not only one sort, do
you think I'm mad? For to myself I seem sane.'
DAM. 'Tell me, when Agave is carrying in her hands the torn-off
head of her ill-starred son, does she then think herself a maniac?'
305 HOR. 'I admit I'm a fool (let me submit to the truth) and even
insane. Just expound this — what mental failing do you think is
making me ill?'
DAM. 'Listen: in the first place, you're building, that is you are
imitating the highups when from top to bottom you measure two
310 feet in all, and yet you laugh at Turbo's arrogant air and swagger
under arms, as being too big for his body: how are you less
ridiculous than he? Or is it right for you also to do whatever
Maecenas does, so unlike him, and so much too small to compete
with him. While the frog was away her young were squashed by
315 the hoof of a calf; one escaped; he tells the whole story to his
mother, how a huge monster crushed to death his brothers and

quantane, num tantum (sufflans se) magna fuisset.
"maior dimidio" "num tantum?" cum magis atque
se magis inflaret, "non, si te ruperis" inquit,
"par eris." haec a te non multum abludit imago.   320
adde poemata nunc, hoc est, oleum adde camino,
quae si quis sanus fecit, sanus facis et tu.
non dico horrendam rabiem.' 'iam desine.' 'cultum
maiorem censu.' 'teneas, Damasippe, tuis te.'
'mille puellarum, puerorum mille furores.'   325
'o maior, tandem parcas, insane, minori!'

---

aERΨ(=φψλl)

317 tantum E V *P interpr.* : tanta R: tandem a Ψ *P^l Porph. codd.*   **318** tantum 1 : tanto *cett.*

sisters. She asks how big, whether, blowing herself up, it was so
big. "Half as big again." "Was it so big?" As she blew herself up
320   more and more, he said, "You won't equal it, not if you burst
yourself." This picture doesn't fall far short of you. Now throw
in your poems, that is, add fuel to the flame; if anyone has
composed poetry sane, you too are a sane poet. I won't mention
your frightful temper.'

HOR.   'Leave off now.'

DAM.   'Your way of life beyond your means.'

HOR.   'Keep away, Damasippus.'

325   DAM.   'Mad passions for a thousand girls, a thousand boys.'

HOR.   'O greater madman, *do* spare a lesser.'

IV

'Unde et quo Catius?'

                'Non est mihi tempus aventi
ponere signa novis praeceptis, qualia vincent
Pythagoran Anytique reum doctumque Platona.'

'Peccatum fateor, cum te sic tempore laevo
interpellarim; sed des veniam bonus, oro.   5
quod si interciderit tibi nunc aliquid, repetes mox,
sive est naturae hoc sive artis, mirus utroque.'

'Quin id erat curae, quo pacto cuncta tenerem,
utpote res tenuis tenui sermone peractas.'

'Ede hominis nomen, simul et Romanus an hospes.'   10

'Ipsa memor praecepta canam, celabitur auctor.
longa quibus facies ovis erit, illa memento,
ut suci melioris et ut magis alba rotundis,
ponere; namque marem cohibent callosa vitellum.
cole suburbano qui siccis crevit in agris   15
dulcior; irriguo nihil est elutius horto.
si vespertinus subito te oppresserit hospes,
ne gallina malum responset dura palato,
doctus eris vivam musto mersare Falerno;
hoc teneram faciet. pratensibus optima fungis   20
natura est; aliis male creditur. ille salubris
aestates peraget qui nigris prandia moris
finiet, ante gravem quae legerit arbore solem.
Aufidius forti miscebat mella Falerno,

---

aERΨ(=φψλl)

4. **2** vincent R φ ψ λ V : -cunt a E l R *var.* : -cant ς   **7** utroque *codd.* : utraque
Praedicow SB (*cf. quae scripsit ad Cic. Att. 15.22*)   **19** musto *Crato* : mixto *codd.* : mulso ς
22 peraget λ φ ψ : perget R : peragit a E l

FOUR

HOR. 'Catius! Where from and where to?'

CAT. 'I've no time. I'm burning to put down notes of these new teachings, of a kind that will outdo Pythagoras and the man Anytus accused and learned Plato.'

5 HOR. 'My fault, I admit, having cut in on you like this at an unlucky moment. But pardon me like a good fellow, please. If anything just now slips your mind, you will soon recover it. Whether this is nature in you or art, you are amazing either way.'

CAT. 'Why, that was my concern, how I might retain it all, because the subject matter was fine-drawn, treated throughout in a fine-spun style.'

10 HOR. 'Pronounce the man's name. Is he a Roman or from abroad?'

CAT. 'The teachings I'll recite from memory, their author's identity will be kept hidden. Eggs which are long in shape, forget not to serve those, as they have a better flavour and are whiter than the round: for they are hard-skinned, and contain a male yolk.

15 Cabbages grown in dry fields are sweeter than those from the suburbs; nothing tastes more washed out than over-watered garden-stuff. If in the evening a guest has suddenly surprised you, in order that a tough hen does not disappoint the palate, you will show your knowledge by drowning it alive in juice from Falernian grapes. This will make it tender. Field mushrooms are the best

20 kind; the others are not to be trusted. One will get through the summers in good health if one ends lunch with black mulberries picked from the tree before the sun becomes oppressive. Aufidius used to mix honey with strong Falernian, a mistake, since you

mendose, quoniam vacuis committere venis   25
nil nisi lene decet; leni praecordia mulso
prolueris melius. si dura morabitur alvus,
mitulus et viles pellent obstantia conchae
et lapathi brevis herba, sed albo non sine Coo.
lubrica nascentes implent conchylia lunae;   30
sed non omne mare est generosae fertile testae:
[murice Baiano melior Lucrina peloris;]
ostrea Circeis, Miseno oriuntur echini;
pectinibus patulis iactat se molle Tarentum.
nec sibi cenarum quivis temere arroget artem   35
non prius exacta tenui ratione saporum.
nec satis est cara piscis averrere mensa
ignarum quibus est ius aptius et quibus assis
languidus in cubitum iam se conviva reponet.
Umber et iligna nutritus glande rotundas   40
curvet aper lances carnem vitantis ineptem;
nam Laurens malus est, ulvis et harundine pinguis.
vinea summittit capreas non semper edulis.
fecundae leporis sapiens sectabitur armos.
piscibus atque avibus quae natura et foret aetas   45
ante meum nulli patuit quaesita palatum.
sunt quorum ingenium nova tantum crustula promit.
nequaquam satis in re una consumere curam,
ut si quis solum hoc, mala ne sint vina, laboret,
quali perfundat piscis securus olivo.   50
Massica si caelo suppones vina sereno,
nocturna si quid crassi est tenuabitur aura
et decedet odor nervis inimicus; at illa
integrum perdunt lino vitiata saporem.
Surrentina vafer qui miscet faece Falerna   55
vina, columbino limum bene colligit ovo,

aERΨ(=φψλl)

32 *damnat Clausen* murice Baiano *codd. P* : murex Baianus *Snapius, SB*   37 averrere (*P*)]
avertere g ς   39 reponet a E ψ *corr.* : -nit R Ψ *P*   41 curvet ς : -vat *codd.*   44 fecundae V :
-di *codd.*   *P¹ Donat. Ter. Eun.* 426   46 latuit *Peerlkamp* palato ς, *Peerlkamp*   48 est *post
curam add. SB cum Teuffel, alibi alii*

25   should put nothing except the mild into empty veins. You'd do
       better first to rinse your lungs with mild honeyed wine. If your
       bowels are constipated and slow, sea-mussels and cheap shell-fish
       will expel the blockage, and the short-stalked sorrel, of course with
       white wine from Cos. New moons fill up slippery shell-fish; but
30   not every sea produces the choice sorts: [the giant mussel from the
       Lucrine lake is better than the purple from Baiae;] oysters come
       from Circeii, sea-urchins from Misenum; luxurious Tarentum
       boasts of its flat scallops. Let no one rashly claim as his the art of
       dining unless he has first studied the subtle science of flavours. It's
35   not enough to trawl fish from an expensive counter, if you don't
       know which kind a sauce is best for, and which, if grilled, will have
       the drooping guest immediately up on his elbow again. Let the
       Umbrian boar fed on acorns bend the circular silver serving-dishes
40   of him who would avoid insipid meat; for the Laurentian is
       worthless, fattened on sedge and reed. Vineyard-bred roes are not
       always eatable. The connoisseur will hunt the wings of the
       breeding hare. As for fish and fowl, their qualities and best age,
45   no palate before mine has gone into and shed light on that. There
       are those whose powers of invention bring forth only new cookies.
       In no way is it enough to exhaust your care on one thing, as if, for
       example, someone were to take pains only over seeing that his
       wines were not bad, but did not care what sort of oil he poured over
50   his fish. If you expose Massic wine under a clear sky, any
       thickness will be dispelled by the night breeze and the odour
       harmful to the sinews will pass off; but it is spoilt by straining
       through linen and loses its full flavour. He is a canny fellow who
       mixes Sorrentine wine with the lees of Falernian and successfully
55   collects the sediment with a pigeon's egg, since the yolk precipitates

quatenus ima petit volvens aliena vitellus.
tostis marcentem squillis recreabis et Afra
potorem coclea; nam lactuca innatat acri
post vinum stomacho. perna magis et magis hillis   60
flagitat immorsus refici; quin omnia malit
quaecumque immundis fervent allata popinis.
est operae pretium duplicis pernoscere iuris
naturam. simplex e dulci constat olivo,
quod pingui miscere mero muriaque decebit   65
non alia quam qua Byzantia putuit orca.
hoc ubi confusum sectis inferbuit herbis
Corycioque croco sparsum stetit, insuper addes
pressa Venafranae quod baca remisit olivae.
Picenis cedunt pomis Tiburtia suco;   70
nam facie praestant. Vennuncula convenit ollis;
rectius Albanam fumo duraveris uvam.
hanc ego cum malis, ego faecem primus et allec,
primus et invenior piper album cum sale nigro
incretum puris circumposuisse catillis.   75
immane est vitium dare milia terna macello
angustoque vagos piscis urgere catino.
magna movet stomacho fastidia seu puer unctis
tractavit calicem manibus, dum furta ligurrit,
sive gravis veteri creterrae limus adhaesit.   80
vilibus in scopis, in mappis, in scobe quantus
consistit sumptus? neglectis flagitium ingens.
ten lapides varios lutulenta radere palma
et Tyrias dare circum inluta toralia vestis,
oblitum, quanto curam sumptumque minorem   85
haec habeant, tanto reprehendi iustius illis
quae nisi divitibus nequeunt contingere mensis?'

---

aERΨ(=φψλl)

60 et (σχ)] ac E : om. a   **61** immorsus (inm-) (σχ)] in m-ς : inmorsis *coni. Bentley* : immersus
Bothe   **66** qua] quae a l φ ψ   **71** vennuncula E φ ψ : *uariant cett.*   **78** movet] -ent a E l
80 creterrae R φ ψ V: craterae a E λ l   **84** inluta a E R: illota (inl-) Ψ *SB*   **87** nequeant ς

taking the foreign matter down with it. When a drinker is flagging
you will revive him with grilled scampi and African snails; not
60   lettuce, for after wine that floats undigested on an acid stomach.
The stimulated stomach demands to be restored rather by smoked
ham and sausages; in fact it would prefer all those kinds of things
that are brought piping hot from squalid cookshops. 'Tis worth
one's while to master the nature of the two kinds of sauce. The
plain consists of sweet olive oil, which should be mixed with full-
65   bodied unwatered wine and fish-brine, none other than that which
makes the tunny-barrel from Byzantium stink. When you have
combined this with chopped herbs, let it boil, then sprinkle with
Corycian saffron and let it stand, finally add what the pressed berry
of the Venafran olive-tree has produced. Tiburtine apples yield to
70   those from Picenum in flavour; I say this because the former are
better-looking. Vennunculan grapes are suited to potting; Alban
grapes you'd do better to dry by smoking. You'll find it was I who
invented the practice of setting round this grape with apples, I too
wine-lees and pickled-fish paste, I white pepper sifted with black
75   salt in small clean bowls. It's a monstrous fault to give three
thousand each to the fish-monger only to constrict the roving
fish in too narrow a platter. It very much turns the queasy
stomach if a slave has handled the wine cup with hands made
greasy while he was stealing a sly mouthful, or if a nasty
80   deposit has built up on the antique wine bowl. Cheap brooms,
napkins, sawdust – how much do these cost? But neglect here
is an absolute disgrace. To think of your sweeping the mosaic
floor with a grimy palm-broom and putting unwashed valences
around covers of Tyrian purple, forgetting that the less care and
85   expense these involve, the more justifiably you are blamed for
neglecting them than for the absence of those things which can
only belong to the tables of the rich.'

'Docte Cati, per amicitiam divosque rogatus
ducere me auditum, perges quocumque, memento.
nam quamvis memori referas mihi pectore cuncta,   90
non tamen interpres tantundem iuveris. adde
vultum habitumque hominis, quem tu vidisse beatus
non magni pendis, quia contigit; at mihi cura
non mediocris inest, fontis ut adire remotos
atque haurire queam vitae praecepta beatae.'   95

HOR.   'O learned Catius, by our friendship and by the gods I beg you, forget not to take me to hear the next lecture, wherever it is you go. For with however retentive a memory you relay it all to

90   me, nevertheless, as an interpreter, you would not give as much delight. Add the man's expression and appearance, the sight of which you, in your blessedness, count of little value, because you have had that luck. But I have no ordinary desire to be able to approach the far away springs and to drink deep the teachings of

95   the happy life.'

V

'Hoc quoque, Teresia, praeter narrata petenti
responde, quibus amissas reparare queam res
artibus atque modis. quid rides?'
                                    'Iamne doloso
non satis est Ithacam revehi patriosque Penatis
aspicere?'
                        'O nulli quicquam mentite, vides ut   5
nudus inopsque domum redeam te vate, neque illic
aut apotheca procis intacta est aut pecus? atqui
et genus et virtus nisi cum re vilior alga est.'

'Quando pauperiem missis ambagibus horres,
accipe qua ratione queas ditescere. turdus   10
sive aliud privum dabitur tibi, devolet illuc
res ubi magna nitet domino sene; dulcia poma
et quoscumque feret cultus tibi fundus honores
ante Larem gustet venerabilior Lare dives;
qui quamvis periurus erit, sine gente, cruentus   15
sanguine fraterno, fugitivus, ne tamen illi
tu comes exterior, si postulet, ire recuses.'

'Utne tegam spurco Damae latus? haud ita Troiae
me gessi certans semper melioribus.'
                                        'Ergo
pauper eris.'
                'Fortem hoc animum tolerare iubebo;   20
et quondam maiora tuli. tu protinus unde
divitias aerisque ruam dic, augur, acervos.'

'Dixi equidem et dico: captes astutus ubique
 testamenta senum, neu, si vafer unus et alter

---

aERΨ(=φψλ)

5. **1** Teresia (*P*)] tir- λ l g *et codicum* R φ l (tyr-) *inscr.*   **3** doloso] -sos R Ψ (exc. 1): -se ς
5 vides ut...pecus *interrog. feci*   **7** est] sit *coni. L. Müller*   **21** tulit *Crato*

FIVE

UL.   'Answer me this question too, Teresias; I want more than what's been told. By what arts and means can I make good my lost wealth? Why are you laughing?'

TER.   'For the man of many wiles, isn't it enough by now to sail back to Ithaca and to look on his ancestral home?'

5   UL.   'O you who have spoken false to no one, do you see how I'm returning home destitute and resourceless, according to your prediction, and there neither the wine-cellar nor the flock has been left untouched by the suitors? Yet both lineage and manliness (unless you have money to go with them) are worth less than seaweed.'

10   TER.   'Since it is poverty you shudder at, to put it unambiguously, learn in what way you can become rich. If you are given a thrush or anything else for yourself, let it fly off to the place where great wealth gleams, and the owner of it is an old man; sweet fruit and whatever beauties the tilled farm brings you, let him taste sooner than the Lar, the rich man more to be worshipped than the Lar; however perjured he may be, of no family, stained with a

15   brother's blood, a runaway slave, nevertheless don't you refuse, if he asks you, to walk on his outside.'

UL.   'What! Am I to cover dirty Dama's side? This wasn't the way I behaved at Troy, always pitting myself against better men.'

TER.   'Then you will be poor.'

20   UL.   'I will order my steadfast soul to endure this; in past times I have borne even more. You tell me at once, seer, from where I may shovel up riches, heaps of cash.'

TER.   'I *have* told you and I am telling you: be cunning and hunt everywhere for old people's wills, and, if a crafty one or two gets away from the fisher, after taking the bait off the end of the hook, don't give up hope, or drop the practice because you've been

insidiatorem praeroso fugerit hamo,   25
aut spem deponas aut artem illusus omittas.
magna minorve Foro si res certabitur olim,
vivet uter locuples sine gnatis, improbus, ultro
qui meliorem audax vocet in ius, illius esto
defensor: fama civem causaque priorem   30
sperne, domi si gnatus erit fecundave coniunx.
"Quinte," puta, aut "Publi" (gaudent praenomine molles
auriculae) "tibi me virtus tua fecit amicum.
ius anceps novi, causas defendere possum;
eripiet quivis oculos citius mihi quam te   35
contemptum cassa nuce pauperet. haec mea cura est,
ne quid tu perdas neu sis iocus." ire domum atque
pelliculam curare iube. fi cognitor ipse;
persta atque obdura, seu rubra Canicula findet
infantis statuas seu pingui tentus omaso   40
Furius hibernas cana nive conspuet Alpis.
"nonne vides" aliquis cubito stantem prope tangens
inquiet, "ut patiens, ut amicis aptus, ut acer?"
plures adnabunt thynni et cetaria crescent.
si cui praeterea validus male filius in re   45
praeclara sublatus aletur, ne manifestum
caelibis obsequium nudet te, leniter in spem
adrepe officiosus, ut et scribare secundus
heres et, si quis casus puerum egerit Orco,
in vacuum venias; perraro haec alea fallit.   50
qui testamentum tradet tibi cumque legendum,
abnuere et tabulas a te removere memento,
sic tamen ut limis rapias quid prima secundo
cera velit versu; solus multisne coheres,
veloci percurre oculo. quandoque recoctus   55
scriba ex quinqueviro corvum deludet hiantem
captatorque dabit risus Nasica Corano.'

---

aERΨ(=φψλl)

36 cassa] quassa *codd.*   **39** findet (*P¹*) -dit *Serv. G. 3.363*   **41** conspuit *Quint. 8.6.17*   **48** ut et *codd.* : ut g: uti *Heindorf, SB* : ut ad(scribare) *Apitz*   **55** quandoque *scripsit SB (cf. 1.9.33, Tac. Ann. 6.20.8, quandoque degustabis imperium, Hist. Aug. 20.19.5)*: plerumque *codd. P¹*

25   fooled. If one day a case of greater or less moment is being
contested in the Forum, whichever party is rich and childless, a
scoundrel, the sort who recklessly and unprovoked would sum-
mons a better man into court, of that man be the advocate: spurn
30   the citizen with the better name and case, if he has a son or fertile
wife at home. "Quintus," let's say, or "Publius" (sensitive ears
delight in first names), "your excellence has made me your friend.
I know the law's ambiguity, I can defend cases;   sooner will
35   someone pluck out my eyes than hold you in contempt and make
you the poorer by a nutshell. My concern is this, that you lose
nothing and not become a laughing-stock." Tell him to go home
and look after his precious hide. Become his attorney yourself.
Stand fast and endure, whether the red Dogstar splits unspeaking
statues or whether, swollen with rich tripe, Furius bespatters the
40   wintry Alps with white snow. "Don't you see" somone will say,
nudging his neighbour with his elbow, "how long-suffering he is,
how serviceable to friends, how keen?" More tunny will swim up
and the fish-ponds will grow. If someone, moreover, has a son
45   who is not very well, yet has been acknowledged and is being
raised in opulence, then, so that the flagrant servility paid an
unmarried man does not unmask you, be attentive and gently
worm your way into the hope of being written down second heir
and also into the hope that if some mischance should despatch the
50   boy to Orcus, you come into the empty place. Very rarely does this
gamble fail. If anyone hands you his will to read, be sure to refuse
and push the tablets away from you, but so that you snatch with a
side-glance what the second line of the first page prescribes; scan
with swift eye to see if you are sole heir or co-heir with a multitude.
55   Some day the civil servant cooked up from a minor magistrate will
dupe the raven with its beak gaping open, and the hunter Nasica
will provide Coranus with a laugh.'

'Num furis? an prudens ludis me obscura canendo?'

'O Laertiade, quidquid dicam aut erit aut non;
divinare etenim magnus mihi donat Apollo.'   60

'Quid tamen ista velit sibi fabula, si licet, ede.'

'Tempore quo iuvenis Parthis horrendus, ab alto
demissum genus Aenea, tellure marique
magnus erit, forti nubet procera Corano
filia Nasicae metuentis reddere soldum.   65
tum gener hoc faciet: tabulas socero dabit atque
ut legat orabit. multum Nasica negatas
accipiet tandem et tacitus leget invenietque
nil sibi legatum praeter plorare suisque.
illud ad haec iubeo: mulier si forte dolosa   70
libertusve senem delirum temperet, illis
accedas socius; laudes, lauderis ut absens.
adiuvat hoc quoque; sed vincit longe prius ipsum
expugnare caput. scribet mala carmina vecors?
laudato. scortator erit? cave te roget; ultro   75
Penelopam facilis potiori trade.'
                                        'Putasne
perduci poterit tam frugi tamque pudica,
quam nequiere proci recto depellere cursu?'

'Venit enim magnum donandi parca iuventus,
nec tantum Veneris quantum studiosa culinae.   80
sic tibi Penelope frugi est; quae si semel uno
de sene gustarit tecum partita lucellum,
ut canis a corio numquam absterrebitur uncto.
me sene quod dicam factum est: anus improba Thebis
ex testamento sic est elata: cadaver   85
unctum oleo largo nudis umeris tulit heres,

---

aERΨ(=φψλl)

74 scribit R φ ψ *pr.*   **79** magno ς (*sed cf. Epist. I.18.75*)   **87-6.33** *deest E*

UL.   'Are you raving? or are you deliberately making fun of me with your veiled prophecy?'

60   TER.   'O Laertes' son, all that I say either will come to pass or not; for great Apollo gives me this gift of foretelling the future.'

UL.   'None the less tell me, if it is allowed, what this story of yours is getting at.'

TER.   'At that time when a youth dreadful to the Parthians, scion descended from high Aeneas, shall be mighty on land and sea, to gallant Coranus shall be wed the stately daughter of Nasica,

65   anxious not to repay his debt in full. Then shall the son-in-law do this: he will give his will to his father-in-law and beg him to read it. After frequent refusals Nasica will finally take it and will read it in silence and will find nothing bequeathed to him and his but — to go to hell. This too I recommend: if a crafty woman or freedman

70   happens to have sway over a senile old man, join them as partner. Praise them, so that you may be praised in your absence. This too helps; but it's better by a long way to storm the principal himself. If he's a maniac writing bad verse, praise it. If he's a womaniser,

75   don't wait to be asked. Be obliging, of your own accord hand over Penelope to the better man.'

UL.   'What? Do you think she can be procured, so honest and so pure, she whom the suitors have not been able to swerve from the right path?'

TER.   'Yes, because it was youth that came, frugal in giving a lot,

80   devoted not so much to Venus as to the kitchen. That's why your Penelope is honest. But if once she's tasted a nice little profit from one old man, in partnership with you, then, like a dog from a greasy hide, she will never be scared away. When I was old, what I am going to tell you happened: at Thebes a wicked old woman, in

85   accordance with her will, was carried out to burial as follows: the

scilicet elabi si posset mortua; credo,
quod nimium institerat viventi. cautus adito;
neu desis opera neve immoderatus abundes.
difficilem et morosum offendet garrulus; ultra   90
"non", "etiam" sileas. Davus sis comicus atque
stes capite obstipo, multum similis metuenti.
obsequio grassare; mone, si increbruit aura,
cautus uti velet carum caput; extrahe turba
oppositis umeris; aurem substringe loquaci.   95
importunus amat laudari? donec "ohe iam!"
ad caelum manibus sublatis dixerit, urge,
crescentem tumidis infla sermonibus utrem.
cum te servitio longo curaque levarit
et certum vigilans "quartae sit partis Ulixes"   100
audieris "heres:" "ergo nunc Dama sodalis
nusquam est? unde mihi tam fortem tamque fidelem?"
sparge subinde et, si paulum potes illacrimare, est
gaudia prodentem vultum celare. sepulcrum
permissum arbitrio sine sordibus exstrue; funus   105
egregie factum laudet vicinia. si quis
forte coheredum senior male tussiet, huic tu
dic, ex parte tua seu fundi sive domus sit
emptor, gaudentem nummo te addicere. sed me
imperiosa trahit Proserpina. vive valeque.'   110

aRΨ(=φψλl)

89 opera *Siesbye*: -rae *codd.*   90 offendet (V)] -dit l φ ψ   91 *dist. Samuelsson*   92 multam *Bluemner*   100 sit] est R *pr.*: esto ς   103 *dist. post* potes *et gravius post* illacrimare *SB*

heir carried the corpse, generously oiled, on his bare shoulders,
her hope evidently being she might slip away from his grasp when
dead; because he had pressed her too hard in life, I suppose. Make
a careful approach; neither fall short in service nor be inordinately
90 overflowing with it. A chatterer will offend the cantankerous and
peevish; beyond "no", "yes," be silent. Be Davus in the comedy
and stand with head bent sideways, with a great look of fear. Assail
him with servility; if the breeze has grown stronger, warn him to
cover his dear head; get him out of the crowd using your shoulders.
95 Cock an attentive ear if he is talkative. Is he an insatiable lover of
praise? Until he says "Steady on!" hands raised to the sky, press
on, blow up the swelling bladder with hot air. When he has
released you from long slavery and anxiety and you hear, sure
100 you're wide awake, "Of the fourth part let Ulysses be heir," throw
in now and then a "And so now Dama my dear friend is no more?
Where will I find one so brave and so loyal?" and, if you can weep
a little, you can hide the expression betraying joy. If the tomb has
105 been left to your discretion, build it not meanly. Let the neigh-
bourhood praise a funeral brought off exceptionally well. If one
of the co-heirs, an older man, has a bad cough, tell him that, should
he be a buyer for a farm or a house from your share, you would
gladly assign it to him for a song. But as for me, stern Proserpina
drags me away. Live long, goodbye.'

VI

Hoc erat in votis: modus agri non ita magnus,
hortus ubi et tecto vicinus iugis aquae fons
et paulum silvae super his foret. auctius atque
di melius fecere. bene est, nil amplius oro,
Maia nate, nisi ut propria haec mihi munera faxis.   5
si neque maiorem feci ratione mala rem
nec sum facturus vitio culpave minorem,
si veneror stultus nihil horum, 'o si angulus ille
proximus accedat qui nunc denormat agellum!
o si urnam argenti fors quae mihi monstret, ut illi,   10
thesauro invento qui mercennarius agrum
illum ipsum mercatus aravit, dives amico
Hercule!', si quod adest gratum iuvat, hac prece te oro:
pingue pecus domino facias et cetera praeter
ingenium utque soles, custos mihi maximus adsis.   15

Ergo ubi me in montis et in arcem ex urbe removi,
quid prius illustrem satiris Musaque pedestri?
nec mala me ambitio perdit nec plumbeus Auster
autumnusque gravis, Libitinae quaestus acerbae.
Matutine pater, seu 'Iane' libentius audis,   20
unde homines operum primos vitaeque labores
instituunt (sic dis placitum), tu carminis esto
principium. Romae sponsorem me rapis: 'eia!
ne prior officio quisquam respondeat, urge.'
sive Aquilo radit terras seu bruma nivalem   25
interiore diem gyro trahit, ire necesse est.
postmodo quod mi obsit clare certumque locuto
luctandum in turba et facienda iniuria tardis.
'quid tibi vis, insane?' et 'quam rem agis?' improbus urget

---

aRΨ(=φψλl)

6. **7** ve R l φ ψ : que a λ **10** o a l φ *uar.*: heu R φ ψ : *om.* λ **16** et (*P*)] ut *Peerlkamp*
29-31 'quid...recurras?' *sic dist. SB* **29** quam rem a- *Bentley* q- res agis *codd.*: quas res g *SB*
urget *codd.* : -es ς *SB*

SIX

It was this I used to pray for: a parcel of land (not too big), where there would be a kitchen garden and a spring of ever-flowing water close to the house and, above them, a little bit of forest. The gods have provided better and more generously. I am content. I ask for
5 nothing more, O son of Maia, except that you make these gifts mine for ever. If I've neither made my wealth greater by evil means nor am going to make it smaller by waste or neglect, if I don't, like a fool, make any of these prayers, 'O if only that corner my neighbour owns were added on; it now spoils the shape of my dear little farm! O if only some stroke of luck would show me a
10 pot full of silver, as it did to that man who, after he found a treasure, bought and ploughed that very field, which he used to work as a hired labourer, made rich by Hercules' friendship!', if I am pleased by and grateful for what I have, with this prayer I beseech you: make my flock fat, and everything else I am master of, except my brains, and, as is your custom, be at my side, my most powerful
15 protector.

And so, when I've withdrawn from the city to my mountain citadel, what should I celebrate first in my satires, with my Muse who goes on foot? Neither damnable ambition is the death of me nor the leaden Southerly and oppressive autumn, a source of
20 profit for pitiless Libitina. Father of Morning, or 'Ianus' if you so prefer to be called, you from whom men begin the labours of their daily life (so the gods decided), be the beginning of my song. At Rome you rush me away to stand surety: 'Come on! so that no one answers the call of duty before you, get a move on.' Whether the
25 North wind is sweeping the lands or whether mid-winter pulls the snowy day on a narrower circuit, go one must. When I've said loud and clear what could do me harm one day, I have to wrestle in the crowd and do injury to the slow. 'What's the idea, you lunatic?' and 'What are you up to?' a rude fellow insists with angry curses.

iratis precibus; 'tu pulses omne quod obstat,   30
ad Maecenatem memori si mente recurras?'
hoc iuvat et melli est, non mentiar. at simul atras
ventum est Esquilias, aliena negotia centum
per caput et circa saliunt latus. 'ante secundam
Roscius orabat sibi adesses ad Puteal cras.'   35
'de re communi scribae magna atque nova te
orabant hodie meminisses, Quinte, reverti.'
'imprimat his, cura, Maecenas signa tabellis.'
dixeris 'experiar': 'si vis, potes' addit et instat.

Septimus octavo propior iam fugerit annus   40
ex quo Maecenas me coepit habere suorum
in numero, dumtaxat ad hoc, quem tollere raeda
vellet iter faciens et cui concredere nugas
hoc genus, 'hora quota est?', 'Thrax est Gallina Syro par?',
'matutina parum cautos iam frigora mordent'   45
et quae rimosa bene deponuntur in aure.
per totum hoc tempus subiectior in diem et horam
invidiae noster. ludos spectaverat una,
luserat in Campo: 'Fortunae filius!' omnes.
frigidus a Rostris manat per compita rumor: 50
quicumque obvius est, me consulit: 'o bone, nam te
scire, deos quoniam propius contingis, oportet,
numquid de Dacis audisti?' 'nil equidem.' 'ut tu
semper eris derisor!' 'at omnes di exagitent me
si quicquam!' 'quid? militibus promissa Triquetra   55
praedia Caesar an est Itala tellure daturus?'
iurantem me scire nihil mirantur ut unum
scilicet egregii mortalem altique silenti.

Perditur haec inter misero lux, non sine votis:
'o rus, quando ego te aspiciam? quandoque licebit   60
nunc veterum libris, nunc somno et inertibus horis

---

aERΨ(=φψλl)

30 precibus] pedibus *SB*   tu ... recurras *interrog. fecit Peerlkamp*   **34** *redit* E   **44** thr(a)ex a R φ
ψ V   **48** spectaverit g   **49** luserat (σχ)] -rit ς   **57** mirantur a E λ l : miratur R φ ψ *SB*
59 perditur *codd.* σχ : deperit *L. Müller SB*

30 'Must you shove everything in your way, if you are running back
to Maecenas, thinking of nothing else?' This is pleasing and sweet
as honey, I won't deny it. But as soon as I get to the black
Esquiline, a hundred affairs of other people surge up all over my
head and round my side. 'Roscius requests that you meet him at
35 the Well, tomorrow, before the second hour.' 'Quintus, about an
important new matter of mutual interest, the treasury officials
request that you remember to come back today.' 'See to it that
Maecenas puts his seal to this document.' Suppose you have said
'I will try,' he adds 'You can if you want to,' and insists.
40   The seventh year, closer to the eighth, will soon be gone,
since Maecenas began including me in the number of his follow-
ers, just as a person he might wish to take along in his carriage
when making a journey and to whom to entrust small-talk of this
sort, 'What's the time?', 'Is Chicken, the Thracian, a match for
Syrus?' 'The early morning frosts are already nippy if you don't
45 take care,' and things which it's safe to deposit in a leaky ear.
Throughout all this time from day to day and hour to hour, our
friend is more exposed to envy. Had he watched the games
together with him, had he played on the Campus with him, 'Lucky
devil' all would say. A chilling rumour from the Rostra runs from
50 street corner to street corner: whoever comes across me, seeks my
opinion: 'Dear fellow, you ought to know, you see, because you're
in closer contact with the gods, have you heard anything about the
Dacians?' 'Nothing at all.' 'What a joker you will always be!'
'May all the gods drive me mad if I've heard anything!' 'Tell me,
55 the farms he has promised to the veterans, is Caesar going to give
them in Sicily or Italy?' When I swear I know nothing they
marvel at me as if I am, can you believe, the one and only
mortal of uncommonly deep silence.
        I suffer as the day is wasted amid these occupations, with
many a prayer: 'O country estate, when will I look on you? And
60 when will I be allowed, now with books of ancient authors, now
with sleep and profitless hours, to drink in pleasant forgetfulness

ducere sollicitae iucunda oblivia vitae?
o quando faba Pythagorae cognata simulque
uncta satis pingui ponentur holuscula lardo?'
o noctes cenaeque deum! quibus ipse meique   65
ante Larem proprium vescor vernasque procaces
pasco libatis dapibus. prout cuique libido est,
siccat inaequalis calices conviva, solutus
legibus insanis, seu quis capit acria fortis
pocula seu modicis uvescit laetius. ergo   70
sermo oritur, non de villis domibusve alienis,
nec male necne Lepos saltet; sed quod magis ad nos
pertinet et nescire malum est agitamus: utrumne
divitiis homines an sint virtute beati;
quidve ad amicitias, usus rectumne, trahat nos;   75
et quae sit natura boni summumque quid eius.

Cervius haec inter vicinus garrit anilis
ex re fabellas. si quis nam laudat Arelli
sollicitas ignarus opes, sic incipit: 'olim
rusticus urbanum murem mus paupere fertur   80
accepisse cavo, veterem vetus hospes amicum,
asper et attentus quaesitis, ut tamen artum
solveret hospitiis animum. quid multa? neque ille
sepositi ciceris nec longae invidit avenae,
aridum et ore ferens acinum semesaque lardi   85
frusta dedit, cupiens varia fastidia cena
vincere tangentis male singula dente superbo;
cum pater ipse domus palea porrectus in horna
esset ador loliumque, dapis meliora relinquens.
tandem urbanus ad hunc "quid te iuvat" inquit, "amice,   90
praerupti nemoris patientem vivere dorso?
vis tu homines urbemque feris praeponere silvis?
carpe viam, mihi crede, comes. terrestria quando

---

aERΨ(=$\phi\psi\lambda$)

63 simulve *Usener*   **67** prout a E l ψ *corr.* : cum ut R ϕ ψ *pr.* : ut λ **70** lentius *Peerlkamp, SB*
78 nam si quis ς **83** ille] illi ς **92** *redit* z   **93** *post* comes *levius dist. vulg.*   quando] *anne*
cuncta *SB*

of my harrassed life? O when will the bean, Pythagoras's relative, be served, and with it greens sufficiently oiled by fat bacon?' O

65   nights and feasts of the gods! When I myself and my friends eat before my own household god and I feed the cheeky homeborn slaves after making a food-offering. Just as each one pleases, the guests, freed from crazy laws, drain dry unequal cups, whether the hard-headed one takes his drinks undiluted, or whether with

70   moderate ones he grows mellow more happily. And so conversation arises, not about other people's villas or town-houses, nor whether Lepos dances badly or not, but we discuss what has more relevance to us and not to know is an evil: whether it is wealth or virtue that makes men happy; or what leads us to friendships, self-

75   interest or rectitude; and what is the nature of goodness and what its highest form.

Amid this talk my neighbour Cervius prattles away telling old wives' tales that are to the point. For if anyone praises Arellius's wealth, unaware of the troubles it brings, he begins like

80   this: 'Once upon a time, they say, a country mouse entertained a town mouse in his poor burrow, host and guest being friends of old. He was rough and careful with his store, but so as, nevertheless, to loosen his tight disposition for hospitality's sake. Why say more? He was not the one to grudge the chickpea he had put away,

85   nor the long oat, and, bringing them in his mouth, he offered a raisin and half-eaten morsels of bacon, wishing by the variety of the meal to overcome his friend's disdain, as he scarcely touched them one by one with his contemptuous tooth; while the father of the house himself, stretched out on fresh chaff, ate emmer wheat and darnel, leaving the better parts of the feast. Finally the

90   townsman said to him "Why should you be happy, my friend, to live in hardship on a steep wooded ridge? Do please choose

mortalis animas vivunt sortita neque ulla est
aut magno aut parvo leti fuga — quo, bone, circa, 95
dum licet, in rebus iucundis vive beatus,
vive memor quam sis aevi brevis." haec ubi dicta
agrestem pepulere, domo levis exsilit; inde
ambo propositum peragunt iter, urbis aventes
moenia nocturni subrepere. iamque tenebat 100
nox medium caeli spatium, cum ponit uterque
in locuplete domo vestigia, rubro ubi cocco
tincta super lectos canderet vestis eburnos
multaque de magna superessent fercula cena,
quae procul exstructis inerant hesterna canistris. 105
ergo ubi purpurea porrectum in veste locavit
agrestem, veluti succinctus cursitat hospes
continuatque dapes nec non verniliter ipse
fungitur officiis, praelambens omne quod affert.
ille cubans gaudet mutata sorte bonisque 110
rebus agit laetum convivam; cum subito ingens
valvarum strepitus lectis excussit utrumque.
currere per totum pavidi conclave, magisque
exanimes trepidare simul domus alta Molossis
personuit canibus. tum rusticus "haud mihi vita 115
est opus hac" ait et "valeas. me silva cavusque
tutus ab insidiis tenui solabitur ervo." '

---

aERΨ(=zφψλl)

103 arderet *Peerlkamp, coll. Verg. A. 4.262*   **106** ubi *om.* R Ψ (*exc.* 1)   **108** ipse *Lambinus* : ipsis *codd.*   **109** praelibans ς *SB* : -labens g   afflat R (?) Ψ (exc. l)

civilisation before the wild woods. Take my advice, step out on the
road, as my companion, since earthly creatures have been allotted
mortal souls and there is no escape from death for big or small —
95   therefore, my good fellow, while you may, live a happy life amid
pleasant things, live mindful of how brief your lifespan is." These
words struck the countryman. He bounds lightly from his home;
then the pair carry on to the end of their purposed journey, since
they were eager to creep up to the city walls while it was still night.
100 And now Night had reached the mid-point of her heavenly jour-
ney, when the two plant their footsteps in a rich house, of the kind
where covers dyed with rich scarlet blazed on ivory couches and
many a dish was left over from a great dinner, in baskets piled up
105 aside from the day before. Well then, when he had settled the
countryman in his place, stretched out on the crimson coverlet, the
host, with his clothes tucked up like a waiter's, scurries around and
keeps the feast coming and also performs himself the duties of a
homeborn slave, licking everything he brings first. The other,
110 lying back, rejoices in his change of fortune, and, since things were
going well, plays the happy guest; when suddenly a huge crash
of doors scared them both right off the couches. They ran in fright
all over the dining-room, and their terrified panic was greater as
soon as the high house resounded with Molossian hounds. Then
115 the countryman said, "I don't need this kind of life" and "Farewell.
My burrow in the wood safe from surprise attack will keep me
happy with simple vetch." '

VII

'Iamdudum ausculto et cupiens tibi dicere servus
pauca reformido.' 'Davusne?' 'ita, Davus; amicum
mancipium domino et frugi quod sit satis, hoc est,
ut vitale putes.' 'age, libertate Decembri,
quando ita maiores voluerunt, utere. narra.'   5

'Pars hominum vitiis gaudet constanter et urget
propositum; pars multa natat, modo recta capessens,
interdum pravis obnoxia. saepe notatus
cum tribus anellis, modo laeva Priscus inani,
vixit inaequalis, clavum ut mutaret in horas;   10
aedibus ex magnis subito se conderet unde
mundior exiret vix libertinus honeste;
iam moechus Romae, iam mallet doctus Athenis
vivere, Vertumnis quotquot sunt natus iniquis.
scurra Volanerius, postquam illi iusta cheragra   15
contudit articulos, qui pro se tolleret atque
mitteret in phimum talos, mercede diurna
conductum pavit; quanto constantior isdem
in vitiis, tanto levius miser ac prior illo
qui iam contento, iam laxo fune laborat.'   20

'Non dices hodie quorsum haec tam putida tendant,
furcifer?' 'ad te, inquam.' 'quo pacto, pessime?' 'laudas
fortunam et mores antiquae plebis, et idem
si quis ad illa deus subito te agat, usque recuses,
aut quia non sentis quod clamas rectius esse   25
aut quia non firmus rectum defendis et haeres
nequiquam caeno cupiens evellere plantam.

---

aERΨ(=zϕψλl)

7. **13** doctus E l (*de a n. l.*)] doctor (V) *SB* **18** isdem z R a V : idem E *alt.* l *corr.* **19** ac
prior Ψ : acrior a E R V   illo ς σχ: ille *codd.*   **20** iam...iam λ l σχ : iam...quam a : tam...quam
R z ϕ ψ : iam (*alt.* iam *om.*) E

SEVEN

DAV. 'For some time now I've been listening. I want to tell you a few things, but, being a slave, I'm scared to.'

HOR. 'Is that Davus?'

DAV. 'Yes, Davus, his master's friend, though a bought slave, and an honest fellow, honest enough, that is, not to be thought too good to live.'

HOR. 'Come on, take advantage of December's freedom, seeing that our ancestors wanted it so. Speak out.'

5

DAV. 'Some people are consistent in the enjoyment of vice and pursue their chosen course; the majority waver, at one moment making for the right, sometimes at the mercy of what is wrong. Priscus was often noticed sporting three rings, but sometimes with his left hand bare. He lived so inconsistently that he would change his stripe from hour to hour. From a great house, he would suddenly go to earth in the kind of place a fairly respectable freedman could scarcely appear from with any decency. First he preferred to live as an adulterer in Rome, then as a man of learning at Athens. He was born with all the Vertumni there are against him.

10

15

Volanerius, the playboy, when a well-deserved gout had crippled his finger-joints, kept a man hired by the day to pick up the dice for him and put them in the dice-box. The more consistent a man is in one and the same vice, the less unhappy he is and the more he comes out ahead of him who slogs with the rope now taut, now slack.'

20

HOR. 'Won't you tell me at last where all this rot is heading, you crook?'

DAV. 'At you, I say again.'

HOR. 'How's that, scum?'

DAV. 'You rave about the good fortune and good behaviour of the people of old and yet you would resist to the end if some god were suddenly to take you to all that, either because you don't really think that what you proclaim is the better way or because you aren't steadfast in your defence of what's right and stick fast, vainly longing to pluck the sole of your foot out of the mire. At

25

Romae rus optas, absentem rusticus urbem
tollis ad astra levis. si nusquam es forte vocatus
ad cenam, laudas securum holus ac, velut usquam   30
vinctus eas, ita te felicem dicis amasque
quod nusquam tibi sit potandum. iusserit ad se
Maecenas serum sub lumina prima venire
convivam: "nemon oleum fert ocius? ecquis
audit?" cum magno blateras clamore fugisque.   35
Mulvius et scurrae tibi non referenda precati
discedunt. "etenim fateor me" dixerit ille
"duci ventre levem, nasum nidore supinor,
imbecillus, iners, si quid vis, adde popino:
tu, cum sis quod ego et fortassis nequior, ultro   40
insectere velut melior verbisque decoris
obvolvas vitium?" quid si me stultior ipso
quingentis empto drachmis deprenderis? aufer
me vultu terrere; manum stomachumque teneto,
dum quae Crispini docuit me ianitor edo.'   45

'Te coniunx aliena capit, meretricula Davum:
peccat uter nostrum cruce dignius? acris ubi me
natura intendit, sub clara nuda lucerna
quaecumque excepit turgentis verbera caudae
clunibus aut agitavit equum lasciva supinum,   50
dimittit neque famosum neque sollicitum ne
ditior aut formae melioris meiat eodem.
tu, cum proiectis insignibus, anulo equestri
Romanoque habitu, prodis ex iudice Dama
turpis odoratum caput obscurante lacerna,   55
non es quod simulas? metuens induceris atque
altercante libidinibus tremis ossa pavore.
quid refert, uri virgis ferroque necari
auctoratus eas an turpi clausus in arca,
quo te demisit peccati conscia erilis,   60

---

aERΨ(=zϕψλl)

34 fert E l] feret *cett.* V (?)   **35** fugis (σχ)] furis V *Pl*   **42** ipse E R *corr.* l

Rome you long for the country, but, when living in the country,
you praise the far-off city to the skies. Inconsistent! If you happen
30   not to have been invited out to dinner anywhere, you praise your
carefree greens, and, as though you went out anywhere under
duress, you declare youself lucky and hug yourself because you're
not expected to be boozing somewhere. Should Maecenas invite
you at lighting-up time to come to his house as a last-minute guest:
"Hurry, someone, bring the lantern-oil! Does anyone at all hear?"
you blether with a great hue and cry and are off. Mulvius and the
35   other hangers-on leave, cursing you in unrepeatable terms. "Oh
yes," Mulvius might say, "I admit that I'm a fickle slave of the
belly, my nose leans back at the smell of cooking, I'm weak, lazy,
add, if you want anything more, a greedy-guts. Why should you,
though you are what I am and maybe worse, gratuitously abuse me
40   as if you were better, and cloak your vice in fine words?" What
then if you're found out to be a bigger fool than I myself, bought
for five hundred drachmas? Give over trying to frighten me with
your looks, and keep your hand and bile in check, while I pass on
45   what Crispinus's doorkeeper taught me.

'You are captivated by another man's wife, Davus by a
tart. Which of us more deserves crucifixion for his fault? When
irresistible nature sets me up for sex it doesn't matter who, naked
in the bright lamplight, has received the blows of my swollen tail
50   or, free of inhibitions, with bouncing buttocks has ridden me on my
back as her horse. She lets me go with reputation intact and not
worried in case one more wealthy or better-looking piss in the
same place. But you, when you've thrown off your signs of rank,
your knight's ring and Roman dress, and appear in public not a
55   juror, but a Dama, a degenerate, with a cloak covering up your
perfumed head, are you not what you're disguised as? Full of fear
you're brought inside, and you quake to your very bones as panic
disputes against lust. What does it matter whether you sell yourself
as a gladiator to be branded, and slain with rods and the sword or,
60   shut up in a foul chest (the maid, the accomplice of her mistress's

contractum genibus tangas caput? estne marito
matronae peccantis in ambo iusta potestas?
in corruptorem vel iustior; illa tamen se
non habitu mutatve loco peccatve superne.
[cum te formidet mulier neque credat amanti]   65
ibis sub furcam prudens dominoque furenti
committes rem omnem et vitam et cum corpore famam?
evasti: credo, metues doctusque cavebis:
quaeres quando iterum paveas iterumque perire
possis, o totiens servus! quae belua ruptis,   70
cum semel effugit, reddit se prava catenis?'

' "Non sum moechus" ais. neque ego, hercule, fur, ubi vasa
praetereo sapiens argentea. tolle periclum,
iam vaga prosiliet frenis natura remotis.
tune mihi dominus, rerum imperiis hominumque   75
tot tantisque minor, quem ter vindicta quaterque
imposita haud umquam misera formidine privet?
adde super dictis quod non levius valeat: nam
sive vicarius est qui servo paret, uti mos
vester ait, seu conservus, tibi quid sum ego? nempe   80
tu, mihi qui imperitas, alii servis miser atque
duceris ut nervis alienis mobile lignum.'

'Quisnam igitur liber? sapiens, sibi qui imperiosus,
quem neque pauperies neque mors neque vincula terrent,
responsare cupidinibus, contemnere honores   85
fortis et in se ipso totus, teres atque rotundus,
externi ne quid valeat per leve morari,
in quem manca ruit semper Fortuna. potesne
ex his ut proprium quid noscere? quinque talenta
poscit te mulier, vexat foribusque repulsum   90
perfundit gelida, rursus vocat: eripe turpi

---

aERΨ(=zφψλl)

64 ve a E : que R Ψ (exc. l) SB : ne ꟗ P^l superne codd. P : pudice SB (pudenter iam Peerlkamp)
65 seclusit SB   67 dist. Shütz   80 quid z ꟗ : quod cett.   81 aliis Ψ (exc.z)   83 qui R l : que
cett. V (cf. Nilsson, Eranos, 52, 1954, 195 sqq.)   93 sic dist. Klingner, aliter SB

fault, has put you there), pull in your head until it touches your
knees? Does the erring wife's husband have lawful power over
both parties? In the case of the seducer it is even more justified.
The wife at any rate doesn't change dress or place or lie on top as
she sins. [Since the woman fears you and does not trust you, her
lover] will you deliberately put your head in the stocks and hand
over to a raging master your whole substance and life and repu-
tation along with your body? You've escaped: surely you'll be
afraid and take care now you've learned your lesson: no, you will
seek to know when again you may be terrified, when again you
may perish, O time and time again a slave. What wild beast, when
it has got safely away once, is so perverse as to return to its broken
chains?

        "'I'm not an adulterer," you say. And I'm not a thief, by
god, when I wisely pass by silver plate. Take away the risk, at once
our nature as the reins are removed will spring out and run wild.
Am I to call you my master, you who are subject to so many and
so great constraints, both of circumstances and of people, you
whom an act of manumission performed three, even four times,
could never release from wretched fear? Here's another point, of
no less force than what I've said: for whether he who obeys a
slave's orders is called a "deputy", as you free men say, or a "co-
slave", which am I to you? One thing's sure, you who give me
orders suffer as the slave of others and are manipulated like a
wooden puppet pulled by strings in someone else's hands.

        'Who, then, is free? The wise man, who has dominion
over himself, whom neither poverty nor death nor chains makes
fearful, having the courage to stand up to his desires and to disdain
honours. He is complete in himself, a smooth, rounded sphere. On
his polished surface nothing from outside can get a hold. On him
the attack of Fortune always falls half-strength. Can you recognise
any of these qualities as your own? A woman asks you for five
talents, torments you, turns you away from her door and drenches
you with cold water. Then she summons you back. Pull your neck
out from the degrading yoke and be free. "I'm free," come on, say

65

70

75

80

85

colla iugo liber; "liber sum" dic, age: non quis.
urget enim dominus mentem non lenis et acris
subiectat lasso stimulos versatque negantem.'

'Vel cum Pausiaca torpes, insane, tabella,   95
qui peccas minus atque ego, cum Fulvi Rutubaeque
aut Pacideiani contento poplite miror
proelia rubrica picta aut carbone, velut si
re vera pugnent, feriant vitentque moventes
arma viri? nequam et cessator Davus, at ipse   100
subtilis veterum iudex et callidus audis.'

'Nili ego, si ducor libo fumante: tibi ingens
virtus atque animus cenis responsat opimis?
obsequium ventris mihi perniciosius est. cur?
tergo plector enim. qui tu impunitior illa   105
quae parvo sumi nequeunt obsonia captas?
nempe inamarescunt epulae sine fine petitae
illusique pedes vitiosum ferre recusant
corpus. an hic peccat, sub noctem qui puer uvam
furtiva mutat strigili: qui praedia vendit,   110
nil servile, gulae parens, habet?'

                         'Adde quod idem
non horam tecum esse potes, non otia recte
ponere teque ipsum vitas fugitivus et erro,
iam vino quaerens, iam somno fallere curam:
frustra; nam comes atra premit sequiturque fugacem.'   115
'unde mihi lapidem?' 'quorsum est opus?' 'unde sagittas?'
'aut insanit homo aut versus facit.' 'ocius hinc te
ni rapis, accedes opera agro nona Sabino.'

---

aERΨ(=zφψλl)

102 nili *scripsit SB* (*v. ad Cic. Att. 2.15* nihili) : nil *codd. P*   **104** *dist. Fabricius (cf. 2.3.187)*
105 qui tu E V σχ (*cf. Pers. 5.130*) : quid tu a z λ : qui dum R(?) l φ ψ : *anne* quid? tu (*SB*)
118 *redit* C

it. You can't. That's because a relentless master rides your mind
hard, plying the sharp spurs when you are tired and wheeling you
round when you balk.

95   'Or when you swoon over a painting by Pausias, you
lunatic, how is it that you're less guilty than I, when, with straining
knees, I admire the red-ochre or charcoal-painted battles of Fulvius
and Rutuba or Pacideianus, just as if they were really fighting,
striking and parrying as they brandish their weapons, real heroes?

100   Davus is a rogue and a dawdler, but you yourself are called a
connoisseur, and a fine judge of old masters.

        'I'm a good-for-nothing, if I'm led astray by a piping hot
cake; does your great strength and nobility of character stand up
to the temptations of rich dinners? Subservience to the belly is
more ruinous for me. Why?   My back is beaten, you see. But

105   aren't you punished just as much when you hunt out those
delicacies which cannot be bought cheaply?   Count on it, an
endless round of feasts begins to turn to gall and the baffled feet
refuse to bear the unsound body. Or is he at fault, the slave who
at nightfall swaps a stolen body-scraper for a bunch of grapes,

110   while there is nothing of the slave about the man who sells his
estates to do his gullet's bidding?

        'Moreover, you can't endure your own company for an
hour, you can't invest your free time properly and you try to get
away from yourself like a runaway or truant slave, attempting to
cheat anxiety now with wine, now with sleep. In vain, for that
black companion anxiety presses close, following you as you run
away.'
HOR.   'Where can I get a stone?'
DAV.   'What for?'
HOR.   'Whence arrows?'
DAV.   'The man is either mad or versifying.'
HOR.   'Unless you take yourself off from here — and quickly
too— you'll be assigned as the ninth labourer on my Sabine farm.'

VIII

'Ut Nasidieni iuvit te cena beati?
nam mihi quaerenti convivam dictus here illic
de medio potare die.'
                    'Sic ut mihi numquam
in vita fuerit melius.'
                    'Da, si grave non est,
quae prima iratum ventrem placaverit esca.'   5

'In primis Lucanus aper. leni fuit Austro
captus, ut aiebat cenae pater. acria circum,
rapula, lactucae, radices, qualia lassum
pervellunt stomachum, siser, allec, faecula Coa.
his ut sublatis puer alte cinctus acernam   10
gausape purpureo mensam pertersit et alter
sublegit quodcumque iaceret inutile quodque
posset cenantis offendere, ut Attica virgo
cum sacris Cereris, procedit fuscus Hydaspes
Caecuba vina ferens, Alcon Chium maris expers.   15
hic erus: "Albanum, Maecenas, sive Falernum
te magis appositis delectat, habemus utrumque." '

'Divitias miseras! sed quis cenantibus una,
Fundani, pulchre fuerit tibi, nosse laboro.'

'Summus ego et prope me Viscus Thurinus et infra,   20
si memini, Varius, cum Servilio Balatrone
Vibidius, quos Maecenas adduxerat umbras.
Nomentanus erat super ipsum, Porcius infra,
ridiculus totas semel absorbere placentas.

---

aCERΨ(=z$\phi\psi\lambda$l)

8. **2** convivam quaerenti *Prisc. GL 3.71* **4** da Ψ (*exc.* l)] dic (V) *SB* **5** placaverit Ψ (*exc.* l) :
pac- a *pr.* C R l : pecc- E **7** *post* circum *dist. Doederlein* **10** ut (*Prisc. G L 2.333*)] ubi a E l
15 *anne* Alco? *SB   post* Chium *dist. SB* **18** miseras ($\sigma\chi$)] miras *D. Heinsius* **22** quos (*P^l*)
quas z g *P* **24** semel C R Ψ : simul a E V (*?*)

EIGHT

HOR.   'How did you like rich Nasidienus's dinner? When I was looking for you as a guest, you see, they told me you were carousing there yesterday from midday.'·

FUND.   'So much so that I never enjoyed myself better in my life.'

HOR.   'Tell me, if it's not troublesome, which delicacy first
5   appeased the angry belly?'

FUND. 'To begin with, Lucanian boar. It was one caught in a gentle Southerly, as the father of the feast said. Around were sharp things, baby turnips, lettuces, radishes, such as excite a tired stomach, parsnip, fish-pickle, tartar of Coan wine. These had been
10   cleared away. A slave with tunic girt-up high thoroughly rubbed down the maple table with coarse crimson cloth and a second picked up whatever was lying useless and that could offend the diners. Then, like an Attic maiden with Ceres' holy vessels, dusky
15   Hydaspes marches in, bearing Caecuban wine, Alcon bearing Chian without sea-water. Hereupon the master said: "If Alban, Maecenas, or Falernian pleases you more than what has been served, we have both." '

HOR.   'The sorrows of the rich! But I am anxious to know with which dinner-companions, Fundanius, you had a wonderful time.'

20   FUND.   'I was at the top and next to me was Viscus of Thurii and below, if I remember, Varius, with Servilius the Buffoon was Vibidius, the extras whom Maecenas had brought with him. Nomentanus was above the master, below him was Hogg, who raised a laugh by swallowing whole cakes at one go. Nomentanus's

Nomentanus ad hoc, qui, si quid forte lateret,   25
indice monstraret digito; nam cetera turba,
nos, inquam, cenamus avis, conchylia, piscis
longe dissimilem noto celantia sucum —
ut vel continuo patuit, cum passeris atque
ingustata mihi porrexerit ilia rhombi.   30
post hoc me docuit melimela rubere minorem
ad lunam delecta. quid hoc intersit, ab ipso
audieris melius. tum Vibidius Balatroni:
"nos nisi damnose bibimus, moriemur inulti,"
et calices poscit maiores. vertere pallor   35
tum parochi faciem nil sic metuentis ut acris
potores, vel quod maledicunt liberius vel
fervida quod subtile exsurdant vina palatum.
invertunt Allifanis vinaria tota
Vibidius Balatroque; secutis omnibus imi   40
convivae lecti nihilum nocuere lagoenis.'

'Affertur squillas inter murena natantis
in patina porrecta. sub hoc erus "haec gravida" inquit
"capta est, deterior post partum carne futura.
his mixtum ius est: oleo quod prima Venafri   45
pressit cella; garo de sucis piscis Hiberi;
vino quinquenni, verum citra mare nato,
dum coquitur (cocto Chium sic convenit ut non
hoc magis ullum aliud); pipere albo, non sine aceto
quod Methymnaeam vitio mutaverit uvam.   50
erucas viridis, inulas ego primus amaras
monstravi incoquere, inlutos Curtillus echinos,
ut melius muria quod testa marina remittit." '

---

aCERΨ(=zφψλl)

28 dissimili notum *Peerlkamp*   **29** atque] assi et ς   **30** porrexerit (V?)] -erat z   **40** *sic dist.*
L. Müller, post omnibus *vulg*.   imi a E R V σχ: imis C Ψ   **52** inlutos *codd.* σχ (in luto,
Scurtillus σχ *uar*.) : illotos ς *SB*   cortillus Ψ   **53** quod] quo V : quam z   remittit C V : -tat
a R Ψ : -tas E

25 role was to point out anything that might happen to escape our
    notice; all the rest of the crowd, you see, the uninitiated, we, I
    mean, were dining on fowl, shell-fish, fish containing a taste far
    different from any familiar to us — as it appeared right from the
    beginning, when he passed me loin of flounder and turbot, which
30 I had not tasted before. After this he told me that honey-apples are
    red if picked when the moon is less than full. What difference this
    makes, you will better hear from the man himself. Then Vibidius
    says to the Buffoon: "If we do not drink him bankrupt, we'll die
35 unavenged," and he asks for larger cups. Pallor then transformed
    the face of the caterer who feared nothing so much as strong
    drinkers, either because they are too free with slander or because
    heating wines dull the subtle palate. Vibidius and the Buffoon
40 upturn whole wine jugs into the Allifanian cups; while all
    followed their lead, the guests on the bottom couch did no damage
    to the flagons.

        'There is brought on a moray eel, stretched out in the dish,
    amid swimming scampi. Thereupon the master says "This was
    caught pregnant, since after spawning it will deteriorate in the
    flesh. The sauce was mixed from the following: oil which is the
45 Venafran cellar's first pressing; fish-sauce from the juices of
    Spanish fish; five-year old wine, but originating on this side of the
    sea, while it is being heated (once it has been heated Chian suits
    better than anything else); white pepper, with vinegar which
    through spoiling has soured the Methymnean grape. I first taught
50 to boil fresh green rocket and bitter elecampane in the sauce,
    Curtillus unwashed sea-urchins, as that which the sea-shell yields
    is better than fish-brine."

Interea suspensa gravis aulaea ruinas
in patinam fecere, trahentia pulveris atri   55
quantum non Aquilo Campanis excitat agris.
nos maius veriti, postquam nihil esse pericli
sensimus, erigimur. Rufus posito capite, ut si
filius immaturus obisset, flere. quis esset
finis, ni sapiens sic Nomentanus amicum   60
tolleret? "heu, Fortuna, quis est crudelior in nos
te deus? ut semper gaudes illudere rebus
humanis!" Varius mappa compescere risum
vix poterat. Balatro suspendens omnia naso
"haec est condicio vivendi" aiebat "eoque   65
responsura tuo numquam est par fama labori.
tene, ut ego accipiar laute, torquerier omni
sollicitudine districtum, ne panis adustus,
ne male conditum ius apponatur, ut omnes
praecincti recte pueri comptique ministrent?   70
adde hos praeterea casus, aulaea ruant si,
ut modo, si patinam pede lapsus frangat agaso.
sed convivatoris, uti ducis, ingenium res
adversae nudare solent, celare secundae."

'Nasidienus ad haec: "tibi di quaecumque preceris   75
commoda dent! ita vir bonus es convivaque comis,"
et soleas poscit. tum in lecto quoque videres
stridere secreta divisos aure susurros.'

'Nullos his mallem ludos spectasse; sed illa
redde, age, quae deinceps risisti.'

                                         'Vibidius dum   80
quaerit de pueris num sit quoque fracta lagoena,
quod sibi poscenti non dantur pocula, dumque
ridetur fictis rerum Balatrone secundo,

---

aCERΨ(=zφψλl)

70 pueri recte C g

'And now the suspended tapestries fell heavily onto the
55   dish bringing down more black dust than the North wind stirs up
from the Campanian fields. We feared worse, but after we realised
there was no danger, we picked ourselves up. Rufus, with head
buried, wept, as though his son had died before reaching manhood.
60   What end would there have been, had not Nomentanus, in
philosophical vein, thus cheered his friend? "Alas, Fortune, which
god is more cruel to us than you? How you always enjoy making
sport of human affairs!" Varius could scarcely contain his
laughter with his napkin. The Buffoon, who turns up his nose at
65   everything, was saying "This is the law of life, and for this reason
fame equal to your effort will never reward it. Are you, in order
that I may be entertained grandly, tormented and racked by every
kind of anxiety, that burnt bread be not served, or a badly seasoned
70   sauce, that all the slaves who serve be girt-up and coiffed correctly?
Not to mention accidents like these, if the tapestries fall down, as
just now, if losing his footing a stable-boy smashes the dish. But
the host's genius, as the general's, adverse circumstances usually
lay bare, while favourable conceal it."

75   'Nasidienus replied: "May the gods reward you, whatever
your prayer may be! You are such a good man and gracious guest,"
and he asked for his slippers. Then on each couch you would have
seen buzz whisperings in different pairs, meant for the private ear.'

HOR.   'I would have preferred to watch no other shows than
these; but come, give over those things you laughed at next.'

FUND.   'While Vibidius is inquiring from the slaves whether
80   the flagon has been broken as well, because no cups are being
given to him, though he asks, and while, with the Buffoon egging
us on, we laugh at pretended jokes, Nasidienus, you return, with

Nasidiene, redis mutatae frontis, ut arte
emendaturus fortunam. deinde secuti   85
mazonomo pueri magno discerpta ferentes
membra gruis sparsi sale multo, non sine farre,
pinguibus et ficis pastum iecur anseris albae
et leporum avulsos, ut multo suavius, armos,
quam si cum lumbis quis edit; tum pectore adusto   90
vidimus et merulas poni et sine clune palumbis,
suavis res, si non causas narraret earum et
naturas dominus; quem nos sic fugimus ulti
ut nihil omnino gustaremus, velut illis
Canidia afflasset peior serpentibus Afris.'   95

---

aCERΨ(=zϕψλl)

88 albae V g (*cf. Bentley*): albi *codd.*   90 tum] cum C E (?)   94 veluti si ς   95 afris a E R
z : atris C Ψ (*exc. z*)

changed countenance, like one about to set bad luck right by skill.

85 Then follow slaves carrying on a great trencher the disjointed limbs of a male crane, sprinkled with plenty of salt, and with flour, and a white goose's liver, fed with fat figs, and hare's wings detached, as much more delicious than if one were to eat them with

90 the loins; then we saw served both blackbirds with burnt breast, and wood-pigeons without the rump, delicious things, had not the lord given an account of their origins and natures; him we fled after taking our revenge in such a way that we tasted nothing at all, as though Canidia, worse than African snakes, had breathed poison

95 on them.'

Commentary

Satire One

The introductory satire of the book presents some intriguing surprises, the first being its form. As a dialogue between the poet and the eminent jurist Trebatius it signals the book's adoption of dialogue as the predominant structural mode and the consequent widening of the range of interlocutors (see Introduction §§4, 5). Trebatius is another surprise. In Book 1 Maecenas had been the dedicatee and privileged addressee (*Sat.* 1.1.1, 1.6.1), but in Book 2, though an important presence, he is not addressed at all. These two new features of the book, dramatic dialogue and diverse interlocutors, are not new to satire. Lucilius frequently used dramatic dialogue and showed himself in conversation with contemporaries (Charpin II, 124, 128-9). Most significantly, the whole idea of this satire, the satirist's justification of his role as satirist, was already in Lucilius. For it appears that, in an introductory satire to his first book (26), a friend advised him to write an epic on the Numantine war, and in what might have been an epilogue to the final book of his first collection (30) he defended his satire against criticism and complaint (10-20N). To this extent then, the opening satire, in which Horace reaffirms Lucilius as his model, is Lucilian in its practice.

If the main subject of the poem is a defence of Horace's satire, very little is said directly about its artistic nature. For this reason it seems far less of a serious statement of literary theory than the other two literary satires (1.4, 1.10), of which in some respects it is a continuation. But rather than repeat his demonstrations of how his satire differs from that of Lucilius in content and form, Horace now aligns himself with Lucilius the man. The assumption is that being a satirist gives him a certain character: he must be 'like Lucilius'. This assumption, taken ironically, underlies both the criticisms to which Horace is subject (1-4), and the whole defence of his satire (Harrison *passim*). The strategy of this defence does involve distinguishing himself from Lucilius, but the differences are attributed to the pressure of circumstances, not to any perceived failings of his predecessor (cf. *Sat.* 1.10.1-4).

Another difference between this and the earlier 'literary satires' is made by the publication of Book 1. The excuse of privacy no longer being available, Horace takes the issue of public reaction to his work head-on (1-4), envisaging possible trouble with the libel law. When asked for advice, Trebatius, as a lawyer, must present the legal, and indirectly, the political, implications of writing satire.

It was not only his stature as a lawyer that made Trebatius suitable for this role in the fictional consultation. His good standing with Octavian (cf. 10-12, 83-5, see Bauman, 123-36) cuts two ways, on the one hand enhancing the authority of his warning, on the other increasing the significance of his final concession to Horace's joking evasion of the law. It is also the reason why he can usurp Maecenas's usual role as recipient of the Augustan poet's refusal to write the epic celebration of the new régime which was now expected (see Fraenkel 1957, 149-50, citing Virg. *G.* 3.16-39; for *G.* 3.1-48 as an anti-*recusatio* see R.F. Thomas, Virgil *Georgics* Books III-IV [Cambridge, 1988], 36f.). Finally, some attractive features of his character help offset the gravity of his professional *persona*. For the Trebatius who succumbs to Horace's punning demolition of the law (83N) has much in common with the Trebatius who tolerated the ponderous legal puns in Cicero's letters to him. If he could take a joke he would not have minded a characterisation which undercut his solemnity (Rudd 1966, 130-1, Anderson 1982, 43-4). In Horace's poem playful allusions to legal language construct him as a lawyer.

We know something of his personality and interests in his younger days from Cicero's letters to him (*Fam.* 7.5-22, see Fraenkel 1957, 145-7, D.R. Shackleton Bailey, *Cicero* [London, 1971], 99-104). When Cicero recommended him to Julius Caesar in 54 B.C., praising his juristic knowledge (Cic. *Fam.* 7.5.3, 'there is also the point that he leads the field in civil law, with his exceptional memory and supreme learning' [trans. Shackleton Bailey], but note Fraenkel's qualification, 145 n.4), he was a young man making his career. Now he is an established figure in his mid-fifties, who condescends to turn his mind to a problem presented by an amusing younger man, who knows the right people. Trebatius was consulted by Augustus on a legal matter (*Institutiones Justiniani* 2.25 pr.) and an opinion of his to do with Maecenas's and Terentia's divorce case is recorded (*Dig.* 24.1.64.). His friendship with Cicero was a lasting one, as is attested by the dedication to him of the *Topica* in 44 B.C. (*Fam.* 7.19, *Top.* 1-5).

In the debate about whether and how Horace will continue to write satire Trebatius argues from the perspective of the law and Horace replies in the terms of poetics. He seeks to show that satire has its own conventions and that Lucilius provides a model of a successful satirist. Literature has its own laws, notably the law of the genre, embodied in earlier writers' works (cf. Juv. 6.635, *legemque priorum*). The metaphorical equation of these two different legalities is adumbrated in the satire's opening lines and the circle is completed in the word-play at the end (82-3). At the beginning and end of the satire the legal and literary are brought together. In between the dialogue is conducted on two different levels (Anderson 1982, 118): in fact, the satire dramatises the independence of literature and the law as 'genres' or verbal systems. Neither of the interlocutors can 'talk to' the other.

In the context of a fictionalised conversation, the law itself is fictionalised. When Trebatius does cite a law, it is not a current one (Cloud in Braund 1989, 67), and Horace evades its application through a pun. This makes it difficult to judge whether Horace was in any real danger of prosecution for his satirical writing. It could be argued that if Horace makes a joke out of the situation he does not take very seriously the possibility of legal action against him (see 82-3N). But this confidence might be due, not to the complete absence of legal danger, but to his knowledge that his satire, at least in Book 2, is not offensive (Rudd 1966, 128-9) and to his confidence that he has the favour of those in power (DuQuesnay, 201 n.10).

Sat. 2.1 was written as a programmatic poem when Book 2 was substantially complete. In Rudd's words (1966, 131), it forms a 'bridge' between the two books, continuing the discussion about the nature of Lucilian and Horatian satire begun in Book 1, but also preparing us for some modifications in Book 2. Several of the new characteristics of Book 2 are foreshadowed indirectly. We have already noticed the use of dramatic dialogue. Then there is the staging of a consultation with an expert in another field, which allows parody of another genre, in this case legal discourse. But in contrast with most of the other dialogue satires in Book 2, in *Sat.* 2.1 Horace himself has a large speaking role. Subsequently, where 'Horace' appears, it is not as 'the satirist' speaking his concerns in his own voice, but as a man who also happens to be a poet who writes satires. Even in *Sat.* 2.2, where Horace is the sole speaker, the doctrine is said to come from Ofellus. So the poet puts the 'satire' into the mouths of others. The ambiguity of this ploy, we realise, is foreshadowed in the ironic stance of *Sat.* 2.1, in which Horace advertises a reduction in personal invective on his own part, but also promises to continue to write critical satire (cf. Langford, 98f.).

In the opening section (1-23) Horace raises the question of the reception of his satire and Trebatius defines the issue as a personal/political one. Winning the favour of Caesar would be better than courting universal unpopularity. Horace's long reply (24-60) reaffirms his role as satirist but he promises to refrain from unprovoked attack. That is, he expounds his dilemma: the only way he can continue to write satire is not to write it in the Lucilian way. Even so, Trebatius rejoins with a warning of social ostracism, to which Horace tendentiously opposes Lucilius's freedom of speech, which did not deprive him of the favour and friendship of Scipio and Laelius.

Horace too has powerful friends (60-79). Conceding the point, Trebatius returns to the letter of the law, which, however, Horace can twist to suit his own case. If Caesar approves and the victims deserve exposure, he will be let off with a laugh (79-86).

Imitated by Pope as *The First Satire of the Second Book Imitated*

1-7:   Horace presents his dilemma to Trebatius and asks for him for advice. Trebatius's first reaction is to tell him to give up writing all together.

Horace presents himself as subject to criticism as a Lucilian satirist, at once too aggressive and too lax stylistically: a writer of *mala carmina* in both senses (Leeman 1982, 162). These are not logically opposite faults (as the contrast between *tendere* and *sine nervis* suggests), but different and compatible. As in *Sat.* 1.4 and 1.10, both spirit and style are the subject of discussion, though style is less important in this poem. Horace does not identify his critics, but they may be thought to be: (a) the wider public, (b) the supporters of Lucilius (LaFleur, 1813, Rudd 1966, 118f.).

1   **ferocious:** *acer* has the same sense as at *Sat.* 1.10.14, 'hostile', 'violent', 'cutting', cf. *Sat.* 1.4.65, *Epod.* 6.11-14. It could also be understood as a stylistic term ('intense', 'passionate'), as at *Sat.* 1.4.46 (cf. Fraenkel 1957, 130 n.5, Freudenburg, 188ff.).

    satire: here by *satira* Horace means 'the kind of poetry that Lucilius wrote' (Gratwick, 168). The word's generic meaning, most probably acquired before Horace, is attested here for the first time, see van Rooy, 67, F. Corsaro in *Studi classici in onore di Quintino Cataudella* III (Catania, 1972), 251-67. An intermediate step may have been its use for an individual 'satire' (cf. *Sat.* 2.6.17), a meaning that some support here, Coffey, 69, Brink on *Ars P.* 135. Lucilius as well as Horace may have used the title *Sermones* (Griffith, 56-72, at 66 n.1, N.M. Horsfall, *BICS* 28 [1981], 103-114, at 108). It has been suggested that Horace uses the precise generic label here (rather than the vague circumlocutions found in Book I) because he is talking to a lawyer (A.L Wheeler, *CPh* 7 [1912], 457-77, at 468).

2   **beyond what is legitimate:** the reference to the 'law' is ambiguous. I take the primary reference as to the law of the land (cf. Leeman 1983, 209) and the phrase as synonymous with 'too ferocious' (Anderson 1982, 118). Lucilius, the inventor of the genre, was conventionally thought to be aggressive, so Horace can hardly be breaking *his* law. For the view that the law is one that reflects Horace's own revisions of the satiric genre, see van Rooy, 70f. The literary concept of 'the law of the genre' (not clearly formulated in Latin before *Ars P.* 135 [*operis lex*], cf. Cic. *Or.* 198, *De Orat.* 2.62, *TLL* VII.2 1248.31ff., Pind. *Nem.* 4.33f., L.E. Rossi, *BICS* 18 [1971], 69-94) of course underlies the whole satire.

    slack (lit. 'without sinews'): the reference is primarily stylistic, see *Ad Herenn.* 4.16, Cic. *Orat.* 62, Brink on *Ars P.* 26. Another Lucilian characteristic can be found in the criticism of facile prolixity turned against Horace himself in 3-4 (cf. *Sat.* 1.4.9-10, 1.10.60ff.). Taken with *nervi* ('sinews'), *tendere* ('strain', 'stretch') hints at a concrete image, most obviously of straining the muscles, or perhaps of stretching the cord of the lyre (Lejay ad loc.) or the bow (West 1969, 62).

4   **spun:** this metaphor for writing poetry is first recorded from Horace, cf. *Sat.* 1.10.43-4. The neoteric nuance ('*finely* spun', cf. Virg. *Ecl.* 6.5, Hor. *Epist.* 2.1.224-5) is not relevant here, W. Eisenhut in *Properz*, W. Eisenhut (ed.), Wege der Forschung, 237 (Darmstadt, 1975), 247-263. If anything, the suggestion is of length and weakness (see Macleod 1983, 305 n.7).

    Trebatius: C. Trebatius Testa, born in (?) 84 B.C. at Velia in Lucania, died A.D. 4, 'the most important lawyer of the period', R.A. Bauman, *Lawyers in Transitional Politics* (Munich, 1985), 2, see 123-136, Sonnet *RE* VIA 2251-61.

5   **Give a ruling**: *praescribere* may be used of authoritative advice from an expert in any field, e.g. law (Cic. *Sen.* 27 of jurisconsults) or medicine (Cic. *Div.* 2.123).
         Take a rest: in *quiescas* various senses are in play: 'repose in sleep', 'stop (writing or whatever else you are doing)' (Ter. *An.* 22f., Cic. *QFr.* 2.13.1), 'take no legal action' (Cic. *Quinct.* 30).

6   **That is my opinion**: expressed with the lapidary *aio*, which, in view of its rarity, K-H (citing Cic. *Mur.* 26) suggest may belong to legal language, *TLL* I 1458.41ff.
         I'm damned: in contrast Horace uses a colloquialism, Catull. 92.2, 4, Hor. *Sat.* 1.9.38, 47 (the pest speaks), Hofmann[3] §39.

7   [*erat*: with impersonal phrases expressing ability, obligation or suitability and verbs such as *possum* and *debeo*, Latin regularly uses the indicative where in English we use a modal expression. The imperfect tense expresses a nuance of regret or reproach, cf. 16 below, Cic. *Fin.* 4.2 (*illud erat aptius*), Virg. *Ecl.* 1.79, Ernout-Thomas, 246-8, L-H-S II 328.]
         I can't sleep: like *quiescere*, *dormire* can mean 'keep quiet', 'do nothing'. But Trebatius takes Horace literally. There is a further implication in that it was to a poet's credit that he lost sleep over his work (Call. *ep.* 29.4, Hor. *Epist.* 2.1.112f., Juv. 1.51). Horace humorously turns this round and claims his poetry is a result of insomnia, see *Epist.* 2.2.54 (*ni melius dormire putem quam scribere versus*) with Brink's note.

7-9   **Let those ...** : Trebatius's remedy ('get plenty of exercise and drink a lot before going to bed') is expressed in formal language which would suit legal advice or a medical prescription. 'Thrice' is often used of ritual repetition (Virg. *Ecl.* 8.73, Tib. 1.2.54, Hor. *Epist.* 1.1.37). The so-called legal imperatives (*transnanto, habento*, cf. Cic. *Leg.* 3.8, Virg. *Aen.* 6.153, Woodcock §127n.) are most suitable in the mouth of the lawyer. 'Deep' sleep is a solemn poeticism (Lucr. 3.465f., Virg. *Aen.* 6.522 with Norden, Livy 7.35.11).

7   **rub themselves with oil**: cf. *Sat.* 1.6.123, *Odes* 1.8.8, 3.12.7ff. The older Trebatius advises the younger Horace to undertake a strenuous regime of exercise, athletics on the Campus before a final swim in the Tiber. It is humorously appropriate advice in Trebatius's mouth, since in his youth he was himself a keen swimmer (Cic. *Fam.* 7.10.2, *studiosissimus homo natandi*) and possibly a bit too fond of a drink (at least Cicero got tipsy [*bene potus*] with him, *Fam.* 7.22).

10-20:   if Horace *must* write, Trebatius advises him to write panegyric of Octavian, in epic, or failing that, in Lucilian satire. Horace excuses himself from the first by claiming lack of capacity and from the second by saying that it would not be tactful at the moment.
         The whole passage must be set in the wider context of other such apologies, of which it is one of the first. The Augustan refusal to celebrate contemporaries in epic (labelled the *recusatio*) has a model in Callimachus's rejection of derivative epic (Call. *Aet.* I fr.1.22-8, *Ap.* 105-13, N. Hopkinson, *A Hellenistic Anthology* [Cambridge, 1988], 98-101, Virg. *Ecl.* 6.3-8, *Odes* 1.6, 2.12, Prop. 2.10, Brink, 170 n.1, Thill, 250ff., Wimmel 1960, *passim*), the Callimachean passages having the function of prologue and epilogue. Whether in the development of the 'Callimachean' themes in this satire there is any specific allusion to Callimachus is doubtful (*pace* Clauss). Lucilius too provided a model for a conversation in which the satirist is advised to write epic, or to give up satire and so avoid giving offence. Such themes have been detected in Lucilius Book 26, in Lucilius's introductory satire to his first book (691, 713, 714W, Charpin II, 125 n.9, Christes, 72ff.) and Book 30, in the epilogue to his first collection (1061ff.W, Griffith, Christes, 141ff.).
         For a detailed analysis of the panegyrical motifs involved in 10-20 see Doblhofer, 22-45.

10   **dare**: implies a compliment to the subject, but also the poet lifting his sights from a lower to the highest genre, cf. *Epist.* 2.1.258 (another Horatian apology), Prop. 2.10.5-6, Vell. 2.86.1 (in the context of Actium).

11   **invincible Caesar's deeds**: C. Iulius C. filius Caesar, commonly referred to as 'Octavian', did not receive the cognomen 'Augustus' until 27 B.C. Horace elevates him by giving him an epithet which belongs to a hero (Scipio at Ennius *Var*. 3, *Scipio invicte*, Achilles at *Epod*. 13.12) or a god (Jupiter at *Odes* 3.27.73). If the satire was written in 30 B.C., we must reckon with a climate of post-Actian propaganda, and the existence of expectation that the poets would celebrate the victory over Antony and Cleopatra (*Epod*. 9, *Odes* 1.37, Virg. *G*. 3.16-39, Fraenkel 1957, 149f.) In these circumstances Augustan poets adapted Callimachus's poetic rejection of epic to their excuses for not celebrating contemporary military exploits. This is the first such apology 'to' Octavian (Wimmel 1960, 163).

    deeds: *res* = *res gestas*, the proper subject matter of epic, *Ars P*. 73.

11-12   **rewarded**: besides recognition as a poet (cf. *Odes* 1.1.29), Trebatius must also mean the financial rewards poets could expect to receive from their patron, cf. *Epist*. 2.1.246-7. (Wimmel 1960, 163 n.1 thinks 11 refers to a concrete offer of Octavian). Augustus eventually did 'enrich him', [Suet.] *Vit. Hor*. 2.19-20 Klingner. The ancient commentators also record Augustus's generosity to Virgil and Varius, to whom he is said to have given 1,000,000 sesterces each (ps.-Acro on *Epist*. 2.1.245-50, the MS note to Varius's *Thyestes*, *pro qua fabula sestertium deciens accepit*, with H.D. Jocelyn, *CQ* 30 [1980], 387-40, cf. Donat. *Vit. Verg*. 13). Horace imitates a passage of Lucilius in which an imaginary interlocutor advises the poet to celebrate Scipio Aemilianus's victory in the Numantine war (713f.W), *hunc laborem sumas laudem qui tibi ac fructum ferat/...percrepa pugnam Popili, facta Corneli cane*.

    [*laturus*: the participle stands for a whole clause, *Epist*. 2.2.38, *Ars P*. 155.]

12-15:   now Horace makes two moves that are to become standard in the Augustan poet's apology: the claim that the poet does not have the capacity for epic themes is joined to a small sample of illustrative epic encomium, appropriate in diction and metrical regularity.

12   **revered sir**: cf. the patronising 'young man', 60. The respectful tone of the refusal (Fraenkel 1957, 149) is perhaps humorously exaggerated.

12f.   **the strength fails me**: a succinct statement of the incapacity topos, which appears first here (Wimmel 1960, 165), cf. *Epist*. 2.1.257, Brink on *Ars P*. 38f., Lucil. 691W (?).

13-14   **columns bristling with javelins**: the expression is reminiscent of archaic epic, cf. Enn. *Ann*. 267Sk., 384Sk., *horrescit telis exercitus asper utrimque*, Livy 44.41.6.

    javelins: *pila* (the Roman throwing-spears) characterise the Roman legions, who are seen in marching order, while the Gauls and Parthians are depicted in defeat (K-H).

14-15   **Gauls ... Parthian**: why Gauls and Parthians? Why not Actium? The references may just be typical, to dangerous enemies on the borders at the opposite extremes of the Roman world. The unsuitability of the Actian victory for epic narrative may have turned the poets to other, foreign, wars, see J. Griffin, 'Augustus and the Poets: "Caesar qui cogere posset",' in F. Millar and E. Segal (edd.), *Caesar Augustus. Seven Aspects* (Oxford, 1984), 189-218, at 198. Some commentators look for more contemporary relevance, pointing to the victories over the Germans and Gauls celebrated on the first day of Octavian's triple triumph in 29 B.C. (Dio Cass. 51.21.5-6, the mention of Germans and Gauls 'not entirely trustworthy', Reinhold ad loc.) and Octavian's present activities in Syria which may have led to engagement with the Parthians (cf. Virg. *G*. 2.170ff.), against whom Antony had campaigned unsuccessfully in 36 B.C. However, this passage must be set in the context of the frequent references in Augustan poetry to conquest of Britain and the Parthians (cf. *Sat*. 2.5.62, Wimmel 1960, Index s.v. Parthersymbol). That such 'romantic' aspirations were compatible with Augustus's pragmatic foreign policy was argued by P.A. Brunt, *JRS* 53 (1963), 170-176 at 173f., 176; see now E.S. Gruen, 'Augustus and the Ideology of War and Peace,' in Winkes, 51-72, on claims of world rule as the dominant propaganda of the era. 'The poet decried civil strife in the 30's for it kept Rome from her real business — that of expansionistic wars.' (57). If part of the point here is to flatter Octavian by comparing him with Julius Caesar who had conquered the Gauls and planned to move against the Parthians (Griffin [above], 198), there may also be a reminder to Trebatius of his time in Gaul with Caesar. Even in the 30s Gaul was still being pacified.

shattered lance: the Gallic spear (*gaesa*, Virg. *Aen.* 8.662, Polybius 2.22.1 with Walbank's note) has not withstood the impact with Roman armour.

from his horse: the Parthian technique of fighting from horseback, showering the enemy with arrows while riding away, was not forgotten by the Romans, who were unprepared for it at Carrhae in 53 B.C., cf. Hor. *Odes* 1.19.11-12, 2.13.17f., Virg. *G.* 3.31. The description may be more appropriate, however, to the heavily-armed cavalry, the cataphracts, who were rendered helpless if knocked off their horses, M.A.R. Colledge, *The Parthians* (London, 1967), 65f., Reinhold on Dio Cass. 49.20.1-3.

15   [*describit*: the present indicative is generalising, cf. *Epist.* 1.17.36, *Ars P.* 263.]

16   [*poteras*: see 7N.]
      justice and magnanimity: virtues of peace (Doblhofer, 27f.).

17   **wise:** in the sense of worldly wise.
      Lucilius: 180(?)-103-2 B.C. Gaius Lucilius from Suessa Aurunca was Horace's acknowledged satiric model, *Sat.* 1.4.56f. (See in general Coffey, 35ff., Gratwick, 162ff.) On his friendship with Scipio Aemilianus see 64N. The equation suggested between Octavian and Scipio Aemilianus — the heroic ideal of the preceding generation — is a compliment to Octavian. None of the surviving fragments of Lucilius may indubitably be identified as praise of Scipio, but, basing himself on Horace's evidence, Christes, 168ff. has linked a number to this theme, cf. 1014W, *haec virtutis tuae cartis monumenta locantur*. To suggest that such panegyric is part of Horace's inherited genre is a clever reply to his refusal, and it opens the way to implicit criticism of Lucilius for going beyond the genre's limits (Christes, 195 n.238, 200).
      the scion of Scipio: it was Ennius who, first faced with the metrical intractability of Scipio's name, invented the solution of using a grand Homeric patronymic for the oblique cases. Later poets gratefully followed, cashing in on the poetic associations, Lucil. 424, 255W, Lucr. 3.1034, Virg. *Aen.* 6.843.

17-20: again Horace professes willingness, but now his excuse is that such praise may not be appropriate for the present circumstances. He is not in the same relationship of easy intimacy with Octavian as Lucilius was with Scipio.

17   *haud mihi deero*: cf. *Sat.* 1.9.56!

18   **time is right:** the right moment (*kairos*), was an important consideration in dealing with rulers. Reluctance to importune the great man is a standard topic of proemial dedications, cf. *Epist.* 1.13, Brink on *Epist.* 2.1.1-4, Vitr. 1 pref. 1 (probably referring to the time of Actium), *metuens ne non apto tempore interpellans subirem animi tui offensionem*, Mart. 5.6. Octavian was away from Rome engaged in the settlement of the East in 30 B.C. (cf. *Sat.* 2.6.38N).
      Floppy: Horace uses his cognomen Flaccus, which means 'flap-eared' or 'with drooping ears' (Varro *Rust.* 2.9.4, Cic. *Nat. D.* 1.80) twice, here and at *Epod.* 15.12, see N.M. Horsfall, *Philol.* 117 (1973), 136-8. In both cases there is a pun (Doblhofer, 43). In contrast to Horace's drooping ear, Caesar's is 'pricked'. The contrast between the names also underlines their difference in social status.

20   **kick out:** the image of the horse (cf. noticed by ps.-Acro, cf. Cic. *Cael.* 36) comes suddenly to life and makes us reinterpret the whole sentence. Rudd 1966, 129-30 speaks of 'that amazing metaphor which begins with a pun on Horace's name and ends with a comparison of the emperor to a nervous horse', cf. 256f. on the limits to panegyric in satire. In the light of this image *attentam* and *palpere* regain their literal meanings ('pricked') and

('stroke'). Bauman, 133 interprets the image as a reference to Octavian's tribunician sacrosanctity, while Langford (102) sees it as a 'satiric' motif, comparable to an animal fable. The *princeps* is said to have jokingly equated himself with an elephant, Macrob. *Sat.* 4.3, Suet. *Aug.* 53 (for his sense of humour see Z. Yavetz, 'The Personality of Augustus', in Raaflaub and Toher, 21-41, at 36ff.). Clauss, 201ff. argues for a re-writing of Call. *Hymn* 2. 105-7.

[*recalcitret*: the subjunctive normalises the correspondence of moods in the conditional sentence. *Palpere* is an indef. second person subj.]

21-3: Trebatius shifts from advice to write a more acceptable kind of poetry to warning Horace more directly against satire. The terms of the criticism recall the charges brought against the satirist in *Sat.* 1.4 (see 22-5, 33ff., 70, 78-9), echoing Lucilius Book 30 (Griffith, Christes, 141ff.).

21 **abusing**: for *laedere*, ('to injure', 'defame') the appropriate word for the context, see 67, *Sat.* 1.4.78, Lucil. 1075W, Trebonius ap. Cic. *Fam.* 12.16.3, Cic. *Rep.* 4.11.

22 **"Grab-all …**: this line is a quotation of *Sat.* 1.8.11 (as at *Sat.* 1.4.92 Horace quotes 1.2.27 in his own defence). Thus Trebatius gives an example of the sort of satire (direct attack against named individuals) which may be offensive. (Horace instantly replies with a scurrilous comment about Milonius.) At 1.8.11 these two are said to be likely to end up in a pauper's grave; the hit is gratuitous and this may be Trebatius's point. 'Grab-all', according to the ancient commentators, was a nick-name acquired by a Mallius Verna from his habit of trying to scrounge a loan. They also attribute it to the Lucilian *scurra* Maenius (*Epist.* 1.15.26).

the scrourger: for the *scurra* see *Sat.* 2.7.15N.

Nomentanus: is probably Horace's favourite victim. He first appears at *Sat.* 1.1.102 in his character of prodigal, cf. 2.3.175, 224. The ancient commentators identify the present Nomentanus as a Cassius Nomentanus, who lived in Cicero's time, or perhaps Horace's own, and spent huge amounts on food and sex, cf. Sen. *Vit. Beat.* 7.11.4. A Lucilian Nomentanus depends on corrections of the Lucilian text, cf. Lucil. 82, 80W, Rudd 1966, 142 and 294 n.28. (For the Nomentanus of *Sat.* 2.8 see 2.8.23N.)

with acid verse: cf. Lucil. 1084W, *tristibus dictis*, Hor. *Odes* 1.16.26 (*criminosi iambi* are also *tristia*). The emphasis seems to be more on the tone than the style (cf. *Sat.* 1.10.11 with K-H ad loc.), but see Christes, 157.

22 is a four-word verse. Virgil has relatively few four-word verses in comparison to Homer (*Ecl.* 5.73, *Aen.* 3.549, 4.542, 7.410, 8.158), while I have counted nine instances in the two books of Horace's *Satires* (1.2.1 has only three words), see S.E. Bassett, *CPh* 14 (1919), 216-33.

23 **fears … hates**: cf. *Sat.* 1.4.33, *omnes hi metuunt versus, odere poetas*.

not been injured: cf. 45, Lucil. 142W.

24-60: in this speech Horace gives the heart of his case, ending with the bold declaration that he will continue to write satire (60). In the course of explaining that he is a satirist by nature, following the personal and polemical model set by Lucilius, he distinguishes between the use of satire as an offensive and a defensive weapon.

24-9: by comparing his own writing of Lucilian satire (*me*) with a selection of ill-assorted enthusiasms (Anderson 1984, 38), Horace avoids making any grand poetic claims. Whatever amusement one chooses is all a matter of caprice. This is an abbreviated version of a comparative schema (called a 'priamel') used by Horace and other poets to emphasise their personal preferences, see N-H on *Odes* 1.1.29ff., Tib. 1.1.1-5, Prop. 3.9.7ff., Pers. 5.52-62, W.H. Race, *The Classical Priamel from Homer to Boethius* (Leiden, 1982), 124 and n.14. A similar argument can be found in other apologies, e.g. Prop. 2.1.43f. and may have been in Lucilius, see 702, 701W.

24   **I can't help it:** repeats the earlier *quid faciam* (5), but in an idiomatic sense, Brink on *Epist.* 2.2.57, Persius 1.12. Horace picks up Trebatius's reference to his 'passion for writing' (10) and, in admitting that he cannot restrain himself, 'implicitly provid[es] comic justification for a *second* book of satires' (Harrison, 51).

Milonius: unknown.

dances: cf. *Sat.* 1.9.24f. The riotous atmosphere of a drunken party was the only excuse for such disreputable behaviour. Dancing was regarded as effeminate, and not approved of by Romans of the old school (Scipio minor *ORF⁴* 30, Cic. *Pis.* 22, *Mur.* 13). In the last passage Cicero suggests that the accusation is conventional, and so Horace's satire may again be of the harmless kind (cf. *Sat.* 1.4.92).

wine-struck: the drunk are regularly 'wine-struck', *Anth. Pal.* 9.325.5, Plaut. *Cas.* 639, *percussit*, Tib. 1.2.3, *percussum*.

25   **the number of the lighted lamps:** seeing double, Juv. 6.304f., Petron. *Sat.* 64.

[*accessit*: the verb is taken with both nouns (but with a slightly different sense), wittily underlining the connection between cause and effect.]

26   **Castor:** an example from mythology. Castor and his identical twin brother Pollux were the sons of Jupiter and Leda. (Helen and Clytemnestra were born from the other egg.) They were famous for their different skills which they had, so Horace suggests, in spite of the closeness of their origin (cf. use of 'twin' at *Sat.* 2.3.244). The rather hackneyed example (Hom. *Il.* 3.237, Hor. *Odes* 1.12.26, Prop. 3.14.18) is topped off with an adaptation of a proverb, *quot homines tot sententiae*, Ter. *Phorm.* 454, Otto, 166-7.

born: *prognatus* is a solemn word, in keeping with the mythological context, Catull. 64.1, Cael. ap. Cic. *Fam.* 8.15.2, Fraenkel 1957, 82 n.4. Rudd 1966, 130 notes the complexity of effect achieved by its juxtaposition with the undercutting *ovo*.

28   **enclosing words in feet:** or 'versifying', cf. *Sat.* 1.4.40f., 1.10.59. In the earlier contexts Horace is critical of Lucilius, suggesting that if he lived now he would write with more artistic control but here he does not differentiate himself from Lucilius, implying that satire uses metrical form, but does not rise to the status of poetry (Harrison, 49f.).

29   **a better man than either of us:** a catchphrase, in which the meaning of 'better' need not be pressed, cf. Lucr. 3.1026 (based on Hom. *Il.* 21.107). As inventor of the genre (*Sat.* 1.10.48-9), Lucilius is an authority to whom both must defer, though the difference between legal and literary precedent is something that Horace will demonstrate (see Lejay ad loc.).

30-4: Lucilius's writings contained an unvarnished record of his reactions to the vicissitudes of his life and this is why he is now so vivid a literary character. This famous passage is often discussed out of context, see Introduction §3 and Harrison, 38-52 for detailed discussion and bibliography. Here we should ask what it contributes to the argument as it is summed up at 58-60. The main point is that writing for Lucilius was a kind of private recreation. His more often mentioned polemical stance underlies 34ff.

30   **entrusted his secrets ... as though to ... friends:** the image of books as close friends may have come to Horace from Lucilius (ps.-Acro ad loc, Brink 1963, 173 n.2). The ancient commentators quote Aristoxenus (a philosophical follower of Aristotle and a musical theorist) to the effect that the early lyric poets, Sappho, Alcaeus and Anacreon, 'had their own writings in the place of friends' (fr. 71b Wehrli). The association puts Lucilius's writings in the class of personal 'confessional' writings, in contrast to the epic or encomium rejected in 10-20.

secrets: information about personal feelings, as at *Epod.* 11.14 (secrets of the heart). These are the sort of feelings one shares with friends, cf. Cic. *Fin.* 2.85, *at quicum ioca seria, ut dicitur, quicum arcana, quicum occulta omnia.* For an argument that *arcana* means 'secrets of others', 'indiscreet gossip' see Harrison, 40ff., and for satire's disclosure of secrets, Lucil. 672-3W, Braund 1988, 169ff.

31   [*cesserat*: Bentley's defence of this reading against *gesserat* (which needs a direct object) has been universally accepted, but not with the meaning he gave it, 'whether what he had written turned out well or not', see Harrison, 46f. whose interpretation, in line with Bentley's, i.e. that Lucilius kept writing satire, whether it was well received or not, is worth considering.]

32-4   **old man**: there seem to be two meanings in play. If the birth date of 180 B.C. is correct (on the plausible hypothesis that the consuls for 180 were confused with those for 148 B.C., the date of birth given by Jerome [Marx, xxiii]), then Lucilius would have been about 50 when he began to write in the 130s B.C. (Marx, xxviff.) But, as a poet of the past, he may also simply be an 'ancient', cf. *Sat*. 1.10.67, Virg. *Ecl*. 6.70 (Hesiod), Persius 1.124 (Aristophanes).

whole life: the point is not that he narrated a life history but that he provided a mirror of his human existence in its totality (*omnis* is stressed by its wide separation from *vita* [Fraenkel 1957, 152]). His satires were like a diary or notebook — indiscreet, personal and revealing of character, cf. *Sat*. 1.4.134-39.

votive tablet: usually shows dangers miraculously surmounted or misfortunes requiring divine assistance, cf. Hor. *Odes* 1.5.13-5, Pease on Cic. *Nat. D.* 3.89, F. T. van Staten, in *Faith, Hope and Worship* ed. H. S. Versnel (Leiden, 1981), 65-151, at 96f. If one presses the comparison (with Anderson 1982, 31 and Harrison, 48f.), it implies that Lucilius's work was naive and inexpert, an amateur production.

34-9:   the sequence of thought is devious. Horace follows Lucilius in writing satire; but satire, by definition, is polemical, and he too has inherited this trait from his war-like forbears.

34   **I follow him**: *sequor* is used of literary dependency, e.g. *Sat*. 1.4.6-7 (Lucilius follows the poets of Old Comedy except in metre), *Epist*. 1.19.24f. (Horace follows Archilochus in metre and spirit). The deceptive transition moves us on to a new point — the fighting spirit of Lucilian satire.

whether as a Lucanian or Apulian: K-H seem to be the only commentators who have understood what Horace is saying here. In 291 B.C towards the end of the Third Samnite war the consul L. Postumius Megellus took Venusia. The native Samnite population was driven out and a large and important Latin colony founded (Dion. Hal. 17, 18.4, 5, Salmon, 26 n.2, 275, Fraenkel 1957, 2ff, Brunt 1971, 542). Venusia was strategically sited on a ridge between Lucania to the south west and Apulia to the east, protecting an important road to the south (Salmon, 19, 275 n.4). Horace claims descent not from the farmer-colonists but from one of their war-like neighbours, some of whom were no doubt captured and enslaved. The servile status of Horace's own father may have a more recent origin, however, in the fate of the Venusine rebels after the town's capture in the Social War (Diod. 37.2.10, Salmon, 369 n.4). Horace plays with the idea of being Lucanian not only to associate himself more closely with Lucilius's fighting spirit, but perhaps also to remind Trebatius of his own origins (in Velia in Lucania, Fraenkel 1957, 146); Salmon (357 n.4) connects him with a Trebatius who was a rebel leader in the Social War, 'praetor of the Venusini perhaps'. The alternative view is that Horace is claiming descent from the Roman defenders of the colony.

36   **Samnites**: *Sabelli*, 'a fierce race of men', Virg. *G.* 2.167. *Sabelli* was a term for the Oscan-speaking Italic peoples (see Salmon, 32ff. on its origin and meaning).

37   [*quo ne*: a difficult, because unparalled, phrase. With other commentators I take *quo* as the final conjunction, 'in order that by these means' (*OLD* s.v. *quo* 3), followed by the regular negative *ne*.]

39 **threat:** *incutere* is literally 'to strike against'. It has a regular metaphorical extension of the producing or instilling of emotions (*OLD* s.v. *incutio* 3a). Here and at 81 the verb gives a stronger impact to the notion of 'threaten' or 'cause'.

39-46: now Horace introduces a qualification — the idea of self-defence is brought in first here (LaFleur, 1815) — and begins his reply to the accusation that he is 'too fierce', repeated in Trebatius's warning in 21-3. He will not make unprovoked attacks but if he is disturbed he threatens appropriate retaliation. Rudd's (1966, 128) description of the whole satire as 'shadow-boxing' fits this section particularly well, with its melodramatic prayer to Jupiter.

39 **pen:** the pen is turned into a weapon through the explicit comparison to a sword. The actual similarity between the *stylus* and the dagger is at the basis of Cicero's famous remark (*Phil*. 2.34), but does not allow us to speak of a pun.

40 **sword:** *ensis* belongs to high style (cf. *Sat.* 1.9.31, Axelson, 51). Juvenal portrays Lucilius as an epic hero (1.20), with drawn sword (1.165), perhaps following Lucilius himself (Courtney ad loc), cf. Stat. *Silv*. 4.5.51.

42 **thugs:** such as might attack a traveller at night or on a lonely road, cf. *Sat.* 1.4.65-70. They belong to the sword simile and stand for anyone who might attack Horace.

42-4 **O Jupiter:** the prayer is high-flown, with archaic *ut* for *utinam*. Commentators point to a stylistic similarity with Catull. 66.48, *Iuppiter, ut Chalybon omne genus pereat* = Call. *Aet.* IV fr. 110.48-9Pf.

45 [*commorit*: = *commoverit*, cf. 71 *remorant*, *Sat.* 1.9.48 *summosses*.]
     leave well alone (lit. '[it will be] better'): a threat-formula, cf. Ter. *Ad*. 180, Livy 3.48.3.

46 **talked about:** the relevant meaning of *cantare* is 'to repeat over and over again' (Plaut. *Trin*. 287b, 350, Ruckdeschel, 20), so that circulation of insulting verse is not necessarily implied. The victim will simply become 'the talk of the town' as a result of Horace's satiric attack (cf. Ov. *Am*. 3.1.21, Hor. *Sat.* 1.4.36ff.).

46-60: another but more elaborate priamel-like movement (cf. 24ff.) underpins this section (Anderson 1984, 39ff. Just as Horace's pen is his natural weapon, others too have their special weapons. This phenomenon can be subsumed under a universal law of nature, applicable to individuals as well as to species (50-56). As for Horace (*me*), whatever happens he will continue to write. Is there significance in the cases analogous to Horace's? He mentions two perverters of justice and two poisoners. Satire is a kind of correction of crime, and poison is an analogy for malicious language (*Sat.* 1.4.100-1, Anderson 1982, 81 and n.16), but the difference is that Horace's motives are good (85).

47-56: the names have a double function. Within the pattern of the priamel they are the vicious 'others' to whom Horace is compared. But when satire uses proper names we look for criticism of a satiric victim. So they are analogues for the satirist in one way, but he is also distinguished from them, cf. the way Horace differentiates himself from Sulcius and Caprius at *Sat.* 1.4.60ff. *Sat.* 2.1 contains more proper names than any of the other satires in the book (Lejay, 293). Unfortunately it is not possible to determine whether the references are to real people alive now, or dead but still vividly remembered (Rudd 1966, 139-40). The names could possibly be being used for their value as satiric innuendo (hinting at Octavian's political opponents?, LaFleur, 1815 n.69, Nisbet 1984, 9 [on Canidia and the Antonian Canidius Crassus], cf. DuQuesnay, 54-5).

47 **Cervius:** apparently an informer. Informers brought criminal accusations and profited from convictions. The only known Cervius of the period is Verres' legate in Sicily, P. Cervius (Cic. *Verr*. II 5.114 , Broughton *MRR* II 112, 119), hardly likely to be the same.
     voting urn: the urn in which the jurors in the court deposited their votes, written on tablets, cf. Prop. 4.11.49.

48 **Canidia:** in *Sat.* 2 a poisoner (cf. *Sat.* 2.8.94-5), a witch in *Epod*. 5, 7, *Sat.* 1.8, though the distinction was not clear cut in antiquity. Nothing definite can be said about her identity, see Rudd 1966, 148f. Porphyrio on *Epod.* 3.8 claims that Canidia is a cover name for a Gratidia. Her mention may have some significance, apart from the connection it makes with Book 1 (cf. 22), in the implication that the satirist attacks those who deserve to be attacked, see further Anderson 1982, 81, E. Oliensis, *Arethusa* 24 (1991),107-37, at 117.

Albucius's poison: Albucius and his connection with Canidia are unexplained. (The Albucius of *Sat.* 2.2.67 is a different person.) As a subjective genitive *Albuci* implies that he is a famous poisoner (see Porph. and ps.-Acro ad loc.), but if it is objective, 'the poison used against Albucius', he is one of her famous victims, his name being part of the threat, cf. Rudd 1966, 140f.

49   **Turius:** a severe judge (cf. Lupus, Lucil. 805-11W). A candidate for identification is the praetor (Cic. *Brut.* 237) and judge for a scandalous trial in the extortion court in 75 B.C. (also said to be Furius, Broughton *MRR* II 97). This was rather a long time ago. 'Big trouble' is a colloquialism, see Plaut. *Cas.* 729a.

50-56:   the claim that he writes satire by instinct prepares for Horace's refusal to give it up. The didactic tone of the argument has encouraged commentators to identify a philosophical doctrine behind it, but if there is such an allusion it is hardly serious. K-H quote Cic. *Off.* 1.110 (Panaetius) but that is part of a discussion of *decorum*, a concept which is not in play here. The Lucretian parallel (5.1033ff.) is not in itself philosophical, but a commonplace analogy, as here.

Nature: instinct, or an inborn predisposition (cf. *Sat.* 1.3.113), not the Stoic cosmic power.

51   **join with me in thus inferring:** *sic collige* is a prosaic phrase, from Greek philosophising, Brink on *Epist.* 2.1.119.

52   **the wolf... :** even if this is not a proverb, the thought is traditional, Anacreontea 24.1-2, Cic. *Nat. D.* 2.127. We are reminded of the comparison of the satirist to a wild bull in *Sat.* 1.4.34ff.

53   **Lefthand:** *Scaeva* is a well-known Roman *cognomen*. The reference could be to a real case, with the pun on *dextera* added for fun (Rudd 1966, 293 n.16). For the satiric idea, that the wastrel cannot wait to inherit, see Juv. 14.250f.

56   **honey:** the poison is concealed in a drink of *mulsum*, honey mixed with wine, *Sat.* 2.2.15N, cf. Pliny *HN* 25.152, 'taken in wine hemlock is invariably fatal'. Cf. D.B. Kaufman, *CPh* 27 (1932), 161.

57-60:   the tone changes from that of apology to defiance and the style abruptly rises from the prosaic (*ne longum faciam*, *Sat.* 1.3.137 [introducing a conclusion], cf. Lucil. 973W) to the lofty. Whatever the consequences Horace will continue to write satire.

58   **Death ... on sable wings:** the personified figure of 'black-winged' death recalls the Euripidean Thanatos, Eur. *Alc.* 843, 262, *Hec.* 705, cf. Ar. *Av.* 695, Tib. 2.1.89, Brink on *Epist.* 2.2.178-9. Horace's high-sounding description may have influenced Virgil, cf. Virg. *Aen.* 2.360 with Austin ad loc., 6.866, *nox atra caput tristi circumvolat umbra*.

60   **I will write:** 'satire' understood. The hyperbaton (dislocation of the normal word-order) throws *scribam* into relief. Other bold instances in the Satires are *Sat.* 1.5.72, 2.3.211, see Fordyce on Catull. 66.18.

shade: 'condition', 'complexion', 'style,' cf. Hor. *Epist.* 1.17.23. If, as Brink ad *Ars P.* 86 suggests, the 'muffled' metaphor is from painting a picture (cf. Cic. *Brut.* 320), then there would be a further link with 30-34.

60-79:   Trebatius replies with a further warning, this time of the danger of losing favour with a powerful friend. But Horace argues that Lucilius, as the establisher of the genre, attacked leading politicians and the populace at large but was none the less a friend of Laelius and Scipio, because his satire had a moral basis. Horace may appear vulnerable because of his relatively insignificant status, but he can rely on the 'great' men, to whom he is attached, to protect him.

61   **long for this world:** *vitalis* as at *Sat.* 2.7.4. Trebatius picks up the life/death opposition
from Horace's last words. There is perhaps a reference to the capital punishment ordained
for defamation in the Twelve Tables (Cic. *Rep.* 4.12), a provision which was no longer in
force. The real danger for Horace was of losing the support of patronage, which would
have been a serious blow for one of no independent social standing. The 'death' threatened
is social death (Leeman 1983, 211). There is some sort of allusion in play as well, to a
proverb (Lejay ad loc.), to medical language (cf. 5N, Fraenkel 1957, 147 n.2) or to what
Thetis says to Achilles (Hom. *Il.* 18.95): 'You will be doomed to an early death, my child,
from what you say.'

[***maiorum***: a partitive genitive depending on *quis*. For the meaning of *maiores* ('high
society') see *Epist.* 1.7.2. The words could also be taken more simply as 'a friend of the
great', i.e. someone well-connected.]

62   **chill:** like the English phrase 'a cold reception', as in Persius's adaptation, 1.108-9, *vide sis
ne maiorum tibi forte/limina frigescunt*, but with the additional suggestion of active
disapproval. This metaphorical meaning may occur at Cic. *QFr.* 2.10.1, 5 (A.W. Lintott
RhM 110 [1987], 65-9); later, *frigus* is opposed to *amicitia* at Sen. *Epist.* 122.11.

Lucilius: as *inventor* he set the pattern for the genre (cf. *Sat.* 1.10. 48, *inventore minor*, *Ars
P.* 73ff., 275 [on 'first founders' generally]), cf. 17N.

62f.   **dared first:** such collocations are found elsewhere in claims to have, or acknowledgements
of, founding status in a genre (cf. Lucr. 1.117-19, Prop. 3.1.3-4, Hor. *Odes* 3.30.10-14, A.
Kambylis, *Die Dichterweihe und ihre Symbolik* [Heidelberg, 1965], 155-62), but this
passage has a different emphasis. The 'daring' points more to the fearlessness of Lucilius's
satire, cf. Juv. 1.153-4 (the words are as if quoted from Lucilius), *cuius non audeo dicere
nomen?/quid refert dictis ignoscat Mucius an non?* Whether or not the aggressive element
really dominated Lucilius's satire, it suited later satirists to portray him this way (for
discussion of this complex topic, see Bramble, 169 and n.1 on 'the falsification of the
Lucilian persona', Anderson 1982, 33f., Christes, 154 n.57, DuQuesnay, 29ff.).

***carmina*:** cf. 82.

64   **strip off the skin:** satire exposes hidden faults (cf. Bramble, 153-4 on the contrast between
inside and outside). The image of the skin (cf. Hor. *Sat.* 1.6.22, *Epist.* 1.16.45, Persius
4.14) may possibly be drawn from the fable of the ass in the lion's skin (*Aesopica* 358 Perry
= Babrius 139 [Perry, 1965]), though the fable's moral is not relevant.

in public (lit. 'before men's eyes'): cf. Sall. *Jug.* 30.10.

65-7 **Laelius or he who ... offended:** see 71N below. As Scipio Aemilianus died in 129 B.C.
Lucilius's earliest satire must have included some such outspoken comment on
contemporary political figures (Astin, 84, 313), cf. W.J. Rashke, *JRS* 69 (1979), 78-89,
Hermes 115 (1987), 299-318.

66   **took his well-deserved name:** the monumental periphrasis identifies Scipio by the deed
which was the high-point of his military career and established him also as a leading
politician in Rome — the capture and destruction of Carthage in 146 B.C. He had inherited
the cognomen *Africanus* from his adoptive grandfather (cf. *Odes* 4.8.17-9 with S.J.
Harrison, *JRS* 80 [1990], 31-43, at 39), but his ambition to emulate the first Africanus
culminated in his winning it in his own right (*meritum* may hint at this, Cic. *Rep.* 6.11,
eritque cognomen id tibi per te partum, quod habes adhuc a nobis hereditarium [Astin, 21,
cf. 75-79]). Scipio was, to later generations, an ideal (and idealised) figure, as general,
statesman, orator and patron of letters (Cic. *Amic.* 6, *nec enim melior vir fuit Africano
quisquam nec clarior*). Cicero portrays him as learned in Greek philosophy (see *De
Republica*), and his patronage of the Stoic Panaetius shows he had an interest in it. His role
as literary patron was significant, even if the group around him was less politically and
intellectually cohesive than has been claimed (Astin [294-306] on the 'Scipionic Circle'.

J.E.G. Zetzel, *HSCP* 76 [1972], 173-9 with further lit.). Maecenas and Octavian would not have objected to the comparison (DuQuesnay, 31-2).

7   **natural bent:** English commentators suggest the translation 'wit', but the idea of inborn disposition is important here.

Metellus: Metellus and Lupus were political opponents of Scipio. Q. Caecilius Metellus Macedonicus (consul 143 B.C., censor 131 B.C., Astin, 85f., 312-5) was the leader of the old aristocratic party. He and Scipio, once 'friends', became political enemies, though Cicero speaks of 'estrangement without acrimony' (*Off.* 1.87, *Amic.* 77, *Rep.* 1.31).

8   **Lupus:** L. Cornelius Lentulus Lupus (consul 156 B.C., censor 147 B.C., leader of the senate 131-125 B.C., Marx, xxxvi, Broughton MRR I 500-1). An example of a Lucilian attack is 805ff.W (Book 28). The most famous was in the parodic Council of the Gods in Book 1, from after Lupus's death. Astin (92, cf. 73) calls him a 'shadowy personality'.

 overwhelmed: a metaphorical extension of the Latin phrase for 'stoning' (*lapidibus cooperire*, Cic. *Verr.* II 1.119), bringing back the idea of satire as a weapon (cf. Catull. 116.4, 7). Stoning was a form of judicial punishment.

9   **arraigned:** cf. *Sat.* 2.3.224. It is not clear if *arripere* is used in a semi-judicial sense (cf. Cic. *Planc.* 54, *Ac. Pr.* 2.63, *TLL* II 640.70ff.) or as an extension of the meaning 'attack' (*OLD* s.v. *arripio* 8b). A judicial nuance would suit the context.

people's leaders: cf. Persius 1.114, *'secuit Lucilius urbem,/te Lupe, te, Muci, et genuinum fregit in illis'*, Cic. *Nat. D.* 1.63 (1138f.W). There is a succinct illustrative survey at Gratwick, 163.

tribe by tribe: the Roman citizens were organised 'by tribes' for various official purposes (cf. Cic. *Flacc.* 15). Even though there are references to tribes in Lucilius (1132, 1133W) we should not take Horace's wording too seriously: Lucilius's criticisms were comprehensive, across the population, cf. *Sat.* 1.10.3-4, *sale multo/urbem defricuit*.

10   **well-disposed:** cf. the accusations against himself for being 'unfair' (*improbus*) that Lucilius quotes, Lucil. *catal.*, 929f.W.

to Virtue alone: cf. *Sat.* 1.4.3, 2.1.85. *Virtus* for Lucilius (1196-1208W) summed up the aristocratic ideal of 'good character', 'right action in the political and social sphere', perhaps with a tinge of the Stoic *arete* ('goodness') (see W.J. Rashke, *Latomus* 49 [1990], 352-69): 'virtue is giving that which in all truth is due to honour, being an enemy and no friend of bad men and manners, and on the other hand being a defender of good men and manners; prizing greatly the latter, wishing them well and being a life-long friend to them' (1203ff.W)

On the connection of virtue and friendship in Stoic theory (Cic. *Amic.* 18, 20, 27 with Powell's notes), see K. Büchner, *Horaz* (Wiesbaden, 1962) 10-11.

The personified *Virtus* is linked to Scipio, the personification of *Virtus* (72). Scipio Aemilianus had built a temple to *Virtus* in 134 B.C. to commemorate the capture of Numantia (Plut. *De fort. Rom.* 5; *Mor.* 318D, Astin, 23, 79, Rudd on *Epist.* 2.1.231, H.L. Axtell, *The Deification of Abstract Ideas in Roman Literature and Inscriptions* [Chicago, 1907, reprinted 1987], 25f.)

11-3   **brave scion of Scipio** (lit. 'Scipio's valour'): an epic-style periphrasis (cf. Hom. *Il.* 13.248, 'the strength of Idomeneus', Lucil. 1240W, Lucr. 3.996, parodied at Hor. *Sat.* 1.7.1), as is 'Laelius's gentle wisdom', cf. Stat. *Bell. Germ.* 1 (Morel, 134), *Nestorei mitis prudentia Crispi*. The grand style is appropriate for the public identity which is being laid aside.

gentle, wise Laelius: Laelius (consul 140 B.C., date of death unknown) was remembered for his friendship, exemplary in its closeness and constancy, with Scipio. Hence Cicero makes him the main speaker in his dialogue *On Friendship*. (Cf. Astin, 81, Cic. *Amic.* 15, 103-4). Some modern scholars believe Laelius's *cognomen* (the 'Wise') came more from political caution than from a philosophical formation, Astin, 81, Münzer *RE* XII.1 399-410, at 407, Plut. *Tib. Gracch.* 8, though Cicero does derive it from Greek learning and philosophical interests, cf. *Fin.* 2.24, *Laelius ... dictus est sapiens* [quoting Lucil. 200-5W], *Amic.* 1, 6-7. Cf. G. Panico, 'Caton et Lélius chez Cicéron: sagesse grecque ou sagesse romain?', *Mélanges d'études offert à M. Lebel* (Quebec, 1980), 257-66; G. Petrocchi, ' Lelii, gli Scipioni e il mito del "sapiens" in Cicerone', *Ciceroniana* 1.2 (1959), 20-77.

gentle: may refer to his policy in the particular crisis mentioned by Plutarch (M. Massaro, ' "sapere" e i suoi derivati in Orazio', *SIFC* 46 [1974], 85-128, at 86-7) or to his generally calm and cheerful character (Cic. *Mur.* 66, *comior, ... iucundior, quis illo gravior, sapientior?*).

stage: there was a proverb comparing public life to the theatre, Cic. *Ad Brut.* 17.2, Otto, 311. For further references see Powell on Cic. *Amic.* 97.

fool around: cf. *Epist.* 1.18.60, *interdum nugaris rure paterno.* There are vivid descriptions of the friends' 'childish' behaviour in Cic. *De Orat.* 2.22, 'Often I heard from my father-in-law, when he was talking about his father-in-law Laelius, that he always used to stay in the country with Scipio, and that they used to revert to boyhood in an inbelievable manner, when they had escaped to the country from the city as if from inprisonment. would not dare say this of men of such stature but all the same so Scaevola used to tell the story that at Caieta and Laurentum they used to pick up sea-shells and pebbles (?) and stoop to all kinds of mental relaxation and play,' Val. Max. 8.8.1. Ps.-Acro also has an anecdote of Laelius coming upon Lucilius chasing Scipio around the dining room with a twisted napkin. These accounts may derive from contemporary sources, including Lucilius himself (Münzer loc. cit. [71-2N]). Lucilius is a companion of their relaxation as Horace is of Maecenas's (cf. *Sat.* 2.6.40-49), see J. Perret, *Horace* (Trans. B. Hunez, New York University, 1964), 57 on the appeal of this relationship to Horace.

casual clothes: lit. 'unbelted tunics,' informal dress as opposed to the *toga* of official civic occasions or the military uniform. The metaphorical sense of 'at ease' is also implied, cf Ov. *Am.* 1.9.41, *discinctaque in otia*, with McKeown's note.

74   **vegetables:** the simple meal of the countryside implies a particular spectrum of values, to be explored further in Book 2. Cf. Cic. *Fin.* 2.24 quoting Lucil. 200-5W (Laelius's praise of sorrel). Lucilius himself attacks extravagent spending on food, 1234, 1235W.

75   **fortune:** Lucilius came from a rich and noble Latin family, thought to be senatorial already in his father's generation, Wiseman 1971, 188 n.2. He had estates in southern Italy, and could afford to serve in the cavalry in the Numantine War. It is possible that his brother was Manius Lucilius, a senator. As an aristocrat in his own right he could address his contemporaries as an equal and was less in need of protection from a patron than Horace. His status gave him immunity from prosecution for defamation, Crook, 253-55.

76-7   **Envy:** what sort of envy? In Book 1 (1.6.45ff.) Horace is envied for his friendship with Maecenas (cf. *Sat.* 2.6.47f., N-H on *Odes* 2.20.3-5), something which is owed partly to his success as a poet. McGann 1969, 69 n.1 draws attention to the prominence of the theme of envy in the satires and M.W. Dickie, (*Papers of the Liverpool Latin Seminar* 3 [1981], 183-208) explains it as a foil that draws a contrast between social criticism motivated by *invidia* and Horace's own satire. The context here is literary, and the unpopularity that aroused by the *Satires* (cf. 1-4, 21-3). The Callimachean motif of the poet's triumph over envy is also relevant, Call. *Epigr.* 21.4, *Hymn* 2.105-12, Hor. *Sat.* 2.3.13, *Epist.* 1.19.35f., 2.1.89, *Odes* 4.3.16, Wimmel 1960, 166f., Clauss.

lived with the great: in the sense of being an intimate friend (*Sat.* 1.4.81, 1.6.47, *convictor,* Cic. *Pis.* 68, *Ac. Pr.* 2.115). This was a source of pride to Horace (*Epist.* 1.17.35, 1.20.23).

77-8   **tooth ... something solid:** damage to the tooth is an appropriate punishment for 'biting' envy (*Odes* 4.3.16, *Epod.* 6.15 etc., Clauss, 205). Whatever the underlying image, the point lies in the contrast between *fragili* and *solido*. Horace is not as soft a target as he appears. A reference to the fable of the serpent and the blacksmith's file (Phaedrus 4.8, Fiske, 168, Rudd 1966, 291 n.65) would be appropriate, for, though *solido* does not point to the fable's moral (that the file can bite back), retaliation is a function of Horace's satire. P.H.L Eggermont, (*Mnemosyne* 10 [1942], 69-76) argues for a contrast between different kinds of nuts (cf. Pliny *HN* 15.88). There would be further point in the nut's smallness.

● **dissenting opinion**: Horace invites Trebatius to give his legal assessment. *Sentire* and its compounds *adsentiri* and *dissentire* can have a legal nuance. See Cic. *Fam.* 7.22, *ego tamen Scaevolae et Testae adsentior*, which Fraenkel (quoting *Dig.* 43.20.1.17) notes 'prettily mimics the manner in which jurists used to conclude their discussions of controversial issues' (1964, 80, *TLL* V.1 1456.45ff.).

●-86: Trebatius admits the force of Horace's reply to his earlier warning, but now reminds him that there are laws against defamation. The wording of the law he cites lends itself to an equivocation on the senses of 'good' and 'bad'. If his work is not 'bad', i.e. malicious, Horace claims, the law will not apply to him. His work is 'good' in the sense that it is well-written, and also in that it has a moral basis. Such a positive judgement answers the criticisms raised at the beginning of the satire (Leeman 1983, 212) and hints at the plea with which Horace would defend himself (the *color*, Griffith, 63 n.1). In such circumstances (the naming of Caesar is crucial), Trebatius concedes, the matter will not go to trial.

● [*diffindere*: offers more sense than the other readings. The literal meaning is 'to divide', 'slit open', hence here 'to split off.' There is not so much an allusion to the legal formula *diem diffindere* ('to break off', 'defer the day of trial', Lex XII tab. 2.2, Livy 9.38.15, Ulp. *Dig.* 2.11.2.3, Rudd 1966, 130, 291 n.65) as a hint of the word's legal flavour.

● **take care**: with an allusion to the legal sense of the word. One of the three functions of the jurisconsult was *cavere* 'to safeguard a client' (Cic. *De Orat.* 1.212), which meant 'to draft a form of words which seeks to take precautions against various eventualities, as legal documents do', H.F. Jolowicz and B. Nicholas, *Historical Introduction to the Study of Roman Law*[3] (Cambridge, 1973), 96 n.5 (see Leeman 1983, 211f.).

2-3 **harmful verses** (lit. 'bad'): a law is quoted, but which law? According to R.E. Smith *CQ* N.S. 1 (1951), 169-179 the reference is to Sulla's *Lex de iniuriis*, while for A.D. Manfredini, *La diffamazione verbale nel diritto romano* I, *Età repubblicana* (Milan, 1979), 186ff. it is the provision of the Praetor's Edict (*actio iniuriarum*) *ne quid infamandi causa fiat* ('Let nothing be done with intent to defame ...'). But the wording seems close to a law from the XII Tables (the earliest Roman legal code), one provision of which was against using incantations to cast spells on people (*malum carmen*, Lex XII tab. 8.1b *ROL* III = Pliny *HN* 28.17), while another treated as criminal *occentare* (creating a public disturbance against someone, 8.1a). Of this Cicero (*Rep.* 4.12) says 'If any person had sung or composed against another a song such as was causing slander or insult to another ...' Fraenkel 1984, 397-415 has argued that this is the law to which Horace refers, and that Horace has confused the two provisions (see also A. Momigliano, *JRS* 32 [1942], 120-24, Brink on *Epist.* 2.1.152f.). Horace had to balance the requirements of his pun against the need for Trebatius to show legal accuracy. From the fact that an archaic law is cited the inference has been drawn that there was no real legal danger in writing satire (Cloud in Braund 1989, 67), but others argue that Horace makes Trebatius cite the old law for its venerable moral authority, when what we are meant to have in mind are the modern revisions (LaFleur, 1819, cf. Watson 1974, 111-22). For further discussion of this vexed passage see Crook, 251ff., Coffey, 231 n.83, Griffith, 61, LaFleur, 1817 n. 73, 1820ff., K.J. Reckford, *Horace* (New York, 1969), 37-8.

law and the courts: a civil procedure under the Praetor's Edict is envisaged. A preliminary hearing was held before the *praetor* to establish which law would guide the subsequent investigation of the facts (*in iudicio*), in many cases before a single judge (*unus iudex*). See Crook, 73-83.

84   **judge:** through his literary judgement Caesar can obviate the legal judgement. He was also the ultimate legal authority, having obtained some form of appellate jurisdiction through a plebiscite of 30 B.C. (Dio Cass. 51.19.7 with Reinhold ad loc.), Lejay, 294, G. Broggini *Iura* 9 (1958), 261f. A.H.M. Jones, *Studies in Roman Government and Law* (Oxford, 1960), 54, 94ff. interprets this as the 'appeal to Caesar' in capital cases involving citizens. The allusion would be topical.

85   **barks:** Horace reaffirms his status as a satirist by using an appropriate image, cf. Lucil (Book 30) 1000-1W, Hor. *Epist.* 1.2.66, Persius 1.109f., W.S. Anderson, *CQ* N.S. 8 (1958), 195-7, F. Muecke in P. Petr, D. Roberts, P. Thompson (edd.), *Comic Relations* (Frankfurt am Main, Bern, New York, 1985), 113-122.

86   **tablets:** tablets were used for legal documents and official records of all kinds (cf. *Sat.* 2.3.70, 2.5.52). *Tabulae* is also found at *Epist.* 2.1.23 for the XII Tables. The exact meaning of the phrase here has not been determined. J. Elmore (*CR* 33 [1919], 101-2) argued for 'records of proceedings in court', R. Düll (*ZRG* 92 [1975], 270-1) the tablets with the praetor's formula, which are 'opened' in court to general amusement when it is found not to fit the case. Others prefer 'laws' (LaFleur, 1817 n.72) or the indictment (Rudd 1966, 128, 30). Cf. Lejay, 289-90, Manfredini (cited at 82-3N), 185f.

     let off: rather than formally acquitted, since the trial will not be concluded.

Satire Two

Horace gives a lecture on the topic of the 'simple life.' The source for his teachings is the farmer Ofellus, whom he knew as a boy, but the setting is Rome and the audience Horace's far from perfect contemporaries. Why does he bring in Ofellus? It is important to realise that, unlike Damasippus and Davus in *Sat.* 2.3 and 2.7, the speaker of this lecture does not use the words or take on the character of his *auctor*, the old farmer. In fact, as Kiessling-Heinze saw, Horace speaks thoughout and there is very little (if anything) that can be said to belong to Ofellus, before his quoted speech at the end. The attribution of the substance of what is said to Ofellus is a Platonic distancing device (see 2N) — Ofellus stands to Horace as Socrates to Plato — and we need not, with Rudd (1966, 171), criticize it as 'feeble', or an experiment in form which does not come off. Once again Horace allows himself to appear as the speaker of a 'diatribe' or philosophical sermon (as in *Satires* Book 1), but his ironic sophistication appears in the more self-conscious adoption of this role, as well as in his reluctance to set himself up as the moral authority in the case (cf. 1-8). All the same, the grounding of the satire in personal experience of the Italian countryside gives a different picture of the satirist from that of the urbane protégé of Octavian in *Sat.* 2.1.

     Rather than being satirised as the source of the doctrine, or for his 'excessive zeal' (Anderson 1982, 44), Ofellus has the function of an exemplary figure (*magnum documentum, Sat.* 1.4.110) who could have been pointed out to Horace by his father 'when he was urging me to live sparingly and frugally, as one satisfied with that which he had provided me with' (*Sat.* 1.4.107-8) and is now held up for emulation by Horace himself as an example of the good old ways. As such he belongs to the stereotyped ideal of the frugal life in the countryside, the 'myth of the peasant patriarch' (Garnsey, 37) especially celebrated in Augustan poetry as an image of civic virtue (e.g. Cic. *Sen.*

51ff., 56, Virg. *G.* 2.467-74, Hor. *Epist.* 2.1.135, 'the farmers of old, sturdy and happy with little', Kenney, xxxviii-xl).

These country values implicitly underpin the satirical criticism of the irrational extravagance, lack of proportion and self-destructive indulgence of the urban gluttons. However, the point of the poem is to be found not so much in the traditional contrast of city and country as in the revelation that the wisdom of a Socrates, seen as the founder of Hellenistic ethics, can actually be lived by an Italian farmer. For, if Ofellus's 'voice' is that of the old country values, there is another voice in the satire, that of Hellenistic moralising. These voices are not at odds, but supplement each other. The philosopher can say why the simple life is good, but the good man can prove the teaching true in his own life (cf. *Sat.* 1.4.115-6).

Therefore the development of the argument owes little to Ofellus. In spite of the directness with which the topic (the benefits of frugality) is introduced in 1, straightforward discussion of it is postponed to 70, by which point the simple diet has been established as the desirable mean (54), between luxurious consumption and squalid penny-pinching. Meantime, from the explanation of why he rejects the symposium as the occasion for his lecture the speaker has moved into an analysis of right and wrong ideas of pleasure in the enjoyment of food, and the perversion of values involved in gluttony (8-52). The end of the discussion proper is signalled by *contentus parvo* ('satisfied with little') at 110, echoing the opening line. The name of Ofellus articulates the structure at 53 and 112 and his speech draws all the threads together at the end. The urban setting (emphatically not at a dinner) is a negative counterpart of the idealised country dinner at *Sat.* 2.6.59ff. where conversation on the important questions of life arises among friends. Other connections between the two satires are noted in the introduction to *Sat.* 2.6.

In approach, this satire has many similarities with the 'diatribe' satires of Book 1 (see Introduction §4) and like them it combines social criticism and Hellenistic ethics. The philosophical perspective is mainly Epicurean, as the appeal to 'supreme pleasure' (19-20) indicates. Epicurus (*Ep.* 3.130-1) gives the bare bones of the argument, while Plutarch's *Advice about keeping well* (*De tuend. san.*) usefully illustrates the popular moral tradition Horace is drawing on to flesh it out. Several passages on the simple life in Cicero's philosophical works may have helped Horace give life to the theme (*Fin.* 2.90, *Tusc.* 5.89-100, Lejay, 314-6), which, through vivid detail and particularity of example, has been transformed into an exposé of contemporary Roman *mores*. The contrast between traditional values and modern decadence was a favourite theme of Varro's *Menippean Satires*, and *Sat.* 2.2 may have had affinities of structure and theme with Varro's *Manius* (Cèbe 1985, 1147ff., 1158).

Two key philosophical concepts are important for the understanding of this satire and Horace's thought generally. First, there is the idea of the mean, used to define the wise man's way of life at 53-69. According to this system of thought, virtues occupy the position of the just mean between two opposites extremes. Horace has already in Book 1 (e.g. *Sat.* 1.1.103-5, 2.24ff.) shown his preference for the Aristotelian mean, a concept which was highly influential in Hellenistic ethics generally, and was taken up by the Stoic Panaetius, by whom Horace was influenced (Arist. *Eth. Nic.* 2.6, Cic. *Off.* 1.29, 89, 130, McGann 1969, 13). Apart from its philosophical appeal, it was a useful tool of satire in its prosecution of outrageous human excesses. The ideal of self-sufficiency (*autarkeia*), too, was common to the Stoics and the Epicureans, though they had different ways of achieving it. This is the simple life's most important 'virtue', of which Ofellus is the emblem: the modest and self-sufficient life he has always lived has enabled him to take philosophically the reduction in his circumstances. For Epicurus independence from desire does not require continual self-denial, but he recommends living on little for the reason that the person satisfied with what is natural and necessary will be prepared for changes of fortune. The happiness that is the wise man's goal cannot be vulnerable to fortune (Epicurus, *Ep.* 3.134, fr. 584 Us., Cic. *Tusc.* 3.49, *RAC* I 1039-44, s.v. Autarkie).

Ofellus's equanimity in misfortune is demonstrated through his reaction to a contemporary historical reality, the land-confiscations, by which farmers were evicted from their land in favour of returning veterans. (See Virg. *Ecl.* 1 and 9, and L.J.F. Keppie, *Colonisation and Veteran Settlement in Italy, 47-14 B.C.* [London, 1983], Chap. 4 ['The Settlement Process'], Chap. 5 ['The Impact of Settlement'].) Because Horace knew him as a boy, Ofellus's farm is presumed to be near Venusia, where Caesarian veterans were settled on appropriated land, after Philippi, probably in 42 B.C. (Appian *B. Civ.* 4.3, cf. Fraenkel 1957, 13 n.6). At the same time Horace lost his father's farm (*Epist.* 2.2.50-1).

Pope imitated 53-88 as his *The Second Satire of the Second Book of Horace Paraphrased*

1-8:   the satire begins as a lecture on a topic of moral philosophy addressed to an imaginary audience (cf. Hor. *Epod.* 7, 16). There is no indication of setting, though the time of day (before lunch) identifies it as a sober inquiry in lecture hours. The speaker rejects the dinner party as an appropriate occasion for his discussion of the virtues of the simple life: the point that luxury dulls the powers of moral discrimination leads into the next section (8-22). This rejection may have polemical point; not to mention the *Symposia* of Plato and Xenophon, Varro's *Modius* may have been a dialogue on temperance in a banquet setting (cf. Varro, *Sat. Men.* 315, 317, 318, 321B, Cèbe 1987, 1339). On the moral symbolism of the banquet see Bramble, 46f.

1   **What a virtue:** the dependent question (cf. *Sat.* 2.6.72-6N) introduces the theme as a philosophical topic and hints at the didactic intention, which becomes explicit with the postponed *discite* ('learn'), and *disquirite* ('conduct an investigation').
         good sirs: in the singular this form of address is familiar from Plato (*agathe*, e.g. *Prt.* 311a), and in Latin *O bone* or *bone* ('my dear fellow', 'my good man') is a colloquial form of address which is mostly found in satire (e.g. Hor. *Sat.* 2.3.31 [beginning Damasippus's harangue], Pers. 3.94). The plural is much less common than the singular (in Greek see Plato *Leg.* 7.821b.5, Ar. *Eq.* 843). Here the apostrophe makes the audience present and may characterise them as a philosophical audience (Rudd 1966, 170, West 1974, 75), listening to a particular kind of speaker. Horace is playing the preacher (cf. Lucr. 3.206).
         living on little: in ancient moralising asceticism was particularly associated with Socrates and the Cynics (see Bion fr. 17 Kindstrand). The Epicureans advocated a less extreme version of the simple life. Technical details of Epicurean thought can be recognised in 14-20 and 25 and in general the satire's praise of the simple life corresponds to Epicurus's programme. See Epicurus, *Ep.* 3.130-1, Cic. *Tusc.* 3.49, 5.89 (speaking of Epicurus), 'With how little is he himself in fact content. No one said more about plain living (*tenuis victus*)', Lucr. 5. 1118-9, *divitiae grandes homini sunt vivere parce/aequo animo; neque enim est umquam penuria parvi*, Hor. *Odes* 1.31.15, 2.16.13 with N-H's note, R. Vischer, passim.

2   **this talk isn't mine:** cf. *Sat.* 2.4.11. A 'validating formula' (T.C.W. Stinton, *PCPhS* N.S. 22 [1976], 60-89, at 66) quoted from one of Euripides' most famous speeches (fr. 488N from *Melannipe the Wise*, where it introduces information about the origin of the world, which the heroine had learnt from her mother). Plato alludes to it (*Symp.* 177a, see Fraenkel 1957, 136) as does Callimachus (*Hymn* 5.56). This complex of allusions alerts us to the sophistication of Horace's poem, in contrast to the straightforwardness of his claimed authority (Bond 1980, 117). The Latin word *sermo* (in contrast to the Greek *mythos* ['the *tale* is not mine']) here refers to the kind of discourse the poem purports to be, a lecture (in Greek *homilia*).
         Ofellus: the name, which has an Oscan origin (Schulze, 291, 452, 463), is attested in an inscription. Nevertheless, with its close connection to *ofella* ('a pork cutlet', R.L.

Dunbabin, *CR* 49 [1935], 9-12, at 10, cf. Apic. 8.4) it is humorously appropriate to the subject matter (Rudd 1966, 143-4).

the countryman: frugality is associated with the countryside (cf. *Epod.* 2.55ff., Vischer, 151). To this extent Ofellus is an appropriate source of wisdom. Though *rusticus* is potentially ambiguous, we are not meant to feel its negative associations (slowness, uncouthness, naivety), but rather the positive implication of unsophisticated decency.

an irregular philosopher: Horace brings out the paradox of relying on Ofellus as his authority, and raises a puzzle that is not resolved until the end of the poem. Though untaught and without intellectual pretensions, he can be called 'wise'. The collocation of words is not meant as criticism of Ofellus, but does point to the doubleness of the satire, in which Ofellus's country values are transmitted in the terms of Hellenistic ethics.

[*Abnormis*, which might also be translated by 'unschooled' (Palmer ad loc.), is found only here in classical Latin. Its rarity has caused problems of text and translation. *Abnormis* is best taken as adjectival with substantival *sapiens* (cf. *Sat.* 1.4.115). *Abnormi* spoils the autonomy of the proverbial *crassa Minerva* (Bentley). The nearest parallel is Cic. *Amic.* 18, where Cicero says men judged wise in the Roman past could not be said to be wise 'by the standard of your Stoics' (*ad istorum normam ... sapientes*).]

of homespun wisdom (lit. 'with a thick/fat Minerva'): Ofellus is a man of plainspoken, shrewd commonsense. The allusion to the proverbial *pinguis Minerva* ('fat Minerva') (Cic. *Amic.* 19, Otto, 224) resolves the puzzle of *abnormis sapiens*. Minerva, the goddess of wisdom, stands for 'native wits' or 'intellect', but she also presided over weaving. This may give double point to *crassa*, which means 'dull' or 'thick' of the mind, or 'coarsely woven' of cloth (cf. *toga ... crassa, Sat.* 1.3.15).

crazy glitterings: *insanus* is used here in the active sense of 'maddening' (*TLL* VII.1 1834.81f., Bond 1980, 122-3), with reference to the state of mind induced by such surroundings. Such exaggeration is in the character of the 'diatribe' speaker.

inclined to: in Latin this is a rare metaphor, requiring interpretation. One possibility is an allusion to a term from Stoic ethics, *euemptôtos* ('prone to'), Posidonius fr. 163.18, 30 Kidd, cf. *proclivitas* (Cic. *Tusc.* 4.27-8), Bond 1980, 123, I.G. Kidd, '*Euemptosia* — Proneness to Disease' in W.W. Fortenbaugh (ed.), *On Stoic and Peripatetic Ethics: The Work of Arius Didymus* (New Brunswick, 1983), 107ff. The neuter plurals *falsa* and *meliora* belong to philosophical discourse (N-H on *Odes* 1.29.16).

7	**unlunched**: cf. Hor. *Sat.* 2.3.257, early morning is the time for school, and Pers. 3.85, eating hampers clear thinking.

join me in an investigation: the verb *disquiro* does not occur elsewhere in classical Latin, though the noun *disquisitio* is found, mainly in legal contexts. There may, then, be a connection with 'judge' in 9. On the other hand *disquirite* may be meant to suggest the Greek *diazêteo* (Pl. *Resp.* 258b) and the more common Platonic *zêtêsis* ('philosophical enquiry').

-22:	it is an error of judgement to seek pleasure through luxurious foods, when true pleasure comes from the satisfaction of natural desires. In fact indulgence removes the ability to enjoy. The underlying idea is the Epicurean distinction between natural and 'vain' desires (see Epicurus, *Ep.* 3.127.8, 130.9, *Sent.* 29, 30), but it is presented through vivid, concrete examples, bringing the familiar maxim ('hunger is the best sauce') up to date. In this section there is a shift from the plural address of the introduction to the generalising second person ('you' = 'one') of the 'diatribe' style, and the speaker goes on to use other techniques of the moralising harangue: questions (e.g. 18-19), direct address (33, 104) and the imaginary interlocutor (99-101).

f.	**corrupt**: picked up by 'corrupted' (25). The image is of bribery. J.A. Coulter, *CPh* 62 (1967), 39-41 suggests that there may be an allusion to Arist. *Eth. Nic.* 1109ᵇ8-9, 'On every occasion, what we should guard against is the most pleasurable ... for we do not judge pleasure impartially.' (Trans. Apostle)

weighs: *examino* is rare in poetry. Here it belongs to prosaic legal phraseology (*TLL* V.2 1169.35ff.).

10-14   **After chasing the hare:** the syntax is mannered. In the Latin the conditional clause beginning 'if either the swift ball' has no verb, and no apodosis. Lambinus's solution endorsed by Housman (*Classical Papers* II 546-7, comparing *Epist.* 1.3.23-5), was to supply what is missing from the parallel clause ('or the discus'), implying the apodosis 'go play with the ball', cf. Rudd 1966, 170 n.17. At the end of 14 the long and involved sentence is broken off unfinished and resumed with the simpler restatement 'when work has hammered out ...'

10f.   **playing the Greek:** the contrast beween Roman and Greek is unmistakeable. It is not simply between Roman toughness and the softer and more decadent Greek way of life denoted by the compound verbs *congraeco* and *pergraecor* in Plautus (see Barsby on *Bacch.* 743), but between Roman and Greek sports, as at *Odes* 3.24.54ff., the Greek sport being further marked, as Rudd has noticed (170), by the use of words imported into Latin from Greek (*austerum, aera* and *disco*). *Graecor* conveys a sneer at the fashion of Greek athletics, but though the Greek ball-games may seem less arduous, they are still strenuous enough. See Harris, 57-8.

Roman military drill: this refers to the sports just mentioned (hunting and riding), but by way of a metaphor. The idea that hunting is an exercise which resembles military training begins to appear in the late Republic, Cic. *Nat. D.* 2.161 with Pease's references, see also Balsdon, 159ff. For discussion of the context and origins of Horace's view of hunting and riding as traditional Roman activities (cf. *Epist.* 1.18.49-52) see J. Aymard, *Essai sur les chasses romaines* (BEFAR 171, Paris, 1951), 92-3, M. Dickie, *Papers of the Liverpool Latin Seminar* 5 (1985), 165-221, at 188ff. On the Augustan encouragement of equestrian exercises and exhibition riding see N-H on *Odes* 1.8.5ff.

11   **ball:** a Greek sport also at Prop. 3.14.5. See Harris, 75-111, Gardiner, 230- 38.

12   **softly beguiling the harsh work:** the mannered word order draws attention to the juxtaposition of opposites, *molliter austerum*. The expression in the next line is also teasing ('go for the yielding air').

harsh: cf. *Ars P.* 342. In poetry (where it was rare) the metaphorical force of *austerum* would still be felt, though in Cicero it has already been transferred from 'dry', 'harsh', 'bitter' of taste to 'hard', 'severe' of people (Cic. *Cael.* 33, *Pis.* 71). See Fedeli on Prop. 3.3.50 Tränkle, 128-9, N-H on *Odes* 1.27.9.

13   **discus:** as a Greek sport also at Cic. *Orat.* 2.21, Hor. *Odes* 1.8.11, Prop. 3.14.10. See Harris, 38-9, Gardiner, 154-68.

14   **hammered out:** or 'hammered into shape', a metaphorical extension of the literal meaning which belongs to metal-work. The expression is vigorous, even if the application of the metaphor cannot be precisely explained.

choosiness: cf. *Sat.* 1.2.116f., 'when you're hungry do you turn up your nose at everything but peacock and turbot?'

15   **honey from Mt. Hymettus:** with this periphrasis Horace refers to the drink called *mulsum*, made from honey and wine, which accompanied the *gustatio* (*hors d'oeuvres*), see *Sat.* 2.4.24-7, Petron. *Sat.* 24.7 (*promulsis*), André[2], 166. Here it is made with the best honey (see N-H on *Odes* 2.6.14) and a luxurious wine (proper names are used to identify the best, as at *Epod.* 2.49ff.). Cf. Varro in his *Logistoricus, Catus* fr. 28 Riese (advocating exercise), 'to the thirsty water seems *mulsum*, to the hungry black bread seems made of wheat.' Cicero (*Fin.* 2.17) asks Torquatus the Epicurean if *mulsum* gives the same pleasure to a person who is not thirsty as to one who is.

16   **The butler:** *promus* was the slave who 'brought out' provisions from the storeroom, cf. Plaut. *Pseud.* 608.

17   **bread and salt:** proverbial according to Varro ap. Pliny *HN* 31.89; see Otto, 305. For the poor, salt (a necessary supplement to the cereal diet) goes with the bread in place of the *pulmentarium* (an accompaniment consisting of meat, vegetables or fish). The fisherman at Plaut. *Rud.* 937a who has not caught a fish says he will lunch on vinegar and salt.

18   **growling stomach:** cf. the stylistically more pretentious phrase at *Sat.* 2.8.5. The metaphorical use of *latrare* ('bark', 'clamour for') has epic parallels, Hom. *Od.* 20.13, Enn. *Ann.* 481Sk., Lucr. 2.17, cf. Hom. *Od.* 7.216, where the persistent belly is 'dog-like' (Rudd 1966, 170). The vivid image makes the point that you are really hungry.
            [*qui partum*: cf. 31, *Sat.* 2.1.52. *Qui* ('how') is an interrogative adverb (for its use in the Satires see Lejay on *Sat.* 1.1.1, and 359); *partum* is in apposition to a cognate accusative understood as describing the action of 'calming down' from the previous sentence.]

19-20   **The supreme pleasure:** the *summum bonum* of the Epicureans. Epicurus (*Ep.* 3.131) said 'barley-bread and water give the supreme pleasure, when one comes to them in need.' See Cicero's criticisms (at *Fin.* 2.90ff.) of inconsistencies in the Epicurean position.

19   **aroma:** Greek *knisê*, the savoury cooking smell, cf. *Sat.* 2.7.38, Juv. 5.162, Lilja 1972, 97-104. Plutarch (*Advice* 124F-125A) compares empty repute to an attractive aroma. Perhaps there is a suggestion here of the smell's insubstantiality.

20   **Earn your sauce** (or 'appetiser', 'relish'): *pulmentarium* (Greek *opson*) was anything eaten with bread (Cato, *Agr.* 58, Varro, *Ling.* 5.108, Pers. 3.102). The saying, 'hunger is the best sauce', attributed to Socrates in various forms, (e.g. Xen. *Mem.* 1.3.5, Cic. *Fin.* 2.90, *Tusc.* 5.97, Socr. ap. Porph. *Abst.* 3.26, ap. Ath. 4.157E) and to the Scythian sage Anacharsis (Cic. *Tusc.* 5.90), is very common in works influenced by Cynicism (see Kindstrand on Bion fr. 17). Horace's wording is his own (cf. *Epist.* 1.18.48), and, in keeping with the 'diatribe' style, he has cast it in the form of an injunction.

21   **excess has made bloated:** in contrast to the 'growling belly'. Those who over-indulge cannot find pleasure even in the most costly delicacies. The point is developed at 41ff., 76-7, cf. Plut. *Advice* 128D, ' ... but in those who are captious or suffering from a debauch, or in a bad way, all things lose their intrinsic agreeableness and freshness.'
            pale: pallor as a sign of over-indulgence, cf. 76, Pers. 3.94ff., Sen. *Ep.* 95.15-18, Hippoc. *Salubr.* 3.76.
            oysters: shell-fish, fish and fowl are typical elements of a menu (cf. *Sat.* 2.8.27), but here choice and rare kinds are specified (as at *Epod.* 2.49ff.), cf. Varro, *Sat. Men.* 549B., 'neither the helops, a costly fish caught in the ocean, nor even those big oysters (...) could arouse the palate.'

22   **parrotfish:** the *scarus* has been identified as the parrotfish or wrasse (*Euscarus cretensis* L.), see D'Arcy Thompson 1947, 238-41, André[2], 101. Vividly coloured, it is a fish of the Eastern Mediterranean (*Epod.* 2.50-2), rare and costly in Italy. In Pliny's day it was the most highly prized fish (*HN* 9.62-3, cf. 32.151).
            ptarmigan: the *lagois* is more likely to be a bird than a fish. Unknown outside Horace, it may be the same bird as the *lagopus* (Pliny *HN* 10.133f., D'Arcy Thompson 1936, 190, cf. André[2], 125 n.191), which lived in the Alps. Pliny says the *lagopus* was tasty but could not be kept outside its own region, and this would give good point to 'exotic'.

23-52: in this section the Epicurean theme of 'empty opinion' (*kenodoxia*, see Fiske, 379), which was hinted at in 8ff., becomes explicit in 'corrupted by vanities'. The false estimation of values has two distinct bases, both immaterial: appearance and fashion. The speaker first focuses on the glutton, who is located in contemporary Rome, castigating his foolishness and perverted judgement, then at 40ff. reacts to the unregenerate attitude he has just exposed. The train of thought becomes a little hard to follow. Lucilius (see 47N) was an important source here, and something in the Lucilian context where Laelius spoke in praise of sorrel and attacked the luxury and gluttony of the *nouveau riche* Publius Gallonius (Cic. *Fin.* 2.23-5) may have helped the transition at 43-4 from the gluttons' longing for vegetables to the example of Gallonius. For the highlighting of the gourmets' obsession with fish as a 'satiric routine' see E. Flintoff, *Papers of the Leeds International Latin Seminar* 6 (1990), 121-37, at 129ff.

23   **a peacock:** Varro (*Rust.* 3.6.6, cf. Pliny *HN* 10.45) tells us that the orator Q. Hortensius Hortalus (consul 69 B.C.) was the first to serve peacock. For Cicero it is still a luxury (*Fam.* 9.18.3-4, 9.20.2). For further information see Courtney on Juv. 1.143, D'Arcy Thompson 1936, 279.

24   **brush:** *tergere*, usually taken as 'to stimulate', 'arouse' is hard to translate. There is a suggestion of vigorous physicality, and Wickham explains it as implying that the stimulation of the palate requires effort. This continues the thought of 21-2.

25   **sells for gold:** Varro (*Rust.* 3.6.1-6) calculates the profits to be made from raising peacocks. A single bird sold for 50 denarii (200 sesterces), i.e. one tenth the price of the slave at *Sat.* 2.7.43. It was 'the most profitable of all fowls'.

26   **rare bird:** the expression is literal here, a catch-phrase at Pers. 1.46, cf. Juv. 6.165. It becomes proverbial, Otto, 51-2.

28   **beauty:** abstract for concrete, as at *Epod.* 11.6, 'December has cast down the beauty from the woods'. With the thought cf. Lucil. 761-2W, 'The cook does not care that it is remarkable for its tail, provided it be fat', where the reference to a tail is not quite certain.
      [*num*: the only instance in Horace of 'prosodic hiatus' after -*m*. The syllable is short. Cf. Lucr. 2.681, 3.1082, see J. Soubiran, *L'Élision dans la poésie latine* (Paris, 1966), 374.]

[29-30:   the textual problems have not been satisfactorily resolved and there are almost as many solutions as there have been editors. Whatever we read, the sense seems to be that the glutton chooses peacock not for its taste, but for its appearance, under the influence of 'empty opinion', cf. Martial 13.76, *rustica sim an perdix, quid refert si sapor idem est?/carior est perdix: sic sapit illa magis.* Reading *petere* the emphasis falls more on *imparibus forma deceptum*, another reference to the appearance of the birds before cooking (cf. *Odes* 1.33.10). For the acc. and infin. of exclamation without -*n(e)* see *Epod.* 8.1.]

31   **From what evidence:** in the case of peacock vs. chicken there was an (irrelevant) difference in appearance, while in this case there is none. The speaker ridicules the claim that a difference in taste could be detected.
      bass: the sea-bass (*perca labrax*), found in the sea, in salt-water lakes and the lower reaches of rivers, 'a fish of outstanding flavour', Macrob. *Sat.* 3.16.17. The period of the bass's greatest popularity followed that of the sturgeon, bass caught in rivers being preferred (Pliny *HN* 9.61, 169). In the Rome of Lucilius's time and later there was a vogue for bass 'caught between the two bridges' (C. Titius *ORF* 51.2, Lucil. 603W, *hunc pontes Tiberinus duo inter captus catillo*, Macrob. *Sat.* 3.16.12). See D'Arcy Thompson 1947, 140-2, André², 99, G. Giangrande, *Hermes* 95 (1967), 118-21.

32   **between the bridges:** the bridges (perhaps the *pons Sublicius* and the *pons Aemilius*) cannot be positively identified. Because at Macrob. *Sat.* 3.16.12 the fish is said to feed on sewage, and the vexed passage Juv. 5.104-6 probably connects it with the *Cloaca Maxima* (the main sewer), one of the 'two bridges' may be downstream from the sewer outlet. Courtney ad loc., however, envisages the fish passing the sewer outlet as they swim upstream! (In late antiquity the Tiber Island was known as 'between two bridges', see Courtney on Juv. 5.104-6 and Platner-Ashby, 281-2.)

33   **the Etruscan river's mouth:** the Tiber rose in Etruria (Virg. *G.* 1.499 etc). Horace's word order brings the source close to the mouth.

33f. **a three-pound mullet:** that is, over a kilo according to the modern standard. The highly regarded mullet has been identified as the red mullet (*mullus surmuletus*) which is still prized for its delicate flavour. On the high prices paid for mullet see Pliny *HN* 9.67 and Courtney on Juv. 4.15. Pliny (*HN* 9.64) says a two-pounder is rare. See further D'Arcy Thompson 1947, 161-2, André², 100.

you lunatic: the direct address is characteristic of the 'diatribe' style, cf. *Sat.* 2.3.184, 326, 2.7.95, Cic. *Parad.* 17.

lengthy bass: bass could grow up to a metre long.

37 **short weight:** the unusual collocation brings together the two aspects in which the mullet differs from the bass — its length and its weight. The wit underlines the irrationality of the glutton's attitudes, if his preferences are based on appearance. The rare large mullet is favoured, while the common, larger bass is despised.

38 [**The empty stomach ... :** a most unconvincing line here, condemned by Bentley. It interrupts the continuity (L. Müller), and though it fits the context better if we take *raro* with *ieiunus* as many commentators advocate ('The stomach that is rarely empty despises what is commonly available,' i.e. lengthy bass), this is hardly the natural way to take the line, and *raro* is not usually found with an adjective (K-H). Also, there seems to be no good reason for the poetic and rare *temno* in a flat sententious statement (cf. *Sat.*1.1.116)].

39 **big ... big:** the repetition is grandiose, Hom. *Il.* 16.776, Virg. *Aen.* 10.842. For an analysis of the epic parody see A. Traina, 'Il pesce epico. Hor. *Sat.* 2.2.39', *MD* 23 (1989), 145-50.

40 **the gullet:** or 'the glutton', metonymy with personification, cf. Cic. *Att.* 13.31.4, Juv. 14.9f., Ruckdeschel, 66. The blunt term is in tension with the mythological reference. *Gula* denotes the vice of gluttony, *Sat.* 2.7.111, *Epist.* 1.6.57, *RAC* IX 350-1.

snatching Harpies: see Ap. Rhod. *Argon.* 2.178ff., Virg. *Aen.* 3.217-8, 'faces always pale with hunger,' 256, Hyg. *Fab.* 19, Rose, 28f. The Harpies in Apollonius were hideous and ravenous birds, with the faces of maidens, who punished Phineus by fouling and snatching away his food. Hence in Horace's choice of adjective there is etymological play on the name of the Harpies, which was taken to mean 'Snatchers'.

41 **South Winds:** here the reference is to the sultry Scirocco, which brought sickness and death in summer and autumn, *Odes* 2.14.15, *Sat.* 2.6.18f.N. See Juv. 4.58-9, where Picens hurries to Rome with the turbot 'as though the South Wind were pressing him on'. The winds are summoned as gods to 'come' (cf. *Odes* 1.35.2, 3.5.2f., *Epist.* 2.1.15-7 with Brink's note), so that they can exercise their power, and turn the luxurious foods bad.

Though in fact: the connection of thought is difficult: there is no need to spoil the gluttons' food, for their very excess brings them to the point at which they cannot face boar and turbot, and long instead for the sharp tasting vegetables which provoke the appetite (cf. *Sat.* 2.8.7-9). Once vegetables used to make up the whole dinner, but, today, even with changing fashion, olives and eggs are still served as part of the greatest dinners, because they meet natural needs.

42 **boar:** wild boar was a luxury food, first served whole by P. Servilius Rullus in the generation before Cicero (Pliny *HN* 8.210, cf. *Sat.* 2.3.234, 4.40, 2.8.6-10, Juv. 1.141, Petron. *Sat.* 40.3, Plut. *Ant.* 28).

turbot: *rhombus*, 'noblest of the flat-fish', D'Arcy Thompson 1947, 223. The Latin name comes from its lozenge shape. The best came from Ravenna (Pliny *HN* 9.169), cf. *Sat.* 2.8.30, *Epod.* 2.50, Pers. 6.23, Juv. 11.121, André², 101.

[**Since:** *quando* in causal sense, common in Plautus, Terence, Lucretius, cf. Hor. *Sat.* 2.5.9, 2.6.93, 7.5.]

43f. **radishes** (lit. 'baby turnips'): the diminutive of *rapum* is found only here and at *Sat.* 2.8.8, where the *rapula* are sharp and used to stimulate the appetite.

elecampane: *Inula Helenium*. Here, as at Pliny *HN* 19.91ff., it is a tonic for the digestion. The part eaten was the root, cf. *Sat*. 2.4.44, 2.8.51, André², 18.

45-6 **cheap eggs and black olives**: in the elaborate dinner party these were part of the *hors d'oeuvres* (cf. *Sat*. 1.3.6, 'from the egg to the apples'), but for country people they were a staple. Cato (*Agr*. 58) gives instructions about the sparing (!) distribution of olives to the farm workers as *pulmentarium*. See André², 90f.

47 **the auctioneer Gallonius**: Gallonius is mentioned twice by Cicero for gluttony and extravagant spending on food (*Quinct*. 94, *Fin*. 2.90), besides the passage at *Fin*. 2.23-5, where the quotation from Lucilius occurs (see next note). As an auctioneer (a 'crier'), a lucrative but disreputable occupation (see Nisbet on Cic. *Pis*. Frag. IX, R. MacMullen, *Roman Social Relations* [New Haven, 1974], 72, 140), he was probably satirised as a wealthy upstart.

notorious for sturgeon: if the *acipenser* is correctly identified as *acipenser sturio* (D'Arcy Thompson 1947, 7-8, André², 97), it is a large fish with a maximum length of four metres. Gallonius's notoriety consisted in his conspicuous consumption, not in his being the first to serve sturgeon (so Palmer ad loc., see Rudd 1966, 166 n.13). The point is that in Lucilius's day it was the most highly regarded fish (Pliny *HN* 9.60, Macrob. *Sat*. 3.16.1-8), though rare (Cic. *Fat*. Frag. 4 ap. Macrob. *Sat*. 3.16.3f., an anecdote about Scipio Aemilianus, may derive from Lucilius [*RE* XXII.I 34]). In Lucilius the criticism of Gallonius is put into Laelius's mouth (Cic. *Fin*. 2.25, Lucil. 203-5W, cf. Fiske, 161):

'O Publius, O glutton Gallonius, you're a poor fellow,' says he,
'You've never been dining well in your life, neither when wasting all you have
on that shrimp, nor when on a sturgeon, in size a number ten.'

49 **the stork's nestlings** (lit. 'with a safe nest'): 'nest' for 'nestlings' by metonymy, *OLD* s.v. *nidus* 2. The ancient commentators tell us that it was the young which were eaten. Stork was no longer eaten at the time of Pliny (*HN* 10.60), who quotes Cornelius Nepos to the effect that it had been more popular than crane in the Augustan period.

50 **an authority of praetorian status**: we do not know who is meant, since a variety of names is offered by the ancient commentators. The most likely is C. Sempronius Rufus (or Asellio Rufus) a contemporary of Cicero (*Att*. 5.2.2, *Fam*. 8.8.1, *RE* IIA 1436f., Broughton *MMR* II 465, E. Badian, *PACA* 11 (1968), 1-6, D'Arms 1981, 48ff.). A satirical epigram quoted by Porph. (p.175 Morel) interprets his defeat at an election as the revenge of the storks. His view is that this was the praetorian election, but in the light of Horace's *praetorius*, it might have been consular (Rudd 1966, 167 n.15).

51 **decree**: the technical term for the issuing of public notices, or edicts, by magistrates and other authorities, picking up *praetor*, cf. *Sat*. 2.3.227.

52 **the youth of Rome**: this ironically echoes Ennius, *Ann*. 563Sk. (cf. 499, 550), 'the excellent youth of Rome with noble hearts'. Virgil adapted the formula for the Trojans (*Aen*. 1.467 etc.), cf. Hor. *Odes* 4.4.46. A climax of absurdity has been reached.

53-69: the simple life now appears in a new philosophic light, as the mean between the extremes of greed and luxury and squalid stinginess, the first being represented by Gallonius, as we realise in retrospect, and the second by Avidienus. After an opening which tended to Epicureanism, but also had Cynic moments, Horace now rejects the radical poverty of Cynicism (see Dudley, 32ff.), symbolised by Avidienus. The topic of dining is widened to include contrasting styles of hospitality.

53f. **in the judgement**: an echo of 8-9. Ofellus is a more reliable guide than the just-mentioned 'authority of praetorian status'.

the simple diet: an expression that Horace may have picked up from Cicero (e.g. *Tusc*. 3.49, *Fin*. 2.90, *Parad*. 12), whether or not the latter formulated the Latin phrase (*tenuis victus*) as Lejay (316) suggested. (For the Greek *litos bios, litê diaita* see Vischer, 22-7.)

4: cf. *Sat.* 1.2.24ff., 'when fools are avoiding vices ... they run in the other direction ... there is no moderation', *Epist.* 1.18.9.

5 **to go askew:** or 'bend yourself so as to be warped in another direction' (*pravum* is proleptic). Coulter (cited at 8f.N) thinks the image may come from Arist. *Eth. Nic.* 1109^{b}5-7 (though Aristotle's point is different), 'We should then drag ourselves towards the contrary extreme, for by drawing ourselves well away from our disposition to error, we shall be more likely to arrive at the mean, like those who straighten warped sticks by bending them in the contrary direction.' (Trans. Apostle)

Avidienus: both Avidienus and Aufidienus (codd. det.) are attested names (Schulze, 105, 428, 203). Aufidienus could easily become Avidienus, and presumably this is why Shackleton Bailey prints it. Though the first syllable of Avidienus is long, word-play with *avidus* ('grasping') is possible; Palmer adduces Sagana (*saga*) from *Sat.* 1.8.25; see Austin on Virg. *Aen.* 2.607. Rudd 1966, 143 thinks Avidienus may have been a real person.

6 **'Dog':** dogs, as scavengers of refuse and worse, were 'dirty', *Epist.* 1.2.26, S. Lilja, *Dogs in Ancient Greek Poetry* (Helsinki-Helsingfors, 1976). The deliberate squalor of his life was one of the reasons why the Cynic Diogenes was called 'Dog' (Dudley, 27, Lilja 1976, 115-6).

7-62: an example of the character sketch exemplifying a type. These portraits, full of finely drawn and amusing detail, were one of Horace's important contributions to the techniques of literary satire. (On the critical 'character' in later satire see M. Hodgart, *Satire* ([London, 1969], 163ff.) He himself was drawing on Peripatetic ethical theory and character studies (see especially the *Characters* of Theophrastus), comedy and perhaps rhetorical *characterismos* (see Quint. 6.2.17, Brink on *Ars P.* 152). The miser is a favourite character of satire, cf. *Sat.* 1.1.95ff., 2.3.84ff., 111ff., 142ff., Pers. 6.19-21, Juv. 14.119ff.

7 **five-year-old olives:** they are kept for too long because he eats them sparingly.

cornel-berries: mentioned as food for animals or for poor country folk living off the land (Virg. *Aen.* 3.649, Ov. *Met.* 8.665, Pliny *HN* 16.105, André^2, 82). They represent an extreme of hardship.

8 **turned:** cf. *Sat.* 2.8.49-50 (a definition of vinegar), *Sat.* 2.3.117.

9 **oil:** cf. *Sat.* 2.3.125, Juv. 5.86ff.

60-61 **dressed in white:** the appropriate dress for festivities. In antiquity such celebrations had a religious, ritual dimension, cf. Cic. *Vat.* 31, Tib. 2.1.13, Pers. 2.40, Petron. *Sat.* 65.3, Balsdon, 122.

wedding: the *re-* in *repotia* implies a return to drinking (Varro, *Ling.* 6.84). The party might be at the house of the bridegroom the day after the wedding (Festus p.281M), or on the seventh day at the bride's parents' (ps.-Acro). Avidienus's extreme stinginess is shown by the fact that he does not improve his diet at all even on feast days, when he has guests, cf. 116ff., *Sat.* 2.3.142ff.

birthday: another occasion for splendid feasting. Plaut. *Pseud.* 165 is the earliest reference to a private birthday celebration. The feast was in honour of the *genius*, friends were invited and gifts were brought or sent (Virg. *Ecl.* 3.76-8, Cic. *Phil.* 2.15, Juv. 5.37, *RE* VII.1 1135-1149).

he himself: imitated by Pers. 6.21, cf. 68-9. He does not trust a slave with the storage jar.

62 **aged vinegar:** Palmer ad loc. (followed by Rudd 1966, 166 n.4) takes this as a second reference to vinegary wine, citing *Sat.* 2.3.115-6. Perhaps Avidienus's only concession to the feast is to pour out more *bad* wine, being paradoxically generous in his meanness (Stack, 289 n.3). Cf. Persius 4.32. But K-H take it that the oil and vinegar together dress the cabbage, the point being that the cheap vinegar drowns the oil. In Apicius (3.16) we do find oil and vinegar as salad dressing, and old wine and oil as dressing for cabbage (3.9). Elsewhere in Horace cabbage is simply oiled (*Sat.* 2.3.125).

63: the question is typical of the 'diatribe' style, cf. *Sat.* 2.7.83.

64 **as they say:** this phrase marks the proverb (*TLL* I 1459.2), for which see Plautus *Cas.* 971, Otto, 199. Trapped between two dangers, one does not know which way to turn. Rudd 1966, 143 suggests that the wolf symbolises the glutton, the dog 'the Dog'.

65: the topic here is the general running of the dinner party, the quality of service and the appointments. This was probably a commonplace of food writing, cf. Varro, *Sat. Men.* 339B (a satire on this topic), 'the host of the party should not be so much grand as without squalor', Hor. *Sat.* 2.4.78-87, *Odes* 3.29.14-15, *Epist.* 1.5.7, 21ff.

refined: the answer to the dilemma of opposite extremes is the mean, often invoked in prescriptions of good behaviour. Cf. Cicero (*Off.* 1.130) on *munditia* (simplicity, neatness, understated elegance) of appearance: 'We must use besides an elegance that is not offensive nor too exquisite, but only enough to avoid boorish and uncivilised slovenliness. The same rule is to be followed in regard to dress, in which, as in most things, the mean is best.'

66 **in either direction:** i.e. in either extreme, a set phrase in the context of the mean, cf. Ter. *Haut.* 440ff., 'you are too excessive in either direction, either too prodigal or too mean', Nep. *Att.* 13.5.

[*cultus*: a genitive of respect or reference, denoting that with respect to which he is 'wretched', cf. *Sat.* 1.9.11-12, Woodcock §73 (6).]

67 **old Albucius:** old and strict. The contrast between Albucius and Naevius focuses on their preparations for a dinner party. This Albucius is not the same as at *Sat.* 2.1.48. He has been speculatively identified with the T. Albucius of Lucilius Book 2, a philhellene who studied philosophy in Athens and came out 'a complete Epicurean' (Cic. *Brut.* 131). If we put together the fact that he was an Epicurean with a possible reference to an Albucius in Varro, *Sat. Men.* 127B which may suggest an interest in food (the text is uncertain) we get a gourmet Albucius who fits here (Rudd 1966, 141 n.19; Cèbe 1977, ad loc. is unconvinced).

68 **cruel to his slaves ... :** cf. Ballio giving orders for his birthday dinner, *Pseud.* 131ff., Juv. 14.59ff., 'a scene from comedy', Courtney ad loc.

Naevius: a Naevius of a different character (a spendthrift) appears at *Sat.* 1.1.101, where Porph. comments, 'Naevius was so close-fisted that he was rightly thought squalid in Lucilius'. (Lucil. after 1257-8W) Obviously this does not fit the context in *Sat.* 1.1, and may have come from a careless reading of the present passage. Doubt therefore remains about whether Naevius was a Lucilian character (Rudd 1966, 141-2).

68-9 **greasy water:** the water was for washing the hands before dinner, cf. *Sat.* 1.4.88, Petron. *Sat.* 31.

69 **a big fault:** cf. *Sat.* 2.4.76, 'it's a monstrous fault.'

70-93: now that the simple diet has been shown to be the desirable mean its positive aspects can be enumerated, in terms familiar from the philosophers. The simple diet promotes good health and a feeling of well-being, whereas the luxurious diet causes physical discomfort and dullness of mind. It also allows scope for greater indulgence should appropriate circumstances arise (here there is a contrast with Avidienus, who does not allow himself anything better (55ff.]). On the other hand, the example of Ofellus (116-25) shows how such enjoyments can be kept simple. This train of thought follows Epicurus, *Ep.* 3.131: a frugal and simple diet is healthy and allows one to face up unafraid to the compulsions of life, to cope with occasional luxury in a better frame of mind and to be unafraid of what chance may bring. Horace enlivens this doctrine with vivid expressions and concrete examples. The problematic section on the preference of a past generation for high boar (89ff.) connects to the extent that it is an example of keeping a luxurious food for a suitably festive occasion. Rudd 1966, 169 also shows that it provides a telling contrast with 41ff., where even fresh boar revolts the habitual gluttons.

70   **Now listen:** a didactic formula, cf. *Sat.* 2.3.46.

71   **good health:** a commonplace in discussions of the simple diet, cf. Cic. *Tusc.* 5.99-100, 'add soundness of health; compare them sweating, belching, stuffed with feasts like prime cattle' (this comes from an Epicurean passage, where it is argued that those who pursue pleasure the most attain it the least). See Plutarch *Advice on keeping well*, Vischer, 64-5.

    a mix of things: cf. *Sat.* 2.6.86 where the country mouse aspires to the elegance of a *varia cena*. It was considered harmful to mix foods which might be digested at different rates, cf. Arist. [*Pr.*] 1.15 (a varied diet causes disease), Celsus, *Med.* 1.6.1, 'do not use a variety of foods', Macrob. *Sat.* 7.4. Epicurus (*Sent. Vat.* 69) attributes to dissatisfaction the desire for a variety of foods (*poikilmata*, translated by Lucretius [2.22] as *delicias*).

73-4   **boiled with roasted:** perhaps Horace has in mind the system of humours which prevailed in ancient medicine (Phillips s.v. humours). Since boiled is wet and roast is dry (Hippoc. *Salubr.* 1) this combination would involve the mixing of opposites.

    shellfish with thrushes: the wet/dry opposition again?

    thrushes: or fieldfares (D'Arcy Thompson 1936, 148-50, André², 122). Their delicate flavour made them popular eating, cf. Hor. *Epist.* 1.15.40-1, 'there is nothing better than a plump thrush', but they were cheap because they were plentiful, cf. Varro, *Rust.* 3.2.15, Hor. *Sat.* 1.5.72, *Epod.* 2.34, Petron. *Sat.* 65. Cf. E. Romer, *The Tuscan Year* (London, 1984), 120, on its 'dark, perfumed flesh'.

    bile ... phlegm: medical terms. Again the opposition of humours suggests itself, bile being hot and phlegm cold, cf. Hippoc. *HNHom.* 4, Arist. [*Pr.*] 1.29. See Cato *Agr.* 156.4 (on cabbage as a cure for constipation), 'he will throw out so much bile and phlegm, that he himself will be amazed it is so much'.

75   **revolt:** the remedy for indigestion is vomiting, cf. Celsus, *Med.* 4.12.5. The political image was established in medical and moral contexts, e.g. Plutarch (*Advice* 128F) interprets the elegiac poet Crates' use of the image of 'civil war' (ap. Ath. 4.158B) to apply to discord of the body ('derangements and diarrhoeas'), see *Mor.* 661C.

77   **perplexing dinner:** the phrase occurs here and at Terence *Phormio* 342 where it is part of a riddling joke: 'A dubious dinner was laid.' 'What sort of a word is this?' 'Where you are dubious what to take first.' Since the explanation Terence gives fits the Horatian context, we are probably meant to recall it.

77-9:   the argument rises to philosophical seriousness, the tone contrasting with the unaffected business-like style of 80-1. It is no longer a case of corruption through appearances; the mind now risks subordination to the body and loss of its ability to control its destiny independently. For an analysis that makes this passage the key to the thought of the poem see L. Scarpa, 'Adfigit humo divinae particulam aurae', in *Dignam dis, a G. Vallot. Silloge di studi suoi e dei suoi amici* (Venezia, 1972), 229-237.

    laden: heaviness is an effect of 'overloading',Plut. *Advice* 128A-B, cf. Epicurus, fr. 461Us.

78   **weighs down the soul:** the rare *praegravat* is emphatic, Brink on Hor. *Epist.* 2.1.13. For the thought cf. Cic. *Tusc.* 5.100 (Plato's dinners were pleasant on the following day), 'Why so? Because we cannot make proper use of our minds when our stomachs are filled with meat and drink,' Plut. *Advice* 127B, Cic. *Div.* 1.60-1.

79   **nails to the ground:** at Plato *Phaedo* 83d (in an Orphic-Pythagorean context) pleasures and pain 'nail' the soul to the body and make it corporeal.

    that particle of divine breath: in Stoic doctrine the soul was part of the divine *pneuma* or rational fire, cf. Cic. *Tusc.* 5.38, 'the soul of man, derived from the divine mind', *Nat. D.* 2.37 with Pease's note, Virg. *Aen.* 6.730. Here the Stoics were influenced by Platonic-Pythagorean doctrine, cf. Cic. *Sen.* 78 (Pythagoras). The Stoic term for 'particle' was *apospasma*, *SVF* I 128, II 633 (Zeno and Chrysippus), Arr. *Epict. Diss.* 2.8.11. See F.H. Sandbach, *The Stoics* (London, 1975), 82ff.

80-1:   **sooner done than said**: 'a turn from lively descriptive style' Austin on Virg. *Aen.* 1.142 with further examples, Cic. *Phil.* 2.82, Petron. *Sat.* 74, 131, Ruckdeschel, 163.

   refreshed his limbs: the more usual phrase is 'refresh the body', cf. Lucr. 2.31, 5.939, Livy 9.37.7, 25.38.22, *OLD* s.v. *curo* 1b. Skutsch on Ennius, *Ann.* 367 points out that the phrase 'excludes any idea of over-indulgence', troops being ordered to 'refresh their bodies' on the night before a battle or a strenuous march.

   sleep: the point is he does not linger over dinner, and is able to fall asleep when he wishes. On the importance of sleep, see Plut. *Advice* 129B; sleep should not follow immediately on dinner (133EF).

82-88:   the occasional indulgence is a sign of the temperate man and is in keeping with Epicureanism, Democritus fr. 230, Epicurus, *Ep.* 3.131, fr. 182 Us., Lucr. 2.20ff., N-H on Hor. *Odes* 2.3.6ff.

83   **the returning year**: cf. Lucr. 1.311, Virg. *Aen.* 8.47, Hor. *Odes* 3.8.9, 18.10.

85   **gentler**: *mollius* is picked up by *mollitiem* ('softness', 87). Note the contrast with *dura* ('harsh', 'hard', 88).

88   **dragging old age**: the phrase may be from Ennius, *Trag.* 300J, cf. Virg. *Aen.* 9.610f., Tib. 2.2.19-20.

89-93:   this is a strange passage which Gow and Palmer tried to discredit on points of Latinity, and A.Y. Campbell (*CQ* N.S.1 [1951], 139-42) to transpose (suitably emended) to between 38 and 39. With ironic pomposity, Horace pretends to praise the hospitality of good old days, at the same time satirising their well-meaning naivety. The scene of rustic hospitality in Callimachus's *Hecale* (with its incongruous realism) was read as praise of the simple life in antiquity (Vischer, 127); on the hospitality theme in Latin poetry see A.S. Hollis, *Callimachus Hecale* (Oxford, 1990), 349ff., and on Ov. *Met.* 8.664ff. See further J.G. Fernández, 'Parerga', *Emerita* 30 (1962), 132-5, Lilja 1972, 105.

91   **arrived rather late**: cf. 118. The boar is kept aside for the unexpected guest, cf. *Sat.* 2.6.84.

92f.   **heroes**: in an appropriately elevated tone Horace mocks the poets' nostalgia for a golden age of heroes (see Hes. *Works and Days* 106-201), cf. Catull. 64.22f., Virg. *Aen.* 6.649.

94-111:   a new argument against extravagant eating. Wasting of one's substance on ostentatious and luxurious foods leads to disgrace and penury, but, on the other hand, there are some ways of spending that will enhance one's reputation. In a most un-Epicurean fashion the social and civic consequences of an individual's prodigality are followed through to the end. 106-111 is a transitional passage, connected to the main theme of the section by *risus* (ridicule and rejection by one's fellows). With its emphasis on the self-sufficiency (*autarkeia*) of the man who lives modestly it sums up the satire so far and prepares for the example of Ofellus.

94   **more welcome than song**: this is illustrated by some Greek anecdotes; Porph. ad loc. tells a story about the Cynic Antisthenes telling a 'luxurious' young man given to pleasures of the ear that 'the best pleasure of the ear is praise of yourself' (see Kindstrand, 252), cf. Xen. *Hier.* 1.14, 'praise the sweetest of all sounds'.

95   **big turbots**: imitated by Pers. 2.42. The repetition and alliteration (*damno dedecus*) underline the sententious tone, cf. Sen. *Ep.* 95.18, *multos morbos multa fercula fecerunt*.

   dishes: the *patina* is usually taken to be the dish in which the fish is cooked, cf. *Sat.* 2.8.43, Juv. 4.72 (where Courtney cites Mrs Beeton's 'turbot kettle'), Mart. 13.81, Hilgers, 245ff.

96-99:   a quick sketch of the prodigal's progress. Aristotle's *asôtos*, who wastes his substance and ruins himself (*Eth. Nic.* 1107^{b}12, 1120^{a}1), is contrasted with his liberal and magnificent man (see below).

97   **an angry uncle**: the uncle on the father's side was proverbially stern, since it was his duty to uphold the welfare of the family, cf. Cic. *Cael.* 25, Hor. *Sat.* 2.3.88, *Odes* 3.12.3, Pers.

1.11, Otto, 268, J.P. Hallett, *Fathers and Daughters in Roman Society* (Princeton, 1984), 191-2.

neighbours: for hostile neighbours see *Sat*. 1.1.85.

9   **the price of a noose:** hanging is the last resort of desperation. This sounds like comedy, and commentators cite Plautus *Pseud*. 88, where Calidorus asks to borrow a drachma to buy a rope to hang himself. Cf. Otto, 298.

Trausius: the name is attested in inscriptions (Schulze, 245), but its bearer here unknown. Satire of a named individual is put into the imaginary interlocutor's mouth.

101ff.:   the wealthy man is urged to spend less selfishly. K-H adduce Xen. *Oec*. 11.9, where the uses of wealth are to honour the gods magnificently, help friends in need, and adorn the city. General remarks about giving to the city or the gods belong to the Greek ethical tradition, Socrates ap. Stob. *Flor*. 94.34M, Cic. *Off*. 3.63, *Tusc*. 5.90, Lejay, 317, Coffey, 232 n. 85. On liberality (the mean between the extremes of meanness with money and prodigality) see Arist. *Eth. Nic*. 4.1-2, and for magnificence in expenditures connected with the gods and the city, 1122^b; as the speaker claims the resources of three kings he ought to be both liberal and magnificent. For Rudd 1966, 172 this is the only passage in the *Satires* which leaves the sphere of private morality. Roman writers repeated the commonplace public/private contrast, e.g. Sall. *Cat*. 9.2, Cic. *Flac*. 28, *Mur*. 76, 'the Roman people hate private luxury, but love public magnificence' (in another context [*Off*. 2.60] Cicero criticises public extravagance), Hor. *Odes* 2.15.15.

102   **spend the surplus:** cf. Men. *Dysc*. 807-10 with Handley's note, A.R. Hands, *Charities and Social Aid in Greece and Rome* (London, 1968), 75, 'classical benefactors normally gave out of regular income ... or from past savings, rarely out of capital'.

103   **undeservedly:** see Hands, 74ff., on 'goodness' and 'worth' as necessary criteria for receiving help, cf. Arist. *Eth. Nic*. 1120^{b}3f., Cic. *Off*. 2.54, *Tusc*. 4.46. Pers. 6.27ff. describes charity to a friend, Juv. 3.215ff. to the wealthy.

104   **temples ... falling down:** in the triumviral period Octavian restored the temple of Jupiter Feretrius on the Capitol at the suggestion of Atticus (Nep. *Att*. 20.3), but he was not alone in commissioning new building. Later, the restoration programme, centered on Augustus himself, had the moral dimension hinted at here, Hor. *Odes* 2.15.20, 3.6.2, *Mon. Anc*. 19-21, esp. 20.4, Suet. *Aug*. 29. See P. Zanker, *The Power of Images in the Age of Augustus* (Trans. A. Shapiro, Ann Arbor, 1988), 65-71, 102-10.

[*deum*: the old genitive in *-um*, cf. *Sat*. 1.3. 117, *Epist*. 2.2.33.]

reprobate: the rebuke marks the climax, cf. Lucr. 3.1026, Hor. *Sat*. 2.3.200.

106   **always ... later on:** the hint that fortune may change is the main idea of the transition (Rudd 1966, 169). For parallels with a section of Lucilius Book 27 (769ff.W, on the variability of fortune, cf. Book 18) see I. Mariotti, *Poesia latina in frammenti. Miscellanea filologica* (Genova, 1974), 133-39.

be all right: the expression is colloquial, *OLD recte* 9b, *Sat*. 2.3.162, Ruckdeschel, 116.

107   **laugh:** 'laugh' for 'laughing-stock' as at Prop. 3.25.1, Ov. *Fast*. 1.438, cf. *Sat*. 2.5.37.

109   **accustomed ... to abundance:** cf. Virg. *G*. 2.472, 'accustomed to a little'.

11   **in peace ... has got ready:** the military image sounds proverbial, but is paralleled only by the maxim of Publ. Syr. *Sent*. P 16, 'one ought to foresee in time of peace that which helps war' (Otto, 54), cf. Pl. *Leg*. 8.829a. *Aptare* is often used in military contexts (*TLL* II 326.83) but Palmer ad loc. is wrong to think of putting on weapons.

12-136:   the poem ends with Ofellus's speech, which illustrates the exemplary coherence of his principles and his way of life (cf. *Odes* 1.7). Because he lived frugally before he lost his farm, he has not had to change the way of life in which he is happy. The main themes of the poem are subtly recapitulated: the simplicity and moderation which can rise to generosity on a special occasion, the informal hospitality that gives pleasure to host and guests, the natural piety, and the strength given by self-sufficiency. The power of the passage comes from the rich detail of the description of the country feast, and then from the force of Ofellus's statement of independence (126ff.), all this set against the grim background of the dispossessions (Stack, 68-70). E. Flintoff, *Latomus* 32 (1973), 814-' analyses the differences in verse technique between this section and the earlier part of th poem and suggests an allusion in 114-5 to Virg. *Ecl.* 9.3-4. On the difference in tone from *Ecl.* 9 see Williams 1968, 314-6.

112: note the interlacing word order which links Horace with Ofellus. For the theme see Plate *Charm.* 156a, Cic. *Sen.* 30 with Powell.

114 **cut back:** see *OLD* s.v. *accido²* 3. In a metaphorical sense the verb is often used of resources in the context of war (*TLL* I 299.18f.).
  surveying: the farms were surveyed before they were given, often with differen boundaries, to the new owners. *Metor* is the technical term, *Dirae* 45.
  plot: a diminutive is used in the Latin, cf. *Sat.* 1.6.71 (of Horace's father), *macro pauper agello*, *Sat.* 2.6.9, Virg. *Ecl.* 9.3, 'the new-comer who has taken over my plot', *Dirae* 45.

115 **sturdy:** *fortis* is a key term in the myth of the independent farmer, cf. *Epist.* 2.1.139, Virg. *G.* 3.288, Tib. 2.2.14.
  tenant-farmer: see *OLD* s.v. *colonus* 2, Cic. *Caec.* 94, *Dig.* 19.2.14 and 25, Garnsey, 38.
  gnatis: see *Sat.* 2.3.169N.

117 **vegetables:** cf. *Sat.* 2.6.64, 2.7.30, cf. Pers. 6.69-70. A dish of peas, beans or especially cabbage, flavoured with the fat of salt or smoked pork, was the basic food of peasants and simple folk in Mediterranean Europe for centuries.
  a foot of smoked ham: the term 'foot' is strange (*OLD* s.v. *pes* 12d, the small end), but may be suggested by Varro's etymology (*Ling.* 5.110, *perna a pede*). Ham might be both salted and smoked (Cato *Agr.* 162, Columella, *Rust.* 12.55, André², 142). The *perna* (frequently mentioned in Plautus) was the traditional food of Italy, see J.C.B. Lowe (*CA* 4 [1985], 72-102, at 77), 'Later writers speak of it as the humble food of the early Romans before they acquired a taste for luxuries.'

120 **we enjoyed ourselves:** a colloquialism, see *OLD* s.v. *bene* 9b, cf. Plaut. *Men.* 485, Hor. *Sat.* 2.8.4, Ruckdeschel, 115.
  not with fish: fish was an urban luxury, and expensive even in the city (see Plut. *Quaest. Conv.* 668C on Cato complaining about a fish being more expensive at Rome than a cow, André², 96). None of Ofellus's feast has to be specially bought (cf. Cic. *Sen.* 56, *Epod.* 2.48, Mart. 10.48); its luxury consists in the animals being killed for the occasion.

121-2 **dessert:** dessert consisted of fresh fruit when this was available, cf. Ov. *Met.* 9.92, Juv. 5.146-55, 11.72. Nuts and figs are part of the slave feast at Plaut. *Stich.* 68-91.
  hung-dried grapes: hanging was only one of the methods for drying grapes, see Varro, *Rust.* 1.68, Pliny *HN* 14.16, 15.67, 23.10-22, Plaut. *Poen.* 312 (with a pun on *pensilis*), André², 90.
  split figs: the figs were split to be dried, with the two halves remaining joined, see Pliny *HN* 20.52, André², 87.

123 **After this:** that the drinking begins only after the meal is mentioned specifically, in order to contrast the traditional country custom with the city dinner party, at which it begins after the *gustatio* (*Sat.* 2.8.10ff., Sen. *Ep.* 122.6).
  the sport: may simply be the drinking itself, Lucil. 1020W, Virg. *G.* 3.379, *TLL* VII 1790. On *potare* see *Sat.* 2.7.32N.
  [***captu ... magistro:*** this is Housman's (*Classical Papers* I 146ff.) emendation of the difficult *culpa... magistra* ('with fault as mistress') of the MSS. The situation is the same as at *Sat.* 2.6.67-70, another rustic dinner, where 'just as each one pleases, the guests, freed from crazy laws, drain dry unequal cups, whether the hard-headed one takes his drinks

undiluted, or whether with moderate ones he grows mellow more happily'. That is, there is no *arbiter bibendi* (*Odes* 2.7.25f.) or *magister convivii* (Varro ap. Non. 142.8M, Catull. 27.3 [*magistra*]) to specify the amount and the strength of the wine all drank alike, but each drinks as much as he can carry. Porph. takes the phrase in the MSS to apply to a drinking party without a 'master' or symposiarch, but cannot explain *how* it means this. (Attempts to explain *culpa* as 'forfeit' fail because a forfeit seems incompatible with the freedom that the context seems to require. In Plutarch [*Quaest. Conviv.* 620Aff.] forfeits are prescribed for not drinking in the way the symposiarch required, and at Plaut. *Stich.* 725 the forfeit for making a slip in the dance is to be *deprived* of a cup of wine.) Bond 1980, 124-6 argues for *culpa* = conscience.]

24   **Ceres**: a libation to Ceres, the patron goddess of field crops, begins the drinking at *Odes* 4.5.31ff., where Horace explicitly contrasts the Roman custom of making offerings to the Lares with the Greek one of invoking a deity. Farmers usually pray to Bacchus and Ceres together (e.g. Varro, *Rust.* 1.1.5, Virg. *Ecl.* 5.79-80).

25   **smoothed away**: one of the standard powers of wine is to give freedom from worry, cf. *Odes* 3.29.16, *Epist.* 1.5.20. The idea of worry turns into specific dangers in the next line.

26   **Let Fortune rage**: the tone rises to epic grandeur, perhaps echoing Ennius, see Vretska on Sall. *Cat.* 10.1, Virg. *G.* 1.5ll, 'lawless War rages through the world', 3.551, Tib. 1.3.70, 1.5.58. Fortune has philosophical symbolism here, see above P.105 and 106N.

27-8   **How much ... less sleek** (lit. 'more sparing in our prosperity'): this contrasts Ofellus with Avidienus, cf. *parcit* (58) and *parcus* (62). *Niteo* ('I prosper') is used of the 'flourishing' of crops and farm animals (Cato *Agr.* 1.2, Plaut. *Bacch.* 1124) but is also appropriate to the youthful sleekness of the sons, see *OLD* s.v. *niteo* 3b, 4, Plaut. *Pseud.* 774, Hor. *Epist.* 1.4.15.

     settler: in opposition to *erus* 'master', 'owner' in the following line.

29:   the connection of thought is: we have not really lost anything, for no one can own anything for ever; our well-being depends on ourselves, cf. *Epist.* 2.2.158-74 with Brink's commentary. This is a commonplace of popular morality, cf. Bion fr. 39 A-D Kindstrand, 'Fortune has not given their goods to the rich, but lent them'. (See further Kindstrand, ad loc., Dover, 174f., Lucil. 857-8W, Lucil. 777, 781W, with Fiske 385f., Lucr. 3.971 with Kenney's note, Cic. *Tusc.* 1.93, Arr. *Epict. Diss.* 1.1.31-2.) Here of course it is made pointedly appropriate to Ofellus's own situation. The use of the personal pronouns, finally appearing as the proper names in 133, underlines this.

31   **worthlessness**: see Cic. *Tusc.* 3.17-18 on *nequitia*.

     the tricksy law: cf. *Sat.* 2.5.34. *Vafer* is used of personal cunning, cf. *Sat.* 2.3.21, 2.4.55 etc.

32   **an heir**: one of the arguments deployed against greed and miserliness was that your wealth would pass to an heir, who did not have to be a close relative, and could even be a stranger (Pers. 6.33f., 41) or a plausible hanger-on (*Sat.* 2.5), cf. *Sat.* 2.3.122f., *Odes* 2.14.25 with N-H's note, *Epist.* 1.5.13f.

33   **Umbrenus**: the man cannot be identified, but his name occurs at Sall. *Cat.* 40.1, Cic. *Cat.* 3.14. The new settlers were Roman veterans.

34   **my use**: 'use' has a hint of the legal meaning, by which the right to use contrasted with the idea of ownership, cf. Lucr. 3.971, *Epist.* 2.2.159, Watson 1968, Chap. 9.

35   **bravely**: cf. Epicurus, *Ep.* 3.131, 'unafraid in the face of chance'. The courage is that of the self-sufficient person (*autarkês*), cf. *Sat.* 2.7.85-6. There is a hint of a military image (cf. Virg. *Aen.* 8.151), picking up 111. The 'golden' line (abCAB, Wilkinson 1985, 215-6) creates a strong sense of closure, as does the exhortation based on a general truth; the end with a speech that points a moral is also found in *Sat.* 2.6.

Satire Three

In the first satire of this book we saw how the poet's practice of his gift for satire might involv
him in controversies with legal and social ramifications. The context is the urban literary scene
In the second, from the perspective of the alienated city-dweller, he advocates the ideal of th
simple life associated with the countryside. Now we find him spending the winter holiday in th
country, at his newly acquired Sabine estate. Here Damasippus (see 16N) descends upon him
bringing with him the city's discontents. Damasippus, a failed speculator, has suffered a disastrous
loss, but far from enduring this 'with a brave heart' and demonstrating the worth of his principles in
his own life, as Ofellus did, he, after being saved from suicide and converted to philosophy, takes
his new understanding that he is not unique in his folly as licence to berate others, finding plenty to
criticise in Horace the countryman and townsman alike.

Damasippus is the main speaker in the satire, but most of his words are not his own. The long
central section (77-295) is devoted to a lecture on a Stoic dogma, that those who are not wise are
mad (43-5), quoted as from Stertinius, a follower of the eminent Stoic philosopher Chrysippus
Stertinius, who is portrayed as a popular philosopher, assumes the Stoic dogma as proved, and
devotes all his efforts to illustrating it from the behaviour of his fellow men and persuading
Damasippus of its truth. Five common vices are treated and shown to be forms of madness
avarice, ambition, extravagance, love and superstition. The orderly introduction (77-81) and
presentation of the topics is characteristic of an academic approach, not of Horatian satire'
conversational mode (cf. Persius 3, Juvenal 10, called 'sermon' poems by Braund 1988, 44ff.
183ff.).

Stertinius's method is to present his argument through individual examples, often of
antithetical extremes, in order to win his listener's agreement to the general proposition. Examples
drawn from Roman life (Staberius, Opimius, Oppidius, Nomentanus etc.) predominate, but
interspersed are anecdotes about philosophers (Aristippus and Polemo) and cases drawn from
tragedy and comedy (see Fraenkel 1957, 143 n.1, McGann 1954, Appendix). Some of these
anecdotes are told as self-contained narratives, while others are integrated into Stertinius's
arguments.

These aim to remove the distinctions between behaviour that is regarded as truly mad and
other instances of aberrant beliefs and action. This approach perhaps parodically reflects the
original Stoic arguments for the dogma (K-H on 102). We cannot imagine Horace endorsing it or
even taking it seriously. As a speaker Stertinius has a didactic tone, bombarding the listener with
hectoring questions, either addressed directly to him or to imaginary characters. Even conclusions
may be presented in question form (see Fronto, *Ep. ad M. Ant. de eloquentia* 1 on the rhetorical
style of Chrysippus's teaching [at Lejay, 383]).

Stertinius's doctrine and lecturing style are marked as distinctively Stoic in other ways (see
Lejay, 356ff.). He appeals to the authority of Chrysippus (44, 287). He pays lip-service to the
importance of definitions (41N), and he uses the key Stoic terms 'reason' (82f.N) and 'fool' (158)
The image of the passions as mental illness, common to the 'diatribe' tradition, was particularly
exploited by the Stoics. For example, Cicero (*Tusc.* 4.23) criticises the excessive attention paid by
the Stoics, especially Chrysippus, to the parallel between diseases of the soul and the body. We do
not know how Chrysippus approached the topic of the paradox (but see Ath. 11.464D). Cicero in
arguing for it (*Tusc.* 3.7-11) took care to distinguish between mental 'unsoundness' (*insania*) and
madness proper (*furor*), but these are deliberately confused by Stertinius (A. O'Brien Moore,
Madness in Ancient Literature [Diss. Princeton, 1924], 36ff., 44 n.4). The very variety of
expressions for madness used in Horace's satire shows, however, that there is no intention of

giving Stertinius a philosophical defence of the paradox. Instead he exploits its power to dazzle a naive audience.

The Stoic framework should be kept in mind when we notice the similarities of some aspects of Stertinius's lecture to moral topics found elsewhere in the satires, especially the treatment of avarice in *Sat*. 1.1 (see Perret, 61-2) and luxury in *Sat*. 2.2. Sometimes Stertinius's anecdotes sound just like Horace's (e.g. Oppidius, 168-81) — not just wittily expressed and full of vivid detail but also pointing a similar moral. This is partly because Horace's 'diatribe' satires draw on the same tradition of popular philosophy as figures such as Stertinius and Crispinus (*Sat*. 1.1.120-1, 2.7.45N) and partly because a parody of a prolix speaker cannot afford to be boring as well as long. Therefore the satirist in Horace uses Stertinius to expose irrational extremes of human behaviour, his usual target, while he dissociates himself from the Stoic's rigid dogmatism, which swamps the listener without encouraging him to reach the balanced perspective and sense of reality which Horace himself offers elsewhere (cf. *Sat*. 1.3.76ff., Cèbe 1966, 262-3).

The satire's plot and structure, too, help distance Horace from Stertinius's doctrine. A recent convert, Damasippus has taken down and recorded the homily of Stertinius (see Lejay, xv, 384, 448). Wishing to put his new profession into practice, he begins the satire by finding fault with Horace, and concludes it by identifying the failures which make the poet too 'mad'. These two closely connected passages of dialogue between Horace and Damasippus (1-31, 296-326) act as a framing introduction and conclusion. The scene at Horace's villa that begins the satire is a sequel to an earlier scene, narrated in the bridge passage (31-46). Here we learn how Damasippus became Stertinius's disciple after going bankrupt. Bond 1987, 7 even suggests that the philosophical conversion of Damasippus is a parodic echo of the coming to philosophy of Chrysippus himself, after the property he had inherited was confiscated by the state (Diog. Laert. 7.181, Hecato of Rhodes). Damasippus in his role of intermediary does not distort Stertinius's doctrine in the retelling, but his misuse of what he has heard, to attack others rather than reform himself, does interpose an element of irony. That despite his naivety his criticisms of Horace ring true is also ironic (see Anderson 1982, 45).

The Stoic 'paradox' that 'all fools are mad' has a history in both Roman satire and philosophy (see Rudd 1966, 186ff.). The fragments of Varro's Menippean satire *Eumenides* (see Lejay, 381f., Cèbe 1977, 525ff.) show that Varro made satiric use of the notion that obsessive passions are mental illnesses (see also his *Aiax stramenticius*). Porphyrio on *Sat*. 2.3.41 tantalisingly refers to a Lucilian definition of madness. Unfortunately the treatment in Cicero's *Stoic Paradoxes* 4 does not survive.

In structure and idea *Sat*. 2.3 and 2.7 are very similar. *Sat*. 2.3 is on a much larger scale, however. This is partly due to the nature of its paradox, which readily becomes all-inclusive, since all passions and vices can be treated as symptoms of insanity (77-81), with the result that we soon leave the specific case of Damasippus behind. There is a closer link between the Saturnalian setting and the paradox in *Sat*. 2.7, even if it too becomes more general in its central homily.

1-16: like 2.1, 2.3 begins with the opening of a conversation, the setting and situation of which we have to piece together from hints given in the course of what Damasippus says. Damasippus, it becomes clear, is bursting in on Horace in his rural retreat (5, 10) — why, we are never told. It is the Saturnalia, the time of the mid-winter holiday, but Horace had left home in order to find some peace in which to read and write. Damasippus takes the smallness of Horace's poetic production as evidence of laziness and gives him a piece of good advice (14-16), applying to Horace's case a precept (to accept loss with equanimity) that did not occur to him in his own crisis (37ff.). At the same time as we are led to recognise Damasippus's zeal as that of the new enthusiast for philosophy, we also realise that he misunderstands Horace's reasons for writing little: his high poetic standards and his need for leisure (*otium*).

Persius 3 imitates 2.3, with a similar opening scene in which a young student sleeping off a hangover is rebuked for not engaging in worthwhile activity.

1 [*sic raro scribis*: K-H argue that the abruptly introduced accusation suits the situation of Damasippus's interruption better than the more oblique conditional clause preferred by many editors. With the reading *si ... scribes* it is necessary to supply an adverb with *raro ... ut* (but see Brink on *Epist.* 2.2.87). On the other hand, the difficulty with *scribis* is that its final syllable must be lengthened before *ut*, a licence which Horace permits himself at this position in the line (before a third foot caesura) but elsewhere only with verbs in the third person singular (as at *Sat.* 1.4.82).]

so infrequently: the reproach of unproductivity rings true because elsewhere Horace has made a virtue of writing little (see *Sat.* 1.4.18, 'of one speaking infrequently and very little') especially in comparison with the fluent Lucilius who was too lazy to bother with the work that should go into writing (*Sat.* 1.4.9ff.).

2 **parchment**: the singular refers to the material, see C.H. Roberts and T.C. Skeat, *The Birth of the Codex* (London, 1987), 20. *Membranae* were probably notebooks in codex form for work in progress, cf. *Ars P.* 388-9 with Brink's note, Pers. 3.10, Courtney on Juv. 7.23. The finished poem was copied onto *charta*, paper made of papyrus (*Sat.* 1.5.104).

unweaving: the verb (*retexo*) is found only here in Horace. There is an allusion to Penelope's web, which was intended never to be finished (Cic. *Ac. Pr.* 2.95, Ov. *Am.* 3.9.30). At the same time weaving is a metaphor for writing (the work is a *textum*), cf. Pindar fr.179 Snell, Call. fr.532 Pf. (?), *Ciris* 9, 21ff., Quint. 9.4.17, Wimmel 1960, 67f. Therefore what Damasippus intends as a criticism can also be read as evidence of the care Horace takes to revise his drafts (*Sat.* 1.10.72-3, *Ars P.* 389).

3 **wine and sleep**: Damasippus assumes that drinking and sleeping prevent the poet from writing, and they are indeed regarded as alternatives at *Sat.* 2.1.5-9 and *Epist.* 2.2.54. But since elsewhere sleep symbolises the leisure of the poetic life (*Epist.* 2.2.78), and wine is traditionally associated with Bacchic inspiration (*Epist.*1.19.1-11), Damasippus may be casting the cold eye of common sense on Horace's poetic pretensions.

4 **compose** (lit. 'sing'): cf. *Epist.* 2.2.79-80. 'Singing' usually implies lyric or epic, genres higher than the satires, and the reference to *Sat.* 2.6 as a *carmen* (22) shows awareness of its exceptional nature. Hence some commentators see a reference here to the *Epodes*, which were being written during the same period as the *Satires*. However, if *sermone* is ambiguous (see below) the tension between the apparently incompatible *sermone* and *canas* may suit the ambivalent nature of conversational poetry (cf. *Sat.* 2.6.17N, Introduction §2). On Horace's various uses of *carmen* see Brink on *Epist.* 2.2.25, 59-60.

worthy of talk: the phrase *dignum sermone* imitates the Greek *axion logou* ('worthy of mention', 'worth talking about'), but may also hint at a punning reference to Horace's own *sermones* ('talks').

5 **the Saturnalia**: see *Sat.* 2.7.4N. Lejay suggests that the setting of these homilies at this time undermines their seriousness (xxxiv).

sober: the adjective indicates the purpose and result of Horace's flight. It is not to the point that he is sober when he is asked to recite, but that he has had the opportunity to do some work. The punctuation adopted in the text (that advocated by Bentley; Lejay ad loc. argues against it) is supported by K-H's observation that (except in questions) *ergo* is always in first place in Horace.

6 **you've promised**: probably something more specific than general expectations (K-H), see Brink on *Epist.* 2.1.52, *Ars P.* 138.

It's no use: *nil est* is an idiomatic expression, Plaut. *Cas.* 286, *Truc.* 851, Cic. *Rosc. Am.* 58.

7. **reed-pens**: see Pers. 3.11-14, 19. The reed was split and cut to a point like a quill-pen, see D. Diringer, *The Book before Printing: Ancient, Medieval and Oriental* (New York, 1982), 556ff., illustrations, 549.

give a hard time to the innocent wall: the wall is personified. The poet thumps the wall near his writing couch when he feels frustrated, cf. Pers. 1.106 (banging on the back of the couch).

the wrath of gods and — poets: the anger of the gods means bad luck (see *Sat.* 2.7.14N), but it is the bad luck of this wall to have met an angry poet, Horace. Anger is part of Horace's self-characterisation, cf. 323N.

threatening: an unusual use of the verb (cf. Hor. *Epist.*1.8.3, Phaedr. 4.23.1), probably in imitation of the Greek *apeilein* which can mean 'promise', 'threaten' and 'boast'. It sounds an ironic note.

0 **the little farmstead**: the diminutive expresses affection, cf. Cic. *Att.* 8.9,3, Hanssen, 127. The congruence of themes with *Sat.* 2.6 (15-6, 60-2, sleep, leisure, books of ancient writers, escape from worries), the satire in which Horace thanks Maecenas for the gift of the Sabine estate (between 34 and 31 B.C.), and the hint of building in progress (308), strongly suggest that the setting is the newly acquired country house. It was situated near modern Licenza, in the hills to the ENE of Rome (*Epist.* 1.18.104-5). The remains of a villa found in this area are commonly regarded as being those of Horace's villa, see G. Lugli, *Monumenti Antichi* 31 (1926), cols. 456-598.

free time: cf. *Sat.* 1.4.138f., *Odes* 1.32.1f., *si quid vacui sub umbra/lusimus tecum. Otium* is necessary for poetic composition, but this is something Damasippus does not understand.

warm shelter: the countryside is praised for its temperateness, its warmth in winter, and cool in summer, cf. *Epist.*1.10.15, 1.16.8. The ready availability of fuel makes it a good place to be in winter, Xen. *Oec.* 5.9, Cic. *Sen.* 57.

1 **to pack in**: *stipare*, as a technical term for packing in cargo, Varro, *Ling.* 5.182, is appropriate for the books as physical objects. Another sense ('to crowd closely with attendants') comes into play when the books are thought of as people, K-H ad loc. and on *Sat.* 1.3.138, *OLD* s.v. *stipo* 2.

Plato: the philosopher, not the poet of Old Comedy with the same name who was a slightly younger contemporary of Aristophanes. The names are of Greek authors who are of particular relevance to the writing of *Satires* Book 2 and the *Epodes*. Plato is cited as a master of the philosophical dialogue, Menander for his famous skill in characterisation (E.H. Haight, *CPh* 42 [1947], 147-55, E. Fantham, *TAPhA* 114 [1984], 299-309 at 302). Eupolis (the poet of Old Comedy) and Archilochus stand for the satiric spirit of iambic. Horace claimed that the genre of satire descended from Greek Old Comedy (*Sat.* 1.4.1ff.) and he makes Archilochus his model in the *Epodes* (*Epod.* 6.13-4, *Epist.* 1.19.25, 28).

2 [*Archilocho*: Bentley's reading, supported by only one MS, is attractive because of the neat balance it produces.]

take ... companions away: now the books are personified. *Educere* is the technical term for taking people away to the country or on journeys, Cic. *Cat.* 1.9, *Pis.* 83, cf. *Sat.* 1.6.101ff., *TLL* V.2 117.81ff.

3 **envy ... what you excel in**: for 'envy' or 'unpopularity' see *Sat.* 2.1.77N., *Sat.* 2.6.47f.N. The unpopularity may be due to Horace's success as a poet, but also to his poetry's nature, satire being a genre that arouses enmity. Hence some commentators give this whole line a reference to satire, taking *virtute relicta* as, e.g., 'by deserting the cause of virtue' (Rudd 1966, 173), cf. *Sat.* 2.1.70. But, as Damasippus is talking about smallness of output generally, we should take *virtus* as 'energy', 'effectiveness' (Shackleton Bailey 1982, 39 n.15) or *arete* ('excellence', Bond 1987, 5-6), in contrast to *desidia* (15).

14   you'll be despised: Pers. 3.21. K-H cite Sen. *Ep.* 14.10, 'precautions must be taken, lest fear of envy bring us into contempt'.

poor fellow: the vocative rather than the nominative allows emphasis on 'despised' as the result.

you must avoid: Damasippus's advice is tactlessly blunt and dogmatic. He implies that without evidence of intellectual activity, Horace's *otium* can only be construed as *desidiosum*, see J.-M. André, *L'otium dans la vie morale et intellectuelle romaine des origines à l'époque augustéenne* (Paris, 1966), 243, 276, 336.

14f.   the shameless Siren Sloth: the Sirens lured men to destruction by the beauty of their singing, which seemed to promise them their heart's desire (Homer *Od.* 12.39ff.); hence they became proverbial of temptation (Otto, 324).

16   with equanimity: equanimity belongs to both popular wisdom and the philosophical tradition (see N-H on *Odes* 2.3.1), *aequo animo* occurring at the beginning and end of nature's diatribe at Lucr. 3.939, 962. That Damasippus resorts to this notion (which is important to Horace elsewhere, see McGann 1969, 19ff., 61, 82 on *euthumia*), when he so obviously lacks it himself, demonstrates his unsuitability as a student of philosophy.

16-18   Gods and Goddesses: there is an unexpected twist in Horace's reply (Lejay and Palmer ad loc., Fraenkel 1931, 127 n.1). Horace begins with a formula which suggests a curse (cf. Plaut. *Pseud.* 37, *Mostell.* 655, Catull. 28.14), in keeping with his angry nature and Damasippus's intrusion, but masters his temper and turns the curse into an ironic piece of good advice. His acquiescence in Damasippus's interpretation of his own situation is also ironic.

16   Damasippus: wrongly named Iunius Damasippus by ps.-Acro. D.R. Shackleton Bailey (*Two Studies in Roman Nomenclature* [American Classical Studies no.3, 1976], 46f.) suggests he was a son of the Licinius Crassus Damasippus who died with Metellus Scipio ([Caesar,] *B. Afr.* 96). He can be identified with a contemporary of Cicero's, who appears in some letters of 46-45 B.C. (*Fam.* 7.23.2-3, *Att.* 12.29.2, 12.33.1) in connection with the buying of statues and real estate. He was essentially a speculator in various kinds of luxury property, rather than a connoisseur of art, E. Rawson in M.I. Finley (ed.), *Studies in Roman Property* (Cambridge, 1976), 100-102, D'Arms 1981, 50. The Damasippus with whom Cicero dines at Macrob. *Sat.* 2.3.2 may be the same person. We do not know if he was still alive at the time of the composition of the *Satires*.

17   a barber: the first hint of Damasippus's conversion to philosophy, if there was not one already in the advice that he has just given Horace. At a time when men were clean-shaven, philosophers were conspicuous with their beards, cf. Varro, *Sat. Men.* 419B., Hor. *Sat.* 1.3.133, Pers. 1.133, 4.1, 5, Juv. 14.12 with Mayor ad loc. On the significance of the Stoic's beard see A.C. van Geytenbeek, *Musonius Rufus and the Greek Diatribe* (Trans. B.L. Hijmans, Utrecht, 1963), 119f.   Note that Damasippus later (35) also puts his conversion in terms of the change in his external appearance.

18-31:   Damasippus explains his new occupation (taking an interest in other people's business) as the result of his bankruptcy, and Horace diagnoses his transformation as the mere substitution of one unhealthy obsession for another.

18f.   shipwrecked: the metaphor (cf. Cic. *Rosc. Am.* 147, *tamquam e naufragio, Phil.* 12.19) is continued in the next line: he has been 'tossed out' like the steersman (Virg. *Aen.* 1.114, 6.353) from the management of his property.

at the central Janus: for a full discussion of the ancient evidence pertaining to this archway see Platner-Ashby s.v. *Ianus.* According to the scholiasts it was in the forum near the Basilica Aemilia. Two references in Cicero (*Off.* 2.87, *Phil.* 6.15) make it clear that it was the place where the money-lenders did business, J. Andreau, 'L'espace de la vie financière à Rome', in *L'urbs*, 158, 171f. 173., cf. *Epist.* 1.1.54 with D.P. Fowler, *CQ* 38 (1988), 262-3.

affairs: the word also means 'business'. Damasippus has already shown himself to be a meddler in other men's affairs, and here he naively acknowledges it. He has the defence, however, that certain philosophies (especially the Stoic) advocated concern for the welfare of others. See Plutarch, *On Being a Busybody* 2.7, *Mor.* 515D-516A, 518E for the busybody and Arr. *Epict. Diss.* 3.22.77, and 97, 'he is not meddling in other people's business when he is overseeing the actions of men, but these are his proper concerns' (of the idealized Cynic philosopher).

21 **in what bronze piece**: after the destruction of Corinth by Mummius in 146 B.C. (cf. Plin. *HN* 34.6 for the unbelievable story that the invention of Corinthian bronze was an accidental result of the burning of the city) Corinthian bronzes became collectors' items in Rome, much sought after and highly priced. There are many references to this craze, see Cic. *Parad.* 13, *Rosc. Am.* 133, *Verr.* II 2.46, Suet. *Aug.* 70.2, *Tib.* 34.1, cf. *Sat.* 1.4.28, *Epist.* 1.6.17.

Sisyphus: the legendary founder of Corinth, like Odysseus proverbial for his craftiness (Hom. *Il.* 6.153-4, Cic. *Tusc.* 1.98, Otto, 325).

washed his feet: there could hardly be a more antique piece of Corinthian bronze than Sisyphus's footbath (for another such fabulous attribution, cf. *Sat.* 1.3.90-1; Stat. *Silv.* 4.6.59ff. is more plausible). It is referred to, and described as 'lion-footed', in one of Aeschylus's Sisyphus plays, *TGF* III fr.225 Radt, H.W. Smith, *Aeschylus* II (London and Camb. Mass., 1946), fr.121 (225). For discussion and illustration of this type of bronze footbath see M. Milne, *AJA* 48 (1944), 26-63. The legendary pedigree was an important selling point (Chevallier, 111, 127ff.), no doubt in this case invented by Damasippus himself (Rawson 1985, 89).

22 **carved**: here the reference is to sculpture in marble, on which see Pliny *HN* 36.9ff. The reading *scalptum* is defended by Ernout-Meillet s.v. *scalpo*.

cast too stiffly: for artists in cast bronze see Pliny *HN* 34 passim. *durus* ('stiff') is contrasted with *mollis* ('fluid', 'life-like') in accounts of the development of artistic technique from primitive roughness to greater skill and polish, Cic. *Brut.* 70, Quint. 12.10.7, cf. Virg. *Aen.* 6.847. Damasippus claims his expertise enables him to recognise antiques from their technique.

23 **invest**: some commentators have taken *ponere* as 'put a price on', 'fix the value of' but it seems more likely that Damasippus speculated by buying statues for resale. *Ponere* meaning 'put a price on' is usually accompanied by the word for 'price'. For *ponere* ('invest') see *Sat.* 1.2.13.

24 [*mercarier*: the use of the archaic infinitive throws the verb into prominence before it is picked up by *Mercuriali* (with etymological play). The tone of the archaic infinitive in Horace's hexameter poetry is difficult to pin down, see Brink 1982, Appendix 6.]

without equal: *unus* could mean 'only' (cf. 283) but the idiomatic 'especially' is better, cf. *Sat.* 2.6.57-8, *Epod.* 12.4, *Ars P.* 32 with Brink's note.

25f. **street corners**: places where gossip is spread, *Sat.* 2.6.50, Cic. *Mur.* 13, Prop. 2.20.22 etc.

"Mercury's man": the Roman god Mercury, whose name is etymologically connnected with *merx* ('merchandise', 'trade') was the god of gain, commerce and good luck (cf. *Sat.* 2.6.4-5N). See Plaut. *Amph.* 1ff., *Stich.* 404., Petron. *Sat.* 29.3, 67.7, 77.4. Damasippus's nickname derives from his financial success. For other meanings of *Mercurialis* see N-H on *Odes* 2.17.29.

[*Mercuriali*: the MSS read *Mercuriale*, as an adjective with *cognomen*, but this has no exact parallel and would mean 'of Mercury' rather than 'favoured by Mercury'. The regular constructions are either with the name in the dative assimilated to the case of the personal pronoun (as in 47-8, and often in Plautus, cf. *Rud.* 5, 934, *Stich.* 174, Sall. *Iug.* 5.4) or with the name in the same case as *cognomen*, in apposition to it (cf. *Mercurialem* of codd. det.).]

27   **cleared**: *purgatum* is used as a medical term, perhaps implying a cure for mental illness, cf. *Ars P.* 302 (purging with hellebore).

illness: Horace deftly introduces one of the *leitmotifs* of the satire, the disease metaphor (see 80, 121, 254, 306-7). Talking about vices as 'mental illnesses' was an approach especially associated with the Stoics, though not confined to them (*SVF* III 421-30, Cic. *Tusc.* 3.7, 4.23-4, Lejay, 364, Long, 175-8). Damasippus's disease must have been avarice (see 300).

27-30:   the attribution of *atqui ...urget* is problematic. Against the old tradition that Damasippus is the speaker two considerations are of relevance: 1) it is unlikely that Damasippus would say of himself that a new illness had replaced the old, 2) something is needed to provoke Damasippus to reply 'you are mad too' at 31ff. In essence, what Horace says is that Damasippus's original vice, has, like a physical illness, turned itself into another. But, through his analogy from mental illness in 30, Horace hints that Damasippus has become mad, and therefore Damasippus embarks on his rejoinder (see Rudd 1966, 297 n.20). Thus the main topic of the satire is introduced almost accidentally, as Palmer notes ad loc., and the change of direction at this point is reminiscent of the technique of the 'diatribe' satires in Book 1.

28   [*mire*: obelised by Shackleton Bailey. The conjunction with *ut solet* can be handled by limiting this phrase's relevance to physical disease. *Mire* then deliberately repeats *miror*.]

28f.   **transferred itself**: according to Porphyrio *traicere* is a technical term of medicine for an illness changing its seat.

stomach: it is difficult to know whether to translate as 'stomach' or 'heart', since in Greek medical terminology *kardia* meant both the heart and the mouth of the oesophagus and doctors disputed about which was the primary seat of disease, C.R.S. Harris, *The Heart and the Vascular System in Ancient Greek Medicine from Alcmeon to Galen* (Oxford, 1973), 432ff.

30   **lethargic**: the Greek term occurs here first in Latin, as an appropriate technical term. For the illness see Celsus, *Med.* 3.20.1. It is contrasted with *phrenesis* (3.18.1), which is manifested in delirium, hallucinations, raving and violence. Medical treatments of lethargy aimed at arousing the patient (cf. 142ff.). K-H quote from Sext. Emp. *Math.* 11.135-6, a passage, perhaps deriving from polemic against dogmatic philosophy, where 'the philosopher, who introduces one perturbation after the other', is said to be like 'the physician who removes pleurisy (*pleuritis*) and causes inflammation of the lungs (*peripneumonia*) or cures frenzy (*phrenitis*) but in its place introduces lethargy'.

31   **it**: the new illness.

31-40:   a transitional passage which leads from the introductory dialogue to Stertinius's lecture via the narrative of Damasippus's salvation. On the use of subordinate clauses (33-4) to effect an indirect transition here, see U. Knoche, *Philologus* 90 (1935), 471-2 = D. Korzeniewski (ed.), *Die römische Satire* (Darmstadt, 1970), 306-7.

31   **My dear fellow**: see *Sat.* 2.2.1N.

32   **all foolish people**: Damasippus quotes the so-called Stoic paradox 'all fools are mad'. For the Stoics all except the wise man were 'fools', that is, not wise (cf. *Sat.* 1.2.24, 1.3.77, 2.7.42, Pers. 5.93, 121). Folly, or ignorance of the truth, implies moral unsoundness, and moral unsoundness madness (cf. Cic. *Tusc. Disp.* 3.7ff.). The paradox plays on the confusion between the special and normal meanings of the words and suppresses the middle term.

pretty well: cf. *Sat.* 1.3.98, *Epist.* 1.6.1, *Ars P.* 432. *Prope* modifies the hyperbole of the statement, but does not change its meaning. See *OLD* s.v. *prope* 8, Becker, 141 n.24.

33   **Stertinius:** see *Epist.*1.12.20 (where ps.-Acro tells us he wrote 220 books on Stoicism in Latin verse!), Rudd 1966, 145. Nothing more is known about him, and there is no evidence for the view that he and Crispinus (*Sat.* 2.7.45N) are to be imagined as quasi-Cynic 'street-preachers'. On this, Rawson 1985, 53 is sceptical, and for her they are primarily writers, but Wiseman 1987, 271-2 takes Stertinius's role in this satire as his main support for the statement 'philosophers too sought a public audience for their moral preaching.' For the question of when Stoics began writing and teaching in Latin at Rome see Rawson 1985, 49, 53, 284f. She suggests (53) that Stertinius might have been from the family of the Stertinii attested at Delos (as wealthy business men) and that he might have studied at Athens. In this case he would have been a cut above the ambulatory Cynic-Stoic preacher, if they existed at this time. His name may have comic resonance (cf. *stertere*: to snore).

    rattles off: *crepat* has a disrespectful tone, which has been interpreted variously. Rudd thinks it is Horace's joke which jars in Damasippus's mouth (1966, 175). .It is better to take it (with Lejay ad loc. and 286) as unconscious irony and a touch of characterisation. The old pragmatic and unintellectual Damasippus shows through (see Bond 1987, 10f.).

    marvellous: perhaps there is a hint of the paradoxical nature of the teachings, Cic. *Fin.* 4.74, *admirabilia*, Sen. *Ep.* 87.1, *mirabile*.

35   **nurture a philosophic beard:** the grand expression, modelled on the use of the Greek *trephô* (cf. Hom. *Il.* 23.142, Virg. *Aen.* 7.391) is the answer to 17, showing that the beard is not to be scoffed at.

36   **the Fabrician bridge:** the stone bridge leading from the Campus Martius to the Tiber Island, built by L. Fabricius in 62 B.C. (Dio Cass. 37.45) and named after the builder.

37   **after my financial failure:** see 74, *OLD* s.v. *gero* 9. The ablative absolute suggests officialese, or commercial jargon (Lejay ad loc.), cf. Plaut. *Stich.* 402, *Trin.* 1182, Macrob. *Sat.* 3.6.11 (the context is *mercatura*).

37f.   **covered my head:** it was customary to cover the head at the approach of death, cf. Xen. *Cyr.* 8.7.28, Plato *Phaedo* 118A, Livy 4.12.11. For a full list of examples, with discussion, see R. Waltz, *REL* 17 (1939), 299-308.

38   **he stood at my right hand:** the idea is that he appeared suddenly, like a divine saviour. See Brink on *Epist.* 2.1.205. *Dexter* also means 'favourable', 'propitious', cf. Virg. *Aen.* 8.302.

    [*Cave faxis*: the shortening of the final syllable of the iambic imperative was already a feature of the language of Plautus and Terence, cf. 177. *Faxis* is an old subjunctive (with optative suffix), which was preserved in such fixed forms as prohibitions and prayers (cf. *Sat.* 2.6.5), L-H-S I 622. A colloquial expression, Ruckdeschel, 107.]

39   **unworthy of you:** Damasippus's situation is not such as to justify suicide in Stoic theory, according to which the moment and the reason had to be right. His specific misfortune, poverty, as an external, should not affect him (cf. *Sat.* 2.7.84N), and his general condition, folly, which he shares with most men, was not enought to justify suicide, according to Chrysippus (Plut. *Stoic Self-Contradictions* 18, *Mor.* 1042A). See Rist, Chap. 13, M. Griffin, *G&R* 33 (1986), 64-77, 192-202. His *method* of suicide is also *indignum*, cf. Tacitus's disapproval of a young man jumping out of a window (*Ann.* 6.49, 'sudden and ugly'). Methods such as hanging, drowning and jumping off heights (cf. 277) were not practised by the upper classes (Y. Grisé, *Le suicide dans la Rome antique* [Montreal/Paris, 1982], 94).

    tortures (lit. 'chokes', 'strangles'): a strong word (*TLL* II 48.32ff.), which recognises the intensity of his mental suffering, cf. Cic. *Tusc.* 3.32 (in an ethical context) and *angor* at Lucr. 3.903, 993.

40   **to be thought mad:** at 46-8 we are told that some people now call Damasippus 'madman', just as he was called 'Mercury's man' when he was successful. He feels the humiliation so deeply that he wishes to kill himself. There may be a hint that Damasippus has been legally designated mad and removed from the administration of his property, cf. 74 and Cic. *Sen.* 22, *nostro more male rem gerentibus patribus bonis interdici solet.* In any case, it is this possibility which accounts for the appellation.

41-76:   the introduction to Stertinius's lecture. Here he defines the general proposition to be proved, but keeps Damasippus's case closely in mind, showing that those who accuse him of madness suffer from a corresponding and antithetical kind themselves. He takes great pains to set out his argument clearly and systematically (see 50-1, 52, 56). 46ff. and 53ff. differ in emphasis (the first illustrates the general rule, the second illustrates the principle of antithesis) but there are links between them (52, *nihil ut sapientior*; 56, *nihilo sapientius*). In the final section the argument is applied to Damasippus and his creditors.

what it is to be mad: Porphyrio comments 'He demonstrates what madness is, like Lucilius', after 1247W, cf. 744W.

Stertinius begins in proper philosophical style, with a definition, a procedure often explicitly followed by Cicero, e.g. *Off.* 1.7, 'Every systematic development of any subject ought to begin with a definition, so that everyone may understand what the discussion is about', *Fin.* 2.1ff. (discussion arising from the point that the Epicureans do not consider definition necessary), 4.8, *Tusc.* 4.11, 53 ('your [i.e. Stoics'] definitions'), see Lejay, 356-7, Rudd 1966, 185-6. We have the titles of treatises of Chrysippus which were collections of definitions (*SVF* III App. II, fr.15). The promised definition, which is a clarification of the paradox, is given at 43-5.

43   **ignorance of the truth:** for the Stoics only the wise man had perfect knowledge and moral goodness. Wisdom (or knowledge of what is really good and really evil) is the virtue of reason, the vice of reason being ignorance (*SVF* III 256, Gould, 168-71). The link between folly and madness is made through ignorance, or 'blindness' (*SVF* III 663).

44   **the portico and flock:** the Stoics took their name from the Painted Portico (or Stoa) in the Agora at Athens in which the founder of the school (Zeno of Citium) began teaching in about 300 B.C. See Pers. 3.54. 'Flock' can be derogatory in tone (see Rudd 1966, 175, 297 n.22), but need not be here, see *Epist.* 1.9.13, Cic. *Fin.* 1.65, *De Or.* 1.42, *TLL* VI.2 2333.64ff.

Chrysippus: the two occurrences of his name (here and 287) frame Stertinius's homily (see also *Sat.* 1.3.127, *Epist.* 1.2.4). Head of the school after Cleanthes (232 B.C.), he wrote extensively, leaving a comprehensive exposition of Stoic doctrine (see the catalogue of his works at Diog. Laert. 7.189-202). He was regarded as responsible for the survival of the school (Diog. Laert. 7.183, 'If there had been no Chrysippus, there would be no Stoa'). See *OCD²* s.v. Chrysippus, Gould, Chap.2.

45f.   **maintain:** *autumo* is found only here in Horace. Though it is frequent in Plautus, in later writers it would be felt as archaic in tone and solemn rather than colloquial (Quintilian [8.3.26] says 'tragic'), cf. Lucil. 835W, Catull. 44.2, Pac. *trag.* 366ff.R, *philosophi ... autumant.* Here it adds to the formality of tone.

This general rule: *formula* does not occur elsewhere in Horace. The binding force of the dogma is expressed through a metaphor from Roman legal terminology. Cicero (*Off.* 3.19-20, cf. Sen. *Ep.* 117.6, Lejay, 366) had already applied the legal term *formula* to the ethical sphere, *TLL* VI.1 1114.81ff. *Formulae* were established forms of legal procedure applying in various areas of law in which cases could be brought. 'Excepted' continues the legal metaphor, see T.E. Kinsey, *Pro P. Quinctio Oratio* (Sydney, 1971), App.1, 'After the *formula* would be set out a list of *exceptiones* ...', 285N., *TLL* V.2 1249.61ff. *Tenet* and the ablative absolute phrase also have the ring of legal terminology. For the usual exception of the wise man see *SVF* III 668.

46   **Now learn:** cf. *Sat.* 2.2.70.

47   **all:** not the whole of mankind, as at 81, but the group defined in the relative clause.

49   **mistake** (lit. 'deviation'): the illustration is based on the literal sense of the word *error*, but the secondary meaning 'derangement' (63) must have influenced the choice of term.

48f.   **wander here and there:** in a famous passage Lucretius (2.7ff.) speaks of those who have attained the heights of wisdom being able to look down on those 'wandering here and there and seeking the right road of life'. This passage must have been in Horace's mind, since the Lucretian *palantes* is used only here in Horace (similarly Ovid uses it only once in a passage which echoes the same Lucretian context, *Met.* 15.150). *Trames* may also point to Lucretius, cf. 6.27, 'the small track by which we can pass on to it [the highest good]'. For the metaphor of 'the path of life' see Brink on *Ars P.* 404.

50f.   **each makes:** depends on 'Just as ...'

53   **a tail behind:** cf. 299. The point is that they are foolish without realising it. Porphyrio says hanging tails on people without their knowledge was a children's game. The idea also sounds proverbial (ps.-Acro, Otto, 79).
     One kind of folly: the same example is found at Xen. *Mem.* 1.1.14 (in a list of antithetical kinds of madness), 'Some do not fear terrible things, others fear things that are not frightening.'
     folly: i.e. madness, cf. 43.

54f.   **fires, precipices:** the illustration may be generated by the proverbial lack of sense of those who cannot see obstacles in their path, cf. *Epist.* 2.2.135, *Ars P.* 459 with Brink's note.

56   **divergent** (lit. 'bandy-legged'): cf. *Sat.* 1.3.47. For the figurative use see Pers. 6.18, *OLD* s.v. *varus* c.

57f.   **his dear mother:** the punctuation and the distribution of epithets have been much discussed. The solution which points to the Homeric use of *philos* (e.g. Hom. *Il.* 1.351 etc.) is already in Porphyrio. Other commentators are happy to take *amica* as 'loving' (cf. *TLL* I 1905 62ff.), but K-H object to this collocation and interpret 'mistress', arguing that the whole range of friends and relations need not apply to the one person.

58   **relatives:** on the role of relatives in the care and custody of the mad see 217f.N.

60-2:   Cicero refers several times (*Tusc.* 1.106, *Ac. Pr.* 2.88) to the impressive scene in Pacuvius's *Iliona* in which the ghost of Deiphilus rose from the earth to ask his mother for burial. According to the legend, Polymestor, king of Thrace, killed his own son Deiphilus, thinking he was Polydorus. Iliona, his wife, one of Priam's daughters, had charge of Polydorus, her younger brother, and in order to protect him she pretended he was her son. Apparently the actor playing Iliona had fallen into a real drunken sleep, and when he did not respond to his cue, the audience joined in with the words of the actor playing Deiphilus.

60f.   **Fufius ... Catienuses:** Fufius and Catienus were the actors playing the roles in a revival performance of the work. Second century B.C. comedy and tragedy was well-known and influential in the late Republic and early Augustan periods because it was still staged, Griffin, 200ff. The mishap has ensured the memory of the actors' names. That of Catienus indicates that his patron was Italian, C. Garton, *Personal Aspects of the Roman Theatre* (Toronto, 1972), no.63, E. Rawson, *Roman Culture and Society* (Oxford, 1991), 486. Fufius was perhaps a Greek (Garton no.84).

61   **sleeping through the part of Iliona:** as if 'sleeping off' a hangover, cf. Cic. *Phil.* 2.30. See also the acc. of the name of a character after *ago*, as in English 'act Iliona', Cic. *QRosc.* 20.
     twelve hundred: meant as an indefinitely large number (it is the double of 'six hundred' which is often used in this way).

62   'Mother, I beseech you': the opening words of the famous aria of the ghost, Pac. *trag.* 197ff.R = *ROL* II 205-10. R. Kassel *ZPE* 42 (1981), 11-20, at 17 comments on the fitting of words originally in another metre, iambic octonarii, into the hexameter. See also E.W. Handley, *BICS* Suppl. 51 (1988), 166-74.

62-76: a new stage in Stertinius's exposition begins (cf. *docebo*), the application of the general principle (48ff.) and the illustration (53ff.) to Damasippus's case in order to cure him of his false sense of shame. Though some details in this passage remain obscure, the main point is clear: the creditors who financed his speculation were just as mad (and as bad businessmen) as he, since they cannot force him to repay what he no longer has.

64-5:   note the parallelism of expression, which reminds us of the antithesis between the two kinds of madness above.

66-8:   Take ... : in this context *accipio*, *reddo* and *praeda* are used in specialised senses from the financial sphere. *Accipio* means 'borrow', *OLD* s.v. 4c, Plaut. *Curc.* 480, Cic. *Verr.* II 3.169, *Sen.* 51; *reddo*, 'pay back', *OLD* s.v. 1, Cic. *Sen.* 51; *praeda*, 'gain', 'profit', *OLD* s.v. 3, *TLL* X.2 526.65ff.

68   **propitius Mercury:** cf. 25N. For *praesens* see *Sat.* 2.2.41N, but here the presence of the god is not emphasised.

69-76: some light is cast on this obscure passage by T. Maguire, *Hermathena* 3 (1879), 134ff., and G.E.M. de Ste Croix, 'Greek and Roman Accounting' (in A.C. Littleton and B.S. Yamey (edd.), *Studies in the History of Accounting* [London, 1956], 14-74) gives useful information on legal aspects of lending and borrowing and the keeping of accounts. See also R. Villers, in *Studi in onore di Emilio Betti*, IV, (Milan, 1962), 465-463. On the names see Rudd 1966, 147.

The general sense is clear: whatever precautions a creditor may take, he cannot force the defaulting debtor to pay. We should begin with the technical senses of *scribe ... a Nerio* (69). It is almost certain that this means 'record as paid ... through Nerius', *scribere* here meaning 'to enter in one's account-books as lent' (Cic. *QRosc.* 2, Servius on Virg. *Aen.* 7.422, Andreau, 566f.). This makes Nerius a banker (for *a* indicating a source of payment see *OLD* s.v. 17d, Plaut. *Capt.* 449, Cic. *Att.* 16.15.5), though Andreau, 701-3 follows the scholiasts' view that he is a money-lender. The point in paying through a banker is that they were obliged to keep books which could be produced in legal proceedings as evidence. The problem here is *decem*, with which we have to understand *sestertia* ('so many thousand sesterces'), cf. Hor. *Epist.* 1.7.80, Sall. *Cat.* 30.6, Catull. 103.1; there is a parallel for its omission at Paul. *Dig.* 12.1.40 and 10,000 sesterces is a typical sum in the *Digest*. It still remains awkward followed by *centum* and *mille*. There was an older view which supplied *tabulas* ('a legal bond') with *decem* and took *tabulas* and *centum* together.

69-70 **Cicuta's knotty contract:** the translation treats *nodosi* as a transferred epithet. In the light of 175 it appears Cicuta ('Hemlock') must be a second banker or money-lender, not some kind of lawyer, though the epithet 'knotty' suggests the complications of the law (cf. Juv. 8.50, 'the law's knots'). *Tabulas* here is probably 'legal document' (*OLD* s.v. 8), rather than 'account-books' (*OLD* s.v. 7). K-H suggest Cicuta was a writer of bonds.

chains: this picks up the literal meaning of 'knotty' and anticipates the image of Proteus.

71   **Proteus:** a god of the sea with prophetic powers. His name became proverbial for deviousness (Otto, 289), cf. Hor. *Epist.* 1.1.90, 'with what knot may I hold Proteus as he changes his aspect'. His transformations, described in Hom. *Od.* 4.417ff., 456-8 (imitated by Virgil at *G.* 4.396ff., 440ff.) were intended to get him out of difficulties. Horace shows independence from the Homeric version. Like Virgil, he begins with the boar, and he ends with the Homeric tree (dropped by Virgil). The bird and rock (cf. Ov. *Met.* 7.735) are new. On 'the old man of the sea' see P.M.C. Forbes Irving, *Metamorphosis in Greek Myths* (Oxford, 1990), 174-9.

72   **hale him to court**: the standard phrase, cf. *Sat.* 1.9.77, Plaut. *Poen.* 1336, *Rud.* 859.

   laughs with jaws not his own: the phrase has not been satisfactorily explained. It is Homeric (*Od.* 20.347), but there the context is quite different. The suitors laugh hysterically, their wits deranged by the intervention of Athena. Here *alienis* suggests 'borrowed' — 'laughing at another's expense', 'as if beside himself'?

75   **Perellius**: according to the interpretation of 69-70 outlined above, Perellius is Damasippus's chief creditor.

76   **dictates**: in the sense of 'laying down terms' but also, literally, to a scribe for signing by the borrower. This is brought out by the connection with *rescribere* 'to write back', 'to pay back' (Ter. *Phorm.* 922).

77-81:   Stertinius turns from Damasippus to introduce his lecture proper, gathering a crowd around him, as if he is a quack-doctor selling cures (K-H), cf. the satirist's procedure at *Sat.* 1.4.25-32, where anyone in the crowd may suffer from avarice, ambition or passion. The audience is told to settle itself comfortably for a long session (77, here he sounds like a Plautine prologue), and prepare itself for the treatment of a series of illnesses, or topics. Giving the topics in advance like this is not an Horatian procedure, but the length of the satire may require it. The topics do not appear in the advertised order, but as follows: avarice (82-157), ambition (158-223), *luxuria* (224-46), love (247-80), superstition (281-95). These are the main vices attacked in the popular-philosophical tradition (the one missing, discontent, becomes the subject of *Sat.* 2.7.). Persius follows Horace with his five enslaving passions in 5.132-88: avarice, luxury, love, ambition and superstition.

78   **is pale**: the external sign of the illness, cf. Pers. 4.47 (of avarice). For the collocation of avarice and ambition, see 158-66N. Cicero (*Tusc.* 4.24-7) puts desire of glory among the sicknesses of the soul (a Stoic context).

80   **is feverish**: cf. *Epist.* 1.1.33, *fervet avaritia miseroque cupidine pectus*, Cic. *Quinct.* 38, Chrysippus *SVF* III 465, 474.

81:   [sense requires the punctuation after *ordine*, which goes well with *doceo* and the didactic stance, see Virg. *G.* 4.4, *TLL* IX.2 951.50ff., Lucil. 202W, 'Laelius ... reproaching all our gluttons one by one' (*compellans gumias ex ordine nostros*).]

82-157:   the leading place in Stertinius's homily is given to *avaritia*, an important topic in Hellenistic popular philosophy and Roman Satire (see Rudd 1966, Index s.v. Greed), and contemporary political discourse, e.g. Sall. *Cat.* 10.3-5. See Plut. *On Love of Wealth, Mor.* 523D-528B, and, in Horace, *Sat.* 1.1, *Odes* 2.2, 3.16, 3.24, *Epist.* 1.1, 1.6.31ff., 2.2.141ff. The similarity here to the treatment in *Sat.* 1.1 is particularly close, with the use of anecdote and concrete detail, and the illustration of the different facets of avarice, or love of wealth (Lejay, 377).

82f.   **the largest share**: because most people suffer from this disease, cf. 120-1.

   hellebore: from the Greek *helleboros*, see Celsus, *Med.* 2.13.2-3, Pliny *HN* 25.47ff., 60, Brink on *Ars P.* 300. White and black hellebore are both mentioned as remedies for madness, the white by inducing vomiting, the black as a purgative for bile in the case of melancholy (an excess of black bile was thought to cause a type of madness, Plaut. *Amph.* 727, *Capt.* 596), see Rudd 1966, 181f. Care has to be taken in the use of hellebore 'which does not always help the sick, and always injures the healthy' (Celsus, *Med.* 2.13.3), see Pigeaud, 208ff.

   lovers of wealth: this general class contains two types, those whose insatiable passion to acquire wealth drives them beyond the limits of civilised behaviour (*aiskhrokerdeia*, cf. Arist. *NE* 4.1121ᵇff.) and even into criminality (cf. Lucr. 3.59ff., Juv. 14), and those whose love of wealth is manifested as meanness or lack of generosity (*aneleutheria*, cf. Arist. *NE* 1121ᵇ13; Theophrastus also treats *mikrologia* [*Char.* 24]). The latter disposition was seen as characteristic of old age. On the depiction of the miser in satire see *Sat.* 2.2.57N.

Reason: also used as a key-word to signal the beginning of a new topic at 225 and 250 (McGann 1954, 12, 13 n.1). It probably implies something like 'a correct interpretation according to us Stoics'. For the Stoics, reason (*logos*) was the fundamental principle of the universe, cf. Long, 144ff.

Anticyra: cf. 166, Brink on *Ars P.* 300, Pers. 4.16. Two towns of this name were famous for hellebore, one in Phocis, on the gulf of Corinth (Strabo 9.3.3), the other in Malis near Mt Oeta.

84-99: the anecdote begins abruptly, cf. 142ff., 168ff., 281ff., 288ff. The section on avarice begins with the example of Staberius, and ends with that of Opimius, both of whose perverted values are shown in relation to their deaths. Though the handling of the examples in this satire shows great virtuosity and variety (Lejay, 372ff., McGann 1954, Appendix, Fraenkel 1957, 143 n.1), some of the detail in this anecdote is unclear, while at times the point seems to be laboured, see L.A. MacKay, *CJ* 36 (1940), 164-6.

84 **Staberius**: to be presumed dead (Rudd 1966, 138), if he is not entirely fictitious. We know no more about him than is given here.

the sum total he had bequeathed: though we have a parallel in an inscription (*CIL* XI.5400 [a freedman from Assisi], 'on the day before he died he left an estate of 520,000 sesterces'), the provision is clearly eccentric and misguided, in the manner of Trimalchio's epitaph (Petron. *Sat.* 71.12), 'God-fearing, brave, faithful, he grew from little; he left 30,000,000 sesterces, and never listened to a philosopher', on which see Th. Mommsen, *Hermes* 13 (1878), 106-21, D'Arms 1981, 108ff.

85f. **obliged**: a legal term for obligations specified in wills, see *OLD* s.v. *damno* 7, where the other examples are all from the *Digest*.

entertain the people: in the Republic great men's families celebrated their funerals with games (including gladiatorial shows and theatrical performances) and banquets, spending huge amounts, see J.M.C. Toynbee, *Death and Burial in the Roman World* (London, 1971), 54, 56, Veyne, 416ff., Ville, 57-58, Hopkins, 202 n.2, 204.

a hundred pairs: cf. Pers. 6.48. The point lies in the extravagance of the figure, especially for a nonentity such as Staberius. We have no contemporary figures (according to Livy 39.46 there were 120 men in the games for P. Licinius Crassus in 183 B.C.). In 22 B.C., as a reform measure, Augustus limited the praetors to no more than two shows per year, and no more than 120 men (Dio Cass. 54.2.4), but we would expect greater lavishness at shows given by magistrates. Staberius wants to perpetuate the memory of his wealth, either by record in the epitaph, or by requiring his heirs to spend an unforgettable amount on benefactions, cf. Balsdon, 332.

Arrius: cf. his sons, 243. A very rich contemporary of Cicero's (see Wiseman 1971, 121, 214), Q. Arrius in 59 B.C. gave a funeral banquet for 'many thousands' in memory of his father (Cic. *Vat.* 30-32, cf. *Brut.* 242).

discretion: a further technical term, cf. *Sat.* 2.5.105. Wills might name a third party who was to decide the amount spent on the funeral, see *CIL* I.1578 = 1199, Scaev. *Dig.* 34.2.40.2, *TLL* II 410.57ff. Arrius would not have stinted the expense.

87 **as much ... corn**: the clause, tacked on to the preceding one without a connective, is explicative of the banquet.

Africa: the reference is a hyperbolic one (cf. *Odes* 1.1.10 with N-H) to the province which was one of the traditional mainstays of the corn supply for Rome in the Republic, see G. Rickman, *The Corn Supply of Ancient Rome* (Oxford, 1980), 61-71, 231-5.

The corn could have been distributed separately as a *frumentatio* (cf. the distribution of meat at the funeral of a Flaminius in 174 B.C., Livy 41.28). There are not many references to *frumentationes* of private individuals, but the immensely rich M. Licinius Crassus gave Roman citizens living in Rome enough wheat to live on for three months (Plut. *Crass.* 2).

7f.   **Whether I am ...** : this is usually taken as Staberius replying to objections that could be voiced by his heirs, but for Lejay (wrongly) it is the final clause of the will.
don't act the uncle: see *Sat.* 2.2.97N. For the whole phrase see Pers. 3.96. It looks like a catch-phrase, and this would account for the preservation of the present subjunctive (instead of the perfect) in the prohibition, see Woodcock §128.

9   **This**: is either the disapproving attitude of the heirs (K-H, Palmer), which he 'had in mind', or the reasoning given in 91ff., esp. 98-9, (which he 'foresaw', Lejay ad loc.), but this is less likely.

9-91   **What then ... ?**: Stertinius's lecture gets a particular tone from the frequency with which he uses questions, see Lejay, 360f. These may be rhetorical questions addressed to the listener (e.g. 108-10), or to an imaginary character (122ff., 272ff.). Here the question is followed directly by its answer, ref. 295. Whether he puts it into the mouth of an imaginary interlocutor (Orelli, Palmer), is not easy to say.

1-9:   Staberius's 'philosophy' is now unveiled. He is suffering from a bad case of inverted values. Not only does he identify his worth with his wealth, but he attributes to wealth the status of the *summum bonum* (the highest good), which, for a Stoic like Stertinius, was virtue. For Staberius it is the rich man (*dives*), not the Stoic wise man, who is the epitome of human excellence.
poverty: should not be thought of as penury, see *Sat.* 2.5.8N.

3   [*perisset*: was explained by Bentley as the subjunctive equivalent to the future perfect of direct speech. Lejay and Palmer prefer *periret* because he has not yet died.]

4-8   **'Everything, you see ...** : Staberius's beliefs are quoted in his own words. The equation of a man's worth with his wealth was old and proverbial, cf. *Sat.* 2.5.7-8N.
subservient to beauteous riches: wealth is elevated to the position of ruling power of the universe, and is therefore beautiful, like the gods (K-H), or as an object of love, cf. Cic. *Fam.* 9.14.4, *nihil est ... virtute formosius, nihil pulchrius, nihil amabilius*. This inversion of values is frequently castigated, cf. Ar. *Plut.* 146, Hor. *Epist.* 1.1.53, 1.6.36. *Virtus* (excellence) should be that which controls human endeavour (Sall. *Cat.* 2.7).

6   **amassed**: the verb implies the image of the heap, symbolic of great wealth, cf. *Sat.* 1.1.44, *Odes* 2.2.24, Cic. *Leg. Agr.* 1.14, *Phil.* 2.97.

7   **illustrious, brave, just**: the string of epithets recalls the *elogium* typical of the epitaph, e.g. *CIL* I² 7, *fortis vir sapiensque*, cf. Trimalchio's epitaph quoted on 84, *CIL* I² 10, *honos fama virtusque gloria atque ingenium*. Staberius is discounting the traditional Roman values of military prowess and civic virtue as well as the Stoic theory which attributes all the virtues to the wise man. It is the word 'king' which makes us realise that Staberius is also challenging the supremacy of the Stoic sage, cf. Lucil. 1189-90W, Varro *Sat. Men.* 245, Hor. *Sat.* 1.3.124-5, *Epist.* 1.1.106f., *sapiens uno minor est Iove, dives,/liber, honoratus, pulcher, rex denique regum.*
[*sapiensque*: most editors read *sapiensne*, taking it as an interpolated question that Stertinius asks himself, or his listeners, as he sarcastically reports Staberius's beliefs.]

8f.   **This**: the fact, recorded in the epitaph, that he had died rich, takes the place of the usual virtues and achievements (the *laudatio*).

9-103:   the contrary example also turns on the point of value. Staberius values wealth above all else, Aristippus cares for it so little that he can throw it away. This also contrasts with the next topic — the hoarder.

9f.   **Aristippus**: a companion of Socrates and the founder of the Cyrenaic school of philosophy, cf. Hor. *Epist.* 1.1.18, 1.17.23. There are many anecdotes about Aristippus, some concerning his extravagance, see Griffin, 37 n.27. The present one, illustrating his independence of wealth, is found in a less colourful form in Diogenes Laertius (2.77 =

Aristippus 68A,B Mannebach, Bion fr.40A Kindstrand); cf. Lucil. 835W, Fiske, 16▮ Lejay, 374-5).

the Greek: in contrast to the materialistic Romans (cf. Hor. *Ars P.* 325f.), of who▮ Staberius is an example (K-H).

anything like: Staberius and Aristippus are a contrasting pair who fit Stertinius's theory o▮ divergent kinds of madness in 47-76. Shackleton Bailey conjectures *dissimile*, whic▮ makes a more logical transition.

101 **in the middle of Libya:** the detail not only adds colour to the anecdote, but reminds us o▮ the philosopher's association with Cyrene.

102 **Which ... is more insane?:** that this criticism of Aristippus's attitude to externals i▮ consonant with the doctrine of Chrysippus is shown by Plut. *Stoic Self-Contradictions* 3▮ *Mor.* 1047E-1048C = *SVF* III 138 (see Gould, 177), 'he says they are raving mad who set a▮ nought wealth and health etc.'.

103 **There is no point:** a maxim that underlines the pointlessness of the preceding question▮ The fact that Aristippus's extreme indifference to wealth may also appear mad means tha▮ his case cannot function as an example of more reasonable behaviour than Staberius's.

104-28: Stertinius now attempts to show that the lover of wealth's madness consists in his refusa▮ to use what he accumulates. For this argument against avarice see 166-7, *Sat.* 1.1.28ff. Teles fr. IVa pp.33.4-34.5, 38.3-4 (Hense[2]), Bion fr.37 with Kindstrand, Plut. *On Love of Wealth* 4, *Mor.* 524F, '[it is] madness and misery when a man refuses to put on a cloa▮ because he is cold, to eat a loaf because he is hungry, or to use wealth because he loves it▮ Rudd 1966, 183.

The articulation of the argument is clear: three short hypothetical examples with ▮ conclusion (104-110) are picked up by three longer hypothetical examples (111ff., 115f. 117ff.) and a surprise conclusion (120-1).

104-7: examples drawn from skills and trades were traditional in moral philosophy afte▮ Socrates. For the musician see Varro, *Rust.* 2.1.3, Arr. *Diss. Epict.* 4.8.16, 3.23.6ff., Otto, 84; for the cobbler, *Sat.* 1.3.124ff., Arr. *Diss. Epict.* 3.23.8; the trader, *Odes* 1.1.16 (with N-H). The mode of questioning has been identified as 'Socratic', by McGann 1954, 1▮ (following F. Klingner, *SB* Leipzig 88 [1936] Heft 3, 6 n.2), cf. *Epist.* 2.2.1ff., 146ff. The▮ philosopher elicits agreement on a series of obvious points, in preparation for a mor▮ difficult proposition to follow.

108-10 **is he different ... ?:** cf. 251, 260. This mode of reasoning (the elision of distinctions i▮ order to provoke the listener's recognition of the folly of ordinary behaviour) may be typica▮ of popular moralising. Elsewhere Horace follows the Peripatetic method of drawin▮ distinctions (*Epist.* 2.2.192ff.).

the one who ... : in contrast to Staberius and Opimius, and for the sake of variety, the▮ typical miser remains unidentified, and is presented through the hypothetical form of the▮ argument. Nonetheless the details bring him vividly to life.

hides away: cf. 173, *Sat.* 1.1.42.

cash: *nummi* (not found in Virgil or in Horace's lyric poems) is an ordinary word for money, see Brink on *Epist.* 2.2.16.

not knowing how to use ... as if it were sacred: 109-14 are closely related to *Sat.* 1.1.70-3, cf. H. Herter, *RhM* 93 (1950), 187-8 on a possible source in comedy.

fearing: cf. 113 'dare'. 'Sacred' suggests the analogy of treasure dedicated to the gods, plunder of which would be sacrilege.

111 **a huge heap:** in pointed contrast with 'grain' (*granum* occurs only here in Horace).

112 **watching over:** picked up by 'keep safe' (123), cf. *Sat.* 1.1.76.

3   **touch a grain:** the repetition of *contingere* from 110 (in the same place in the line) has offended some editors, but Lejay ad loc. defends it as underlining the similarity of the specific example to the general case.

4   **dine ... on:** if *vescor* is grander than *edo* (see N-H on *Odes* 2.14.10) there may be a contrast with the poor food, cf. *Sat.* 2.2.27, 2.6.66.

       bitter leaves: this may be wild chicory (*Cichorium intubus*), see *Odes* 1.31.16, Virg. *G.* 1.120, Pompon. *com.* 128 (the food of *rustici*), André², 27.

15   **Chian and old Falernian:** choice Greek and Italian wines, suitable for festive occasions. Caesar is recorded as serving both Chian and Falernian at a feast (Pliny *HN* 14.97). If Hortensius left over 10,000 jars of imported Chian (Pliny quotes Varro) there is no need to think of the miser as a wine-merchant (*contra* K-H ad loc.).

16f. **sharp vinegar:** cf. Greek *oxinês*, cheap sour wine, cf. Pers. 4.32, Martial 10.45.5, Juv. 3.292, Tchernia, 12.

17   **look:** *age* puts emphasis on the last example of the series, cf. Cic. *Sen.* 24, *Nat. D.* 2.120.

17f: for tmesis between two lines see *Sat.* 1.2.62-3, 6.58-9, *Ars P.* 424-5, *Epist.* 2.2.93-4 (all verbs). Porph. on *Epist.* 2.2.93-4 calls the procedure 'Lucilian and archaic'.

       straw: used for bedding in the good old days (Pliny *HN* 18.14).

       a banquet for moths and grubs: cf. *Epist.* 1.20.12, Lucil. 1104W. 'Banquet' (*epulae*) is grand, cf. *Sat.* 2.2.45, 2.7.107, *TLL* V.2 701.80ff.

20f. **a very few:** the unexpected conclusion (cf. 107), when explained, becomes an additional proof.

       the greatest part of mankind: the same phrase is found at Lucil. 188W.

       tosses: cf. Cic. *Cat.* 1.31, 'they toss with heat and fever', Lucr. 3.507.

22-8:   the old miser is now addressed directly as if he were present, to bring home the folly of his (and most people's) reasons for hoarding. In *Sat.* 1.1 the miser's reason is that he is making provision for old age, but here he is already old, and still stinting himself. In contrast, the heir will know how to enjoy the good things of life, see N-H on *Odes* 2.14.25ff., Plut. *On Love of Wealth* 7, *Mor.* 526A, 'they preserve and lay up their goods for children and heirs until a wicked one comes along and uses it all up'.

       heir: see *Sat.* 2.2.132N.

22f. **god-forsaken:** a Latin version of a common Greek phrase 'hated by the gods' or 'ill-starred', cf. Hes. *Theog.* 766, Ar. *Eq.* 34. K-H quote Stob. 2.7.p.106W = *SVF* III 661,15ff., 'for the Stoics every fool is an enemy of the gods'.

       drink ... up: the verb *ebibo* occurs only here in Horace and, in spite of its established metaphorical sense (Plaut. *Trin.* 250, *Truc.* 156), must evoke a picture of the heir carousing, cf. *Odes* 2.14.25ff.

       run short: cf. *Sat.* 1.1.43, 'But if you drew on it, it would be reduced to a paltry penny.'

24   **how very little:** *quantulus* occurs only here in Horace, cf. *tantuli*, *Sat.* 1.1.58. The diminutive emphasises the idea of smallness, Hanssen, 152-3.

       clip off: *curto* is a rare verb, picked up by Persius (6.34) in a similar context, *TLL* IV 1539. 63ff.

25f. **oil:** used both for dressing vegetables (*Sat.* 2.6.64, Pers. 6.68) and for the personal toilet, *Sat.* 1.6.123-4. Hair is usually dressed with 'unguents', perfumed oils. For the miser's use of bad oil see *Sat.* 2.2.59.

       scurf: Celsus (*Med.* 6.2.1-2) recommends combing as the best treatment.

127 **if the least thing fills your needs:** the miser's self-imposed penury is a parody of the wise man's contentment with little, one of the principal moral ideas in Horace, cf. 178N, *Odes* 3.1.25, 3.16.21-44, etc., Plut. *On Love of Wealth* 2, *Mor.* 523F, 'in what suffices no one is poor'. *Quidvis sat est* (lit. 'anything is enough') looks like a catch-phrase, cf. Plaut. *Mil.* 750, Turp. *com.* 144R, 'To be sure, as each was happy with a very little, so he lived the

most blessed life, as the philosophers say, those for whom anything is enough.' The miser' refusal to use is often connected with his insatiable eagerness to acquire, both expression of avarice, but irrational if looked at in the light of man's basic needs. This makes the transition to the next section, the rapacious avarice which does not stop short of murder relatives, cf. Varro, *Sat. Men.* 126B (*Eumenides*): if the miser had come into possession of the world he would be driven to steal from himself, Plut. *On Love of Wealth* 6, *Mor.* 525E-F (the avarice of the beast of prey).

do you break oaths ... : cf. Cic. *Parad.* 43, *si cotidie fraudas, decipis, poscis, pacisceris, aufers, eripis ... .*

128-41: the example of Orestes is brought in to prove that crime motivated by avarice must be classed as madness. The argument seems to be that if senseless homicidal mania is recognised as madness, then so must be the killing of a mother or wife in order to inherit Orestes is the classic example of a mad matricide (he was known to Roman theatre audiences from Ennius's *Eumenides*, cf. Cic. *Mil.* 8, *Rosc. Am.* 67, *Pis.* 47). If the perpetrator of such a deed claims that he is not similarly mad he will have to show how his case differs from that of Orestes — always taking into account that the standard version of the story according to which Orestes went mad after the murder must be wrong. What he did at the time when he is commonly said to be mad is in no way comparable to the horror of the murder (cf. 199-204, 221f.).

128 **stoning people:** for stone-throwing as a sign of madness see Hunter on Eubulus fr. 94.10 PCG, A. O'Brien Moore, *Madness in Ancient Literature* (Diss. Princeton, 1924), 58-8.

130 **the very boys and girls:** proverbial for 'everyone', *Sat.* 1.1.85, Cic. *Phil.* 13.45 (more elaborately), Otto, 289; cf. Varro, *Sat. Men.*146B (*Eumenides*).

131 **hang your wife:** the point of comparison lies both in the victims' status and in the less public methods of killing employed. The avaricious criminal chooses methods which allow him to escape detection, cf. *Sat.* 2.1.53-6.

132 **your head is untouched:** i.e. you are judged sane and let off. The ambiguity involves a characteristic (see N-H on *Odes* 1.7.27) variation on a technicality: *incolumi capite = capite haud deminutus* ('not deprived of civil rights'). For this sense of *incolumis* (opposed to *damnatus* 'found guilty') see Cic. *Clu.* 10, Hor. *Sat.* 1.4.98, *Epist.* 1.11.17, and for a pun on this sense of *caput* ('civic status'), Cic. *Fam.* 1.9.15.

133 **the mother who bore you:** the epic/tragic word *genetrix* occurs only here in Horace, and is used here to underline the enormity of the deed.
kill: for the 'lurid' tone of the verb *occido*, a word belonging to popular speech and courtroom oratory, see Lyne 1989, 106-7.
like mad Orestes: Orestes' madness was that of delusion, or hallucinations, Celsus, *Med.* 3.18.19, Tert. *de anima* 17.9. Only he could see the Furies who hounded him after he killed his mother, and hence, for some authors, they are the projections of his own anguish of mind (e.g. Cic. *Pis.* 46). Varro's Menippean satire *Eumenides* took Orestes as the typical madman, and he also treated the theme in his *Orestes, vel de Insania* (from the *Logistorici*, Gell. *NA* 13.4.1). For further references see Austin on Virg. *Aen.* 4.469ff., Pease on Virg. *Aen.* 4.471ff., Otto, 258-9.

134 **parent:** *parens* for *mater* may have a legalistic flavour, cf. *Epod.* 3.1.

135 **terrible Furies:** the Furies can incite to crime as well as punish it (Cic. *Sull.* 76). It is best to print *Furiis* with a capital letter and allow a reference to the Furies in Aeschylus's *Eumenides*, even though Stertinius, with the orators, rejects the mythological explanation of Orestes' madness. On the ambiguity of *furiae/Furiae*, see Lyne 1989, 28-9 on Virg. *Aen.* 3.331. The absence of the preposition *a* is not decisive (K-H), as it may be omitted in poetry.

36 **warmed his sharp steel**: the diction is epic, *tepefacio* occurring only here in Horace, see Hom. *Il.* 16.333, Virg. *Aen.* 9.418f., 701, 'the steel grew warm in the pierced lung'.

37 **in a less than safe**: there is a double meaning. Orestes is both 'mad' and 'dangerous'. In medical terminology (Celsus, *Med.* 2.3.2 etc.) 'safe' means 'free from disease'. For the negative sense of *male* see N-H on *Odes* 1.9.24.

40f.: the symptoms of Orestes' madness are merely 'insults', that is, false appellations caused by his disordered perception. For philosophical discussion of Orestes' hallucinations see Sext. Emp. *Math.* 7.170, 245 (= Chrysippus, *SVF* II 65,20), 249, cf. *SVF* III 668,33, see Pigeaud, 95ff., 105f.

  calling her a Fury: the allusion is to Eur. *Orestes* 264, where Orestes mistakes his sister for a Fury. We know of no comparable incident with Pylades, Orestes' friend and companion.

41 **glittering**: black bile (*melancholia*, cf. Celsus, *Med.* 2.1.6) is described thus by Galen (7.245K), *splendens* ('shining') in the Latin translation, cf. Pers. 3.8, *uitrea bilis* ('glassy bile'). In Greek medicine it was a physiological cause of madness, but here it is just another synonym for madness, cf. Cic. *Tusc.* 3.11, *quem nos furorem, melancholian illi vocant*, P. Toohey, *ICS* 15 (1990), 143-161.

42-57: the new anecdote suddenly transports us from the world of Greek mythology to that of contemporary Rome. The case of the rich man who prefers to die rather than spend makes a suitable climax for the discussion of avarice, though it adds nothing new to the argument.

42 **Opimius**: the name, that of a well-known Roman *gens*, with its connotation of 'richness', was chosen not only for the sake of the oxymoron with *pauper*, see Rudd 1966, 141. There may also be an ironic allusion to the celebrated *vinum Opimianum*, a vintage of Falernian dated by L. Opimius's consulship in 121 B.C. (Pliny *HN* 14.55, Petron. *Sat.* 34.6). For *pauper* with the genitive see *Sat.* 1.1.79, *Odes* 3.30.11.

43 **on holidays**: a similar contrast between work days and holidays is made at *Sat.* 2.2.55-62. Opimius chooses for best a bad local *vin ordinaire* (for Veientine see Pers. 5.147, Mart. 1.26.6, 103.9 etc.) and for every day, spoiled wine (cf. Hor. *Sat.* 1.5.16, Pliny *HN* 14.125, Mart. 12.48.14).

44 **a ladle from Capua**: in early authors a *trulla* is a long-handled ladle (Cato *Agr.* 11.3, 13.2, cf. Apic. 4.2.14); later it perhaps comes to mean a drinking-cup or chamber-pot (Martial 9.96, Juv. 3.107f.), *RE* VIIA 700-1. Like the articles mentioned at *Sat.* 1.6.118 the ladle is made of bronze (Pliny *HN* 34.94, *Dig.* 33.10.3.1, Hilgers, 291-2), which was cheaper than gold or silver (a silver *trulla* is mentioned at *CIL* X.6.4). (But see *TLL Suppl. Onom.* II.126.31-2 s.v. *Campana*.)

45 **lethargy**: cf. 30, an old man's disease. *Lethargus* (only here in Horace) is the Greek technical term, cf. Celsus, *Med.* 3.20.1, Lucr. 3. 465.

46 **cash-boxes**: *Sat.* 1.3.17, *Epist.* 2.1.175, Mayor on Juv. 1.89.

  keys: cf. *Odes* 2.14.26 with N-H's note.

  jubilant: like a victorious warrior, cf. Virg. *Aen.* 10.500. The verb *ovo* is found only here in Horace, only three times in Cicero, but often in Virgil and his followers.

47 **quick-witted**: the usual explanation of *celer*, see *TLL* III 750.71ff, *OLD* s.v. *celer* 3. Shackleton Bailey (citing Eur. fr.1072N) thinks cleverness rather than quickness is the quality required, cf. R.G.M. Nisbet, *CR* 36 (1986), 233, J. Delz, *Gnomon* 60 (1988), 501, D.R. Shackleton Bailey, *Philologus* 134 (1990), 216f.

  multum with an adjective is colloquial, cf. *Sat.* 1.3.57, 2.5.67, 92, *Odes* 1.25.5 with N-H.

48 **brings him to**: See 30N.

49 **a number of people**: this is a nice touch, emphasising the extent of the wealth.

51-57: the anecdote ends in a lively dramatic dialogue, cf. *Epist.* 1.7.91ff. (M.J. McGann, *RhM* 97 [1954], 347 n.14).

151 **directly:** for similar uses of *iam* with the future see *Sat.* 1.1.16, 2.7.74, *Ars P.* 468. The greedy heir is conventional, cf. 122f., *Odes* 4.7.19.

152 **be wide awake:** this has a double meaning: 'wake up (from his coma)', and 'watch over', 'protect', cf. 112.
Look sharp!: or 'pay attention', 'take care', cf. *Epist.* 1.18.88. *Hoc age* is an idiom current in everyday speech, frequent in Plautus and Terence and, after Horace, found, for example, at Sen. *Ben.* 3.36.2 (*TLL* I 1380.52ff.). It is thought to have developed from a ritual expression ('Do it!') used at sacrifices at the moment of killing the victim (Suet. *Calig.* 58, Plut. *Num.* 14, *Coriol.* 25, Otto, 9f.).

153 **weak:** that is, with a weak pulse, due to a deficiency of blood in the veins.

154 **strong buttressing:** the language is humorously exaggerated, for though *fulcire* is often used of sustaining food (e.g. Lucr. 2.1147, 4.867, Sen. *Ep.* 95.22, cf. Plaut. *Curc.* 367 *stabilimenta*), the noun *fultura* is rare in a transferred sense, and revivifies the metaphor. *Ruenti* is also more vivid than the standard *cadens*. On the shape of the line see D. West, *The Imagery and Poetry of Lucretius* (Edinburgh, 1969), 118.

155 **rice:** the exotic word comes with emphasis. In Italy at that time rice was known mainly for its use in medicine, see André[2], 54. Doctors recommended it because it was easily digested (Celsus, *Med.* 2.18.10, 2.24.1 etc.), but it had to be imported from India (Pliny *HN* 18.71) or Mesopotamia (Strabo 15.1.18) and was therefore more expensive than the local barley (*tisana*).
gruel: *tisanarium* (the word occurs only here) seems to be the broth made of *tisana*, cf. *pulmentarium* from *pulmentum*. Ps.-Acro suggested it was the pottery vessel in which the *tisana* was cooked, cf. Hilgers, 289.

156 **Eightpence:** lit. 'eight *asses*'. Compare the two *asses* to be spent on lupins at Petron. *Sat.* 14.3.

158-223: the second 'disease of the soul', ambition, or lust for glory (*gloria*, 179, *vitrea fama*, 222) was much castigated by ancient moralists, often in conjunction with love of wealth (e.g. Cic. *Fin.* 1.59-61, Hor. *Sat.* 1.4.26, *Epist.* 2.2.206-7 with Brink). In a powerful passage at the beginning of Lucretius Book 3, *avarities et honorum caeca cupido* drive men to crime (59-63) or to death (78). Sallust too combines them in his influential moral analysis of Rome's political ills (Sall. *Cat.* 10-13, see D.C. Earl, *The Political Thought of Sallust* (Cambridge, 1961), idem, *The Moral and Political Tradition of Rome* (London, 1967). Hor. *Sat.* 1.6, which deals with *ambitio* from an autobiographical perspective, is also, according to Rudd 1966, 36-53, 'a thoroughgoing critique of the aristocratic-republican system'. See C.A. van Rooy, 'Horace, *Sat.* 1,1 and 1,6 and the Topos of Cardinal Vices', in *Antidosis, Festschrift für Walther Kraus, Wiener Studien,* Beiheft 5 (1972), 297-305. Stertinius's first criticism is the pragmatic one of useless extravagance (182-6), while the second and major part of the discussion puts more emphasis on Agamemnon's abuse of power in killing his daughter than on his personal ambition as the cause of the Trojan war, or on Ajax's pride as the motive of his suicide.

155-66: in argumentative style this passage makes the transition from *avaritia* (158) to *ambitio* (165). Rudd 1966, 184 sees the transition as clumsily managed and the attempt to connect *avaritia* and *ambitio* unconvincing. But the thematic link is through the enormous expenditure that political advancement in Rome required and the opportunities for enrichment it provided (therefore ambition is a special type of *avaritia* [Kenney on Lucr. 3.995-1002]). Initially ambition is typified by reckless extravagance in contrast to the meanness just illustrated. For the explicit summary the basic metaphor of vice as mental illness returns and again analogy from physical illness supports the key point: freedom from one sickness, or vice, does not mean freedom from all (cf. *Epist.* 2.2.205-12).

58   **Who is sane then?**: cf. *Sat.* 2.7.83. The form of the questions with their logical progression (cf. 220-3), as well as the doctrine, is typically Stoic, see Cic. *Fin.* 4.7, Lejay, 360. Stertinius either interrogates himself, or quotes an interlocutor who interrogates him (some texts show this by putting all the questions in inverted commas).

60   **Why, Mr. Stoic?**: the form of address need not imply an imaginary interlocutor, cf. Arr. *Diss. Epict.* 2.20-22, 24.

61   **heart-burn**: see 29N. It is difficult to know if this is a stomach-complaint (cf. Plin. *HN* 23.50, 14.96, Juv. 5.32) or something more serious. Stomach pain (*kardiôgmos*) is to be distinguished from the acute *cardiaca passio* (see Caelius Aurelianus *Acute Diseases* 2.163, esp. 2.180, Celsus, *Med.* 3.18.16, 3.19.1ff.), which involved delirium in the final stages (cf. Cic. *Div.* 1.81), see Harris (cited at 29N), 438.
         Craterus: a practitioner of the time of Cicero, who mentions him with approval when he was treating Atticus's daughter (*Att.* 12.13-4). Galen records two of his drugs (a pain reliever at 13.96K, and an antidote at 14.147K). Horace gives the impression of a figure of some authority, and Persius (3.65), while borrowing the name from Horace, implies a doctor of such status could command high fees.

62   **all right**: see *OLD* s.v. *recte* 9b. An expression of every-day speech. Cicero often uses it in his letters when talking about health, e.g. *Fam.* 16.4.3, *Att.* 12.23.3, 14.16.4.

63:   the line is repeated (with small differences) at *Epist.* 1.6.28. It is needed to provide an alternative complaint to which ambition may correspond. For arguments against its appropriateness here, see G. Jachmann, 'Zur Frage des Verswiederholung in der augusteischen Dichtung', in *Studi in onore di Ugo Enrico Paoli* (Florence, 1956), 393-421, at 397f.
         acute: a medical term, cf. Celsus, *Med.* 3.1.1-2, 'Some illnesses are brief and acute. They either carry the person off quickly or themselves come to a quick end.'
         attacking: the verb *tempto* is regularly used of physical affliction, cf. *Sat.* 1.1.80, Lucr. 3.147.

64f.   **let him ... sacrifice a pig to the well-disposed Lares**: the point is that such a person is deemed free from madness, until his further symptoms are observed, but commentators disagree on the sacrifice's significance. The usual interpretation takes the sacrifice as a thank-offering to the Lares, as if for recovery from illness. Similar thank-offerings, for example, were made after a safe return from war (Tib. 1.10.25-6, Macrob. *Sat.* 6.9.4, Gell. *NA* 16.6.7). A pig was a normal offering to the Lares (see Plaut. *Rud.* 1206-8, Hor. *Odes* 3.23.4, Tib. loc.cit.), not to be connected with the madman's sacrifice of a pig as a scapegoat at Plaut. *Men.* 289ff. and 314. Orelli, however, considering that one would not thank the Lares for a cure for madness, but Aesculapius, or the like, argues that the sacrifice is a regular one, from which the mad would normally be excluded. Lejay follows this, making 'let him sacrifice' etc. a question (= 'is he then sane?'), parallel to 'is he all right?'
         Lares: in the plural as at *Odes* 4.5.34, cf. Enn. *Ann.* 619Sk., *Lares tectum nostrum qui funditus curant* ('Lares who protect our house from the foundations'). They were guardians of the crossroads, the farm, or the individual household. In this last function a single Lar is often mentioned. See *OCD²* s.v. Lares, *Sat.* 2.5.14, 2.6.66.

166f.   **Anticyra**: see 82f.N. The Anticyra in Phocis may have been the best place to take the cure, Pigeaud, 208. The recall of Anticyra here signals the arrival of the new topic.
         consign whatever you have: the antithesis between the spendthrift and the miser returns, but now the reckless spender is to be identified as the *ambitiosus*, cf. Cato's boast (*ORF⁴* 173.6-7), *numquam ego pecuniam meam neque sociorum per ambitionem dilargitus sum.*
         a bottomless pit: cf. 241-2, and the vivid metaphorical use of *barathrum* (Greek *barathron*) at *Epist.* 1.15.31.

never use what is available: this translation accepts the special philosophical meaning explained by N-H on *Odes* 1.31.17, citing Epicur. fr. 469 Us., Lucr. 6.9f. etc. According to the Epicureans in particular, the primary needs of man are 'at hand', supplied by nature However, the reference here may simply be to the hoard of the *avarus*. See 109-110, 'not knowing how to use what he has accumulated'.

168-81: the example illustrates the general antithesis, and the specific case of ambition temporarily drops out of sight. Like Staberius, Oppidius reveals his values in his last wishes. In its beginning the death-bed scene is reminiscent of Call. *Iamb.* 1.35ff. (Bathycles the Arcadian), but that takes a different turn. The topos of two brother typifying opposed ways of life has mythological and tragic sources (e.g. Castor and Pollux [*Sat.* 2.1.26f.], Amphion and Zethus in Euripides' *Antiope* [cf. *Epist.* 1.18.41-4]), but Brink on *Epist.* 2.2.183-9 argues that in its application to everyday life Horace was inspired more by the tradition of Greek popular philosophy (Teles fr. 2, p. 12.2ff. [Hense²], Xen. *Conv.* 4.34-5) and New Comedy (e.g. Terence, *Adelphoe*), cf. Cic. *Sen.* 65, *Sat.* 2.2.57-62N.

168-70   **It is said:** the expression indicates that the story is one that has been handed down, cf. *Sat.* 2.6.80, *Odes* 1.16.13, T.C.W. Stinton, *PCPhS* 22 (1976), 60-89, N. Horsfall, *Papers of the Leeds International Latin Seminar* 6 (1990), 49-53.

Servius Oppidius: though the man (a figure reminiscent of Ofellus, and Horace's father. cf. *Sat.* 1.4.107-8) is otherwise unknown, the anecdote is precisely located in a region known well to Horace. Canusium (modern Canosa) was in Apulia, on the right bank of the Aufidus (cf. *Sat.* 1.5.91-2). The name Oppidius is attested only on the borders of Apulia in Southern Samnium (*RE* XXVIII.1 708).

Note the word play *duo ... dives ... divisse ... duobus*.

old days: like Ofellus, Oppidius lives in an older world and personifies old-fashioned values.

sons: *gnatus* for *filius* (the form is confined to the *Satires*) may have an old-fashioned tone, cf. *Sat.* 1.1.83, 2.2.115, 2.5.28, Ruckdeschel, 110, Brown on Lucr. 4.1234 (*gnatus* survives colloquially).

boys: the sons are still young (*pueri*, but cf. *Sat.* 2.2.128). Their father is worried because he can conjecture from their play how they will act as adults, cf. Sen. *Dial.* 2.12.1, Väterlein, 32ff. (The idea is no doubt a piece of folk-wisdom, cf. Hdt. 1.114ff., the mode of the child Cyrus's play reveals his true identity.)

171f.   **knucklebones and nuts:** there are many references to knucklebones and nuts as children's toys, see Ar. *Vesp.* 295f., [Ov.] *Nux* 73-86, Suet. *Aug.* 83, Pers. 1.10, Väterlein, 34ff., M. Manson, *Mél. Éc. Fr. Rome* 90 (1978), 260, D-S 4.1.115, fig. 5337.

loose fold: Roman men carried money in the fold of the toga across the breast, as if in a pocket or purse, cf. Prop. 2.16.12, Juv. 1.88. It had to be kept tight enough to prevent the contents dropping out.

gamble: *ludo* ('play') acquires its specific meaning from the context, Brink on *Epist.* 2.2.183, cf. Ov. *Ars Am.* 2.203. What we expect is 'lose' (cf. Bentley's *perdere*) but *ludere* does not mean this in Classical Latin.

174   **counting ... hiding:** behaviour typical of the *avarus*, cf. 109, 150.

[*vesania*: is very rare, being used several times by Valerius Maximus and then by Florus and Apuleius. Wickham defends it by pointing out the great variety of terms for madness used in this satire. *Insania* requires lengthening of the preceding -*et* at the caesura, for which we have no other examples in the *Satires*, though this does occur with -*it* at 187 and 260, see N-H on *Odes* 1.3.36, Palmer on *Sat.* 1.5.90.]

175   **Nomentanus ... Cicuta:** the examples are of opposite extremes, whereas the ideal of the mean (cf. *Sat.*1.1.101-7, 2.2.53-70) is to avoid going wrong 'in either direction' (cf. *Sat.* 2.2.60). The prodigal Nomentanus (cf. *Sat.* 2.1.22N) later exemplifies the *luxuriosus* (224), who 'gives away' his inheritance. Cicuta has already been mentioned in this satire (69N). As a grasping money-lender (not just a miser, cf. *Epod.* 1.31ff.), he foreshadows Oppidius's prohibition against increasing the patrimony.

176   **by the house-hold gods**: on the *Penates* see *OCD²*. Properly 'gods of the store-cupboard', they were guardians of the house-hold, like the *Lares*, in conjunction with whom they were often mentioned. See *Odes* 3.23, Plaut. *Merc.* 834, 836, Cic. *Rep.* 5.7.
   gods: Horace uses the more grandiose form *divus* only four times in the *Satires*. See *Sat.* 1.3.117 (a legal reminiscence?), 2.3.206 (a context full of epic-tragic diction), and 2.4.88 (another oath).

177   **nor increase**: cf. *Sat.* 2.6.7-8. Satisfaction with what one has represents the mean. But the warning against increase is not just for the sake of balance. It leads into the climactic injunction against seeking glory, political ambition entailing both great expenditure and the constant replenishment of resources, cf. *Sat.* 1.6.100, Finley² 1985, 53, 55. On the contradictory Roman attitudes to acquiring wealth, see Cic. *De Orat.* 2.225-6, D'Arms 1981, 6, 21f., Finley² 1985, 41ff.

178   **what ... is enough**: see 127N, 1.4.107-8 (the advice of Horace's father), *cum me hortaretur parce, frugaliter atque/viverem uti contentus eo quod mi ipse parasset.* The idea of limits set by nature is Epicurean, cf. Hor. *Sat.*1.1.49, *intra/ naturae finis viventi.* More extensive possessions are not necessary to satisfy the basic wants of life, see Epicur. *Sent.* 15, Cic. *Fin.* 1.45.

179   **Furthermore**: the warning against *ambitio* comes just as we are beginning to wonder about the relevance of the *exemplum*.
   tickle: an Epicurean term, as Cicero tells us (*Nat. D.* 1.113 with Pease). Cicero uses it when talking of the pleasures of the senses, with an apologetic *quasi* to signal the translation from the Greek, see Epicur. fr. 411-4 Us. with suppl. to 416, Lucr. 2.429, Cic. *Sen.* 47. The striking collocation with *gloria* has the effect of belittling the aspiration to fame.

181f.   **whichever of you becomes ...**: the form of words, with the legalisms *fuerit* and *esto*, suggests the actual words of the oath, cf. Lex XII tab. 8. 21, 22.
   aedile or praetor: for the function of these magistrates at Rome see *OCD²*. The point is that the posts involve (along with other duties) the expense of overseeing public games, Cic. *Verr.* II 5.36, *Off.* 2.55-7, Balsdon, 261ff. Office at Rome could be envisaged, and hence greater ambition, or municipal magistracies at Canusium, see S. Demougin, 'Notables municipeaux et ordre équestre à l'époque des dernières guerres civiles', in *Les 'bourgeoisies' municipales aux IIᵉ et Iᵉʳ siècles av. J.C.* (Paris, Naples, 1983), 281. The amphitheatre at Canusium (estimated to hold over 10,000 [Brunt 1971, 368]) probably dates from the first century A.D. (Balsdon, 334 n.208) but inscriptions dated to the late Republic referring to gladiatorial games have been found. The municipal magistrates at Canusium were *IVviri* (for the non-technical *praetor* see *Sat.* 1.5.34; Cic. *Leg. Agr.* 2.92), F. Grelle, 'Canosa. Le istituzioni, la società', in A. Giardia and A. Schiavone (edd.), *Società e produzione schiavistica* I (Rome-Bari, 1981), 181-225, at 210-11.
   outlawed: disbarred from legal acts as a consequence of breaking an oath, *OLD* s.v. *intestabilis* 1, Gaius *Dig.* 28.1.26, Ulpian *Dig.* 28.1.18.1.
   accursed: the offence in this case is breaking an oath made in a god's name, see *OLD* s.v. *sacer* 2, 'of one whose person and property are forfeited to a god by reason of an offence against a divine law', Ogilvie on Livy 3.55.7, Servius on Virg. *Aen.* 6.609.

182-6:   the mention of magistracies leads to a picture of the mad politician, evoked through direct address, cf. 122ff. The sudden transition from Oppidius's words back to Stertinius is no more difficult than the one at 157-8. Many editors give these lines to Oppidius, though it would not be appropriate for him to mention the aedileship of Agrippa (Lejay, app. crit.

ad loc.; the same argument does not apply to Nomentanus and Cicuta since they are probably Lucilian or timeless). *Insane* goes better in Stertinius's mouth.

182   **chickpeas etc.**: distribution of pulses (the food of the poor [see *Ars P.* 249]) would have been the least of the expenses involved in running the games, cf. Varro, *Sat. Men.* 504B, Persius 5.177-9 (following Horace) at the *Floralia.* Dio Cass. (49.43.4) tells us that tokens good for money, clothes etc. were rained on the people's heads in the theatre during Agrippa's games. Reinhold 1965, 51 n.34 sees a reference to Agrippa, but the point should be that the lesser *ambitiosus* ruins himself by an expenditure that Agrippa would not have noticed. On the enormous expense of these games see I. Schatzman, *Senatorial Wealth and Politics* (Brussels, 1975), 84ff., 108, 439 (on Agrippa).

183   **promenade yourself in the Circus and stand in bronze**: here, on the other hand, we might think of Agrippa, since his is the status aspired to (Reinhold 1965, 51 n.36). Horace picks out two types of public recognition, spontaneous applause on the occasion of the games (*Odes* 1.20.4, *Epist.*1.6.7), and an official commemorative statue.
flaunt (lit. 'wide', 'broad'): cf. Sen. *Ep.* 76.31, 80.7, both of actors in grand costume strutting on stage. Is the width that of a voluminous *toga*?, cf. *Epod.* 4.8, *cum bis trium ulnarum toga.*
promenade: *spatior* is used of casual strolling (*Sat.* 1.8.15) or of stately procession (Virg. *Aen.* 4.62, Prop. 2.13.19). There cannot be a reference to the ritual procession in chariots which opened the games (see Ov. *Am.* 3.2.43ff., Courtney on Juv. 10.36). Commentators suggest a promenade or procession on foot during an interval at the games.
Circus: *Circus* in the context of Rome usually means the *Circus Maximus*, the site of the *ludi circenses*, the chariot-races, see J. Humphrey, *Roman Circuses: Arenas for Chariot Racing* (London, 1986), 66-77. It was a declassé market-place (shops, prostitutes, astrologers) at other times (Wiseman 1987, 182-3, *Sat.* 1.6.113-4).
bronze: bronze was the chief material for commemorative statues at this time (O. Vessberg, *Studien zur Kunstgeschichte der römische Republik* [Lund, 1941], 114). In Rome statues were erected for heroic military deeds and public benefactions (as a symbol of ambition, cf. Lucr. 3.78) and achievements of magistrates during their year of office, G. Lahusen, *Untersuchungen zur Ehrenstatue in Rom: literarische und epigraphische Zeugnisse* (Rome, 1983), 95-6. It is not known if magnificent games were so commemorated, but Pliny *HN* 18.16 records the erection of statues of M. Seius, aedile in 74 B.C., for distributing wheat cheaply to the people during his year of office, Cic. *Off.* 2.58.

184:   the shape of this line is similar to that of *Sat.* 1.2.13 = *Ars P.* 421 (cf. Virg. *Aen.* 9.26), but the sense here is neatly reversed, suggesting that Horace is parodying an older original, which he imitates in the other passages, Lejay on *Sat.* 1.2.13, Fraenkel 1931, 125 n.1, but see Jachmann (cited at 163N), 400-3.

185   **Agrippa**: M. Vipsanius Agrippa, 64 - 12 B.C., Augustus's life-long supporter, and greatest general and admiral (see *OCD²*). His famous aedileship in 33 B.C., a critical time for Octavian (see R. Syme, *The Roman Revolution* [Oxford 1939, reprinted 1966], 277ff.), was marked by unprecedented munificence aimed at winning popularity for the regime. There were fifty-nine days of games. See Pliny *HN* 36.104, 121-2, Dio Cass. 49.43.1ff., Veyne, 482, Reinhold 1965, 46-52.

186   **sly fox**: this looks like a fable (cf. Persius's imitation, 5.116-7), but since no corresponding fable can be found (closest is the ass in the lion's skin [Perry *Aesopica* 358]; G. Némethy [*RhM* 61 (1906), 139] suggested Perry *Aesopica* 394, the fox who hunted with the lion), it is perhaps best to take it simply as a proverbial expression (Otto, xxiv-xxv, 189, N. Horsfall, *G&R* 36 [1989], 83 n.73). The cunning consists in the attempt to win the people's favour cheaply.

187-223: the new example begins abruptly, with a question directed to Agamemnon. A mock-deferential cross-examination ensues, best given to Stertinius, who imagines himself back into the past (see the discussion with Agamemnon at Arr. *Diss. Epict.* 3.22.30-37, cf. Cic. *Tusc.* 3.62 = Bion fr. 69 Kindstrand, Diogenes *Ep.* 19, Kindstrand, 35f.). The fictional dialogue takes place in the Greek camp at Troy at the same time when the burial of Ajax was still an issue. Archaic language and allusions to Homer create a tragic/heroic atmosphere. For Ajax's madness and its aftermath see *OCD²* s.v Ajax, and Sophocles' *Ajax*. Like Orestes, Ajax is another famous madman of tragedy known on the Roman stage (Plaut. *Capt.* 615, Cic. *Tusc.* 3.11, Juv. 14.284-6, Celsus, *Med.* 3.18.19, Lejay, 367).
Underlying the example is a strong criticism of ambition as an impulse to horrible crime (cf. 212, 220-23). However, superficially and in keeping with Stertinius's overall argument, the dialogue, in Cynic fashion, presents Agamemnon as a typical *stultus*: he calls Ajax 'mad' but fails to realise that his sacrifice of his own daughter is ample proof of his own derangement.

187   **that no one bury:** the command is cast in the form of a Roman legal prohibition (*nequis ... velit* with the perfect infinitive anticipating the result of the act), cf. *S.C. de Bacch.* (*Remains of Old Latin* IV, 255ff.), Ter. *Hec.* 563, Ov. *Am.* 1.4.38.

188   **'I am the king':** a king has supreme authority, see Soph. *Ajax* 1050, 'such is my will and the great general's will'.
a mere commoner: *plebeius* is found only here in Horace, cf. Enn. *Trag.* 280J. It is equivalent to the Homeric 'man of the people', cf. Hom. *Il.* 2.198ff., where Odysseus restores the authority of Agamemnon.

190   **Greatest of kings:** cf. Hom. *Il.* 9.69, 'you are the most kingly'.

191   **may the gods grant:** based on Hom. *Il.* 1.17ff., the appeal of Chryses to Agamemnon and Menelaus to free his daughter, 'may the gods ... grant that you sack Priam's city and return home safely'.
[*reducere:* the Lucretian *reducere* (1.228, 4.992, 5.1337) is not used in Augustan poetry (L. Müller), but an old-fashioned tone would be appropriate in the context. Most poets use the form *reduco*, with short *re-* (cf. *Odes* 4.2.17, *Epist.* 2.1.181, Munro on Lucr. 1.228), but this does not fit the scansion here. The context and the Homeric allusion require the meaning 'bring home'. Bentley supported *deducere*, presumably with the technical meaning 'bring one's army home to Rome from a province'.]

192   **ask a question:** in the formal context the person who is 'consulted', 'responds', cf. the formula with which the jurisconsult was addressed, *licet consulere* (Cic. *Mur.* 28) and the word *responsa* used for his replies. The king is asked to justify his edict in terms of the law.

193   **the hero next to Achilles:** a formula of epic and archaic poetry, Hom. *Il.* 2.768f., 17.279f., *Od.* 11.550f., Alc. 387 PLF, Soph. *Aj.* 1340-1.

194   **famous for saving the Acheans:** this phrase may be an epic reminiscence, see Norden on Virg. *Aen.* 6.837. For the thought see Soph. *Aj.* 1273ff.

195   **Priam's people and Priam:** another Homeric quotation, *Il.* 1.255, 'truly Priam and Priam's sons would rejoice ... '

196   **deprived of an ancestral tomb:** another epic formula, cf. Virg. *Aen.* 10.558, Sen. *Tro.* 55, V. Fl. 6.314, Petron. *Sat.* 122.137. The irony is that Ajax meets, at the hands of his former friends, the same fate that he had inflicted on the enemy. In the *Iliad* it is assumed that those who die on the battlefield, Trojans as well as Greeks, will not be buried, but will lie a prey for dogs and birds. The unburied enemy was a cause for gloating.

197f.: after the death of Achilles, Ajax and Ulysses competed for his arms. It was their award to Ulysses which made him Ajax's hated enemy. In Sophocles' *Ajax* Athena clouds Ajax's senses, in order to divert his murderous rage from the Greek leaders. He slaughters cattle, thinking he is killing Agamemnon and Menelaus, but one ram, 'Ulysses' he takes back to his tent in bonds. There he ties it to a pillar, whips it and curses it, Soph. *Ajax* 239-44. There may have been another version of the story (perhaps Ennian) in which Ajax thought he was killing Ulysses (Cic. *Ac. Pr.* 2.89, *De Or.* 3.162 [= *trag.inc.* 47f.R], Varro, *Sat. Men.* 125B, Lejay, 367 and ad loc., Rudd 1966, 298 n.36).

197   **gave to death**: the phrase is archaic with the personification of death felt, see Enn. *Trag.* 283J, Plaut. *Asin.* 608, *Merc.* 472.
renowned: *inclutus* occurs only here in Horace. According to Skutsch (on Enn. *Ann.* 146) it had 'an archaic and therefore solemn ring even in the beginning of Latin literature'. See Naev. fr.30 (32).1 Morel, Enn. *Ann.* 123, 146, 155Sk., Virg. *Aen.* 6.479, 562, 781.

199ff.:   when the Greek fleet was detained at Aulis by contrary winds, Agamemnon was advised by the diviner Calchas to sacrifice his daughter Iphigenia to Artemis. For polemical reasons Horace, like Lucr. 1.84-100, follows the pre-Euripidean version, in which Iphigenia was sacrificed by her father's hand (see J.-M. Croisille, *Latomus* 22 [1963], 209-225).

199   **sweet daughter**: a sentimental cliche? Or pathos? Cf. Lucr. 3.895, 4.1234, Virg. *G.* 2.523, *Aen.* 4.33, 2.138.
[*gnatam.*: elsewhere in the *Satires*, but not in the *Odes*, Horace uses the older form with *gn-*. Housman (*Classical Papers* III 1139f.) pointed this out, adding that as short -*e* is not lengthened before *gn*- in Horace, *gnatam* could therefore be restored, see N. Horsfall, *ZPE* 77 (1989), 25-6.]
stand ... before the altars: a ritual expression, Virg. *Aen.* 9.627, Livy 1.45.6, *OLD* s.v. *statuo* 3.

200   **salt and grain**: before a sacrifice a mixture of salt and ground grain was sprinkled onto the forehead of the victim, the hearth and the sacrificial knife (Servius on Virg. *Aen.* 2.133, Pease on Virg. *Aen.* 4.517), cf. *immolare* 164, N-H on *Odes* 1.4.11. The emphasis on the ritual detail underlines the enormity of the deed, cf. Sen. *Thy.* 687-90 with Tarrant.
you shameless man: cf. *Sat.* 2.2.104, Lucr. 3.1026, Persius 4.47.

201   **straight**: straight thinking is the opposite of the derangement of madness, cf. Eur. *Med.* 1129. In the moral sphere *rectum* is also 'the right', 'the good', cf. *Sat.* 1.1.102, 2.6.75 etc.
[*cursum*: Peerlkamp's *cursum* is not universally accepted (but for *rectum ... cursum* see *Sat.* 2.5.78, Lucr. 6.28 [O corr.]). *Quorsum* must be given to Agamemnon, with an ellipse of the verb or *haec* or *istuc*, e.g. 'What's the point of that?' The ellipse, combined with the change of speaker, is difficult.]

202   **laid low ... with the sword**: a poetical expression, not found in prose before the Augustan period. The heroic deed has an incongruous object, as did Agamemnon's ritual actions.

203   **wife and son**: Tecmessa (cf. *Odes* 2.4.6) and Eurysaces. In Soph. *Ajax*, where she plays an important role as wife and mother, she is the abducted daughter of the Phrygian king Teleutas (210).
Teucer: Ajax's half-brother. Both were sons of Telamon.

205   **unfriendly shore**: because it was detaining the fleet against its will.

206   **placated the gods with blood**: cf. Virg. *Aen.* 2.116, *sanguine placastis ventos* (of the sacrifice of Iphigenia). By mentioning the gods Agamemnon intends the defence of piety.

208ff.:   Stertinius now interprets the mythological scene in the light of his own moral and philosophical theory, while keeping Agamemnon as his type case.

208f.   **grasps presentations**: Stertinius brings in a mode of technical philosophical explanation rarely found in the *Satires* (or *Epistles*). In Stoic epistemology knowledge came from a 'grasping' (*katalambanein*) by the mind of 'presentations' (*phantasiai*). In theory it was possible to distinguish true from false presentations, or to know when what you were perceiving was real or not. But in the case of madness the Stoics conceded that, during the hallucination, a person might act on presentations which did not correspond with reality (see Cic. *Ac. Pr.* 2.47-50, 88-90, Sext. Emp. *Math.* 7. 248ff., Pigeaud, 105ff.), but they debated whether the wise man could become mad. On Stoic epistemology see Rist, Chap.8. For *species* as a translation of *phantasia* see Cic. *Ac. Pr.* 2.52 (but cf. Brink on *Ars P.* 6-9). For *katalambanein* Cicero uses *percipere* and *comprehendere* (*Ac. Post.* 31, *Pr.* 2.145).

differing from the true: the Stoic doctrine outlined above strongly supports the reading *veris*, abl. of comparison after *alias*, cf. *Epist.* 1.16.20, 2.1.240 with Brink ad loc.

[*cerebri tumultu*: a major textual crux. *Tumultus* (not used in Cicero's philosophical works) seems to be a live metaphor in need of the support of *cerebri* (cf. *Odes* 2.16.10-11, *tumultus mentis*, and Sen. *Ep.* 56.5). *Sceleris* of most of the MSS gives a reason for the *tumultus*, but does not apply to both Ajax and Agamemnon, as the rest of the sentence suggests it should (cf. *ira*).]

209   **made indistinguishable:** in madness there is no way of distinguishing between true and false presentations, Cic. *Ac. Pr.* 2.48, 52.

     deranged: cf. 278, *commotae ... mentis*, Cic. *Tusc.* 4.11, Zeno's definition of *pathos* as *animi commotio* (cf. 4.47).

210   **it will make no difference:** cf. 48-53, Stertinius's argument that madness may manifest itself in different ways, but is always the same.

211:   [the hyperbaton (interwoven word-order) is odd, cf. *Sat.* 2.1.60N.]

212   **empty distinctions:** for the vanity of ambition see Lucr. 3.995ff., Hor. *Epist.* 2.2.205-6.

     distinctions: (*titulos*), cf. *Sat.* 1.6.17, *Odes* 4.14.4, short accounts of a person's achievements inscribed on a portrait bust or statue, used metonymically for 'fame', 'glory' (cf. Ov. *Ars Am.* 1.692, *Met.* 7.56).

213   **are you in your right mind** (lit. 'standing on firm ground', 'steady'): cf. Enn. *Ann.* 199-200Sk., Cic. *Att.* 5.18.2, *stamus animis*.

     heart: *cor* is here as often the seat of the emotions. When 'swollen' it is often with anger (Cic. *Tusc.* 3.18, Virg. *Aen.* 6.49, 407); but anger is not appropriate to Agamemnon or the context, where we are talking about ambition. The most relevant parallel is Hor. *Epist.* 1.1.36, *laudis amore tumes*?

214-20:   'Socratic' questioning, see 104-7N.

214   **sleek:** the lamb is 'well-groomed' like a favourite girl or youth.

216   **Rufa or Posilla:** frequently found female names, translated by Rudd as 'Ruby or Babs.'

     gallant husband: cf. *Sat.* 2.5.64 (a mock-heroic context). Gow ad loc. suggests an allusion to the story of Iphigenia, who was brought to Aulis on the pretext of marriage to Achilles.

217f.   **praetor ... injunction:** the urban praetor, as judge, dealt with matters of guardianship. According to late evidence (Ulp. *Dig.* 27.10.1, *Tit.* 12.2) both madmen, and heads of families who were prodigal in the administration of family property, were put under an interdiction by the praetor, cf. Cic. *Sen.* 22. In the latter case the praetor's formula concluded *tibi ea re commercioque interdico* (Paul. *Sent.* 3.4a.7, Watson 1967, 155f.). At what stage the interdiction was introduced is unsure, Jolowicz[3], 121-2 n.4.

     guardianship: cf. *Epist.* 1.1.103, *OLD* s.v. *tutela* 3. In the case of madness the technical term was *cura*. Hence some commentators take *tutela* as in apposition to a personal subject of *abeat*, i.e. the madman as 'ward'.

     relations: *propinqui* covers both the agnates and clansmen (*agnatum gentiliumque ... potestas*) of the law of the Twelve Tables (5.7). According to this law a lunatic's relatives were made responsible for him and his property, Varro, *Rust.* 1.2.8, Cic. *Tusc.* 3.11, Hor. *Epist.* 1.1.101ff., 2.2.136 with Brink, F. Schulz, *Classical Roman Law* (Oxford, 1951), 197ff., A. Watson, *Roman Private Law around 200 BC* (Edinburgh, 1971), 41.

220-3:   the logical sounding conclusion rounds off the section, suggesting as well the kind of Stoic syllogistic reasoning praised by Cato at Cic. *Fin.* 3.26-7, *consectaria me Stoicorum brevia et acuta delectant.*

222   **glassy fame** (lit. 'glass-like'): the adjective combines the ideas of glitter and fragility, c Pub. *Sent.* F 24, *fortuna vitrea est: tum cum splendet frangitur.*

thunders Bellona: i.e., he is like a *fanaticus* (cf. *Ars P. 454*), possessed by Bellona. The early Italian war goddess was identified with the Cappadocian Ma when she was introduced to Rome (probably under Sulla, whose invasion of Comana first brought her into contact with the Romans [Plut. *Sull.* 9]). Ma was worshipped by wandering Cappadocian priests and priestesses (known as *bellonarii* or *fanatici*), with wild dances and orgiastic rites involving self-mutilation (Tib. 1.6.45) which offended Roman taste. It is even recorded that remains of human flesh were found when her temple was destroyed in 48 B.C. (Dio Cass. 42.26.2). See Courtney on Juv. 4.123, D. Fishwick, *JRS* 57 (1967), 142-60, esp. 145, 153.

The verb *circumtoneo* is found only here in Horace and is rare elsewhere. It renders the Greek *embrontêtos* 'thunder-struck', i.e. driven out of his wits, Ar. *Eccl.* 793, [Plato] *Alc.* 2.140c, cf. Paus. 3.5.9. The whole line has the flavour of epic parody (Lejay, 369).

224-80:   Stertinius's third topic, foreshadowed at 79, is *luxuria*, extravagant self-indulgence in physical pleasures (especially eating). On the 'life of luxury' in the late Republic and Augustan periods see Griffin, 1-31. An extended anecdote (226-238) is followed by two shorter ones, all concerning extravagant young men, heirs or potential heirs. There is no summarising conclusion to the section, though line 246 rounds it off by bringing us back to the main argument.

The section on love (246-80) is sometimes subsumed under the heading of *luxuria* (e.g. Rudd 1966, 180), but it seems to be introduced as a separate topic (cf. 225, 250 with 83 and it has a different thematic focus (i.e. childish folly rather than prodigality). The 'syllabus' at 77-81 indicates five topics to be discussed, one left unspecified.

224   **Come now:** *nunc age* is a transitional formula of didactic poetry. See Munro on Lucr. 1.265, Kenney on 3.417.

hauling up: *arripe* is a vivid metaphor, the technical sense being 'bring before a court', 'arraign' (*OLD* s.v. *arripio* 2). At *Sat.* 2.1.69 Lucilius and here Stertinius arraign their victims before the bar of public opinion.

Nomentanus: cf. 175, *Sat.* 2.1.22N. Nomentanus is the standing example of the spendthrift.

225   **Reason will prove:** cf. 83, 250, *Sat.* 1.3.115.

He: *hic* may be taken as referring back to Nomentanus beyond the generalising 'spendthrifts' (ps.-Acro says *id est Nomentanus.*). Alternatively some editors take *hic* as pointing to a new, indefinite, example, 'one' (cf. *Sat.* 1.9.51, 2.3.23 etc., Lejay ad loc.), possibly because the anecdote sounds contemporary and Nomentanus may be a Lucilian figure. The young heir is depicted not simply as a typical spendthrift; he seems to be someone who seeks to gain popularity from misplaced generosity (cf. Shakespeare's *Timon of Athens*, Acts I and II).

a thousand talents: cf. *Epist.* 1.6.34. The Roman equivalent is 24,000,000 sesterces. Trimalchio claims an estate of 30,000,000 sesterces, 'large but by no means incredible' according to Smith on Petron. *Sat.* 71.12. Atticus inherited about 10,000,000 from his rich uncle Quintus Caecilius, and, significantly, made no difference to his style of life (Nep. *Att.* 5.2, 14.2).

227   **issued a public decree:** or 'made a public announcement' (cf. *Sat.* 2.2.51) as if he were a magistrate convening a meeting and naming the place and time (cf. Livy 28.9.5), cf. 230-1N.

fisherman etc.: similar lists are found at Plaut. *Trin.* 406-12 (the spending of the dissolute young man), and Ter. *Eun.* 255ff. (Gnatho the parasite boasts of his popularity in the market). Cicero (*Off.* 1.150) quotes *Eun.* 257 in disapprobation of *artes ministrae ... voluptatum* ('arts which are providers of pleasures').

228   **the perfumer**: perfumes (in the form of unguents, or ointments) were a luxurious accompaniment of feasting (see Catull. 13, Hor. *Odes* 4.12.16, N-H on *Odes* 1.4.9, Courtney on Juv. 4.108, Griffin, 10f.).

    the godless riff-raff: Plaut. *Curc.* 482, 'in the Etruscans' street, there are the men who sell themselves'.

    the Etruscans' street: see Varro, *Ling.* 5.46, Prop. 4.2.50, Livy 2:14.9, Tac. *Ann.* 4.65. The *Vicus Tuscus* ran from the *Forum Romanum* to the *Forum Boarium,* below the west end of the Palatine, forming the boundary of the *Velabrum* (see below), Platner-Ashby s.v. It was later called the *Vicus Turarius* (street of incense) or *Unguentarius Vicus* (street of unguents), *RE* S IX 1833, cf. *RE²* XIV 1493f. This is probably the street to which Horace refers at *Epist.* 2.1.269, 'the street selling incense and perfumes'.

229   **poulterer**: there is doubt over the meaning of *fartor*. It could be either 'sausage-maker', Donatus on Ter. *Eun.* 257, cf. Plaut. *Truc.* 104, or 'fattener of poultry for the table', Columella, *Rust.* 8.7.1, *CIL* VI.8848.

    covered market: cf. Ter. *Eun.* 255, Varro, *Ling.* 5.147, Hor. *Epist.* 1.15.31, D-S 3.2 1457, Platner-Ashby s. v. *macellum.* In 179 B.C. a new building was constructed for the central market on the north-east side of the Basilica Aemilia in the Forum. It took in the old fish market and other special markets on the site.

    Velabrum: see Varro, *Ling.* 5.43, Tib. 2.5.33, Prop. 4.9.5. It was a low-lying district between the Capitoline and Palatine hills, bounded by the Forum and the Tiber, Platner-Ashby s.v. Wiseman, 1987, 193-4 argues for a more restricted area, 'an open space or piazza', close to the Tiber, and separated from the Forum by the length of the *Vicus Tuscus.* It was a busy market-place, especially for foodstuffs (Plaut. *Curc.* 483, *Capt.* 489, *CIL* VI.9671, Macrob. *Sat.* 1.10.15).

230   [*qui cum* : *quid tum* ('What happened then?', i.e. in the morning) is not impossible but was rejected by Bentley as a pointless interruption disturbing the narrative. Lejay (361-2 and ad loc.) defends the MS reading as a characteristic of Stoic style. But what is emphasised is not the fact that they came, but that they came 'in numbers.'.]

    in large numbers: the session was well attended, a feature of senate meetings on which Cicero takes care to inform Atticus (e.g. Cic. *Att.* 4.1.7, 4.2.3) and Quintus (*QFr.* 2.1.1, 2.6.1). Here, and in the next line, where the pimp is 'leader of the house', the parallel with an official meeting continues (K-H on 226).

231   **was spokesman**: or 'opened the business'. For the meaning of *verba facere* 'to speak in an assembly or the like' see *OLD* s.v. *facio* 6, C. Sempronius Gracchus *ORF⁴* 44, Cic. *Leg. Man.* 27, *Att.* 16.16a.5. The *leno,* the brothel-keeper, is the most disreputable, impudent and unscrupulous, but his offer is a model of courteous generosity.

232   **at home**: an idiomatic expression, frequent in the comic poets, for 'being provided with', 'having at one's disposal'. If 238 refers to the *leno*'s own wife, then the young man has taken his offer literally.

234   [*tu*: seems required by the need to balance *ego*, as well as the following emphatic uses of the pronoun. The young man is addressing different individuals in a crowd, see Plaut. *Pseud.* 157, 162 etc. (Ballio pronouncing his *edictio*). *In* is not necessary, see 48 (*silvis*).]

    Lucanian snow: the best wild boar came from Lucania (*Sat.* 2.8.6), where the forested mountains were rich in game (Sen. *Dial.* 9.2.13). Hunting involved physical hardship, as well as danger (cf. Cic. *Tusc.* 2.40, 'hunters spend their nights in snow').

wearing leggings: cf. Petron. *Sat.* 40.5, D-S s.v. *venatio* (figs. 7360, 7375). Huntsmen usually wore them to protect their legs from injury. The detail points up the dangers of hunting.

235   sweep: *OLD* s.v. *verro* 2, cf. *averrere Sat.* 2.4.37. There is an allusion to the drag-net, *everriculum* (Varro, *Rust.* 3.17.7), cf. Sil. 14.262f.

from a stormy sea: fishermen prefer to stay home when the weather is bad, cf. *Sat.* 2.2.16-17.

237   a million (lit. 'ten times'): probably ten times a hundred thousand sesterces, as at *Sat.* 1.3.15. *OLD* s.v. *decies* 2b.

238   from whose house: *unde* is local, cf. Plaut. *Pseud.* 203, *qui amant a lenone* (D. Armstrong, *Arion* 3,1 [1964], 120).

send for: cf. *Odes* 3.6.30.

239ff. Aesopus's son: M. Clodius Aesopus's son inherited 20,000,000 sesterces from his father (Macrob. *Sat.* 3.14.14), the famous tragic actor (*Epist.* 2.1.82), and friend of Cicero. The story about the pearl is also told by Valerius Maximus (9.1.2) who describes the son as 'of not only abandoned but even of maniacal extravagance'. Pliny mistakenly attributes the exploit to his father, and tells the same story of Cleopatra (*HN* 9.119ff.). See also Macrob. *Sat.* 3.17.14ff. For the context of such anecdotes see Griffin, 36ff.

Metella: for Shackleton Bailey Horace's reference to Metella throws light on Cicero's complaint about the worries caused him by Aesopus's son (*Att.* 11.15.3). Metella, daughter of Q. Metellus Celer and Clodia, former wife of P. Lentulus Spinther the younger, from whom she was divorced in 45 B.C. (*Att.* 13.7.1) had an affair with Aesopus's son. She was also involved with Cicero's son-in-law Dolabella. On Caecilia Metella see T.P. Wiseman in *Cinna the Poet and other Roman essays* (Leicester Uni. Press, 1974), 176-91.

240   a solid: *solidus* is used of entire sums. I also suspect some tension between the meaning 'solid' and the verb 'dissolved' (*diluit*).

241   dissolved: on the practicalities see B.L. Ullman, *CJ* 52 (1956), 193-201. To be dissolvable in cold acetic acid the pearl would have to be pulverized before immersion. The process would then take ten minutes.

242   the sewer: the proverbial expression is stronger than in 166, underlining the foolish waste, cf. Petron. *Sat.* 42.7 (*puteum*), Otto, 86.

243   Quintus Arrius: see 86N. Nothing further is known of his sons.

progeny: *progenies* is a high sounding word used ironically, found in the *Odes* at 3.6.48, 29.1, 4.15.32, cf. Catull. 34.6, Cic. *Cael.* 34 (Appius Claudius Caecus speaking).

244   twins: of similarity in pursuits, tastes etc., see *Epist.* 1.10.3, Catull. 57.6, Cic. *Verr.* II 3.155.

245   nightingales: nightingales were enormously expensive, and it is, of course, perverse to eat birds prized for their song. See Pliny *HN* 10.84 on the price. According to Pliny again (10.141), Clodius Aesopus bought singing birds at 6,000 sesterces a piece for a dinner and Val. Max. 9.1.2 relates the same story about his son.

[*impenso:* only here in Horace. The ellipse of *pretio* is probably colloquial, Cic. *Att.* 14.13.5 (with *pretio*), *OLD* s.v. *impensus* 2a.]

246   marked with chalk as sane: at Catull. 107.6 and Hor. *Odes* 1.36.10 the white (chalk) mark distinguishes a happy day. Here the ancient method of marking the calendar is extrapolated to the marking of people. Pers. 5.108 adapts Horace's words to the distinguishing of things to follow and things to avoid. Perhaps black and white marks might be applied to any list. See N-H on *Odes* 1.36.10, Otto, 64-5 on the symbolism of black and white.

247-80: an adult who persists in childish games is regarded as mad (for the idea that growing up means putting away childish things, cf. Hor. *Epist.* 2.2.141-2, Ovid *Rem. Am.* 23, Pers.

1.9f., Néraudau, 101). But since the way the lover behaves is childish, he should recognise the nature of his aberration. The argument that lovers are childish and therefore mad is combined with the identification of love as a 'mental illness', for which the analogy with physical disease is always available. Erotic infatuation is commonly designated 'mad', see Lucil. 889W, Brown on Lucr. 4.1068-72, Cic. *Tusc.* 4.68-76 (the Stoic view), Hor. *Sat.* 1.2.49, 97, 1.4.49, Fedeli on Prop. 3.17.3-4. The comparison of adult folly with childish irrationality belongs to the tradition of popular philosophy (Lejay, 370-1, K-H ad loc. cite Ariston of Chios in Sen. *Ep.* 115.8). There is also the rhetorical/poetical tradition best illustrated by Prop. 2.12: love is a child because lovers live 'without good sense' (cf. 1.1.6) and give disproportionate importance to trivialities (2-3). In spite of the fact that love is a characteristic aspect of the 'life of luxury' there is no link with the previous section and the repetition of 'building toy houses' (247, 275) marks this passage off as separate. This leaves 275-80 as a kind of after-thought.

47 **building toy houses:** on children's games in general see Balsdon, 91ff., Väterlein, Néraudau. In Latin literature there are remarkably few references to the games children play, perhaps because children themselves are largely ignored in extant literature, Hanssen, 36. For toy houses, see Ar. *Nub.* 879 (compare the whole passage), Tib. 2.1.23-4, Juv. 9.61, Lucian *Hermot.* 33, Väterlein, 50.
tiny cart: the diminutive *plostellum* is unique in this sense. Cf. Ar. *Nub.* 880.

48 **playing at odds and evens:** at Rome the game was played with nuts, cf. Ar. *Plut.* 816, Plato *Lys.* 206e, [Ov.] *Nux* 79f., Suet. *Aug.* 71.4, Poll. 9.101, Väterlein, 36. Ps.-Acro gives the rules: one child holds the nuts or conkers in one hand and asks 'How many?' If the other child guesses correctly he wins the nuts.
riding a hobby-horse: Plut. *Ages.* 25.15, Val. Max. 8.8, Ext.1 (Socrates), Väterlein, 27 and 117, fig.7.

50 **being in love:** further defined in 252, 'love of a call-girl' (*meretricis amore*), cf. *Sat.* 1.3.38, *amator ... amicae*, Ter. *Andr.* 191, 'all those who are in love take it badly if they are given a wife', see Griffin, 118ff. on attitudes to love and marriage.

51-3 **build in play:** the 'work' or 'building' is the accusative object of the verb as would be the name of a game, *TLL* VII.2 1280.73.
in the sand: commentators think of sandcastles, and cite Hom. *Il.* 15.362ff. (the child builds a sandcastle and then destroys it for fun).
weep and wail, tormented: *ploro* is the strongest Latin verb for the expression of grief, with a colloquial tone that excluded it from high poetry, see Hor. *Ars P.* 431, Fedeli on Prop. 3.12.1, Tränkle, 136. For the characterisation of the lover Horace need not have thought further than the lovers of comedy (see Cic. *Tusc.* 4.73 where in Turpilius's *Leucadia* lamenting is taken as a sign of insanity), but contemporary love-poetry could be mocked for its tearfulness, *Odes* 1.33.2-3. The description 'tormented' also sums up the comic or elegiac lover, cf. *Sat.* 2.7.51, Prop. 1.16.39-40 (the shut-out lover), 3.17.42.
love of a call-girl: cf. *Sat.* 1.2.58 (*meretrices* distinguished from *libertinae*), 1.4.49, 111 (*a turpi meretricis amore*), 2.7.46. The phrase sums up the paradoxical condition of the lover obsessed with passion for a girl available to those who can pay, see Griffin, 112ff. The tone of the word *meretrix*, used only once in the *Odes* (*Odes* 1.35.25), depends on the context, J.N. Adams, *RhM* 126 (1983), 321-58. *Sat.* 1.4.49 is revealing: a woman the son calls *amica* 'girl-friend', the father disparagingly calls *meretrix*. See further H. Herter, *RAC* III 1154ff., Griffin, 27-8, J.P.V.D. Balsdon, *Roman Women. Their History and their Habits* (London, 1962), 224ff., S. Treggiari, *CW* 64 (1971), 197.

54 **Polemo:** the lover is urged to reform, following the example of Polemo, who, as a dissolute young man, had burst into a lecture of Xenocrates on self-control and taken it so much to heart that he became a philosopher himself. On Xenocrates' death in 314-3 B.C.

he succeeded him as head of the Academy. At that time the Academy laid most stress ● practical moral teaching. For the anecdote see Diog. Laert. 4.16-7, Lucian *Bis Acc.* 16● Val. Max. 6.9. Ext.1. Lucilius (822f.W) refers to Polemo's succession to Xenocrates . head of the Academy, and there has been speculation that he also told the conversic anecdote (Lejay, 375).

254f.   **badges of your illness:** the comparison depends on the common idea of love as an illnes. The mentally sick lover is like an invalid who goes around wrapped up in protecti● bandages, the signs of his illness, just as Polemo's garlands, which he removed out ● shame, were the signs of *his* dissolute life.

     leg-bands, arm-wrap, scarves: these items, like Augustus's winter leg-warme● (*feminalia, tibialia,* Suet. *Aug.* 82) were worn by invalids or the delicate. Pompe● apparently wore leg-bands for reasons of health (see Shackleton Bailey on Cic. *Att.* 2.3.1 and Quintilian (11.3.144) says ill-health is the only excuse for wearing such scarves an bandages. See Sen. *QNat.* 4b.13.10 (scarves worn by the delicate), Mart. 14.137 (142) *Cubital* occurs only here. Rather than as 'elbow-cushion' (cf. *cervicale, capitale*), I take : (with K-H) as something that was worn (cf. 'elbow-bandage' as the Greek equivalen● *Corpus Glossarium Latinorum* II 216).

     drunk: contrasts with *impransus* of the teacher. The word *potus* is avoided in the *Ode* (except for *Odes* 4.13.5) and is probably the every-day word, Ruckdeschel, 105.

256   **garlands:** sometimes worn around the neck, Lucr. 5.1399, Cic. *Verr.* II 5.27, Tib. 1.7.52● It was the Greek custom to put them on after the meal for the drinking which followe● (Ath. 15.674Cff.); hence they are a sign of revelry.

257   **before ... lunch:** cf. *Sat.* 2.2.7N.

258-71:   a snappy example of childish irrationality leads into the parallel case of the foolish love In spite of the absence of proper names for the characters (cf. 'the locked-out lover', 'th● slave') the source in the first scene of Terence's *Eunuchus* is easy to recognise. In th● passage Horace comes as close to a word for word citation of Terence as is possible give● that they were writing in different metres, cf. *Epist.* 1.19.41 with Fraenkel 1957, 34● Kassel and Handley (cited at 62N). Brown, 136 and n.82 considers the influence of Te● *Eun.* on the psychology of Lucretius's lover, and of Lucretius on Horace. But influenc● from the philosophical tradition represented by Cic. *Tusc.* 4.68ff. seems more likely i● Horace's case, especially as Cicero quotes *Eun.* 59-63 to illustrate the lover's *inconstanti● mutabilitasque mentis* (76). As K-H point out, citation is a technique of prose literature including philosophico-moral essays (e.g. Cic. *Amic.* 87, 93, 98, Arr. *Diss. Epict.* 4.1.19f. cf. *Sat.* 1.2.19-22, a reference to 'Terence's play'). Comedy provides an 'image of everyda● life' (Cic. *Rosc. Am.* 47, cf. Hor. *Epist.* 2.1.16●), but when satire draws on comedy w● should be aware of the close relationship between the two genres, see Hor. *Sat.* 1.4, R.L. Hunter, *Hermes* 113 (1985), 480-490. Later, Pers. 5.161-75 goes back to Menander's *Eunouchos* to show the locked-out lover as a slave of love, see G. Maurach, 'Zu Teren● *Eun.*1.1', *Gymnasium* 88 (1981), 123-38.

259   **pet** (lit. 'puppy'): cf. Plaut. *Asin.* 693f., with other bird and animal names used i● diminutive form as terms of endearment.

259f.   **the locked-out lover:** i.e. Phaedria, Ter. *Eun.* 49, 88 etc. However the formulaic phrase● also refers to a conventional situation and the typical lover. Late at night, usually after party, the lover goes to the house of his beloved, and, when not admitted, voices hi● complaints before the house-door, e.g. Lucr. 4.1177ff., 'But the locked-out lover, in tears often smothers the threshhold with flowers and garlands, and anoints the haughty door posts with marjoram, and plants his kisses, poor wretch, upon the doors;' (trans. based o● Bailey; see Brown ad loc.), *Sat.* 1.2.67, Tib. 2.4.39. See in general F.O. Copley, *Exclusus amator: a study in Latin love poetry* (New York, 1956).

60-62: setting the scene, Horace picks up some words and phrases from *Eun.* 46-7, *non eam ne nunc quidem/quom accersor ultro?* ('Am I not to go to her even now when I am summoned spontaneously?')

61 hangs about: a satirical touch.

62 the doors he hates: this shows his inconsistency. The doors which shut the lover out receive much attention in the discourse which arises from the situation of the 'locked-out lover', see Lucr. loc.cit., Hor. *Epod.* 11.21, N-H on *Odes* 1.25.4, *Odes* 3.10.2-3, Pers. 5.165-6, Copley (cited at 259f.N), 55.

62-64: cf. Ter. *Eun.* 46-9, esp. 49, *exclusit; revocat: redeam? non si me obsecret.* ('She shuts me out; she calls me back. Should I go? Not if she were to beg me.')

63 consider ... putting an end to my pains: this departs verbally from the Terentian model, though remaining close to the thought, cf. Pers. 5.161-2.

65 wiser: see *Sat.* 2.7.2N.
O sir: it is likely that in Terence too Parmeno's speech began here, see B. Bader, *RhM* 116 (1973), 54-9.

66 with reason or measure: Horace's own phrase, replacing *consilio* ('deliberation') and picking up *modum* ('limit', 'due measure') from the previous line. The repetition in 271 (expanding *cum ratione*) is also Horatian. See Brink on *Epist.* 2.1.20 (the phrase has a prosaic tone).

67 evils: Terence has 'flaws', or 'defects', cf. Lucr. 4.1141. Horace's list is very abbreviated, and leaves out the list of words in Terence concerned with lovers' quarrels leading up to 'war', hence G. Lee in M. Whitby, P. Hardie and M. Whitby (edd.), *Homo Viator Classical Essays for John Bramble* (Bristol, 1987), 148-9 suggests that a line has fallen out between *mala* and *bellum.*

68ff. unstable ... weather is: this expands Terence's *incerta* ('unpredictable', 'doubtful'), cf. *Odes* 3.29.43-5, Sen. *Ep.* 99.9. The comparison reinforces the slave's sententiousness.
drifting about by blind chance: the phrase is added by Horace. For the thought, see Cic. *Nat. D.* 3.72 (quoting Terence), *Div.* 2.15.

72-75: two shorter, parallel examples are appended, as in the previous section.

72 apples from Picenum: cf. *Sat.* 2.4.70N. The reference to this kind of apple brings us back to the dinners of the contemporary Roman world where they would be found.

73 hit the ... ceiling: the game consisted in squeezing apple pips between the finger tips to see how far they would go, success being an omen of luck in love. Pollux 9.128 classes it as one of the games played at the symposium, like the cottabus. See Väterlein, 24. For a possible illustration see C. Robert, *Arch. Ztg.* 37 (1879), 82-3.
coffered ceiling: the (Greek) word *camera* is rare in Latin poetry, and is probably a technical term of achitecture, Sall. *Cat.* 55.4, Prop. 3.2.12 with Fedeli, Petron. *Sat.* 40.1, Tränkle, 112. Greek influence on Roman life in art and architecture, clothing, tableware, gastronomy, perfumery, and jewellery was reflected in the technical Greek vocabulary used for such things, Griffin, 6ff., A. Zacchilli, *Sileno* 14 (1988), 115-36, 15 (1989), 89-104.

74 strike: 'strike words on (or from) the palate' is a difficult phrase to explain. Pers. 1.35, 'trip words on the soft palate' is clearer. Palmer suggests the metaphor of coining, as in Juv. 7.55, Gow 'break up words on ... ' K-H quote Ter. *Haut.* 242, *sermones caedimus*, which is almost as strange. *TLL* VI.1 516.64ff. suggests hypallage (*palatum feris verbis*).
baby-talk: for this meaning see Tib. 2.5.94, cf. Ar. *Nub.* 862, 1381. The lover's 'sweet-talk' is also implied.

75-80: an example of a *crime passionnel* is adduced to show that the madness of love is not a harmless aberration, when the true nature of such deeds is understood. Like avarice, ambition and superstition, love leads to death and murder (McGann 1954, 26).

276 **poke the fire with the sword:** this is said originally to have been a Pythagorean maxim explained by Diogenes Laertius (8.18) as 'don't arouse the anger of the powerful', see Ath 10.452D, Otto, 171. What does Horace mean? Get the fire of madness really blazing (K H), or stir up the fire of love to crime (the collocation of *ignem* and *gladio* suggests something like this)?

277 **Hellas ... Marius:** nothing further is known of these people, but their names show that the liaison was between a Roman and a freedwoman of Greek origin, i.e. it was a typical contemporary love-affair.

278 **possessed:** *cerritus* occurs only here in Horace. Examples are very rare after Plautus (*Amph.* fr. vii, xii, *Men.* 890, *Rud.* 1006), which probably indicates the word is colloquial (it is conjectured at Cic. *Att.* 8.5.1, see Suet. *Aug.* 87). In antiquity (see ps.-Acro ad loc.) it was explained as 'pursued by the anger of Ceres', see H. le Bonniec, *Le culte de Cérès à Rome des origines à la fin de la République* (Paris, 1958), 171-5.

280 **related:** *cognata* is very difficult and the line may well be corrupt. The following explanation is the best available. On the Stoic view it is illogical to distinguish between 'crime' and 'madness'. Since there is 'no difference' between them, words which can be applied to both are 'related', i.e. belong to the same class, cf. Quint. 1.5.49. For the Stoic insistence on giving words their true meaning see N-H on *Odes* 2.2.19f.

281-95: there is no transition to the topic of superstition, which was foreshadowed at 79, and i easily recognisable from the first example. The section comprises two typical cases, a freedman and a woman, with a conclusion drawn at the end of each. The kind of madness is not revealed explicitly until the final words, 'fear of the gods' (295).
Attack on superstition was well-established in the moralistic and satiric traditions. Bion criticized superstition (fr. 30-1 Kindstrand), and listed it with avarice and ambition (fr. 3-Kindstrand, for the background see Kindstrand 231ff., 242f.). Theophrastus described the superstitious man in his *Characters* (16), but Plutarch's *De superstitione* has more in common with Horace. Augustine (*De civ. D.* 6.9) quotes from Seneca's lost *De superstitione*, and gives us Varro's definition. In the moralistic tradition superstition was one of the diseases of the mind, the Epicureans associating it closely with fear of death (Cic. *Fin.* 1.60, Lucr. 3.980-3), the Stoics regarding it as a manifestation of fear, one of the cardinal vices (Cic. *Nat. D.* 1.117), cf. Lucil. 524ff.W, Pers. 5.179ff., Sen. *Ep.* 123.16, *superstitio error insanus est* ('superstition is a mad mistake'), S. Calderone, ANRW I.2 (1972), 377-96.

281f. **freedman:** Trimalchio is another example of a superstitious freedman (Petron. *Sat.* 74), obsessed with fear of death (78).
in the early morning: cf. 291, Pers. 5.188. It was not unusual for Romans to pray each morning to their household gods, but going out each morning shows excessive zeal (K-H). Seneca, giving advice on 'how one should worship the gods' forbids 'greeting the gods in the morning and sitting outside the doors of temples', but not as superstition; he is against external display (*Ep.* 95.47).
before ... breakfast: possibly a ritual requirement, cf. 288N. *Siccus* (lit. 'dry', 'before drinking') often means 'sober' as opposed to 'drunk'. Hence some commentators take the freedman's crazy behaviour as belying his soberness. It is better to take it literally, with K-H, who quote Festus (p.472.8L) for the information that wine could be drunk at breakfast cf. *Odes* 4.5.38f.
around the shrines at the street corners: in the city, as well as the country, there were shrines to the Lares at the crossroads. Freedmen probably continued to be associated with the *Lares compitales* even after the prohibition of their *ludi* in 64 B.C. and the abolition of the guilds of freedmen and slaves who ran the *ludi*.

with washed hands: a purification normally required before prayer, Hesiod *Works and Days* 725, 740, Plaut. *Amph.* 1094, Titin. *com.* 86/7.

283 **Me alone**: for *unus* as *solus* see *Sat.* 2.2.106, *Epist.* 2.1.18 etc. Cicero (*Nat. D.* 2.72) derives *superstitio* from *superstites* ('surviving') saying, 'Those who prayed all day and sacrificed so that their own children might survive them, were called superstitious ... ' Perhaps Horace is making paradoxical use of this etymology, for the freedman is asking that he should be the only 'survivor'.

284 **for the gods it's easy**: the sentiment has a long history, e.g. Hom. *Od.* 3.231, 'If a god wishes, he may easily bring a man safe home, even from afar', cf. West on Hes. *Theog.* 28 and 90, Pease on Cic. *Nat. D.* 2.59, N-H on Hor. *Odes* 1.12.31, Ogilvie on Livy 1.39.4, Otto, 108. Prayers often contain a parenthesis expressing the worshipper's confidence in the god's power, cf. Hom. *Od.* 4.237, Call. *Hymn to Apollo* 29, Virg. *Aen.* 6.117.

286 **exclude ... from warranty**: a legal term, referring to the obligation (under a curule edict from the time of Cicero) of the seller of slaves to make specific mention of their faults, physical or moral, see *Epist.* 2.2.16 with Brink, Ulpian *Dig.* 21.1.1.1, *OLD* s.v. *excipio* 4c.

287 **Chrysippus**: see 44N.
Menenius's prolific clan: an unexplained reference, classed as a proverb by Otto, 219. The meaning is probably madmen in general (McGann 1954, 14 n.1).

288ff.: while the point of the anecdote is clear, it is full of obscure details, since, in contrast to the first example, it is based on non-Roman religious practices.

288 **Jupiter**: the supreme deity of the Romans had no special powers in the sphere of health, and as far as we know, had nothing to do with regular fasting, which was not, in any case, a Roman practice, see Le Bonniec (cited at 278N), 404ff. on fasting in the cult of Ceres. Hence commentators take 'Jupiter' as the equivalent of a supreme oriental deity, and 'the day of fasting' as either Thursday (Porph. 'the day of Jupiter') or the Sabbath (P. Lejay, *Revue d'histoire et de littérature religieuses* 8 [1903], 305-335, esp. 313-5).
who send and take away: a religious formula, cf. *Odes* 1.34.13ff., *Epist.* 1.18.111, *Job* 1.21, 'the Lord gave, and the Lord hath taken away'.

289 **mother**: for the mocking of female superstition see Bion fr. 30 Kindstrand, Cic. *Tusc.* 3.72, *Nat. D.* 2.70, Juv. 6.522ff.

290 **shivering quartan fever**: a fever, not usually regarded as dangerous, which recurred every third day, Cic. *Nat. D.* 3.24, Pliny *HN* 28.228, Courtney on Juv. 4.56-8. The name 'quartan' arises from the ancient practice of inclusive counting.

291 **early in the morning**: cf. Pers. 2.16, Juv. 6.523. The time prescribed by ritual to wash away the pollution of the night, but also when the water is coldest.
proclaim: *indicis* is usually taken as a gnomic present, referring to a regular day of fasting, exactly which cannot be stated. We know that Thursday and Monday were days of fasting for the Pharisees (Luke 18.12). The Sabbath was not a Jewish fast-day, though the Romans thought it was (Suet. *Aug.* 76.2, Lejay [cited at 288N], 315-6, Reinhold 1988, 218).
naked: this seems appropriate enough, but is probably of religious significance (see Kindstrand on Bion fr. 30), as well as emphasizing the child's vulnerability.

293 **the point of danger**: in medical language the 'crisis' of the disease, Celsus, *Med.* 2.6.12, 3.18.7.

295 **fear of the gods**: this translates the Greek term *deisidaimonia* ('fear of the gods', 'superstition'). Varro (ap. Aug. *De civ. D.* 6.9) distinguishes between 'revering the gods' and 'fearing' them, and Servius on Virg. *Aen.* 8.187 defines *superstitio* as an 'excessive and crazy fear'. In Roman sources *superstitio* refers not so much to what we think of as superstitions as to extravagant and irrational religious belief which goes beyond the accepted tradition (Cic. *Nat. D.* 1.117, 2.71ff., *Div.* 2.148, Fordyce on Virg. *Aen.* 8.187,

Calderone [cited at 281-95N], 383). Stertinius's lecture ends abruptly, but on a dogmatic, assertive note.

296-99: Damasippus rounds off his account of what Stertinius said to him, picking up the exposition of his aims at 46-53, twisting them to his own more limited purposes.

296 **the Eighth Sage:** Damasippus is naively proud of his friendship with the great Stertinius and regards him as worthy to join the traditional Seven Sages, cf. Plato *Prot.* 343a, Call. fr. 587Pf., Cic. *Tusc.* 5.7, *Lael.* 7.

298 **hear as much said about him:** cf. Hor. *Sat.* 2.6.20, 2.7.101, Plaut. *Pseud.* 1173, 'if you speak insults, you will hear them'.
as much: *totidem* usually means 'of the same number', cf. *Epist.* 2.2.97. Here, as at Catull. 92.3, there is 'a colloquial usage in which the notion of quantity has slipped into the notion of kind' (Fordyce ad loc.).

299 **at what hangs ... behind his own back:** i.e. the tail of 53. There is no need to bring in the fable of the two bags of faults (Perry *Aesopica* 266, Catull. 22.21, Pers. 4.24) adduced by Porph.

300 **Stoic:** Horace acknowledges Damasippus's conversion, but in the wish that immediately follows he hints that it is only a temporary aberration from his true calling.
as you hope to sell: for the idiomatic form of the request, grounded in the preceding wish, see N-H on *Odes* 1.3.1.

301 **with what folly:** Stertinius has shown that all are insane, but that their folly is manifested in the different vices (77-81, cf. 306-7).

303 **Agave:** the reference is to the legend which was the subject of Euripides' *Bacchae* and many other plays in antiquity. On the Roman stage we know of Accius's *Bacchae* and Pacuvius's *Pentheus*. There is a Latin poetic version of Pentheus's death at Ov. *Met.* 3.708ff. One of the most terrible and memorable scenes in Greek tragedy is that in which Agave returns with her son's head as her trophy and is brought to see what she has done (*Bacch.* 1200ff.), see J.R. March, *BICS* 36 (1989), 33-65. Like Orestes, Agave had entered the moralistic tradition as an example of madness (see Plut. *Whether the Affections ... 3, Mor.* 501C cited by K-H). Agave's madness consisted in her failure to recognise her son (on this as a symptom of madness see Nisbet on Cic. *Pis.* 47). But Damasippus makes a further point: when she was mad she was not aware of being mad, cf. the Stoic/Sceptic debate on madness referred to at 208-10N.
[*abscissum*: *abscissum* and *abscisum* were easily confused by scribes, e.g. at Virg. *Aen.* 4.590, cited by the *TLL* I 151.3 as the first place where *abscindo* is used with parts of the body, some MSS have *abscisa* rather than *abscissa*. *Abscindo* 'tear off' gives a better meaning than *abscido* 'cut off', though this is common with parts of the body. Ovid. *Met.* 3.727 has *avulsum caput* and 731, *membra manibus direpta. Manibus* should be taken with *portat* rather than *abscissum*. In the *Bacchae* Agave appears carrying Pentheus's head in her hands (969, 1140, 1238, 1277); it is less clear that it was her own hands that tore off the head.]

306 **expound:** *edissero* is very rare in poetry. It is found twice in comedy (Plaut. *Asin.* 325, *Capt.* 967) and once in Virgil (*Aen.* 2.149) where Austin concluded that it belonged to the conversational style. Tarrant (on Sen. *Ag.* 966, cf. Sen. *Apocol.* 7.2) suggests that the effect in Plautus and Horace is deliberately pompous.

307 **mental disorder:** *vitio* ('defect', 'vice') is substituted for the expected *morbo* (cf. *Sat.* 1.6.30) to remind us that the disease is a moral fault as well.

307-20: Damasippus first criticises Horace for imitating Maecenas, illustrating his point with a fable, in good Stertinian style, the detail of which, however, is seen, on reflection, to be inappropriate, see Anderson 1982, 131-2. Underlying the insinuation that Maecenas's interest in Horace has caused him to become too big for his boots is a Stoic principle.

Horace's fault is really a transgression against *decorum* ('appropriateness'), a central idea of Panaetian ethics (fr. 97 [= Cic. *Off.* 1.110]), cf. *Epist.* 1.7.98, *metiri se quemque suo modulo ac pede verum est*, McGann 1969, 11. The passage belongs with others which define Horace's relationship with Maecenas, by showing how it is misunderstood, and also stand as compliments to him.

308   **building:** cf. Cic. *Cat.* 2.20, *aedificant tamquam beati*. Denunciation of extravagance in building was a favourite topic of Roman moralists, see N-H on *Odes* 2.18, Horsfall on Nep. *Att.* 13.1, J.E.G. Whitehorne, *AUMLA* 31 (1969), 28-39. Horace was probably building or extending the villa on the Sabine farm, where the conversation is imagined as taking place (10), see Frischer, 78ff. on the evidence of the mosaic decoration. Maecenas's palatial villa on the Esquiline, in which his vast wealth was displayed, was probably built during the period of the composition of the *Satires* Book 1, some years before (*Epod.* 9.3 [31 B.C.], *Sat.* 1.8, *RE* XIV.1 216). Maecenas's villa had a high tower, *Odes* 3.29.10, cf. *longos* ('lofty', 'tall'). See Platner-Ashby s.v. *turris Maecenatiana*.

309   **you measure** (lit. 'of a measure of two feet'): *modulus* is a term used in architecture, so there may be a hint of an equation of the 'size' of the buildings and their owners.
    two feet: elsewhere Horace tells us he was short, and fat (*Epist.* 1.20.24). Augustus teased him about it ('You lack height, not plumpness.') in a letter quoted in Suetonius's *Life* (Klingner 3.9-14), cf. Fraenkel 1957, 20-1.

310   **Turbo:** 'tornado', 'whirlwind', said by Porph. to be a gladiator short in stature, a likely guess. See *Sat.* 2.7.96N. on gladiators' names.

312f.   **Maecenas:** mentioned here for the first time in this book, cf. *Sat.* 1.1.1. Gaius Maecenas (died 8 B.C.), a knight of great wealth and luxurious tastes, became Horace's patron and friend in early 37 B.C. (*Sat.* 1.6.61-2), and presented him with the Sabine estate shortly before the war of Actium (*Epod.* 1.31-2, *Sat.* 2.6). His friendship with Octavian gave him influence and real power. The political and propagandist dimension of his patronage of the poets is much discussed. See further Reckford, 195ff., DuQuesnay, 19-58.
    [*tantum:* cf. the similar confusion in 318. An original *tantum* could have been changed to correspond with *tanto,* or, as is less likely, *tanto* to agree with *dissimilem,* since *tantum* is supported by *Sat.* 2.5.92, *Epist.* 1.10.3, and the fact that *dissimilis* is not a comparative.]
    [*tanto certare minorem:* supply *facere* after *verum est,* and take *certare* as depending on *minorem* (Bentley, adducing Sil. 5.76). This is a poetical construction and characteristically Horatian (cf. Wickham's list, Vol. I, Appendix 2.2).]

314-20:   Horace's telling of this fable (Perry *Aesopica* 376, 376a) corresponds to Babrius 28 more closely than to Phaedr. 1.24 (see Rudd 1966, 176ff.). For both the moral is the danger for the small in imitating the great, the point which Damasippus wishes to convey to Horace. The fable is told in an appropriately simple narrative style (note the historic infin. *rogare* [316], cf. *Sat.* 2.6.113-4).

314   **frog:** Rudd 1966, 297-8 n.26 notes that the emblem on Maecenas's seal was a frog and speculates that this suggested the idea of the fable to Horace, cf. Petron. *Sat.* 74.13, Martial 10.79.9f., Otto, 294.
    calf: even a calf is a 'huge monster' for the little frog, an imaginative detail added by Horace (in Babrius it is an ox) (K-H ad loc).

315   **tells the whole story:** *denarro* is found only here in Horace, and is very rare (elsewhere Plaut. *Truc.* 308, Ter. *Phorm.* 944, Gell. *NA* 1.23.12). It is probably colloquial, Ruckdeschel, 33.

316   **monster:** as if an elephant among men, with connotations of abnormal size, ferocity or strangeness, *OLD* s.v. *belua* 1.

320   **picture:** cf. *Epist.* 1.7.34. *Abludo* is not found elsewhere in Latin. Perhaps Horace invented it as the negative of *adludo,* 'make a playful allusion to', *OLD* s.v. *alludo* 3.

321   **add:** Davus uses the same tactic at *Sat.* 2.7.111.
       fuel to the flame (lit. 'oil to the stove'): a proverb, Otto, 253.

322   **has composed poetry sane:** see *Sat.* 2.7.117. It adds to the point here that the connection
       of poetic inspiration with the frenzy of the possessed was originally made by philosophers.
       N-H on *Odes* 2.19, Democritus fr. 21, Plato *Ion*. 533e, Pease on Cic. *Div*. 1.80, Brink on
       Ars P. 295-8.

323   **temper:** *rabies* can be used of uncontrolled emotion, frenzy, even madness. Horace
       admits being 'quick to anger', *Epist.* 1.20.25, and demonstrates it again at the end of *Sat.*
       2.7.

324   **Keep away** (lit. 'keep yourself to your own [territory]'): a phrase with which evil spirits
       were repelled, cf. Petron. *Sat.* 64.1, Th. Zielinski, *Philol.* 60 (1901), 6. The sense 'mind
       your own business' may also be present, cf. Cic. *Off.* 1.92.

325   **Mad passions:** Horace is accused of being 'woman-mad' or 'boy-mad' as the Greek
       expressions *gynaikomanês* and *paidomanês* have it (cf. *Epod.* 11.3f.). This idiom was
       brought into relation with the Stoic paradox by Chrysippus, according to Ath. 11.464D, see
       Rudd 1966, 187-8.

326   **greater madman:** why is Damasippus the greater madman (leaving aside the point that
       Stoic theory did not allow degrees of madness [Bond 1987, 12])? Is it because his normal
       human folly is compounded by the addition of Stertinius's doctrine, itself a sort of
       madness? Cf. Varro, *Sat. Men.* 148B (*Eumenides*), *sic insanis* (dogmatic philosophers?)
       sani et furiosi videntur esse insani. Horace's concession that he himself is mad is enough to
       give him the last word, since Damasippus's 'weapons' have already been used. Note that at
       31 Damasippus said, 'You are insane ...'
       [**do spare:** for *tandem* with an imperative expressing exasperation see Ter. *Ad.* 794, N-H
       on Hor. *Odes* 2.9.17, *Odes* 1.23.11f.]

Satire Four

Back in Rome Horace meets Catius, who has just come away from a lecture, which, in his view,
has shown the way to the good life. Declining to name his teacher, Catius repeats the salient
points of the lecture, which turns out to be on how to dine well. The precepts are directed towards
obtaining true satisfaction and pleasure from food and avoiding discomfort and danger to health.
The student is also instructed on how to choose good ingredients and avoid spoiling them by
careless handling. At the end of Catius's 'lecture' Horace pretends to be won over by the doctrine
and begs to be taken to hear the teacher himself.

The main target of the satire is gastronomy (or 'gastrosophy') and the gourmet's unquestioning
assumption that there is nothing else to life but knowledgeable dining. Catius's disquisition on
food is presented, both through the ironic framework, and the didactic parody that occasionally
surfaces in it, as a sort of philosophy, and the Lucretian echoes in the last lines point to
Epicureanism. But instead of launching a direct attack on those who confuse good dining with
good living (cf. *Epist.* 1.6.56), as Triarius does when arguing with the Epicurean Torquatus at Cic.
Fin. 2.23, Horace makes his point obliquely, as interlocutor taking Catius as seriously as he does
himself. It is worth quoting the passage where Triarius, having dismissed gluttons from the
argument, turns to a class who sound very much like Catius:

No, but men of taste and refinement, with first-rate chefs and confectioners, fish, birds, game
and the like of the choicest: careful of their digestion ... with drapery, silver, Corinthian bronze.

and the scene of the feast, the banqueting room all in keeping; that these live well or enjoy happiness (*bene quidem vivere aut beate*) I will never allow.

Catius's precepts are aimed at promoting pleasure in eating. That such a doctrine could not seriously be attributed to the Epicureans was something Horace and his contemporaries knew well, yet they were not above making the equation for jocular or polemical purposes, as the Stoic Chrysippus had already done, saying 'the very centre of the Epicurean philosophy is the *Gastrology* of Archestratus' and 'Archestratus was the forerunner of Epicurus and those who adopt his doctrines of pleasure, which is the cause of all corruption' (*SVF* III 709 [Ath. 3.104B, 8.278E] See Introduction §6). The satire's juxtaposition with 2.3 (on a Stoic theme) may also support some connection with Epicureanism. None of this permits us to take the satire as directed against Epicureanism itself. At the most, as Classen concludes (346-7), Horace is 'not merely making fun of Catius, but at the same time warning his friends against misunderstandings and misrepresentations of Epicurus' teaching, and against blind attachment to any school of philosophy.'

Food was a topic, if not of serious philosophy, then at least of popular ethics, as we have seen with 2.2 (see Introduction §6). Catius's teacher's lecture can also be set in a tradition of parodic food writing, both epic and comic (for more information see the notes, and Rudd 1966, 202ff. and Classen). Comedy had already assimilated cooking to various other arts and sciences; the assimilation to philosophy depends on the assumption that they are really incompatible (cf. Pl. *Gorg.* 462dff., Varro, *Sat. Men.* 403-4, 315B with Cèbe's notes, Sen. *Ep.* 95.22ff., 23 'the schools of rhetoric and philosophy are deserted: but look how crowded the kitchens are'.). So, while he knows better, Cicero teases his Epicurean friends by pretending that their main interest is in food (e.g. Cic. *Fam.* 15.18.1, to the Epicurean Cassius, 'Where then is philosophy? Yours is in the kitchen ... '). When he takes up gastronomy in early 46 B.C., Cicero describes himself to the Epicurean Paetus as going over to 'the camp of my old enemy Epicurus' though aiming not 'at the excesses of Rome' but at 'your elegance' (*lautitiam*), a word which well suits the aspirations of Catius's teacher (Cic. *Fam.* 9.20.1). The opponents of Epicureanism, no doubt helped by the inconsistencies of such Epicurean diners as L. Calpurnius Piso (see Cic. *Pis.* 63-7 with Nisbet's commentary, Catull. 47.5, *lauta convivia*), persisted in misunderstanding the philosopher's teaching that 'the beginning and root of all good is the pleasure of the belly' (fr. 409 Us., cf. *Ep.* 3. 132, which may be an early protest against such misunderstanding, C. Bailey, *Epicurus. The Extant Remains* [Oxford, 1926], 397, Pease on Cic. *Nat. D.* 1.113).

The satire therefore indirectly parodies Epicureanism whether or not we accept the identification of Catius recently revived by Classen (343ff.). The ancient commentator Porphyrio (on *Sat.* 2.4.1) identified Catius as an Epicurean who wrote 'four books about the nature of the universe and the highest good'. He is now taken to be T. Catius, an Insubrian Gaul from Northern Italy, who died in 46 or 45 B.C. (Cic. *Fam.* 15.16.1, 15.19.1, 2, Quint. 10.1.124, Pliny *Ep.* 4.28.1). Some are reluctant to accept the identification with T. Catius, mainly because he had been dead for so long, and was a fairly insignificant figure. But these objections have less weight when we consider that Trebatius (admittedly still alive) and Damasippus, are figures known (and possibly 'taken', see S. Treggiari, 'Cicero, Horace and mutual friends: Lamiae and Varrones Murenae', *Phoenix* 27 [1973], 245-61, at 246 n.4) from Cicero's *Letters*. On the other hand, we know of no reason for making this technical Epicurean philosopher the spokesman for gastrosophy, apart from the mistaken popular connection outlined above. The fact that the satire has a philosophic framework does not necessarily mean that the philosophy itself is its target; rather it is used to underline the absurdity of the pretentious gourmet.

Another candidate for the role of Catius is C. Matius, a friend of Julius Caesar and Trebatius Testa (Cic. *Fam.* 9.15.2, *suavissimi doctissimique hominis*, 11.27, 28, 9.15A, Palmer, 314-16). Augustus's friend of the same name mentioned by Pliny (as the inventor of topiary, *HN* 12.13) and

Tacitus (*Ann.* 12.68), may have been his son (Münzer *RE* XIV.2 2210.53ff.). One or other may have been the gourmet recorded by Columella (*Rust.* 12.4.2, 12.46.1) as writing three books, named *The Cook*, *The Fishmonger* and *The Pickle-maker*, to give instructions on refined dining, and by Pliny as giving his name to a kind of apple (*HN* 15.49). He certainly fits the role better, but while we may suspect Horace of using pseudonyms, that he does so has not been proved (Rudd 1966, 147).

There is even less chance of identifying the unnamed source of authority (11, Classen, 345). Can we distinguish between Catius and his teacher, or does he repeat verbatim as much as he can remember, even to the extent of borrowing the first person pronoun (46, 73ff.)? There is little to help answer this question, but the stress on Catius's dependence on memory, together with Horace's eagerness to hear the man himself, incline me to regard Catius as little more than a slightly incompetent mouth-piece.

As in *Sat.* 2.3, the introductory and concluding conversation frames a reported lecture. The lecture itself begins and ends abruptly. There is some order in the arrangement of the topics, roughly that of the presentation of a meal, with a few concluding remarks on service (76-87), but throughout Catius seems to jump from precept to precept in a rather random fashion (see Rudd 1966, 206, Classen, 338-9) and there is a noticeable absence of connectives between them.

1-11:   Horace runs into Catius in the street and persuades him to recount the amazing new teachings he has just heard. The introductory conversation raises expectations of a philosophical discourse, and, at the end, Horace the interlocutor gives no sign of having been disappointed. Catius himself claims that the doctrine he has just heard surpasses that of the great philosophers, and as the conversation progresses we also become aware that the poet is evoking the openings of several Platonic dialogues, thus characterising the dramatic setting as philosophical (Rudd 1966, 301 n. 21).

1   **Catius:** see above.
        Where from: the abbreviated questions are colloquial, *Sat.* 1.9.62-3, Virg. *Ecl.* 9.1. For the opening question see Pl. *Menex.* 234a, *Phdr.* 227a, 'Dear Phaedrus, where to and where from?' There are further similarities with the beginning of the *Phaedrus*, where Phaedrus tells Socrates he has been to hear the speech of Lysias, and Socrates conjectures that he has learnt it by heart (Fraenkel 1957, 136, Anderson 1982, 45, A. M. Prowse, *RFIC* 91 [1963], 199-201; see also the opening situation of Lucian's *Hermotimus*).

2-3   **put down notes** (lit. 'put images'): *signa rerum ponere* at Gell. *NA* 17.7.5 means 'to put down notes' and the meaning 'to make written notes' suits 'from memory' (in 11) as an alternative. On the 'art of memory' see below.
        new: the description is intended to arouse the interest of the hearer (Classen, 335). The claim of novelty also recalls the terms of the rivalry between the philosophical schools, each accusing the others of lack of originality (Reid on Cic. *Ac. Pr.* 2.16).
        that will outdo: the future tense suits Catius's enthusiasm. Pythagoras, Socrates and Plato are cited as the most eminent philosophers of the past (cf. Cic. *Sen.* 77-8, *Tusc.* 5.28ff.). On Pythagoras see *OCD*[2]. It is perhaps relevant that he taught a 'way of life' (Pl. *Resp.* 600b) and required abstention from meat and beans. In spite of the Roman reverence for his wisdom (Cic. *Tusc.* 4.2-4, Pliny *HN* 34.26, E.S. Gruen, *Studies in Greek Culture and Roman Religion* [Leiden, 1990], 161ff.), Horace elswhere is scornful of the doctrines of metempsychosis and dietary purification (*Sat.* 2.6.63, *Epod.* 15.21, *Epist.* 2.1.52). On Pythagoreanism in contemporary Rome see Rawson 1985, 291-4.
        Socrates is called 'the man Anytus accused' partly because his name does not fit into the hexameter, cf. Ov. *Tr.* 5.12.12. Anytus was not Socrates' chief accuser, but, as a wealthy democratic leader, the most influential of them.

7   **this**: this faculty of remembering. The 'art of memory' is expounded at *Auct. ad Her.* 3.28-40, Cic. *De Or.* 2.350-60, Quint. 11.2.1-51. See F.A. Yates, *The Art of Memory* (Harmondsworth, 1969) and H. Blum, *Die antike Mnemotechnik* (Hildesheim, 1969). *Auct. ad Her.* takes for granted that there are two kinds of memory, one natural, the other a product of art, passing over what seems to be an ancient controversy about the extent to which art could supplement nature (3.16.28).

      [*utroque*: an adverb, 'in either point of view', 'both ways'.]

8-9:   in spite of Horace's compliment Catius seems unsure of the powers of his memory to cope with the discourse. Here again the hearer's curiosity is aroused.

9   **fine-drawn**: Catius praises the intellectual subtlety of the lecture (cf. Cic. *Ac. Pr.* 2.43, Pers. 5.93, *tenuia rerum/officia*, Sen. *Ep.* 94.35), but there may be an ironic ambiguity in *tenuis* (also 'slight') which undercuts his claim (Classen, 336 n.23). Note the emphatic juxtaposition *tenuis tenui*.

10-11: the style is formal. For *edo* of oracles see *Sat.* 2.5.61N. *Hospes* in the sense of 'stranger' is old-fashioned and poetic, and *canam* is more suited to the inspired utterance of a poet, prophet or oracle than to Catius's precepts, cf. Hor. *Odes* 1.15.4, Ov. *Met.* 15.147 (Pythagoras). See 91-95.

10   **Is he a Roman ...** : for the question, reinforcing the Platonic atmosphere, see Pl. *Prt.* 309c, 'Is he a citizen or a foreigner?'

11   **will be kept hidden**: concealing the name increases Catius's self-importance. In this there is also another allusion to Plato, where occasional reference is made to an unidentified 'wise man' (*Phdr.* 235c-d, *Resp.* 583b, *Chrm.* 161b-c, cf. Lucian *Par.* 4, *Hermot.* 9, Classen, 342 n.71).

12-14: the lecture is an *ars cenarum* ('art of dining', 35) addressed to a host who wishes to have the best of everything on his table. With the first precept Catius simultaneously meets and disappoints our expectations in that he draws on a controversy of natural science (how to identify male and female eggs, Arist. *Hist. An.* 6.2.2, Antigonus *Mir.* 96, Columella, *Rust.* 8.5.11) to make a gastronomic point (the male are better eating, Pliny *HN* 10.145 follows Horace) which is itself an example of an over-subtle distinction. See Jonathan Swift's use of eggs as the trivial cause of political controversy in the *Big-Endian* rebellion (*Gulliver's Travels, Liliput*, Chap. IV).

12   **Eggs**: eggs, as part of the *hors d'oeuvres*, or *gustatio*, proverbially began the *cena*, see *Sat.* 1.3.6, 2.2.45, Cic. *Fam.* 9.20.1, G. P. Shipp, *CPh* 39 (1944), 117.

      forget not: cf. 89. The solemn locution suits the oracular tone, cf. *Sat.* 2.5.52. It is also used in didactic contexts, e.g. Lucr. 2.66, Virg. *G.* 2.259. The formality of the first precept underlines the discrepancy between the presentation and what has turned out to be the subject.

15-16: again the precept concerns the best flavour, Pliny *HN* 19.138. Since market gardens were located in the vicinity of the city (Varro, *Rust.* 1.16.3, N. Purcell, 'Town in Country and Country in Town', in E.B. MacDougall, *Ancient Roman Villa Gardens* [Dumbarton Oaks Colloquia 10, 1987], 185-203, at 188), because of distribution problems, Catius's refinement would be difficult to put into practice. For vegetables as part of the *gustatio* see *Sat.* 2.8.8, Mart. 11.52.5ff.

15   **Cabbages**: cf. *Sat.* 2.2.62. Only here does Horace use the vulgar form *colis* (Cato *Agr.* 35.2, Varro, *Rust.* 1.31.2, 1.41.6, Ruckdeschel, 91).

17-19: how the modern host will cope with the unexpected guest (cf. *Sat.* 2.2.89-93). With the reference to an evening meal we have left the *gustatio* stage. Catius's instructions on how to prepare a chicken at the last minute so that it is not tough sound like cook's talk (cf. Alexis in Ath. 9.383C [a cook tells how to save a scorched dish of stewed pork]) but the practical advice is elevated to the level of serious instruction (*doctus*). The method of killing (drowning in grape juice) is to prevent the dead bird becoming cold and rigid (Rudd 1966, 209-10 cites a modern parallel, cf. Joliffe, 62 n. 3 quoting Allan Ross MacDougall, *The Gourmet's Almanac* [London, 1931], 242, 'For *Canard Rouennais*, the duck must be killed in a special way, by smothering or strangling, so that none of the blood is lost.').

17   **in the evening a guest**: the coincidence of expression with an unattributed poetic fragment (Callimachean?), *inc. auct. fr.* 766 Pf. (*hesperion xenon*), is worth noting.

19   **juice from Falernian grapes**: the problem with the MSS's reading *mixto* is that we need to be told what the wine is mixed with. *Mustum* is unfermented grape juice, which could be preserved for some time (Cato *Agr.* 120, Columella, *Rust.* 12.29).

20-1: a new topic appears in Catius's precepts — the wholesomeness of the food and its effect on health. In antiquity accidental (as well as deliberate) mushroom poisoning was a source of anxiety (Pliny *HN* 22.92ff.). Mushrooms could probably be used at any stage in the meal, as part of the *gustatio*, cooked with a main dish, or even with dessert (Juv. 5.147). For recipes see Apic. 7.13.1-6.

21   **the others**: i.e. growing on or under trees (Pliny *HN* 16.31).

21-3: the concern with health continues. The advice is typical of that found in the comments of medical writers on food (see Hudson, 'Food in Roman Satire' in Braund 1989, 72). These are quoted *passim* in Athenaeus, and provided Pliny with much material. For examples see below.

22f.   **ends lunch**: for fruit as part of the *secundae mensae* see *Sat.* 2.2.121-2. [*Salubris* is acc. plural.]
           black mulberries: a laxative in Celsus, *Med.* 2.29.11. 'Black' makes the point that they should be ripe (Pliny *HN* 15.97). The mulberry is wholesome and easily digested (Ath. 2.51F), superior to the fig (Ath. 3.75E), which should not be eaten at noon, because it overheats the stomach (Ath. 3.79F-80B). Pliny *HN* 23.135 recommends mulberries as cooling, but warns that they are indigestible unless eaten before some other food.

24-7: Catius returns to the *gustatio*, with which *mulsum* was drunk (see *Sat.* 2.2.15N).

24   **Aufidius**: not known. There was a M. Aufidius Lurco, mentioned at Varro, *Rust.* 3.6.1, Pliny *HN* 10.45 (*RE* IIIA 1837.54ff.) as having made a fortune from selling fattened peacocks. Our Aufidius's practice is criticised on grounds of health, continuing the theme of the previous two precepts. It is usual in didactic writings to expose the mistakes of earlier authorities; here the joke lies in exposing as trivial the pedantic controversy that *cognoscenti* think important (cf. 35-6N.)
           strong Falernian: elsewhere Falernian seems to be the normal ingredient of *mulsum*, cf. *Sat.* 2.2.15. Pliny *HN* 22.113 says it is best made from old wine (if it is to be digestible) and in Macrob. *Sat.* 7.12.9 the proverb is *mulsum quod probe* [cf. *mendose,* 25] *temperes miscendum esse novo Hymettio et vetulo Falerno.* Falernian was regarded as a strong wine (*Odes* 1.27.10, 2.11.19) but Pliny (*HN* 14.63) talks of three kinds of Falernian, dry, sweet and mild. Therefore the point lies in the opposition of 'strong' and 'mild' as a specification of the kind of Falernian to be used.

25   **empty veins**: Pliny *HN.* 23.35, 'nothing excites the veins as much as Falernian'. Nourishment was thought to go straight into the veins, Lucr. 2.1125 etc., Hor. *Sat.* 2.3.153, *Epist.* 1.15.19f., Sen. *Ep.* 122.6, Macrob. *Sat.* 7.12.7.

27   [*prolueris* :   for the fut. perf. with iussive sense see *duraveris* 72, F. Thomas, *Recherches sur le Subjonctif Latin* (Paris, 1938), 187. The colloquial verb *proluere* is used in contexts of drinking at *Sat.* 1.5.16, Virg. *Aen.* 1.739 (see Austin ad loc.), *Copa* 29, Ruckdeschel, 86f.]
           lungs: *praecordia = phrenes*, cf. Juv. 4.138f., *cum pulmo Falerno/arderet,* R.B. Onians, *The Origins of European Thought*² (Cambridge 1951, reprinted 1988), 36, 42f.

27-9: the transition to the expensive sea-food is managed through the remedy for constipation. What Catius recommends sounds very like Cato's purgative stew, of which the main ingredients were cabbage, mussels, snails and lentils, cooked in Coan wine, with Coan wine to be drunk in addition (*Agr.* 158). Catius's mussels were common and cheap, but a smaller kind of sorrel is required, probably Sheep's Sorrel (M. Grieve, *A Modern Herbal*, ed. C.F. Leyel [London, 1931, reprinted 1975], 750ff.); sorrel is symbolic of rustic frugality (despised but good for you, like spinach, see Lucil. 200W, Hor. *Epod.* 2.57, André[2], 31). With shellfish we return to the *gustatio* (cf. Macrob. *Sat.* 3.13.12, the menu for a pontifical dinner), but the interest in health remains: the items served in the *gustatio* had to be easy to digest, e.g. Martial (11.52.5-6) mentions the laxative properties of the lettuce and leeks served first in the meal.

29 **white wine from Cos:** or *leucocoum,* was made by mixing white must with sea-water (Pliny *HN* 14.78-9). It did not have to be made with wine from Cos (Cato *Agr.* 112). Wines treated with sea-water were thought to have laxative and digestive properties (Pliny *HN* 23.79, 27.44, Ath. 1.32D-E).

30-4: the best sea-food identified by time and place. There is a bow here to the tradition of didactic/satiric food writing represented by Archestratus, Ennius, and Varro (see introduction to this satire), which gave the provenance of the best of a particular kind of food, e.g. peacock from Samos etc., cf. Juv. 4.140-2, Stat. *Silv.* 4.6.8-11.

30 **New moons fill out:** a widely attested belief, cf. Lucil. 1222W, *luna alit ostrea et implet echinos*, Cic. *Div.* 2.33 (Pease gives many other references).

32: deleted with W. Clausen, *Philologus* 106 (1962), 205f., and R. Renehan, *AJP* 98 (1977), 133-8. The issue is where the best of a kind is found, not whether something from one place is better than something from another place. Clausen's arguments are: that the line is irrelevant in its context, that the *peloris* is not 'a celebrated delicacy' (see Mart. 10.37.9), that the geography is wrong, and that a three-fold comparison is more elegant (cf. Virg. *G.* 2.109-11).

    giant mussel ... purple: both present at the luxurious pontifical dinner (Macr. *Sat.* 3.13.12.). The *murex* ('purple-shell') is best known for the dye produced from it (Pliny *HN* 9.131, D'Arcy Thompson 1947, 209-19), but it was also eaten (Lucil. *catal.*W, Ennius ap. Apul. *Apol.* 39 (*ROL* I 408), Mart. 13.87, André[2], 104, 105 n.55). On the *peloris* see D'Arcy Thompson 1947, 194.

    Baiae: a town on the Campanian coast between Cumae and Puteoli, a well-known pleasure resort, cf. *Odes* 3.4.24. The Lucrine lake was not far off. The area was famous for oysters, *Epod.* 2.49, Pliny *HN* 9.168, Juv. 4.141, Mart. 13.82.

33 **Circeii:** a promontory and port in Latium. It was one of the candidates for best source of oysters, Courtney on Juv. 4.140-2. Pliny *HN* 32.62-3 gives Circeian oysters the prize. Cf. Pliny *HN* 9.168, Lucius Crassus was the first to judge Lucrine oysters the best.

    Misenum: a town and harbour in Campania, near the promontory of the same name, cf. Virg. *Aen.* 6.162. There is no other evidence for it as a source of sea-urchins. These were a choice delicacy, Plaut. *Rud.* 297, Ennius loc. cit. (cited at 32N), Hor. *Sat.* 2.8.52, Macrob. *Sat.* 3.13.12, André[2], 104.

34 **luxurious Tarentum:** present day Taranto on the heel of Italy. It had a reputation for soft living, N-H on Hor. *Odes* 2.6, pp. 94-6, *Epist.* 1.7.45. Macrobius (*Sat.* 3.18.13) detects and criticises an etymological play here, quoting Favorinus to the effect that *Terentinus* is derived from *terenus = mollis* in the Sabine dialect. For further examples of dialectal etymologies in Horace see N. Horsfall, *LCM* 12.9 (1987), 136.

    scallops: D'Arcy Thompson 1947, 133. In Ennius loc. cit. (cited at 32N) the best are from Mitylene (if the text is sound), cf. Petron. *Sat.* 70.6, Pliny *HN* 32.150, 9.101. 'Flat' refers either to the shape of the shell or to its appearance when opened wide.

35-6: one of the general statements that breaks up the list of precepts, separating them into sections. We move now to items belonging to the main course. Polemical methodological comments (cf. 24, 48-9), themselves entrenched in food writing, also belong to the didactic parody (Classen, 338-9). The implied claim that cooking is a 'science' is often met in the mouths of comic cooks (Classen, 340 n.59, in general H. Dohm, *Mageiros. Die Rolle des Kochs in der griechisch-römischen Komödie* [Munich, 1964], 203ff.).

35 **art of dining:** in a sense the whole lecture presupposes an 'art of dining', a body of scientific knowledge, which the teacher professes. (*Ars* can also mean a 'text-book', Ov. *Tr.* 2.471, Quint. 12, pr. 2.) This is in keeping with the philosophical introduction. See also *sapiens* 44, *quaesita* 46.

36 **subtle:** cf. 9.

science (or 'system'): in Greek, *methodos*. *Ratio* is another word that evokes scientific (or philosophical) didactic, and Lucretius in particular, see Bailey on Lucr. 1.51.

37-9: the example connects the general statement with the next division — the main course — the topic of flavours carrying on to 44.

37 **trawl** (lit. 'sweep away'): cf. *verrere*, *Sat.* 2.3.235. *Averrere* is very rare. 'Trawl' may be used humorously of purchase from the fishmonger, as Gargilius 'hunts' in the market, *Epist.* 1.6.56-61.

expensive counter: on the cost of fish see *Sat.* 2.2.34N. Catius does not criticise expense as such, but expense undermined by ignorance, which does not lead to pleasure, cf. 76-7.

38 [*est*: the indicative in the dependent question is colloquial, L-H-S II 537ff.]
sauce ... grilled: for sauce with fish see *Sat.* 2.8.45ff., Apicius Book 9. According to Apuleius (*Apol.* 39), Ennius's *Hedyphagetica* included information on which method of cooking was suitable for which fish (*qualiter assus aut iurulentus optime sapiat*).

39 **up on his elbow:** the attitude is that of the diner, *Odes* 1.27.8 with N-H, Petron. *Sat.* 27.4, 65.6.

40-4: game was usually part of the main course. The precepts specify the best kind, and, probably, the best age.

40 **Umbrian boar:** opinions differed as to which was best (see Stat. *Silv.* 4.6.10). The implication of *curvet* ('bend') is that the serving-dish is bent by the weight of the animal served whole (Petron. *Sat.* 40.3, Juv. 5.116, Pliny *HN* 8.210, Balsdon, 37-8).

42 **Laurentian:** the Laurentian marsh was quite near Rome, on the coast between Ostia and Ardea, cf. Virg. *Aen.* 10.708ff. Hortensius had a game reserve there, Varro, *Rust.* 3.13.1-3. On Laurentian boars Bentley on *Epod.* 5.28, Bömer on Ov. *Fast.* 2.231. Martial does not seem to scorn them but perhaps he could not afford anything better, 9.48.5, 10.45.3-4.

43 **roes:** they too are affected by their diet. Virgil (*G.* 2.374) mentions their fondness for vine-shoots. In the dinner at Macrob. *Sat.* 3.13 they are served along with boar.

not always eatable: what does this mean? It could be that roes fed on this diet are not at their best at certain months. As food, Celsus, *Med.* 2.18.2, Juv. 11.142, Apic. 8.3.1-3, André[2], 116-7.

44 **connoisseur:** there is a pun which encapsulates the satire's comic equation of gastronomy and philosophy, *sapiens* meaning 'one with a good sense of taste', both physiologically and in the conduct of life, Lejay ad loc., M. Massaro, *SIFC* 46 (1974), 85-128, at 125 n.1.

will hunt: further word-play. *Sectari* would be more appropriately used of hunting the hare in the field, Ov. *Rem. Am.* 201.

wings: for the fore-quarters as the best part, cf. *Sat.* 2.8.89.

breeding hare: hare was a delicacy, Petron. *Sat.* 36.2, Mart. 13.92.2, Apic. 8.8.1-13, 4.3.7, André[2], 118-9. *Lepus* is feminine only here. Bentley supports the reading of V with examples of other animals being treated as of female gender when appropriate, e.g. Plaut. *Stich.* 168, cf. *Sat.* 2.8.88.

5-6: cf. *Sat.* 2.8.92-3:

> suavis res, si non *causas* narraret earum et
> *naturas* dominus;

Catius passes quickly over the fish and fowl of the main course, in a statement that makes a claim for original discovery based on research, whether his own or that of his teacher. The expression again brings philosophical didactic incongruously together with food. The indirect question is typical of summaries of content in didactic, e.g. Lucr. 5.509, 775, *noscere possemus quae vis et causa cieret. Natura* is of course a key word in Lucretius.

5 *foret aetas*: *aetas* has to be taken in the sense of 'peak-period' (K-H). In the light of Celsus, *Med.* 2.18.1 on the *proprietates* of various foods, also differentiated in 8 *aetate ... et membro ... et solo ... et caelo ... et habitu,* Shackleton Bailey's condemnation of *foret aetas* seems hypercritical.

[*foret*: is found frequently in *Satires* Book 1 as a convenient metrical equivalent of *esset*, Brink on *Ars P.* 289.]

6 **no palate before mine**: 'palate' comes unexpectedly at the end of the line. Such discoveries in relation to food were taken seriously, see for example 33N, but there is also a hit at the reverence paid to philosophical discoveries, in particular those of Epicurus, cf. Lucr. 3.2, Cic. *Tusc.* 1.48 (Epicurus as *inventor* and *princeps* of the understanding of nature).

7 **cookies**: see Hor. *Sat.* 1.1.25, Varro, *Ling.* 5.107, André[2], 210ff. They are dismissed as unimportant, perhaps because of their association with children.

8-9: the polemical tone continues, while the new topic of wine is introduced unemphatically, as an example.

0 **oil**: cf. Hor. *Sat.* 2.3.125, Juv. 5.86, *ipse Venafrano piscem perfundit.*

[*securus* with the indirect question is a construction characteristic of Horace, N-H on *Odes* 1.26.5f., *Epist.* 2.1.176.]

1-7: the advice is not about the choice of wines but about ways of treating wines to preserve or improve their flavour. Catius adds refinements to well-known methods, while assuming knowledge of the different qualities of Campanian wines.

1 **expose**: clarification by allowing to stand (Ath. 1.33A for Alban and Falernian, 'set aside in an open place so that the thickness peculiar to their nature may evaporate') also allows the wine-fumes to escape (Pliny *HN* 14.136). Night air is Catius's own idea. See N-H on *Odes* 1.11.6.

Massic wine: the use of the plural here and at 56 is not significant (see N-H on *Odes* 1.18.5). A sub-variety of Falernian, Massic wine came from the slopes of Mount Massicus in Campania, *Odes* 1.1.19, Virg. *G.* 2.143. Pliny *HN* 14.64 compares it to Sorrentine, and Columella, *Rust.* 3.8.5 praises its quality.

3 **odour harmful to the sinews**: Pliny frequently mentions wine's effect on the sinews (*HN* 23.35, 37, 38, 39, 46), but the attribution of the effect to the aroma is original (Lucr. 6.805 talks about harm coming from *odor vini*, but the text is uncertain). See Lilja 1972, 116ff.

4 **straining through linen**: this was a well-known method of clarification, Petron. *Sat.* 73.5, Columella, *Rust.* 9.15.12, Pliny *HN* 14.138 etc. The *saccus* was dipped in myrtle oil (Pliny *HN* 15. 124) which may have contaminated the wine (D-S. s.v. *saccus* [4]). On the topic of straining wine, see also Plut. *Mor.* 692Bf.

5 **Sorrentine**: from near Sorrento on the Bay of Naples. It was lighter than the famous full-bodied Falernian, which came from the foot of Mount Massicus (see 51N). Pliny *HN* 14.64 records that Tiberius called it *generosum acetum* ('well-bred vinegar') and Caligula *nobilem vappam* ('high-born plonk').

lees: the intention is to give body to a lighter wine and improve its flavour and keeping properties, cf. Columella, *Rust.* 12.28.4, J. Cousin, *REL* 17 (1939), 59-62. If the lees were added to the wine in liquid form, there would be need for clarification.

56 **pigeon's egg:** egg white is a standard method of clarification, cf. *Geoponica* 7.22. The pigeon is something new, as is the sinking effect attributed to the yolk.

58-62: the topic of wine continues, and the question seems to be what food best accompanies the serious drinking that began after the meal was finished. Understanding of this section is bedevilled by the difficulty of the transmitted reading, *immorsus*, a rare word, found only twice in classical Latin, and only here in a metaphorical sense. It is usually taken as 'roused', 'excited' (cf. Stat. *Theb.* 2.628). S. J. Harrison (*CQ* 38 [1988], 566-7) argues in support of Bothe's *immersus* 'drowned in drink'. This is not found elsewhere, though *mersus* is common with this meaning. Harrison draws a distinction between two stages of drunkenness, the flagging and the more thoroughly drunk, and takes *immersus* with *potor*: 'the drinker who is really drunk demands rather to be restored by smoked ham and sausages'.

58f. **scampi and African snails:** luxuries. For *squillae* see *Sat.* 2.8.42, Cic. *Nat. D.* 2.123, Pliny *Ep.* 2.17.28, D'Arcy Thompson 1947, 104. African snails were medium-sized (Varro, *Rust.* 3.14.4) and highly regarded (Pliny *HN* 30.44-6). Celsus *Med.* 2.18.3, 24, and Pliny *HN* 30.45 both recommend snails as digestible.

lettuce: is more problematic. For Celsus (*Med.* 2.24.2) it aids digestion, cf. *Sat.* 2.8.8, *Mor.* 74, Pliny *HN* 19.127, but see Apic. 3.18.3. In the time of Martial it was served at the beginning of the meal, whereas, in the old days, it had been served at the end (13.14, cf 11.52.5-6).

acid: cf. Celsus, *Med.* 2.19.2, *aliae [res] facile in stomacho acescunt.* The concern is for digestibility in a stomach heated by wine.

60 **ham and sausages:** ordinary and fairly 'low' foods in this context.

62 **piping hot from squalid cookshops:** cf. Sen. *Ep.* 56.2, Mart. 1.41.9-10. *Popina* is the word for a place where prepared food is sold (Kleberg, 17). The reference is probably to food sold by street-sellers. Ancient take-away food was similar to modern, rich and greasy consisting mainly of dishes of cheap cuts — offal and sausages, cf. Hor. *Epist.* 1.14.21-2, M. Corbier, 'The Ambiguous Status of Meat in Ancient Rome', *Food & Foodways* 3 (1989), 223-264 at 245. *Popinae*, which provided the poor with food they could not cook at home, were not respectable, Cic. *Pis.* 13, Juv. 8.158, Kleberg, 29ff., 93ff., Balsdon 152ff.

63-9: is there any connection with what precedes? Some commentators regard the sauce as an accompaniment for the prawns and snails (cf. *Sat.* 2.8.42ff.). I prefer to take the sauce as a new topic. The arresting *est operae pretium* marks a division (Classen, 339 n. 46).

63f. **worth your while:** cf. *Sat.* 1.2.37, *Epist.* 2.1.229 with Brink ad loc., Juv. 6. 474, *est pretium curae ... cognoscere.* There may be an allusion to Ennius, *Ann.* 494-5Sk., though the phrase *audire est operae pretium* is a conventional introductory formula (Fraenkel 1931, 121 n.1).

to master: the only instance of *pernoscere* in Horace. It is stronger than *cognoscere*, cf. Lucr. 1.1114, 3.181, Cic. *De Or.* 1.17, *Fat.* 10.

nature: *natura* at the beginning of a line and as the object of *pernoscere* may have a Lucretian ring, cf. Lucr. 3.1072, *naturam primum studeat cognoscere rerum* (Classen, 342 n.74).

two kinds of sauce (or 'double sauce'): sauces were a major feature of Roman cooking, see Apicius Books 6, 8, 9. Nasidienus is very proud of his sauce (cf. *Sat.* 2.8.69) and the recipe given at 2.8.45-53 for *ius* is very similar to the one here. Catius uses the terminology of the recipe book. What is not clear is the meaning of *duplex*, what the *ius simplex* consists of, and what the second kind of sauce is. (*Ius simplex* at Apic. 8.1.5. is the cooking liquor.) If we follow Bentley and *TLL* and take *duplex* as 'of two kinds', we still have the problem of *simplex* ('plain', 'uncompounded'). One common explanation is that the ingredients of 64-66 make up the *ius simplex*, while the other kind of sauce is cooked. But the recipe as a whole, except for the adding of oil at the end, is similar in method to many in Apicius. It might be better to take *simplex* as consisting of olive oil alone as at 50.

fish-brine: cf. *Sat.* 2.8.53. *Muria* is an imprecise term, shown by the context to mean brine used 'in packing salted fish products in vessels for transport', Curtis, 7f., cf. 14, 166 n.31. The smell was notorious, e.g. at Petron. *Sat.* 70.12 the cook stinks with it, cf. Lilja 1972, 104.

the tunny-barrel: Byzantium is named as the source of pickled tunny-fish, whether for its own production (cf. Pliny *HN* 9.50f., on the catch there) or as the middleman in the export of Pontic products (Curtis, 127).

chopped herbs: Catius is unspecific about the herbs, though it is the choice of herb which makes the sauce different (cf. *Sat.* 2.8.51-2). Perhaps this throws emphasis on the unusual and exotic saffron.

let it boil: *infervesco* is found only here in Horace. The simple form of the verb is often used by Apicius.

saffron: mostly used for its strong scent, and as a yellow dye. The best came from near the town of Corycus in Cilicia (southern Turkey), Pliny *HN* 21.31 Mart. 9.38.5, L. Robert, *REA* 62 (1960), 333-5. In ancient sources we do not often hear of its use in cookery though André[2], 204, 219 n.46 quotes Apic. exc. 7 *addes propter colorem crocum.*

Venafran: cf. *Sat.* 2.8.45. The oil is the best Italian, Cato *Agr.* 146.1, Varro, *Rust.* 1.2.6, N-H on Hor. *Odes* 2.6.16ff.

0-2: we have now reached the dessert (cf. *Sat.* 2.2.121f.), which appropriately comes last, though it does not conclude the lecture. The repetitions in *suco* and *facie* (cf. 12f.) make a ring of beginning and end. Catius's interests remain the same — the choice and preparation of the best type of a particular food.

Tiburtine: from the orchards on the banks of the Anio at Tibur, N-H on *Odes* 1.7.12-14.

from Picenum: apparently especially good, see *Sat.* 2.3.272, Juv. 11.74, Strabo 5.240, *Priapea* 51.7.

Vennunculan: the origin and the spelling of the word remain uncertain. They are also to be potted in Columella, *Rust.* 3.2.2, cf. 12.45.1, Pliny *HN* 14.34. On methods of preserving table grapes, Pliny *HN* 14.16.

Alban: Alban grapes make an especially sweet wine at Pliny *HN* 14.64.

3-5: a new topic, which is connected to what went before (*hanc*) and makes a transition to 76ff., the cleanliness of the appointments. Exactly what the innovations in the serving of the various items are is unclear. In themselves they are commonplace. Perhaps the point is in 75 — the serving in individual dishes. Lejay ad loc. suggests the discoveries consist in the serving together of things which are different but not incompatible.

wine-lees: as a condiment, cf. *Sat.* 2.8.9, Apic. 2.2.5. It is nothing like as common as *allec.*

fish-pickle paste: *allec* was the decomposed paste of fish fermented in brine, that is, the sediment produced in making the clear liquid *garum*, Pliny *HN* 31.95, *Geoponica* 20.46.2, Flower, 22-3, André[2], 112-3, Curtis, 7, 14, 'a mushy, paste-like substance'.

You'll find it was I who invented: 'as though a history of the art were being written' (Wickham ad loc.). The naming of the 'first inventor' of a technique was obligatory in the histories of all ancient arts and sciences (see N-H on *Odes* 1.3.12). Comedy had already exploited the *topos* in its depiction of self-important cooks (see Classen, 340 n.58, cf. *Sat.* 2.8.51f.), where the claim for higher knowledge is already present.

white pepper: cf. *Sat*. 2.8.49. Milder than black, according to Pliny *HN* 31.83, but not in fact.

black salt: coloured by the charcoal used to extract it, and less refined than pure salt (*Sat* 1.3.14), Varro, *Rust*. 1.7.8, Pliny *HN* 31.83.

75   **sifted**: *incretum* has been taken as 'unsifted' (as at Apul. *Met*.7.15), but it is found as 'sifted in', 'scattered from a sieve' at Cato *Agr*. 48.2, cf. *incernere* at Columella, *Rust*. 5.6.6. It is not clear whether it implies purification, or that the salt and pepper are actually mixed together (K-H).

76-87:   the final topic is that of service, and the correct presentation of the food. Catius inveighs against the discrepancy which is sometimes seen between great expense and careless disregard of detail. In 78ff. the theme becomes cleanliness, cf. *Sat*. 2.2.65ff.

76   **monstrous fault**: cf. *Sat*. 2.2.54, 69.
     three thousand each: the high price implies the much sought after large fish, a symbol of ostentation.

77   **roving**: the juxtaposition *angusto vagos* points the antithesis, whatever the exact sense of *vagus* here, see Fordyce on Catull. 64. 271, 'always on the move'.

78   **It ... turns**: *movet* has the conditional clauses as subject.

79   **while he was stealing**: Lucil. 629W, Hor. *Sat*. 1.3.80-1. The perfect tenses *tractavit* and *adhaesit* indicate that dirt previously deposited has not been removed.

80   **antique wine-bowl**: *creterra* is the form to be preferred in Horace, cf. *Odes* 3.18.7. There too it is a variant, though probably right since the vulgar *cratera*, Clausen suggests, was avoided by the poets, Ennius, *Ann*. 621Sk., W. Clausen, *CQ* 13 (1963), 85ff. The bowl is a *crater* used for for mixing wine and water. The dirt is sediment from the wine, cf. Cato, *Agr*. 152.

81   **brooms, napkins, sawdust**: since napkins are mentioned here in the company of cleaning materials, Palmer suggests they are for wiping the tables, cf. *Sat*. 2.8.11. Elsewhere they are for cleaning the hands, see Stat. *Silv*. 4.9.25. Sawdust was left on the floor during the meal and then swept out, Petron. *Sat*. 68.1, Juv. 14.60.

82   [*neglectis* is abl. abs.]

83   [*ten*: -*n*(*e*) adds a note of incredulity to the exclamatory acc. and infin., cf. *Sat*. 2.8.67ff., Austin on Virg. *Aen*. 1.37, L-H-S II 366. This construction is frequent in comedy and belongs to the lively familiar style, but can also be a passionate construction of oratory, M Porcius Cato, *ORF*[4] 58.6, *eane fieri bonis...*?]
     mosaic floor: a floor of expensive mosaic or slabs of coloured marbles (Cic. *Parad*. 49, Suet. *Caes*. 46.). The history of such floors at Rome is given by Pliny *HN* 36.184-89.

84   [*inluta*: cf. *Sat*. 2.8.52. J. Wackernagel, *SIFC* 5 (1927), 35-7, argues for the earlier 'correct' form *inlutus*, suggesting that *illotus* was formed from *lotus* (the vulgar form of *lautus*).]
     unwashed valences: since these could be washed, they were removable. The Tyrian covers (cf. *Sat*. 2.6.102f., 106) were permanent. For the separation of *circum* from its case see *Sat*. 1.3.70 (*cum*), 1.6.58.
     valences: cf. Hor. *Epist*. 1.5.22, Smith on Petron. *Sat*. 40.1. They generally hung from the couch to cover its feet, G.M.A. Richter, *Furniture of the Greeks and Romans* (London, 1966), 119 and fig. 598 etc.

85   [*haec*: is the subject of *reprehendi* and *illis* is ablative of comparison after *iustius, tanto* being taken with *iustius*. With *haec* and *illis* we have to understand *neglecta/is*.]

88-95:   Horace expresses ironic admiration and a desire to meet the source of such wisdom. It is interesting to compare Chrysippus, quoted by Athenaeus (8.335B-E), 'one may not learn by heart ... the *Gastronomy* of Archestratus with the idea that [it] can contribute anything to better living.'

88-9:   stately and formal lines, corresponding to the tone of 12f.

3   **learned Catius:** cf. *Sat.* 2.1.78. The epithet reminds us of Catius's grand claims in 3.
0   **retentive memory:** picks up 6ff., 11, cf. Lucr. 2.582, *memori mandatum mente tenere.*
        interpreter: Catius repeats the teacher's words, as a priest does the oracles of the god
        (*interpres deorum, Ars P.* 391).
        [*iuveris* is potential subjunctive.]
4-5   **far away springs:** the image of the source is conventional in contexts of learning, cf. Cic.
        Fam. 10.3.4, *Arch.* 13, *De Or.* 1.12, 203, 3.123, but here there is an unmistakable allusion
        to Lucr. 1.927 (4.2). In Lucretius the context is that of poetic inspiration (cf. Lucil. 1061W,
        Virg. *G.* 2.175). Here what is sought from the fountain is the key to the life made happy by
        philosophical wisdom. The adaptation of Lucretius points to the satire's Epicurean
        dimension, and, if we accept Classen's arguments (344-45), hints that Catius (and other
        modern exponents) do not adequately represent Epicurus's true doctrine.
        the happy life: in Greek, *eudaimonia*, the promised goal of every ancient philosophical
        system, cf. Cic. *Tusc.* 5.12ff., *Ac. Post.* 1.33, *Nat. D.* 1.95 with Pease.

Satire Five

In 2.5 Teiresias teaches Ulysses the art of inheritance-hunting (*captatio*), the aim of which is to
win the favour of a rich, childless, old man (or woman) and be made his (or her) heir. The method
is to make oneself an indispensable friend and confidant, ready to undertake whatever services are
required as long as the ultimate reward remains in view. The person who exploited friendship for
the sake of gain, stopping at no lengths of self-abasement, was in antiquity the Flatterer (*kolax*, cf.
Arist. *Eth. Nic.* 1108ª26, Theophr. *Char.* 2, Ribbeck). A type-character was defined (initially with
traits characteristic of the later Parasite, Ribbeck), the Flatterer was shown in action in comedy
e.g. Strouthias in Menander's *Kolax*, Gnatho the flattering parasite in Terence's *Eunuchus*, cf.
Lucil. 762W, *sic amici quaerunt animum, rem parasiti ac ditias*), and treatises on friendship
distinguished the true friend from the flatterer (Cic. *Amic.* 88-100, Plut. *Mor.* 48Eff., *How to tell a
friend from a flatterer*). Flattery in word and deed was one of the inheritance-hunter's chief
weapons. His employment of it, as well as his motivation, is what distinguishes him from the
friend he poses as.
        Inheritance-hunting comes into historical view in the late Republic, but it is uncertain when the
concept crystallised: the technical terms *captare* and *captator* appear for the first time in this
satire. Reasons can be given for the awareness of *captatio* in the late Republic. They include the
huge increase of personal wealth (T. Frank [ed.], *Economic Survey of Ancient Rome* I [Baltimore,
1933], 295ff., 393f.), the freedom heads of families now had to dispose of their property (Crook,
119), a greater degree of childlessness (Hopkins, 99-103) and the general expectation that services
(*beneficia*) performed for the testator would be remembered in the will (e.g. Cicero's inheritances
were an indirect return for his advocacy [Cic. *Phil.* 2.40, Plut. *Cic.* 7], see also Nep. *Att.* 21.1,
Saller, 25ff., 122ff., Brunt 1965, 7, Champlin 1989, 202ff.). On the other hand, the courting by his
relatives of a childless bachelor for inheritances is described as early as Plautus's *Miles Gloriosus*
705ff. in terms that correspond to the later literary commonplace (but cf. J. Hall, *Lucian's Satire*
[New York, 1981], 118). Given the satiric potential of the theme (Ov. *Ars Am.* 2.271f., 329-32,
Petronius *Sat.* 116f., 124f., 140f., Martial 4.56, 6.63, 12.40, 12.90 etc., Juvenal 12.93-130 and
passim) and its connection with other favourite satiric topics such as the denunciation of corruption
and *avaritia* (Pliny *HN* 14.5), it cannot be excluded that Lucilius or Varro noticed it, or that it was
a topic of popular moralising (Cic. *Parad.* 39, 43, 46, Oltramare, 139, Sallmann, 181). Even if it

was an established topic before Lucilius, we should not forget the influence of Cicero on, or at least the evidence he often provides for, the formation and formulation of Horace's moral concerns. In one place (*Off.* 3.74), Cicero condemns inheritances gained by flattery and insincerity: 'I in fact regard even genuine inheritances as dishonorable if they were sought by deceitful flatteries, by simulated and not by sincere services.' In another (*Parad.* 39, see on *Sat.* 2.7), inheritance-hunting is defined as slavery: 'Is there any doubt of the slavery of those who out of desire for funds do not reject any condition of the most oppressive slavery? In their slavery what unreasonable demands do they not undertake, those who hope for an inheritance? What nod of a rich childless old man do they not take heed of? They speak according to his will, do whatever he says. They escort him, sit beside him, give him gifts. Which of these deeds is that of a free man? Which even is that of a responsible slave?'

Conditions existed in Roman society which make it plausible to treat *captatio* as a social phenomenon (Hopkins, 238ff., Corbier 1988; Champlin 1989, 211ff., and Mansbach are sceptical) though this does not necessarily mean that 2.5 should be read as a straight 'social document' (Rudd 1966, 224). In fact, the 'existence' of *captatio* depends on how you interpret certain behaviour. The general context in which discussion of *captatio* should be placed is that of friendship and 'duties', the exchange of services on which Roman friendship was founded (see Cic. *Off.* 3.74, Sen *Ep.* 95.43, *Ben.* 4.20.3, Saller, 11ff, 124-5). '*Captatio* is merely *amicitia* viewed in a negative light; indeed, it springs from the very wide Roman notion of friendship, with its particular emphasis on the exchange of *beneficia*' (Champlin 1989, 212). Satirists and moralists exploit the image of the perverted friendship as a symbol of the undermining of the old values by greed and wealth (Champlin 1991, 101-2).

Friendship in this wider sense, and particularly the ethical nuances of the relationships between those of unequal wealth and social status, is a central theme of Horace, *Epistles* 1, already explored in the *Satires* through the story of Horace's friendship with Maecenas. In this satire Horace does not merely identify some modes of friendship as exploitative, but, and this is the brilliant part of his satiric conception (Sallmann, 181-2), he systematises this exploitation into an 'art' which can be taught, perhaps taking a hint from the parasites of Greek comedy (Antidotos fr.2, Axionikos fr.6, Nikolaus fr.1 *PGC*). Why is it *Ulysses* who is taught? Part of the reason must lie in Ulysses' suitability as an exemplar of wiliness and cunning intelligence, to which it was always possible to give a negative or comic twist — transforming him from Homeric hero to unscrupulous schemer or comic rogue (W.B. Stanford, *The Ulysses Theme*[2] [Oxford, 1963], E. D. Phillips, *G&R* N.S. 6 [1959], 58-67). If duplicity is the key to the choice of Ulysses, doubleness is the keynote of the whole satire. As a prophet, Teiresias is expected to speak ambiguously. This contributes to the pervasive irony of the piece, which also reflects the duplicitous nature of *captatio* as a phenomenon, and the built-in doubleness of parody. Throughout the poem there is an ironic counterplay between the heroic status of the characters and the perversion of values implied in *captatio*, mirrored in shifts between epic style and the informal style of conversation. Above all, the cynicism and immorality of the advice is such that it can only be taken as satiric irony, at least on the author's part. Condemnation of corruption is evident, the stance of Teiresias himself more ambivalent (Langford, 94). We cannot tell if he means his advice to Ulysses seriously, or whether it is meant to ironize Ulysses, who takes it seriously. Here the technique differs from that of 2.4 where Catius does endorse his instructions (which therefore represent him, in however distorted a fashion).

In spite of the contemporary theme, Horace avoids pin-pointing specific individuals as *captatores*, except in the trivial case of Nasica and Coranus. Various explanations of this have been offered, and the question also has a bearing on why Horace chose the framework of the epic consultation. Lejay (482) suggests both that inheritance-hunting was too new a phenomenon to have its type characters and also that reference to contemporaries might have been imprudent (if it was new then there is piquancy in the implication that it is old). However, the decision to give the opic epic distance (Horace could not portray himself as receiving the advice, or, on the other hand, as being criticised for practising *captatio*) and to treat it didactically may have reduced the scope for such references.

Critics agree on the distinctive nature of 2.5 but have found it difficult to define (Rudd 1966, 239ff., Roberts). Though Rudd is right to say that it is 'the product of subject-matter, setting, form and language', and, more specifically, due to the nastiness of both the subject-matter and the portrayal of Ulysses and Teiresias, Roberts has gone a step further in pointing to the aspects of language and imagery which create a dehumanised world completely lacking in moral values (Ben Jonson's *Volpone* provides the best commentary). The victim's complacency as a requisite for success (on which Roberts lays stress) needs to be set against the chance that he may be a rogue himself. As Champlin has pointed out, we should not assume that the *captandus*, the object of the *captator*'s attention, is just a passive victim. From Plautus on, the childless old men (and women) are aware of the power of their wealth, and the advantages to be gained from it (this is what Eumolpus in Petronius attempts to cash in on): 'according to caustic observers the *captandus* might gain anything from sexual favours to free advocacy in court to ostentatious naming in the will of the *captatores* themselves' (212). So, early in his advice Teiresias warns Ulysses of the possibility of losing his bait with the prey (24-5). *Captatio* is a game of give-and-take on both sides (Sallmann, 200, Tracy, 401).

As Roberts shows, the effect also comes from the indirectness of the presentation. Itself remote in space and time, totally unreal, the fictional epic framework reinforces the 'reality' of the world of *captatio* it encapsulates. A further indirectness comes from the strategy of the didactic discourse, so that criticism of the practice the satire exposes must be decoded by the reader, in the absence of the satirist (for comparison with Juvenal 9, see Braund 1988, 143ff.). For Roberts there is no doubt that the reader's reaction must be *indignatio*. The indignation is implicit in the content of the satire' (432). But the very indirectness he points to — the gap between the satirist, the speaker, and the reader, and the possible ambivalence of Teiresias, which he does not acknowledge — leaves room for the humour that arises from a clash of perspectives. The poem's mixture of black comedy and satirical bite is, again, rather like that of Jonson's *Volpone*; we should not underestimate the comic power of the blatantly immoral villain (see Knoche, 88 on the comic effect of the poem).

Through its structure and strategy, 2.5 fits, as a variation, the pattern of Book 2. It has also been shown that the aspect of 2.5 which seems most unusual in this book, the Homeric setting, is drawn from the satiric tradition (Lejay, 474ff.). On the one hand, epic parody and heroic burlesque was natural in hexametric satire (cf. Lucilius Book 1, the Council of the Gods, and 565-73W, a conversation with Penelope). On the other, Ulysses as 'hero' and the idea of an interview in the underworld may come from Menippean satire, though no close dependence can be demonstrated (Menippus himself is said to have written a *Nekuia*; see Varro's *Sesculixes*, and Lucian, *Menippus*, where Menippus consults Teiresias in the underworld, Rudd 1966, 237-8). The uniqueness of 2.5 is partly to be attributed to the skill with which Horace combines all these elements.

In the disposition of satires in the book 2.5 corresponds to 2.1 (see Introduction §5). The differences are more striking than the similarities, however. In the consultation with Trebatius in 2.1 the poet himself is the main speaker. In contrast, 2.5 is the only satire in Book 2 in which 'Horace' is completely absent, a natural consequence of the underworld setting and theme. 2.5 nevertheless corresponds to the general structural pattern of the dialogue satires. Preliminary conversation between Teiresias and Ulysses (1-22) introduces Teiresias's advice, which takes up the rest of the satire. Ulysses intervenes twice (58, 76-8), but Teiresias has the last word. As in 2.4, the main speaker teaches an 'art' (*ars captatoria*), and takes a didactic approach.

It has proved difficult to find convincing sectional divisions, not only because Teiresias gives a loosely connected series of precepts, but also because there are continuities (e.g. the theme of flattery) and parallelisms between sections and disruptions and digressions within them (Roberts,

426-7). Since, overall, Teiresias's art demands the matching of a stratagem to a 'victim', K-H's two-fold division of his 'lecture' into 23-72 (people) and 73-109 (tricks of the trade) is not as compelling as the three-fold one of Roberts (with introduction [1-22] and conclusion [99-110] framing a tripartite middle section [23-44, 45-69, 70-98]), which is based on the presence of transitional *formulae*: 23 (*dixi equidem et dico*), 45 (*praeterea*), 70 (*illud ad haec iubeo*). Within this general framework we should notice that the instruction begins in the introduction (10ff.) and that there is in the satire a kind of narrative progression from the first steps in *captatio*, through the vicissitudes of possible set-backs, to final success.

1-22: Ulysses, having learnt from Teiresias that he will return home impoverished, asks him for further advice, this time on how to restore his lost fortunes. Teiresias tells him to cultivate the elderly and wealthy, regardless of their social or moral standing. Ulysses expresses dismay but soon declares that he is ready to drop his heroic ideals in order to become rich. The incongruity between the Homeric setting and the Roman character of Teiresias's advice points to the satiric theme of this piece — the perversion of values in the contemporary Roman world.

1-3   **Answer:** the word sets the dramatic scene as a consultation. ('Answers' [*responsa*] are sought from oracles and seers, cf. Virg. *Ecl.* 1.44, Ov. *Met.* 3.339f., *ille* [Teiresias] ... *inreprehensa dabat populo responsa petenti*.) The reader is given the illusion of breaking in on a conversation that is already in progress as at the beginnings of Plato's *Symposium* and *Cratylus*. The conversation in the satire is imagined as following Teiresias's speech at Hom. *Od.* 11.100-37: 'Noble Odysseus, you are seeking to return home ... you will return late and in evil plight ... And in your own house you will find mischief, I mean the presumptuous men who are devouring your substance now ... ' (Trans. Shewring). For a full survey of the Homeric reminiscences see Leich, 13ff., Cèbe 1966, 303ff.
Teiresias: it soon becomes clear, from Teiresias's name and the details in the first few lines, that Horace is inserting his scene into the context of Ulysses' consultation of Teiresias in the underworld (Hom. *Od.* 11), and that Ulysses is the first speaker (*doloso, Ithacam*). Teiresias was the mythical seer *par excellence*, and was associated with a range of Theban legends. Alone of all the Homeric ghosts he retained his mental faculties (Hom. *Od.* 10.490ff.) and his prophetic powers endured beyond death. Since he belongs to the grand and remote worlds of tragedy and epic we expect some special wisdom from his revelations.
my lost wealth: filled out by 7, a reference to the daily feasting of the suitors in Ulysses' palace on Ithaca. For some time during his absence a band of suitors, whom Penelope had to entertain at the household's expense, had been trying to persuade her to choose one of them as a new husband.
Why are you laughing?: the question is sandwiched between *artibus atque modis* and *doloso*. Teiresias finds it amusing that Ulysses, famous for his cunning tricks, should ask about 'ways and means', especially after he has been satisfied on the main point of the Homeric consultation, his journey home (*Od.* 11.100). Cf. Lucian, *Men.* 21, 'Going to Teiresias, ... I begged him to tell me what sort of life he considered the best. He laughed and said ... '

3   **the man of many wiles:** the epithet recalls the Homeric designations of Odysseus as *poikilomêtês* 'full of wiles', *Od.* 3.163, 5.203 etc., cf. Hor. *Odes* 1.6.7, *duplicis ... Ulixei* with N-H. See also Athena's recognition speech to Odysseus in Ithaca, *Od.* 13.291ff., 297-8, 'you surpass all mankind in stratagem'.

4   **sail back to Ithaca**: the goal of his journey in the epic, characterised as a *nostos*, 'homeward journey', cf. Hom. *Od.* 1.57-9, 'he would be well content to see even the smoke rising from his own land'.

ancestral home: the phrase *patrios Penates* is used metonymically for 'home' or 'native land', cf. *Odes* 3.27.49. On the Penates (household gods) see *Sat.* 2.3.176N. Even if the phrase has epic colouring (cf. Virg. *Aen.* 2.717), the insertion of Roman detail into the Homeric context is still humorously incongruous (but see Sallmann, 188). The full extent of the Romanising of the scene emerges gradually, see Rudd 1966, 232.

5-8:   Ulysses presses the point of his 'evil plight'. The grandiose opening of his utterance (with the passionate 'O' and the use of the participle [see *Odes* 1.7.30]) contrasts with the colloquial *vilior alga* at its end.

5   **spoken false to no one**: a recognition of his standing as a prophet, cf. Soph. *Ant.* 1092-4, *OT* 298f., 'the god-inspired seer, in whom alone of men truth is inborn'.

[*vides ut...?*: cf. *Odes* 1.9.1, 3.27.17, G. Pascucci, *SIFC* 29 (1957), 193 n.3.]

7   **wine-cellar**: *apotheca* ('storeroom', 'wine-loft'), the Latin version of a Greek word, avoided in the literary language. The word does not add to the Homeric atmosphere but evokes contemporary luxury (cf. *cameram, Sat.* 2.3.273N). The best wine was stored in an upstairs room above the furnace for the baths or the oven for baking (*fumarium*), to be aged in the smoke rising through the chimney, Columella, *Rust.* 1.6.20, cf. Hor. *Odes* 3.8.11, G. Bagnani, *Phoenix* 8 (1954), 25-6 (on the chimney).

8   **worth less than seaweed**: a proverb (Otto, 13), cf. *Odes* 3.17.10, Virg. *Ecl.* 7.42. In *genus* and *virtus* we recognise the highest Homeric values which Ulysses is discounting, cf. Hom. *Od.* 24.508ff., Odysseus to Telemachus, 'My son, when you enter the battlefield where warriors prove their mettle, you need not be told not to shame the lineage of our fathers. In courage and manliness we have long been foremost, the world over.' (Trans. Shewring) The cynical recognition of the importance of wealth is itself proverbial, ' "Money is the man", and no poor man is good or honourable', Alcaeus 360 L-P, cf. Hor. *Sat.* 1.1.62, 'you're valued according to the scale of your possessions', *Epist.* 1.1.53-4, 1.6.37-8, Lucil. 1194f.W, Petron. *Sat.* 77, Otto, 157.

9   **poverty**: the ancients distinguished between 'poverty', which meant having enough to live on modestly (cf. *Epist.* 1.10.39-41) and indigence or destitution (see Cic. *Parad.* 45). Fear of poverty recurs in the *Satires* as a driving force of human motivation (*Sat.* 1.1.93, 2.3.92, 2.7.84, cf. *Odes* 1.1.17f.), but nowhere else is the fear expressed in such strong terms.

to put it unambiguously: or 'without circumlocution', cf. Plaut. *Cist.* 747, Lucil. 1192W, Hor. *Epist.* 1.7.82, Ov. *Met.* 10.19. I follow Wickham, who takes this phrase with the whole sentence, though not as apologising for the bluntness of *pauperies*, as he suggests, but as drawing attention to Teiresias's omission of the standard praises of poverty.

10   **learn**: cf. Hor. *Sat.* 2.2.70, 2.3.46, 233. Teiresias begins to assume the didactic manner.

10-14:   Teiresias imagines Ulysses in the role of the landowner receiving gifts from his own dependents or tenant-farmers. These he is to pass on to the rich man he is cultivating, in order to flatter him (for gifts of food from clients, see Lucil. 159-60W, Saller, 124, Veyne, *Rev. Arch* [1981], 245-282; for the passing on of a client's gift, Catull. 14.6ff.). Delicacies were one of the standard means of *captatio*, cf. Hor. *Epist.* 1.1.77-9, 'others/go hunting wealthy widows with cakes and fruit/or try to trap old men for their reserves' (Trans. Macleod), Juv. 4.15-9, 5.97-8, 6.39-40, Lucian, *Dial. Mort.* 19(9).2. Teiresias does not immediately make it clear to Ulysses how he will benefit by making himself a rich old man's client.

10   **thrush**: *Sat.* 2.2.74N.

11   **fly off**: the lively metaphor is suggested by 'thrush'.

12ff. **fruit ... beauties:** probably the 'first-fruits' which were offered to the deities of the farmland, among whom the Lares are sometimes found. See Tib. 1.1.19-23, 21-4, Hor. *Odes* 3.23.3-4, 'If you placate the Lares with this year's corn'. The rich man is promoted from patron to guardian deity, since it is he who is to bestow future prosperity. On the Lares ('household gods') see *Sat.* 2.3.165N.

beauties: the plural of an abstract noun is concrete, as at Hor. *Odes* 1.17.16, Stat. *Silv.* 4.5.1.

15ff. Teiresias develops the point made by Ulysses in line 9: not only does the absence of wealth cancel out good birth and moral character, but its presence compensates for base origin and criminality.

15f. [*quamvis* + indic. as often in Horace, cf. *Sat.* 2.2.29.]

of no family: either as a former slave (slaves did not have family rights or names) or by forfeiting civil rights (for this definition of *gentilis* [Scaevola's] see Cic. *Top.* 29).

with a brother's blood: one of the ultimate crimes for the Romans, often cited as a symptom of moral decline, cf. Catull. 64.399, Lucr. 3.72, Virg. *G.* 2.510.

a runaway slave: therefore an outlaw, see *Sat.* 2.7.113N, Crook, 186f.

17 **on his outside:** the unusual expression (but see Ov. *Fast.* 5.68, *ibat et interior*) is interpreted in Ulysses' reply. The Homeric hero appropriately uses the originally military expression 'cover the side' (Suet. *Claud.* 24.3, cf. *latus ... apertum*, Virg. *Aen.* 10.314). In the city this means taking the street side, or 'giving the wall', in order to protect the person one is escorting from the passing crowds and traffic. Doing this amounts to a public display of inferior status. Cf. Juv. 3.131, 'here a son of freeborn family covers the side of a rich man's slave', with Courtney ad loc.

[*ne ... recuses*: for another use of the second person of the present subjunctive in a prohibition see 89.]

18f.: Ulysses makes the point explicit: he is being told to perform a servile duty for a slave of low moral character, behaviour unfitting a hero. But when threatened with poverty, he soon drops his objections.

[*utne tegam*: a repudiating deliberative, expressing indignation, see Woodcock §175.]

dirty: *spurcus* (the sole instance in Horace) is emphatic. The man is not only a slave, as his name shows (*Sat.* 2.7.54N), but also of unsavoury character. Cf. Lucil. 173W (of a gladiator).

Dama: see *Sat.* 2.7.54N. Note the name's reappearance at line 101.

always pitting myself against better men: a pithy statement of the competitive heroic code, cf. Hom. *Il.* 6.207ff., (Glaucus) 'He sent me here to Troy and many times commanded me always to be best and distinguished above others', 11.784 (Peleus to Achilles). For a discussion of the predominance of the competitive values in the code of the Homeric heroes see A.W.H. Adkins, *Merit and Responsibility* (Oxford, 1960), 30-60.

20f. **I will order ... even more:** an allusion to Ulysses' famous address to his heart, in the passage where he represses his anger at the shameless behaviour of the suitors, Hom. *Od.* 20.18, 'Have patience, heart. Once you endured even worse than this ... ' At first we think Ulysses is summoning his heroic endurance to submit to poverty, but in fact 'this' refers to the humiliation, cf. Hor. *Odes.* 3.24.42ff., 'poverty, a great disgrace, bids men both do and put up with anything'. *Od.* 20.18 is one of the few lines of Homer approved by Plato as morally improving (*Resp.* 390d), a fact that adds complex humour to the allusion.

21 **tell me, seer, from where:** the Roman term *augur* replaces the Greek *mantis*.

shovel up: the sense of *ruo* here seems to be close to that of *eruo* (*OLD* s.v. *ruo* 9, Varro, *Ling.* 5.134, *rutrum a ruendo*, the formula *ruta caesa*, explained as *quae eruta sunt* [Ulp. *Dig.* 19.1.17.6]). Perhaps he is being asked (metaphorically) to divine a source of buried treasure, cf. *Sat.* 2.6.10ff., Ar. *Av.* 593 (consultation of a *mantis* in order to find a good mining site).

23-44: Teiresias begins, with an exhortation to persistence, his formal instructions on the art now revealed to us as *captatio*. The first example chosen to illustrate aspects of the art is typically Roman — a law-suit. Why is the topic of legal service developed at such length? One reason is that it suits Ulysses' character, enabling him to use the qualities he has shown at Troy, his skill as a speaker and his endurance (K-H). Another is the centrality of legal service in the exchange of benefits by which relationships of mutual advantage were maintained at Rome (Saller, 29). What identifies Ulysses' prospective performance of this service as *captatio* is the choice of 'friend' to benefit, and the cynical intention behind it. (Cf. Cic. *Off.* 2.65ff., where Cicero outlines the ethics of legal *beneficia*. While based on similar assumptions, Teiresias's advice is diametrically opposed to Cicero's.)

23-6: these lines are a preface to Teiresias's 'lecture' as a whole. Now that Ulysses has shown himself receptive, the prophet makes explicit the mode of operation advocated in 10-17 and reveals that it is 'the art of inheritance-hunting'. The advice to persist in the face of failure warns him that the quarry can be clever too (as in the Nasica-Coranus example [55ff.], and frequently in Martial and Lucian, cf. Champlin 1991, 91).

23 [*equidem*: emphatic *equidem*, as at *Sat.* 2.1.78-9, 2.6.53, see J. Solodow, *The Latin particle quidem* (The American Philological Association, 1978), 104.]
[*captes*: iussive subjunctive, cf. 72, 91, 92. On the colloquial use of second person of subjunctive rather than the imperative, see Woodcock §126.]

23f. **hunt everywhere for ... wills**: this is the first known instance of the fishing metaphor applied to the practice of *captatio*, which is best translated as 'inheritance-hunting' (Champlin 1991, 87-9). *Captare* becomes the standard verb, e.g. Petron. *Sat* 116.6, Sen. *Dial.* 5.34.2, Plin. *Ep.* 2.20.7. The source of this imagery would seem to be its common use for intrigue, Fantham, 39-41 (fowling, hunting and fishing), Mansbach, 15, 36. Horace may have coined the terminology himself (Sallmann, 182 n.2, Champlin 1991, 87).

25 **fisher ... hook**: *insidiator*, like *captator*, is not specific in itself, but is defined by *praeroso ... hamo*, cf. Sen. *Ben.* 4.20.3, *captator est et hamum iacit*. Cf. 44, Lucian, *Timon* 22 and often, 'those others who opened their mouths in vain are left looking at one another and mourning in earnest because such a fine fish has made his escape ... after swallowing quantities of bait', Juv. 12.123 (see Courtney). For taking the bait, cf. Lucian, *Dial. Mort.* 16(6).4; the hook, Pliny *Ep.* 9.30, Mart. 6.63, Lucian, *Dial. Mort.* 17(7).

26 **practice**: in Greek *technê*, cf. Sen. *Ben.* 6.38.4, *qui captandorum testamentorum artem professi sunt*, Lucian *Dial. Mort.* 16(6).3, 'there's never been anything like this art (*technê*) you've invented'.

27-31: the principles to be borne in mind when selecting the 'quarry' to benefit through advocacy. The two parties are systematically opposed, *sine gnatis* corresponding to *domi si gnatus erit* and *improbus ... audax qui vocet in ius* to *fama civem causaque priorem*.

27 **case**: a special meaning of *res*, cf. Hor. *Sat.* 1.9.41, Varro, *Ling.* 7.93.

28 **rich and childless**: both emphatic. The childless (*orbi* and *orbae*) were the most obvious targets of *captatio*, cf. Petron. *Sat.* 116, where no one brings up children in the city in which everyone is either a practiser or victim of inheritance-hunting, Pliny *HN* 14.5, Juv. 12.99ff., Mansbach, 29ff.

29 **summons ... into court**: the technical phrase, cf. Cic. *Leg.* 2.9, *Sat.* 2.1.82-3N.
[*esto*: cf. *Sat.* 2.1.83. The solemn 'legal' imperatives enhance Teiresias's didactic tone, cf. *memento* (52), *laudato* (75), *adito* (88).]

30 **advocate**: or 'pleader', see *defendere* in 34 below. The case is to be manipulated to make the aggressor seem the injured party.
[*fama causaque*: ablatives of cause.]

31   **fruitful wife:** even someone who could still produce an heir is to be avoided, cf. Juv. 5.137-40, 12.94-8.

32-7:   the familiar tone of the suggested utterance is that of intimate friendship; the motivation is not disinterested, however.

32   **let's say:** 'suppose' or 'for example', a prosaic expression, not attested before Horace, but probably already in use in everyday language (Servius on Virg. *Aen.* 2.651), cf. Pers. 4.9, L-H-S II 339, Ruckdeschel, 54. *Puta* in this sense usually has a short final syllable, an echo of its pronunciation in ordinary speech, cf. 75, *Sat.* 2.3.38N.

32f.   **first names:** for the use of the *praenomen* alone as a sign of intimacy, see *Sat.* 2.6.37N. But the point here may be rather that the victim is an ex-slave who had received his *praenomen* on manumission, cf. Pers. 5.78-9.
[*auriculae*: the diminutive is sometimes used for the part of body being focused on, Hanssen, 118.]

33   **friend:** that the word is being given the sense of 'true friend' is shown by the appeal to virtue (cf. Arist. *Eth. Nic.* 1156[b]ff., Cic. *Amic.* 27ff., 28, 'excellence of character excites affection'), and the use of the personal pronouns. Here the flattery consists in the claim that the friendship is a true one, based on the ideals of affection and selfless service. Client and patron also called each other 'friends', when the relationship was based on the expectation of a reciprocal exchange of benefits (Saller, 11-15). This does not mean that the different kinds of friendship were not distinguished (Brunt, 1965).

34   **the law's ambiguity:** cf. *Sat.* 2.2.131. The claim is to have the jurisconsult's knowledge of the law, as well as the ability to speak. Advocates did not have to have technical knowledge of the law, though it helped if they knew enough to twist it (Cic. *De Or.* 1.239f., Fraenkel 1964, 77ff. [Cicero and Trebatius on a juristic controversy], C.J. Classen, *Latomus* 37 [1978], 597-619).

35-7   **pluck out my eyes:** the assurance is strongly expressed with a colloquialism, cf. Plaut. *Men.* 156, *oculum ecfodito per solum/mihi, Menaechme, si ullum verbum faxo, Pseud.* 510, Otto, 250. The *captator* sets his own eyes, his most precious possession (Catull. 14.1), against his friend's worthless nutshell.
make you the poorer: becaue if he lost the case he would have to pay monetary compensation (J.M. Kelly, *Roman Litigation* [Oxford, 1966], 69, 'All judgements were money judgements.'). *Paupero* is an archaic word, found only here in Horace, and not used in Classical prose (Ruckdeschel, 24). It coheres with the colloquial tone of the rest of the sentence, cf. Plaut. *Mil.* 729.
nutshell: an empty nut is proverbially worthless, Plaut. *Mil.* 316, *Pseud.* 371, *inanem quasi cassam nucem*, Otto, 248. [The MSS read *quassa*, which should mean 'broken', 'shattered', cf. *Odes* 1.1.18, 4.8.32, ps-Acro ad loc., if *quassa* comes from *quatio*. The spelling *quassa* seems to have arisen from a false etymology deriving *cassa* from *quatio*, Non. p.45,10, Serv. auct. on Virg. *Aen.* 2.85.]
laughing-stock (lit. 'joke'): another familar expression, cf. Ter. *Eun.* 300, Petron. *Sat.* 57.4.

37f.   **look after his precious hide:** that is, lavish attention on himself. Elsewhere in Horace the phrase is *cutem curare, Epist.* 1.2.29, 1.4.15, cf. Pers. 4.18, Juv. 2.105. *OLD* s.v. *cutis* 1c distinguishes it from *corpus curare* 'to look after bodily needs', giving it the meaning 'to take care of one's appearance'. While the diminutive form does not express contempt here, *pellicula* ('hide') for *cutis* ('skin') has a sarcastic tone, cf. Juv. 10.192, *deformem pro cute pellem*, Ruckdeschel, 14.
[*fi*: a rare imperative, cf. Plaut. *Curc.* 87, *Pers.* 38.]
attorney: a *cognitor* was a representative in court with full powers to act for the principal, who did not have to intervene at all, Cic. *QRosc.* 32, 53, Gai. *Inst.* 4.83, 97, 98.

39-41: Cicero, talking of the conferring of benefits by service (*opera*) further defines it as *virtute et industria* (*Off.* 2.53). So Ulysses must be willing to work hard and to undergo hardships, the hardships to be borne being exemplified by the extremes of heat or cold, as at Virg. *Ecl.* 10.64ff., Tib. 1.4.41-4, Ov. *Ars Am.* 2.231-2.

39 **Stand fast:** there may be an allusion to the juridical use of *stare*, cf. *Sat.* 1.9.39. Advocates stood to plead in court, and physical stamina was required.

endure: the only instance of *obdurare* in Horace, cf. Plaut. *Asin.* 322, Catull. 8.11, 12, 19. It probably belongs to everyday speech (Ruckdeschel, 24).

whether the red Dogstar ... white snow: the banal contrast of mid-summer and mid-winter is enlivened by literary parody. Line 41 at least is adapted from a bad epic poet, Furius (41N, Quint. 8.6.17).

red Dogstar: the star, the Sirius A/B system, is not now red, though in antiquity it was said to be so, see Sen. *QNat.* 1.1.7. It may in fact have changed colour in the last 2,000 years (P.J. Bicknell, *LCM* 12.1 [1987], 10f.). The Dogstar was associated with a period of intense summer heat (the 'dog-days', mid-July to mid-August), cf. Hor. *Odes* 1.17.17, Tib. 1.1.27.

splits unspeaking statues: the expected object of 'splits' would be 'fields', cf. Virg. *G.* 2.353, Tib. 1.7.21. Why are 'unspeaking statues' brought in? It could be a parodic quotation, the point of which has been lost with the original context. (Statues are proverbially silent, Hor. *Epist.* 2.2.83, Otto, 331.) If we look for a meaning that makes sense in this context K-H suggest old wooden statues splitting in the heat (cf. *Sat.* 1.8.45-6), or perhaps there is the idea of the statues around the Forum suffering from the relentless court oratory, cf. Juv. 1.12-3, 40.

swollen with rich tripe: again we do not know if the words are Furius's or Horace's, and whether *omasum* is literal or metaphorical. The word is thought to be Gallic, and could point to the undigested content of Furius's epic, on the Gallic Wars, according to ps.-Acro, cf. Bramble, 64-6, 109.

41 **Furius:** Quint. 8.6.17 quotes the (unattributed) line *Iuppiter hibernas cana nive conspuit Alpeis* as an example of a 'far-fetched' metaphor. The poet is probably the Alpinus parodied at *Sat.* 1.10.36f., *turgidus Alpinus iugulat dum Memnona dumque/diffindit (?) Rheni luteum caput*. The style of both is 'swollen' and they both dealt with the Alps in an historical epic. Porph. and ps.-Acro identify Furius as the neoteric Furius Bibaculus. But he is not otherwise known to have written a bad epic and modern scholarship has tended towards rejecting the identification, see M. Schanz and C. Hosius, *Geschichte der römischen Literatur*⁴ I (Munich, 1935), 163, Fraenkel 1957, 130 n.1, Perret, 40, 43, Rudd 1966, 289 n.52, Bramble, 64 n.1. DuQuesnay, 54-5 suggests that Furius Bibaculus may have written a mock-epic on Caesar's campaign in Gaul.

bespatters (lit. 'spits'): the verb to which Quintilian objected, found only here in poetry. See further Bramble, 64-6.

42-3: advocacy has the further advantage of giving scope for publicity. On litigation in Rome as a public spectacle, see Crook, 33.

long-suffering: cf. *Epist.* 1.7.40, *patientis Ulixei*, like the Greek epithet *polytlas*.

43: [the ellipse of the subjunctive of *esse* is common with the third person.]

44: the return of the fish imagery with the alliteration of *cetaria crescent* in a generalising statement closes off the first topic.

More tunny: tunny are appropriate because they swim in shoals; where there is one there will be more (Hdt. 1.62, Opp. *Hal.* 3.639, Otto, 348). Cf. Lucil. 937W, Lucian *Tim.* 22.

fish-ponds: ponds in which fish were kept for subsequent salting, or according to Curtis, 54 n.42 the salting vats themselves, ps.-Acro, *dicuntur proprie loca, in quibus salsamenta* *fiunt*, Pliny *HN* 9.92, cf. 31.94, 9.49. The image suits the practice of *captatio*, which does not provide instant rewards, cf. *Epist.* 1.1.79.

45-69: with nothing more than the transitional *praeterea* we turn to a second case, the unstated connection of thought being that when there is a natural heir it is better to avoid public display and gross flattery in order to conceal one's intentions: different tactics suit different victims. However, as the case of Nasica and Coranus shows, the *captator* should always beware of being deceived by the testator, and make sure he knows what *his* intentions are.

45 **moreover:** *praeterea* marks the transition in didactic style, cf *Sat.* 1.1.23, 2.8.71, Lucr. 1.120 and often.

far from well: *male* is here an understated (or euphemistic) negative, cf. *Sat.* 2.3.137, 6.87, *Odes* 1.9.24 with N-H, Petron. *Sat.* 87.3, Hofmann[3] §133.

45f. **acknowledged and ... raised:** both words are significant. The Roman father had the right to decide whether new-born children should be reared or exposed, and he exercised the right by 'lifting up' (*tollo*, the technical term) the child from the ground. It was common not to rear sick children (Crook, 108).

opulence: cf. *Sat.* 1.2.8. *praeclaram ... rem* looks like a cliché.

46f. **flagrant servility ... attentive:** there is a contrast between *obsequium* and *officiosus*. The latter belongs to the language of friendship and mutual serviceableness between equals (cf. Cic. *Fam.* 13.56.1), while *obsequium* may involve both verbal flattery (it is the opposite of 'truth' at Ter. *An.* 68, cf. Cic. *Amic.* 89, and 'outspokenness' at Hor. *Epist.* 1.18 1-20) and the performance of servile services, cf. Tib. 1.4.40ff.

a childless man: the unmarried man (*caelebs*), with no children and no likelihood of having them, is the opposite of the man in 31.

48 **worm:** the very rare *adrepere* is used only here in Horace. It is also found at Cic. *Verr.* 3.158 of 'worming one's way into a friendship'. Rudd 1966, 233 suggests 'creep slowly', as if stalking game.

second heir: or *heres substitutus*, the technical designation of a person appointed to become heir in the event of the death of an infant son named as heir, (or in the event of the first instituted heir's not taking the inheritance), cf. Cic. *Fam.* 13.61, Paul. *Dig.* 4.2.17, see Watson 1967, 52ff.

49 **despatch ... to Orcus:** in the context the epic phrase is not only parodic, but ironic. Far from cloaking the cynicism, for those who are in the know the high-sounding phrase underlines the hypocrisy, cf. *Odes* 1.28.10f., *Orco demissum*, Virg. *Aen.* 2.398, *demittimus Orco*, Hom. *Il.* 1.3, 'consign to Hades'. Orcus is here the kingdom of the Dead itself, but may be elsewhere the lord of the kingdom's name (G.P. Shipp, *Glotta* 39 [1961], 154ff.). *Orco*: the dative of end of motion is archaic and grandiose (N-H on *Odes* 1.28.10).

50 **the empty place:** a technical expression, see Gai. *Inst.* 4.13.1, Ulp. *Dig.* 38.9.1 etc.

Very rarely: *perraro* may have a prosaic tone. ·It is used by Cicero in speeches and dialogues and is not found elsewhere in Horace.

51-5: a new precept: the *captator*'s discretion about his aims is to be maintained even to the point of what seems to be success — an invitation to look at the will. To be kept in mind here is the fact that Romans frequently revised their wills (F. Schulz, *Principles of Roman Law* [Oxford, 1936], 156). Showing the will is a gambit in the game being played between the hunter and his quarry. Motives for showing the will, including the testator's wish to win gratitude for favours he plans to confer, and to win the affection of friends and followers, or to maintain power over them, are discussed by Champlin 1989, 211f., 1991, 24-5, cf. Petron. *Sat.* 71, 117.10.

51 [*qui ... cumque*: for the tmesis (not uncommon in Horace) see *Odes* 1.9.14.]

52 **be sure:** cf. *Sat.* 2.4.12N, 89.

tablets: or 'will'. Wax tablets were used for official documents, cf. *Sat.* 2.3.70, A. Berger, *Encyclopedic Dictionary of Roman Law* (Transactions of the American Philosophical Society, 43, Philadelphia, 1953), s.v. *tabulae.*

53   with a sideglance: the ellipse of *oculis* is vulgar, Plaut. *Mil.* 1217, Ter. *Eun.* 601, Varro, *Sat. Men.* 260B, Ruckdeschel, 154.

53f.   second line: 'second' because the first named the testator. Next came the institution of the heir. This, as the most important element of a will, without which nothing else was valid, had to come at the beginning, Berger (cited at 52N) s.v. *heredis institutio.*

page (lit. 'wax'): each leaf of the tablets was called *cera*, cf. Cic. *Verr.* 1.92, *in codicis extrema cera*, Livy 1.24.7, Juv. 4.19 with Courtney ad loc., Gai. *Inst.* 2.104.

55-69:   the anecdote of Nasica and Coranus gains prominence through its central position. Teiresias, through his powers of divination, predicts a piece of Roman scandal contemporary with Horace and his readers. Hence its relevance is not clear to Ulysses at first, and, even after further explanation, it remains obscure. If the point is not that an undetected glance at the will protects against later disappointment, it is hard to see what it is (see B.M.W. Knox, 'Silent Reading in Antiquity', *GRBS* 9 [1968], 421-35, at 428ff., *contra* Rudd 1966, 304 n.18, 'the absence of logical rigour is concealed by the oracular darkness of vv.55-60'). For Ulysses the anecdote is a cautionary tale. For the poet, the epic device of prophecy allows a Roman example to be cited without breaking the fictional framework.

55f.   civil servant: a secretary of the magistrates, cf. *OCD²* s.v. *scribae*, *Sat.* 2.6.36N. It was a position of some standing, since public *scribae* were generally freeborn citizens. For their social status see N. Purcell, 'The *Apparitores*: A Study in Social Mobility', *PBSR* 51 (1983), 125-73, at 155, 'In the later Republic the scribes were respected members of the community who could be recognised as standing on the edge of equestrian status.' See also E. Badian, 'The *Scribae* of the Roman Republic', *Klio* 71 (1989), 582-603.

cooked up: the language of the prophecy is deliberately obscure, in imitation of the well-known ambiguity of ancient oracles. Hence *recoctus* may simply mean 'transformed into a new man' or there may also be an allusion to the magical rejuvenation practised by Medea, cf. Plaut. *Pseud.* 869ff., Cic. *Sen.* 83. These passages show that a mistaken view of the legend, implying successful rejuvenation, was current.

minor magistrate (lit. 'member of a board of five'): from the evidence of Cic. *Ac. Pr.* 2:136 *quinquevir* seems to denote a low rank of public servant, cf. Livy 39.14.10; for a parallel case (Cn. Flavius) see Livy 9.46.3.

will dupe: *deludere* is a word from colloquial speech, at home in comedy, but not entirely avoided by the Augustan poets (Virg. *Aen.* 6.344, 10.642, with Lyne 1989, 132-4), Ruckdeschel, 33.

the raven with its beak gaping open: ready to bite or eat; the bird is the predator. Crows and ravens are proverbial for their greed (Otto, 95, in particular, like vultures, for feeding on corpses, cf. Catull. 108.5, Hor. *Epist.* 1.16.48, Petron. *Sat.* 116.9 [*captatores*], Catull. 68.121-4). In this context *inhians* denotes the gaping of greed, cf. Plaut *Stich.* 605, *tuam hereditatem inhiat*, *Mil.* 715, Cic. *Verr.* II 2.134, *avaritia semper inhiante* (see Rudd 1966, 233). The parallels in Lucian provide an interpretative context, cf. Lucian *Tim.* 22, *Dial. Mort.* 16(6).3, 'gape with greed at other people's property ... as a result you provide a good laugh, if your burial comes before theirs'. See also the characters Voltore, Corbaccio, and Corvino in Jonson's *Volpone*, and *Volpone* 1.2.95-7, '... a fox/Stretched on the earth, with fine delusive sleights,/Mocking a gaping crow?' This refers to the fox's trick of feigning death in order to catch carrion birds when they fly down to peck at it (Opp. *Hal.* 2.105-9, Stith Thompson, *Motif-Index of Folk Literature* [Bloomington, Ind., 1958], K.827.4, K.

Varty, *Reynard the Fox* [Leicester, 1967], 91 and plates 147-50), which suits the Horatian context better than the Aesop fable of the fox and the raven (*Aesopica* 124 Perry).

57   **the hunter:** the first known instance of the noun *captator*, which was to become the standard term for the 'inheritance-hunter', cf. Sen. *Ben.* 4.20.3, Petron. *Sat.* 125.3, 141.1, Juv. 5.98.

Nasica (the *captator*) ... **Coranus** (civil servant): unknown. Unfortunately the names, which sound specific, do not help us to situate the anecdote. Since Nasica has an historic *cognomen*, he might be thought of as an impoverished aristocrat, with Coranus, 'a man from Cora' (a town in Latium), a small-town man of property. Though it purports to reflect contemporary gossip about people who were still alive (Rudd 1966, 134), the anecdote may have been updated from some lost literary or sub-literary context (Lucilius or the mime), or may simply be invented, with the circumstantial detail added for the sake of realism.

58   **Are you raving?:** i.e. speaking under the influence of a prophetic seizure (Cic. *Div.* 1.66). 'Horace reaffirms the speaker's identity in a piece of oracular bombast' (Rudd 1966, 229).

59f.   **O Laertes' son:** the comical bombast continues, and the epic patronymic reminds us of the initial Homeric situation, cf. Hom. *Od.* 5.203, 10.401.

will come to pass or not: an ironic ambiguity. The stronger claim is that what he says will be will be, and what he says will not will not, but the line can also be taken as a truism which promises nothing. It is quite possible, as K-H argue, that there is a further joke in an allusion to the Stoic arguments about fate and prediction, cf. Cic *Fat.* 20 (Chrysippus, *SVF* II 952), a syllogism which includes the premise 'every proposition is either true or false' and concludes 'therefore whatever happens, happens by fate'.

60   **great Apollo:** more Homeric language, cf. Hom. *Il.* 1.72, 'the diviner's gift, which Phoebus Apollo gave him' (of Calchas).

[*donat* : *donare* with the infinitive object is very rare, Hor. *Odes* 1.31.17f., cf. Enn. *Ann.* 15Sk.]

61   **tell me:** or 'pronounce', cf. *Sat.* 2.4.10, 2.7.45. The verb *edere* is appropriate for the utterances of oracles, Ennius *Trag.* 58J, Cic. *Fin.* 5.79, 2.20, cf. Lucr. 1.121.

is getting at: or 'means'. *Sibi velle* is a colloquial expression, cf. Ter. *Haut.* 615, Lucil. 1119W, Sen *Apocol.* 12.1.

if it is allowed: a seer may not always reveal everything, Ap. Rhod. *Argon.* 2.311f., Virg. *Aen.* 3 379f., Lucian, *Men.* 21.

62-9:   the prophecy begins in the high style of oracular epic, dropping suddenly to a more vulgar tone at 65. More specifically, it echoes contemporary panegyric (Doblhofer 1966, 46-51; for oracles, see R.G.M. Nisbet, 'Virgil's Fourth Eclogue: Easterners and Westerners', *BICS* 25 [1978], 59-78). The juxtaposition of an allusion to Octavian, the earliest in the *Satires*, with the trivial, local anecdote is obviously jarring, and the 'compliment' itself is parodic, but this is satire, in which straight panegyric would be out of place. For interpretation see Rudd 1966, 255-57.

62-3   **At that time:** Teiresias refers in vague terms (prophets avoid exact definitions of time, Arist. *Rhet.* 1407b5) to a time far in the future, which can nevertheless be identified as after Actium, perhaps 30 B.C. The pattern 'When A. happens, then B. will happen' is typical of oracles, cf. Hdt. 1.55, 6.77, Ar. *Eq.* 197ff., H.W. Parke and D.E.W. Wormell *The Delphic Oracle* II (Oxford, 1956), xxvii, Rudd 1966, 230.

the youth: Octavian, born 63 B.C. Cf. Virg. *Ecl.* 1.42, *G.* 1.500, Hor. *Odes* 1.2.41 with N-H. The emphasis on his youth is a eulogistic topos, Doblhofer 1966, 46-47, cf. Cic. *Phil.* 5.48, D.E.E. Kleiner, 'Private Portraiture in the Age of Augustus', in Winkes, at 112ff.

dreadful to the Parthians: cf. *Sat.* 2.1.15N, *Epod.* 7.9, *Odes* 1.12.53 with N-H. *Horrendus*, sometimes used of gods and heroes, suits the eulogistic tone. The date must be post-Actian, since before then it was Antony who had been involved in war against the

Parthians, Plut. *Ant.* 37-52. The threat of danger from the Parthians was exaggerated in Augustan propaganda, until the negotiated settlement in 20-19 B.C. Here the reference is suitably vague.

scion descended from high Aeneas: an early instance of the Caesarian mythological programme applied to Octavian, see S. Weinstock, *Divus Julius* (Oxford, 1971), 15ff., 80ff., 183, 254, J.N. Bremmer and N.M. Horsfall, *Roman Myth and Mythography* (*BICS* Suppl. 52, London, 1987), 23-4. The best parallels for the grandiloquent language are from Virgil's *Aeneid*, which is, of course, later, cf. Virg. *Aen.* 1.288, *Iulius, a magno demissum nomen Iulo*, 6.500, *genus alto a sanguine Teucri*. Virg. *G.* 3.35 is from the same period as Hor. *Satires* Book 2.

mighty on land and sea: praise particularly suitable post-Actium, cf. Prop. 2.7.5, '*at magnus Caesar'. sed magnus Caesar in armis.* Augustan propaganda placed the *princeps* in the line of Roman conquering heroes, Virg. *G.* 2.169-72, *Mon. Anc.* 3.13, cf. Appian *BC* 5.130.541f. (a golden statue erected in the forum in 36 B.C. commemorating the restoration of peace on land and sea), Hor. *Epod.* 9.27, *terra marique,* Livy 1.19.3, A. Momigliano, '*Terra marique*', *JRS* 32 (1942), 53-64. *Tellus,* for *terra,* is grand. On the echoes of Alexander-panegyric in the context of universal rule (esp. *magnus*) see V. Buchheit, *Der Anspruch des Dichters in Vergils Georgika* (Darmstadt, 1972), 136 n.579, E.S. Gruen, 'Augustus and the Ideology of War and Peace', in Winkes, at 70, *Odes* 1.12.50-60.

64   **gallant ... stately**:   these epithets ironically keep up the epic tone. For *fortis* of the bridegroom see *Sat.* 2.3.216. Stature is a criterion of beauty for epic heroines, e.g. Nausicaa is 'as tall as Artemis', Hom. *Od.* 6.107, 150-2. If Nasica expects to benefit by Coranus's death, he must have married his young daughter to a man a good deal older (and more decrepit) than himself! Marriage alliances were often made between friends, but here the motive is the inheritance, cf. Champlin 1991, 89-90.

65   **his debt in full**:   for the meaning, 'the sum', 'the whole', cf. Cic. *Rab. Post.* 46. *Soldum* is the colloquial syncopated form of *solidum,* cf. Hor. *Sat.* 1.2.113, Ruckdeschel, 98f. There is no way of telling exactly what this debt is, whether the dowry (but *reddere* ['pay back'] does not suit this), or a debt owed by Nasica to Coranus, or Nasica's debts in general.

66-9: a complete change of style to that of simple narrative, with asyndeton and parataxis.

66   **beg him to read it**:   cf. 51N. In such a situation Nasica's normal assumption would be that he had been named. What is Coranus's motive for showing Nasica the will? He has nothing to lose, and makes a fool of the man who has tried to 'catch' him, Tracy, 402. Nasica would expect the will to have been altered in his favour after the marriage, but discovers he has been left nothing.

68   **in silence**:   cf. Suet. *Aug.* 39, another instance of silent reading in public intended to keep the document's contents private from by-standers, a possible motivation here. Knox (cited at 55-69N) sees no necessity for silent reading here because, by taking the will, Nasica has agreed to read it. Hence he takes *tacitus* as 'by himself', 'in peace', cf. *Sat.* 1.6.123.

69   **nothing ... bequeathed**:   not only has he not been named *heres*, but he and his daughter have not even received legacies they might have expected, the wife the legacy of her dowry, or the debtor a legacy in the form of release of debts (Crook, 123). It was an insult to be omitted from a will in which one could expect to be named, see Champlin 1989, 198ff., 204.

      go to hell: imitating the Greek *klaiein* 'to lament', 'go hang' as at *Sat.* 1.10.91, cf. Ar. *Ach.* 1131.

70-98:   Teiresias develops, through a variety of different cases, the theme of suiting tactics to victims. The prevailing method is flattery (cf. Cic. *Off.* 3.74), and Horace draws on the comic-satiric tradition for details (cf. Juv. 3.41ff., 100-08; see above P.177).

70-2: the case of the senile old man, already under the sway of a concubine or freedman. Why would they welcome an ally? Not because they would not be able to inherit themselves, but because normally in such a case a friend of the testator was co-heir (Champlin 1991, 95, 131ff.). Also each could further the interests of the other, cf. Hor. *Sat.* 1.9.45-7, *haberes/magnum adiutorem, posset qui ferre secundas,/hunc hominem velles si tradere.*

71 **senile:** cf. Cic. *De Or.* 2.75, *deliros senes, Sen.* 36 with Powell's refs. On the rare use of *delirus* in verse see Brink on Hor. *Epist.* 2.2.126.

72 **praise them:** the social mechanism that is being perverted is related to that of the 'recommendation', cf. *Epist.* 1.9.3, Cic. *Fam.* 13 *passim.* The recommendation introduces two friends who could be of mutual benefit to each other; similarly, Cicero is scrupulous about passing on a friend's praise to the (absent) person concerned.

74 **storm:** the metaphorical use of *expugnare* is rare though the image itself is not, cf. Plaut. *Bacch.* 929 (Fantham, 108-9), Ac. *Trag.* 503, Sen. *Nat.* 4a pr. 9, *quo apertior est adulatio ... hoc citius expugnat.* It revivifies the image in *vincit* ('it conquers', 'wins',) and probably affects *caput* ('chief stronghold' ?), cf. Livy 37.18.3, *ad caput arcemque regni ... oppugnandam.*

74-5: [the old colloquial paratactic construction of question and imperative has a conditional sense, Plaut. *As.* 93, Petron. *Sat.* 57.9, Hofmann³ §103.]

maniac: *vecors* is found only here in Horace. The unusual word underlines the insanity of writing poetry, cf. *Sat.* 2.3.22N.

praise it: 'praise' is a characterising activity of the Flatterer, e.g.. Eupolis *Kolakes* 159.9K, Ter. *Eun.* 251, *quidquid dicunt, laudo,* Juv. 3. 41-2, 'If a book's bad, I can't praise it and ask for it', 86 etc., 'Socrates' ap. Stob. *Florileg.* xiv 22, 'Huntsmen hunt hares with hounds, flatterers hunt fools with praises'.

womaniser: the only instance of *scortator* in Horace, cf. Plaut. *Amph.* 287. It is a very blunt term, which is incongruous in Teiresias's mouth.

[*cave:* with iambic shortening, see *Sat.* 2.3.38N.]

76 **hand over:** the flatterer also plays pimp for his 'friend'. See the arrangements made by Gnatho, at Thraso's request, in the last scene of Terence's *Eunuchus* (1053f.), Alciphr. 111.3.8, Plut. *de lib. ed.* 17, *Mor.* 13B; sex and *captatio,* Juv. 1.37-41, Quint. *Declam.* 325, Champlin 1991, 89-90.

Penelope: the name of Ulysses' wife, exemplary for her fidelity (e.g. Prop. 2.9.3ff., 4.5.5-8f.), comes as a shock.

better man: *potior* is used for the rival lover at *Epod.* 15.13, *Odes* 3.9.2, Tib. 1.5.69, cf. Greek *kreittôn.*

77 **she can be procured:** *perduci* is the *mot juste,* cf. Cic. *Verr.* II 5.31, Ov. *Am.* 3.12.11, *perductor* ('pimp') ps.-Asc. on Cic. *Verr.* 1.33. Even more telling is the circumstance that Ulysses is not shocked by the suggestion itself, but rather, amazed that Teiresias thinks it will work (Rudd 1966, 231). After he has spoken to Teiresias the Homeric Odysseus is told by his mother that Penelope is faithful (*Od.* 11.177ff.).

78 **the right track:** a banal phrase, cf. Varro, *Sat. Men.* 174B with Cèbe's parallels, Cic. *Off.* 1.118, Quint. 2.17.29.

79f. **youth:** initially an epic-sounding collective (cf. *Sat.* 2.2.52N, *Epist* 1.2.29), it acquires extra point through the contrast with the '*one* old man' in 81-2.

frugal in giving a lot: Teiresias explains Penelope's fidelity on the grounds of insufficient reward. This cleverly perverts the situation of Hom. *Od.* 18.275ff., where Penelope finally shames the suitors into bringing gifts, by contrasting their behaviour with that of normal suitors, who, she says, bring their own cattle and sheep for the banquets and valuable gifts. Odysseus listens and approves of his wife's cleverness (281-3). The motivation attributed to the suitors is also amusingly twisted.

2   **tasted:** the metaphor anticipates the simile.

3   **greasy hide:** there is a reference to the Greek proverb, 'It's a bad thing to let a dog taste afterbirth (*khorion*)', Theoc. *Id*. 10.11, where the context is falling in love (G. Williams, 'Dogs and Leather', *CR* N.S. 9 [1959], 97ff., Otto, 71). The Latin *corium* means 'hide' but is used for the similar sounding Greek word, which has a different meaning.

4-9:   Teiresias has digressed in order to answer Ulysses' question. Now he resumes his instructions with the advice not to go to extremes (88-9), advice drawn from the anecdote introduced without transition in 84. The anecdote shows that wills, by the imposition of conditions, could be an instrument of revenge and public rebuke, cf. Petron. *Sat*. 141 (the *captatores* have to eat the corpse), Champlin 1989, 205.

4   **When I was old:** 'a boy' in normal circumstances, but we are reminded that Teiresias can look back on his whole life.
at Thebes: because Teiresias was associated with the Theban mythological cycles. The humorous anecdote jars with its setting in the heroic past.

7   [*si posset*: the conditional clause without apodosis indicates intention or purpose (*OLD* s.v. *si* 11). The idiom is that of casual everyday speech.]

8   **too hard:** *nimium* leads into *cautus* ('careful').

9   **fall short in service:** the general rule: the right approach takes the middle path between too little and too much (Horace may be sending up his favourite Peripatetic mean).
[*opera*: cf. Cic. *Fam*. 12.28.3. The ablative is required with *abundes*; with the dative *desum* means 'to fail in a situation', e.g. Cic. *Att*. 3.27.]

10f.:   having delivered the warning against excess, Teiresias now illustrates 'not falling short'. The flatterer judges his behaviour according to the nature of his victim, cf. *Epist*. 1.18.89ff.
will offend: from the general truth, the particular instruction follows.
cantankerous and peevish: a standard view of old men, cf. Arist. *Rhet*. 2.13, 1389^{b}ff., Cic. *Sen*. 65 with Powell's note, adding Cic. *Orat*. 104, Hor. *Odes* 1.9.17-8.
"no" "yes" the punctuation is due to J. Samuelsson, *Eranos* 5 (1900), 1-10, who cites Cic. *Ac. Pr*. 2.104, *aut 'etiam' aut 'non' respondere*, *Nat. D*. 1.70, Virg. *Ecl*. 3.2. For the thought see Cic. *Parad*. 39, *loquitur ad voluntatem*.
Davus: see *Sat*. 2.7.2N.
in the comedy: the advice is to use a slave role in comedy as a model for *acting* a slave role in real life; but Davus may well be a clever slave whose submission is simulated!

12   **with head bent sideways:** a gesture that accompanies silent thought at Pers. 3.80 and is characteristic of slaves at Theogn. 535 (slaves are also typically afraid, cf. *Epist*. 1.16.66). The archaic *obstipum* is glossed as *obliquum* by Verrius Flaccus (Fest. p.193M).
a great look of fear: for the familiar tone of *multum* with *similis* cf. *Epist*. 1.10.3, N-H on *Odes* 1.25.5. [The history of the formulaic *similis* + pres. part. has been traced by A. Traina, '*Laboranti similis*: Storia di un omerismo Virgiliano', *Maia* 21 (1969), 71-8.]

13   [*grassare*: *grassor* is not found elsewhere in Horace, nor in Cicero or Caesar. The extended metaphorical meaning ('go to work', 'proceed', Sall. *Jug*. 64.5), often has the pejorative nuance of a hostile approach. The *grassator* was a footpad.]
servility: in deeds as well as words, cf. Tib. 1.5.61ff.

14   **to cover his dear head:** like an invalid, cf. Theophr. *Char*. 2.10, Cic. *Pis*. 13. Rudd 1966, 234, detects a pun in 'dear'.

14f.   **get him out of the crowd:** cf. Tib. 1.5.63-4, Ov. *Ars Am*. 2.210, *Laus Pisonis*, PLM 1.15.134-6. See *Sat*. 2.6.28 and Juv. 3.243ff. for the difficulties of the unescorted pedestrian.

15   **Cock an attentive ear** (lit. 'pin up', 'tie up'): not just so as to 'prick them' for a moment, but so as 'to adopt an expression of rapt attention' in order to flatter the speaker. Cf. Theophr. *Char*. 2.4.

talkative: another characteristic of old age, Cic. *Sen.* 55, *senectus est natura loquacior.*

96-8 **insatiable lover of praise:** it seems best to interpret this instruction on the model of the preceeding one: if he is talkative, keep on listening, if he wants praise, give him so much that even he will beg you to stop (for this meaning of *importunus* see *Epist.* 2.2.185). Other commentators take *importunus* differently as 'rude', 'overbearing' (Cic. *Rep.* 1.50) and therefore suggest that praise is the way to win over the person most people dislike.

96 **"Steady on!":** an impatient interruption, frequent in comedy, cf. *Sat.* 1.5.12f., Ter. *Ad.* 723, 769, Pers. 1.23.

97 **hands raised:** the gesture adds force to the refusal, and liveliness to the scene Horace depicts. This gesture of prayer is usually taken as expressing amazement, cf. Catull. 53.4 Cic. *Ac. Pr.* 2. 63, *Fam.* 7.5.2, Petron. *Sat.* 40.1, C. Sittl, *Die Gebärden der Griechen und Römer* (Leipzig, 1890), 13, 269. A prayer to stop seems more likely (Orelli ad loc.).
[*urge*: most editors supply *et*, with the codd. det., but the asyndeton is not unusual for Teiresias.]

98: a 'silver' line (abCBA), brings this section to an end (Wilkinson 1985, 216f.).
bladder: the reference is to an inflatable leather bag or bladder. The comparison of men in general to bladders, a proverbial expression of their lack of substance (Petron. *Sat.* 42.4 Otto, 359f.), goes back to Sophron in the fifth century B.C.
hot air (lit. 'inflating talk'): for the active sense of *tumidis* see Virg. *Aen.* 3.357.

98-110: success comes when Ulysses is declared heir, but this does not mean the end of all endeavour. Rather, new opportunities to practise the art are opened up. However, the death makes a good conclusion to the poem.

99 **slavery:** now that it is over it can be given its true name, Cic. *Parad.* 39, *durissimae servitutis.*

100 **sure you're wide awake:** that is, not dreaming.
[*certum*: adverbial accusative, cf. *Sat.* 2.6.27.]
the fourth part: this already gives the good news, since the Lex Falcidia of 40 B.C prescribed that the heir should receive at least a quarter of the total estate (Crook, 124 Watson 1967, 170ff.). An estate was divided into fractions of the whole on a duodecima basis, see S.F. Bonner, *Education in Ancient Rome* (London, 1987), 181ff. Horace avoids the legalisms of the actual will, cf. Iul. *Dig.* 28.6.30, Pliny *Ep.* 5.7.1.
Ulysses: his name is used only at this climactic point.

101f. [*audieris*: future perfect. The last syllable was originally short, but is sometimes found long, cf. *Sat.* 2.2.74, E. Ernout, *Morphologie historique du latin* (Paris, 1953), 218-9.]
And so: the word 'heir' triggers the lament, appropriately introduced by *ergo*, see N-H on *Odes* 1.24.5.
Dama my dear friend: Dama has been transformed into a true friend (cf. *Sat.* 2.1.30).
is no more: 'is nowhere', 'is non-existent', Plaut. *Mil.* 1199, Cic. *Tusc.* 1.11, Prop. 3.13.58, Ov. *Met.* 1.587. Probably an idiomatic euphemism, on which Cicero and Ovid play.
so brave and so loyal: his *virtus* is now commemorated in language which would suit the epitaph of a soldier, epitomising the highest Roman ideals, Livy 21.44.2, D.C. Earl, *The Moral and Political Tradition of Rome* (London, 1967), 19ff. Cf. Petron. *Sat.* 71.12, *pius fortis fidelis* (the epitaph of Trimalchio), E. Wölfflin, *Ausgewählte Schriften* (reprinted Hildesheim, New York, 1977), 260.
[*unde ... fidelem?*: cf. *Sat.* 2.7.116. Supply *petam* or the like.]

103 **throw in:** there is some uncertainty about the meaning of *sparge.* I follow Gow and *OLD* s.v. *spargo* 6b, 'intersperse', cf. Juv. 9.84. Lejay ad loc. rejects the parallel of Virg. *Aen.* 2.98, *spargere voces*, and suggests the verb is used of phrases broken up by long silences. Alternatively it is taken as 'repeating here and there' (K-H, Bo).

weep ... hide: the final duty of the *captator* is to simulate the grief which relatives would feel naturally at a death, cf. Lucil. 790W, Stat. *Silv.* 4.7.38, Publ. Syr. *Sent.* H 19, *heredis fletus sub persona risus est.*

[*illacrimare*: interpretation of the text is uncertain. Many editors take *illacrimare* as the infinitive after *potes.* According to Shackleton Bailey's interpretation, it is the imperative of the deponent. This form is not well supported, the only certain instance being in the Digest. (It is a variant at Cic. *Nat. D.* 3.82.) On the other hand, the sequence of thought is better with the two imperatives coordinated by *et*, followed by an independent explanation.] **it is possible:** the usual interpretation takes *est* as equivalent to *licet* (cf. Greek *esti* with the infinitive), *Epod.* 17.25, *Sat.* 1.2.79, 101 etc., L-H-S II 349.

04-6:   if no specific instructions have been left, the performance of a handsome burial will impress other potential testators, and the *captator* should resist the temptation to stint on the expense, cf. Stat. *Silv.* 4.7.37-40. Great importance was laid on the fulfilment of the wishes of the dead, especially in the matter of burial and commemoration (Champlin 1989, 213ff.).

05   **to your discretion:** the will might specify a third party to decide, cf. *Sat.* 2.3.86N, Scaev. *Dig.* 34.2.40.2, *funerari me arbitrio viri mei volo.* Testators were much more likely to leave detailed instructions about their tomb than their funeral (Champlin 1991, 170-1).

07   **has a bad cough:** the linguistic tone is vulgar. *Male* with a verb is rare in good prose (cf. *Sat.* 1.2.22, Ruckdeschel, 144) and *tussio* occurs only here in Horace. The sentiment is cynical; sickness is a reason for cultivating an old man, Petron. *Sat.* 117.9, Martial 5.39.6 and often.

08   [*sit*: potential subjunctive.]

09   **buyer ... for a song:** in fact Ulysses is instructed to offer it as a gift. A legal gift involved a false sale for a token price (on *mancipatio*, Gai. *Inst.* 1.119-22). The conferring of this benefit would put the recipient under an obligation to make a fit return, just as did the gifts mentioned at 10ff. But now Ulysses would be rich and could perform *beneficia* of property as an aristocrat (Saller, 125-6).

10   **stern Proserpina:** cf. *Odes* 1.28.20, *saeva Proserpina.* The conversation comes to an abrupt end, but not before Teiresias has put Ulysses on the path to riches. The final detail takes us back to the Homeric setting. Proserpina asserts her authority in the same way as she sends and disperses the souls of the women in Homer's Underworld (Hom. *Od.* 11.225f., 385f.). Paradoxically, the reminder of the implacability of death brings us back to reality — death is not just a money-making enterprise (see Orelli ad loc., Lejay, 490f.).
goodbye (lit. 'live long', 'farewell'): the everyday expression, cf. Plaut. *Mil.* 1340, Catull. 11.17, Hor. *Epist.* 1.6.67, Suet. *Aug.* 99.1 (dying words). Anchises' ghost is more formal (Virg. *Aen.* 5.738f.).

Satire Six

at. 2.6 is universally recognised as 'one of the best, perhaps the best' of Horace's satires (Brink 965, 4). For Fraenkel (1957, 144) it was 'uncommonly happy', and he unfavourably compared to the other satires in Book 2 (except 2.1). For this reason it has received far more critical attention than the other satires in this book, again with the exception of 2.1. It is not just the poem's excellence which has provoked discussion, however. Its focus on autobiographical details means that it has become important for what it can tell us about Horace's relationship with Maecenas (here *Sat.* 1.6, *Odes* 3.29 and *Epist.* 1.7 are the other key works, see Introduction §1), and, endlessly fascinatingly, about how Horace makes sense of his life. For it is here for the first time

that he essays an interpretation of his life through the series of oppositions or tensions that are
repeatedly explored in his later works, the *Odes* and the *Epistles*: city/country; political/private;
civic duty/leisured uninvolvement (*otium*); Stoicism/Epicureanism; Maecenas's luxurious
townhouse/the Sabine estate; the world/the individual (E. Doblhofer, 'Horaz und Augustus', *ANRW*
II 31.3 [1981], 1922-86, at 1937, Syndikus 1973, 464). Here it seems best to limit the discussion
by regarding the poem as a) an 'autobiographical' construction of relevance to a particular
historical moment, and b) a satire to be read in the context of the other satires of Book 2.

In 2.6 Horace acknowledges Maecenas's gift of the Sabine estate, a generous gift, the
importance of which, in this poetic account, is not so much in the financial independence i
bestows on the poet as the opportunity it gives him for living as he really wants (cf. *Epist.* 1.14.1,
mihi me reddentis agelli). Life on the farm, somewhat playfully idealised, is the kind of life that
suits him and brings him happiness. To show that he knows this and that he owes it to Maecenas
is to express his gratitude to him (see Brink 1965, 10f., Bond 1985, 68ff.; on 2.6 as an
eucharisticon see DuQuesnay, *Papers of the Leeds Latin Seminar* 3 [1981], at 97-101).

Sat. 2.6 must be read in relation to an earlier satire addressed to Maecenas, 1.6. There Horace
acknowledged the importance of their friendship, and explained his choice of a private life
uninvolved in politics. Maecenas had chosen him as a friend for what he was. He too understand
who he is, and is satisfied with a modest, but comfortable, life of freedom and leisure. The satire
ends with a vividly detailed description of how he lives privately (111-31). The vignette
convincingly realistic as it is, also bears a range of symbolic meanings (see Hudson in Braun
1989, 75-6 on the food). This type of unattached life, which finds pleasure in simple fare and
leisure, can be identified as conventionally Epicurean (Lejay on *Sat.* 1.6.128, Arr. *Epict. Diss.*
3.24.39ff., Armstrong 1986, 277-9) and so the description is as much of an ideal as of a reality
(note the divergent interpretations of Brink 1965, 11, Horace is 'poor and unknown', and
Armstrong 1986, 279, *Sat.* 1.6 describes his 'secure, gentlemanly status').

Seven or eight years later circumstances have changed. In marked contrast with the life
described in *Sat.* 1.6.111-31, Horace can no longer live quietly and 'unnoticed' at Rome. Instead of
taking solitary promenades before dinner, he attends the games with Maecenas or plays ball with
him. Instead of spending quiet mornings at home, he must help a friend in court. In town he no
longer has time for writing and reading. Leisure is to be found only in the country. In Rome
Horace has the duties and obligations of friendship that befit his personal station and are only
partly attributable to his closeness to Maecenas. Though it is essentially a private friendship
Maecenas's political importance has brought Horace too into the public eye. What brings him
personal pleasure also exposes him to the nuisance of petitioners.

In the city he longs for the country. The life of leisure is idealised as the *vita beata*, a life
remote from obligations and cares, in which a simple meal is shared with friends and conversation
turns to the great questions of philosophy (59ff.). This conversation is explicitly philosophical
more so than the satirical moralising of *Sat.* 1.1-3, and seems to point ahead to the *Epistles*
(Fraenkel 1957, 144). Here too, in a passage corresponding to the opening lines of the satire, 'in
front of our eyes, Horace turns himself into a philosophical case — the wise man, content with
little' (Brink 1965, 4). The image is of an Epicurean philosophical retirement and satisfaction with
the simple life (see Barbieri).

We do not know exactly when Maecenas gave Horace the Sabine estate (it must have been
before 31 B.C., cf. *Epod.* 1.25-37, *Sat.* 2.6.53ff.N, Fraenkel 1957, 15, perhaps in 33 B.C.
[Reckford 1959, 200], but see Bradshaw for a sceptical survey of the evidence). There are no
references to it in *Satires* Book 1. In Book 2, 2.3 and 2.7 take the possession of the farm for
granted in a casual way. From 2.6 on the philosophical-ethical values of satisfaction with little
that, in the Epicurean tradition, were associated with the countryside (Diog. Laert. 10.120, Lucr
2.16ff., Barbieri, 491ff.), now belong specifically to the Sabine estate. In 2.6 the simple life it
represents is a personal aspiration jeopardised by the opposing factors in Horace's own life (see

Brink 1965, 11 on the 'moral dialectic'). So a general theme of the satires, criticism of insatiable striving for gain (esp. *Sat.* 1.1), may now be linked inversely to Horace's life through the real farm, in such a way that we are allowed to see the disjunction between ideal and reality. It is only in the later works that the meaning of the farm is fully developed: in the *Odes* and the *Epistles* it is transformed into a poetic and philosophical symbol, while retaining the specificity of a real place (see Nisbet and Hubbard 1970, xx-xxi).

A third of the satire is devoted to the fable told by Cervius, retold to us by Horace. Cervius is a rustic sage like Ofellus, and the fable, the form of popular wisdom *par excellence*, suits his *persona*. His fable also suits its context. Told at a rustic dinner party, it opposes two kinds of life by focusing on two contrasting dinners, the simple and the luxurious, and asks which gives the true Epicurean pleasure, free from care. Humorously balanced between the true to mouse and the human equivalent, the meals have an easily recognisable moral message. The country mouse is Ofellus writ small, usually frugal but generous in hospitality, while the town mouse's luxury comes at the cost of loss of freedom and peace of mind.

Is the message of the fable more pointed? If so, who is the addressee? 'Fables are intended to instruct their listeners by implying that there are analogies between the characters in the story and the listeners themselves' (D.L. Clayman, *Callimachus' Iambi* [Leiden, 1980], 28). The moral of the fable, satisfaction with a modest life (cf. Cody, 107 on *tenuis victus* as 'the integrating ethical abstraction'), takes us back to the hymn to Mercury with which the poem begins and its rejection of dissatisfied yearning for wealth (cf. *Odes* 3.16.42-3). The fable is relevant to Horace's case, but the point of the satire is that he has no simple choice, however much he leans to 'country values'. 'The Town Mouse ... is one aspect of the *persona* Horace is presenting, and the Country Mouse is another ....'(West 1974, 78). These aspects correspond to, while casting a new light upon, the contrasted portraits of himself, as townsman and countryman, in the satire as a whole (Brink 1965, 9).

If the fable invites a moral interpretation, and has hints of a philosophical dimension (it could even be seen as the equivalent of a Platonic myth, Bond 1985, 85), what about the rest of the satire? Modern critics (especially Brink and West) stress that the poem, in spite of its wealth of personal detail, should not be read as straight autobiography. Horace is constructing a 'moral dialectic' using himself as an example. Readers are already familiar with this procedure from Book 1 (e.g. *Sat.*1.3.63ff., 1.4.129ff.). Here he goes further and ironically tries on the role of *sapiens* (the wise man). Most of the other satires in the book present a *sapiens*, and these preachers of *vitae praecepta beatae* are shown wanting for one reason or another. Here the inadequacy is not in the vision of the *vita beata*, but in the gap between it and the opposing circumstances of Horace's life.

A personal monologue, opening on the unusual lyric note of a prayer, an indirect expression of thanks to Maecenas, what kind of satire is 2.6? As striking as the autobiographical focus is the absence, in the context of this book, of any overt didactic purpose — the speaker has nothing to prove — and hence any satiric aggression, for which, in most of the other satires, the didacticism provides the vehicle and the target. However, ancient satire was not defined exclusively by attack and the modern sense of 'satire' is not a good guide to the nature of Horatian *sermo*. Book 1 has its 'unsatiric' satires (esp. *Sat.*1.5) and 2.6 has been described as 'a reversion to the type of Book 1, rambling discourse in his own person' (A. Y. Campbell, *Horace* [London, 1924], 184), though more unified in concept and more artistically controlled. 2.6 perfects the ironic Horatian version of the mode of self-portraiture inherited from Lucilius (see Introduction §3, *Sat.* 2.1.29-34N). The poem is also true to Horatian *sermo* in its style, with its 'fusion of poetic and conversational elements' (Brink 1965, 18), in its emphasis on humour, irony and realism, and also in its generic inclusiveness, combining prayer and fable with anecdote and parodic narrative. The occasional lyric touches and the subtlety with which the main themes are suggested, not stated, seem to foreshadow the *Epistles*.

Fraenkel's doubts (1957, 137) that 2.2 and 2.6 are thematically parallel seem excessively cautious. The theme of both is 'self-sufficient life in the country' compared with city life. In 2.2 a farm has been lost, in 2.6 a farm has been won. In both Horace recounts a countryman's words and wisdom and in both the kind of food eaten in city or country signifies a kind of life. There is a formal correspondence too, in that both are monologues, though of very different kind, 2.2 being a lecture, 2.6 a lyric monologue. Yet the dialogue element is also implicitly present in 2.2 through Horace's presentation of another's views, and in this poem through Horace's own doubleness. Both satires end with the countryman quoted in direct speech.

Formal structure is unimportant in this satire. The opening prayer (1-15) turns out to be an introduction of the semi-detached sort that begins *Sat.*1.1-3. The unexpected swerve from country to city recalls similar shifts of subject in those satires. The following section on the city (16-58: 43 lines) is balanced by the fable (77-117: 41 lines), which is introduced by a shorter passage (59-76) setting the scene in the country (for other analyses see Cody, 104). The satire is built on the antithesis of city and country, expressed as an alternation between them. In the fable the narrative moves from country to city and ends with the country mouse's choice of his former life. We see city life through his eyes just as we have seen the town mouse's reaction to life in the burrow. So in the earlier part of the satire the vision of city and country is mediated by Horace's *persona*: there is no fixed location, no real shift of place and no narrative of event, rather 'both the contrary aspects are aspects of Horace's mind' (Brink 1965, 10). Underlying the pattern of unresolved alternation, however, there is an unobtrusive unifying frame, the progression from morning to evening, through the stages of the day (Lejay, 512-3).

Imitated by Pope as *An Imitation of the Sixth Satire of the Second Book of Horace*

1-15: the satire begins with a prayer to Mercury. Horace's prayers for a small farm have been answered beyond his expectations. Now he has no wish to increase his possessions, having obtained a lot more than he wanted, but he hopes to enjoy them as his own, under the protection of Mercury.

1-3: Horace enumerates the desirable components of a small mixed holding — arable land, well-watered garden (Pliny *HN* 19.60) and a wood (Hor. *Epist.* 1.14.1, Columella, *Rust.* 1.2.3-4). His desires were modest, but their particularity shows that he knows the land (Varro, *Rust.* 1.11.2-12.2). For descriptions of the Sabine estate (which supported five tenant farmers as well as the home-farm with a steward) see *Odes* 3.16.29ff., *Epist.* 1.16.8-14. The remains of a Roman villa near Licenza (NW of Tivoli) might be those of Horace's villa, G. Lugli, *Monumenti Antichi* 31 (1926), cols. 456-598.

For parallels to the thought, see *Epist.* 1.18.104-10 (what does he pray for at Digentia?) and *Odes* 1.31.15-20 (what does the poet pray for? To enjoy what is at hand).

pray for: after Philippi Horace had lost, presumably in the land confiscations, his father's small farm at Venusia (*Sat.* 1.6.71, *Epist.* 2.2.50f.). Fraenkel 1957, 138 n.1 suggests that *hoc erat in votis* was a set phrase, citing Virg. *Aen.* 12.259, *hoc erat, hoc, votis ... quod saepe petivi*. See W.S. Maguiness, *Virgil Aeneis XII* (London, 1953), ad loc.

Note the repetition of *votis* ('prayers') at 59, the beginning of the second half of the poem.

parcel of land: *modus* is the technical term, cf. Plaut. *Aul.* 13, *agri reliquit ei non magnum modum.*

not too big ... little bit of ... : Horace wants to avoid giving the impression that he was seeking riches. Because his desires were appropriate to his status, he can now appreciate what he has. In the course of the poem the profession of moderation in his material ambitions will be integrated with his slender poetic stance (Bramble, 22, Cody, 104ff.). See 14f.N, 117N.

[*ubi*+subj.: characterising as at 102.]

spring: necessary for the kitchen garden as well as for domestic use, running water being more healthy, cf. *Epist.* 1.15.15f. Springs also have sacral character, see Austin on Virg. *Aen.* 2.719.

above them: it is difficult to determine the sense of *super*. For *super* + abl. the meaning 'in addition to', 'besides' is rare (Silius 1.60 is the only [?] parallel) but fits the context well. The local meaning (e.g. *Odes* 3.1.17), which is also unusual and poetic (L-H-S II 281²), has been dismissed as irrelevant (Fraenkel 1957, 138 n.2). However, for the proprietor, the disposition of the farm is as important as its constitution (Varro, *Rust*.1.12.1, *danda opera ut potissimum sub radicibus montis silvestris villam ponit*, 1.6.5, P. Brind'Amour, *REA* 74 [1972], 86-93). See also *tecto vicinus*. The wood would be located on the hills above the fields and the villa. Timber had commercial value (Cato *Agr.* 1.7, 6.3, Columella, *Rust.* 3.3.1-3, Meiggs, 260ff.) and would also be used on the farm, especially as fuel for heating, cf. *Sat.* 2.3.10N, D. West, *Reading Horace* (Edinburgh, 1967), 4ff.

I ask for nothing more: this follows on from 'It was this I used to pray for', bracketing the intervening description.

O son of Maia: Mercury. The matronymic suits the prayer style (*Hom. Hymn to Mercury* 514). Here he is invoked as a bringer of wealth and good fortune (*Hom. Hymn* 529, Aesch. *Eum.* 946 [*hermaia*], Pers. 2.44ff.), but elsewhere there are hints of Horace's special attachment to the god, cf. 15, *utque soles custos, Odes* 2.7.13, 2.17.29f., *Mercurialium custos virorum*, Fraenkel 1957, 141, 163ff., N-H 1970, 127f.

mine for ever: the appropriate response to good fortune bestowed by the gods was to pray for its continuation, cf. Ter. *Eun.* 1048f., Suet. *Aug.* 58.2, 'Having obtained my highest hopes, Fathers of the Senate, what more have I to ask of the immortal gods than that I may retain this same unanimous approval of yours to the end of my life', Fraenkel 1957, 138 n.4. [*faxis*: the archaic form appears in prayers and legal formulae, Cic. *Fam.* 14.3.3, *di faxint*, Hor. *Sat.* 2.3.38N.]

5-15: one long sentence, culminating in the actual prayer (14-15), the whole governed by the prayer formula in which an if-clause justifies the prayer (cf. Chryses' prayer to Apollo at Hom. *Il.* 1.39ff, Hor. *Odes* 3.18.1-8). Here there are three such clauses, 6f., 8f., 13.

5-7: **wealth greater ... smaller**: cf. *Epod.* 1.31-4, *Sat.* 2.3.177f.N, Pl. *Resp*.330b, Fraenkel 1957, 139. The important thing is to be able to recognise what is sufficient for happiness.

3: **make any of these prayers**: for this sense of *veneror* see *Sat.* 2.2.124. Its use with the internal acc. only is rare.

like a fool: the folly is that of not knowing one's own good and hankering after something which, once possessed, gives little satisfaction, cf. *Epist.* 1.1.47.

O if: *o si* introducing a wish is rare, occurring first in Augustan poetry, L-H-S II 331². (For Virg. *Aen.* 8.560ff. see Hom. *Il.* 7.132ff., 11.670ff.) Persius 2.9-12 is modelled on Horace. The 'O' makes the wish more emotional.

9: **that corner ... were added on**: in this case Horace criticises the looking further afield, and also echoes the general disapproval of expanding holdings by adding neighbouring properties, N-H on *Odes* 2.18.23, *Epist.* 2.2.177f., Juv. 14.142, Pliny *Epist.* 3.19.1-2, *sollicitat ipsa pulchritudo iungendi*.

spoils the shape: in this sense *denormo* is only found here.

10-13: Porphyrio tells the fable more fully with the moral drawn: there was no point in enriching a man who, by persevering in the same work, showed himself incapable of living happily after his windfall. The foolish wisher has forgotten the moral, but it is not lost on Horace.

10: **pot full of silver**: Horace mocks the standard prayer for wealth, cf. Hor. *Odes* 1.31.3ff., Petron. *Sat.* 88.8, Juv. 10.22ff.

11   **hired labourer:** wealth improves his status, but not his quality of life, Cic. *Off.* 1.41, Varro *Rust.* 1.17.2, Garnsey, 35-48. The wisher shares the ancient aspiration to respectable landed property. see Treggiari, 1979, 53ff.

12-13 **Hercules:** in Porphyrio's version of the anecdote it is through Hercules' intervention that Mercury shows the man the treasure, cf. Persius 2.10-12. It was the custom to sacrifice a tenth part of one's gains to Hercules, which may indicate that he was thanked for bestowing wealth. Otherwise there is very little evidence of Hercules as a giver of treasure-trove though the scholia show traces of an alternative explanation according to which Hercules appeared in dreams as a sprite (*incubo*) to reveal hidden treasure.

13   **If I am pleased:** the third condition states what the previous two have hinted.
           what I have: cf. *Odes* 3.29.32f., *quod adest memento/componere aequus.*
           [*gratum*: I take this as masc. acc. object of *iuvat*, cf. *Epist.* 1.11.22f., *tu quamcumque deus tibi fortunaverit horam/Grata sume manu*, though it could also be neut. with *quod adest, 'a* thing for which I feel gratitude'.]

14-15: Horace's prayer for Mercury's continued protection alludes to Virg. *Ecl.* 6.4f. (Apollo to the shepherd-poet), *pastorem, Tityre, pinguis/pascere oportet ovis, deductum dicere carmen* ('the shepherd, Tityrus, should pasture fat sheep but recite a fine-spun song') and, through that, to Call. *Aet.* I fr. 1.23-4 Pf. (see Fraenkel 1957, 139). The god's admonition has become a prayer, in which Horace plays with the Callimachean stylistic requirement of 'slenderness', or refinement, while showing the integral connection of his poetic existence and his life (Brink 1963, 159-61, Cody, 103ff., Macleod 1983, 242 n.1).
           fat: has a double sense. Applied to the mind, it means 'thick', 'stupid', cf. *Sat.* 2.2.3N., 1.3.58. Its opposite is *tenuis* 'thin', 'refined', 'subtle', cf. *Sat.* 2.4.9N.

15   **as is your custom:** a prayer formula, cf. Catull. 34.23, *antique ut solita es.*
           be at my side: a standard solemn way of asking for a god's help, Virg. *G.* 1.18, *adsis, O Tegeaee, favens, Aen.* 4.578.
           protector: see 5N. Mercury is appropriate as god of flocks ('Nomios') and fertility in general (cf. Pers. 2.44ff.), but, as inventor of the lyre, he is also a guardian of poets Mercury also spirited Horace away from the battle of Philippi, *Odes* 2.7.13ff. On the significance of his substitution for Callimachus's Apollo see H. Dettmer, *Horace: A Study in Structure* (Hildesheim, 1983), 283ff.

16-39: on his farm Horace would write poetry celebrating his escape from the dangers and inconveniences of Rome, where he is caught up in a disagreeable daily round of obligations and duties, some of which are the result of his friendship with Maecenas.

16   **withdrawn:** cf. *Sat.* 1.6.18, 2.1.71 (in both cases *a vulgo*).
           citadel: *arx* (the fortified high point) introduces the idea of security as well as philosophical distance from the world, *Odes* 2.6.21f. with N-H, Braund, 'City and Country in Roman Satire' in Braund 1989, 40 n.36 on the word's symbolic value. The theme of security in the country recurs in the fable (esp. 117).

17   **celebrate first ... ?:** the question hints at hymnic style (cf. *Odes* 1.12.13, Fraenkel 1957, 140), which is continued in the grandiloquent prayer at 20ff.
           satires: cf. *Sat.* 2.1.1N. These two places provide the only uses of the word in Horace. Here the plural refers to individual satires, there the singular is a generic term indicating content and tone.
           Muse who goes on foot: the paradoxical expression further defines the satires as 'prosaic verse'. *Pedester* (the Latin equivalent of the Callimachean *pesdos*, Call. *Aet.* IV fr.112.9 Pf., 'But I will pass on to the prose pasture of the Muses', Quint. 10.1.81) refers to the prosaic, down-to-earth style of satire and comedy (see *Odes* 2.12.9f., *pedestribus ... historiis* with N-H ad loc., *Ars P.* 95 *sermone pedestri* ['prosaic language'], cf. *Sat.* 1.4.42,

48, *Epist.* 2.1.250f., *sermones ... repentes per humum*, *Ars P.* 229, *humili sermone*), while the Muses are more commonly associated with the elevated genres, cf. *carminis* (22).

18-19:   the whole satire celebrates the blessings of the farm but the first reason for rejoicing in it is the escape it provides from the most disagreeable aspects of life in Rome, now described.

18   **damnable ambition:** the meaning one gives to *ambitio* must be determined by the following description of Horace's life in Rome. Nice confirmation comes from the more specific description of the perils of keeping busy in Rome during the hot weather at *Epist.* 1.7.3-9, esp. 8, *officiosaque sedulitas et opella forensis* ('concern for social duties and legal trivialities'). So here he is talking about the services and obligations the Roman system of personal relationships required, the 'going around' and 'seeing people' in order to promote one's interests. Note that at *Sat.* 1.6.129 Horace's way of life demonstrated his freedom *misera ambitione gravique.* Now he can only escape from it in the countryside, cf. Ovid *Met.* 11.765f., *secretos montes et inambitiosa colebat/rura.*

is the death of me: an expression common in comedy, e.g. Plaut. *Cist.* 686, *Epid.* 57.

leaden Southerly: the Scirocco was most dangerous in autumn, see *Sat.* 2.2.41N, cf. *Odes* 2.14.15f., *per autumnos ...|metuemus austrum* with N-H, *Odes* 3.23.5ff., *pestilentem ... Africum/... pomifero grave tempus anno, Epist.* 1.7.5ff., Celsus, *Med.* 2.1, *autumnus longe periculossisimus.*

leaden: this metaphorical use is unique. It suggests the depressing effect of the excessively hot and humid wind, or perhaps the overcast white sky that accompanies it. The collocation (which may be felt as an oxymoron) is explicated by the following *gravis* ('heavy', 'oppressive', 'unhealthy').

19   **Libitina:** the old Roman goddess of burial. The undertakers' equipment was kept in her temple and hired out for use. Thus she made a profit from burials (Plut. *Quaest. Rom.* 269A, Suet. *Ner.* 39, *pestilentia unius autumni, quo triginta funerum milia in rationem Libitinae venerunt, RE* XIII.1, 113-4, Marquardt, 384).

20-3:   in a lofty parody of prayer style (Norden, 146 n.1) Horace invokes Ianus, the god of beginnings, since he presides over the beginning of his day.

20   **Father of Morning:** the title may simply be jocular (cf. Martial 4.8.12), or it may play on the name of an old Italic fertility goddess, Mater Matuta, who had been assimilated to the Greek goddess of dawn, Leucothea (Cic. *Tusc.* 1.28).

'Ianus': was named first in all prayers in his capacity as the god of beginnings (Varro ap. August. *De civ. D.* 7.9), cf. Cato *Agr.* 134, Cic. *Nat. D.* 2.67, Hor. *Epist.* 1.16.59, *'Iane pater'.* He was also god of the New Year, Ov. *Fast.* 1.63ff. The alternative name is a well-known feature of prayer style (Hor. *Carm. Saec.* 15, Norden, 144ff., G. Appel, *De Romanorum precationibus* [Giessen, 1909], 75ff.). Other features of prayer style are the archaic *unde* (*Odes* 1.12.17, Fraenkel 1957, 139 n.5), the formulaic comment in parenthesis (*Odes* 1.33.10, 2.17.15f.) and the use of *tu* and *esto.*

to be called: this use of *audio* (a Grecism, cf. *akouô, kluô, Epist.* 1.7.38) makes an elegant variation on the standard prayer formula.

22-3   **beginning:** cf. Pindar *Nem.* 2.1-3, Aratus *Ph.* 1-5, Virg. *Ecl.* 3.60, *ab Iove principium Musae,* Hor. *Odes* 1.12.13f. with N-H. The hymnic prelude to a song usually starts from Zeus.

song: as if he were going to write a 'poem'. Elsewhere the satires are not so designated, and here Horace immediately reverts to a more conversational tone, Fraenkel 1957, 140-1.

23-39:   depiction of a way of life through a description of a daily routine is a theme that suits satire's mixture of the personal and ethical. See Cic. *Fam.* 9.20.3, Hor. *Sat.* 1.6.111ff., Martial 4.8, Ausonius *Ephemeris* with A.C. Dionisotti, *JRS* 72 (1982), 124 n.84, Lejay, 513. The theme is fully developed in G. Parini's mock-didactic satire *Il Giorno* (published 1763-1802).

23-4   **you rush me away:** second-person address to the god continues, as he is imagined getting
Horace up early in the morning. Through means of this transition the prayer turns into a
narrative account of Horace's harrassed mornings in Rome, Fraenkel 1957, 140. Cf. *Sat.*
1.6.119f., *non sollicitus mihi quod cras/surgendum sit mane.*

to stand surety: an obligation of friendship. In an action before the *praetor* both parties
needed *sponsores*, who promised to cover the costs should their principal default in any
way, cf. *Epist.* 2.2.67, *hic sponsum vocat, Epist.* 1.16.40-3, *vir bonus est quis? ... quo res
sponsore et quo causae teste tenentur.*

Come on!: the god speaks in familiar tones. *Eia* is frequent in comedy and quite common
in satire, cf. Persius 5.132, *surge, inquit Avaritia, eia/surge!*, Hofmann[3] §32.

[*urge*: a rare intransitive, see L-H-S II 339[2].]

25-6:   Horace expresses the extremities of bad weather in parodic epic style 'hereby mocking his
own misery' (Fraenkel 1957, 141).

25   **North Wind:** often associated with storms or cold weather, cf. *Sat.* 2.8.56, Varro Atacinus
(fr. 6 Morel) = Virg. *G.* 2.404, *frigidus ... Aquilo.*

26   **pulls ... narrower circuit:** a metaphor from chariot racing, applied to the sun's course (Cic.
Arat. Phaen. fr.VII.5, *nam cursu interiore breui convertitur orbe*). As the winter days grow
shorter the circle traversed by the sun becomes smaller. 'Pulls' is the simplest translation
for *trahit*. Other suggestions are 'contracts' or 'drags with difficulty', 'drags out'. For *gyrus*
as the course of a heavenly body see Catull. 66.6.

27-8:   the proceedings before the *praetor* being over, Horace makes his way to Maecenas's grand
house on the Esquiline.

27   **loud and clear:** quoting, as it were, the legal phraseology with which the sponsor was
asked for his promise, cf. Sen. *Apoc.* 1.3, *certa clara*, P.T. Eden ad loc. (Ter. *Hec.* 841, Cic.
Att. 16.13a.2).

do ... harm: because he may have to pay the debt of the defaulter.

one day: *postmodo* should be taken with *obsit*, cf. *Odes* 1.28.30f. with N-H ad loc. These
are the only two examples in Horace. There was a saying well-known in antiquity:
'become a guarantor and disaster is at hand' (*engua, para d'ata, corp. paroem. gr.* CGL II
18).

28   **in the crowd:** we are reminded of the comic 'running slave', who must push through
crowds in the street in order to deliver news, cf. Plaut. *Merc.* 115ff., *aspellito,/detrude,
deturba in via ... et currendum et pugnandum et autem iurigandum est in via.* Vivid
descriptions of the bustling scenes in the narrow, crowded streets of Rome add colour to
city/country contrasts at Hor. *Epist.* 2.2.72ff., Juv. 3.232-67, see Braund in Braund 1989,
36ff.

29-31:   the remonstrations of someone Horace has shoved in his attempt to pass through the
crowd. Even the man in the street enviously sneers at Horace's friendship with Maecenas.

29   [*quid tibi vis*: as transmitted this line is unmetrical. *Quid tibi vis* is an idiomatic phrase
(Ter. *Eun.* 559, Hor. *Sat.* 1.2.69 etc.) which may stand with Bentley's correction of *quas res
agis* to *quam rem agis* (cf. Ter. *Haut.* 749, 942). (The metre may also be restored by
deleting *tibi* or *agis*.) For a more radical solution see Shackleton Bailey 1982, 84.]

32   **This:** the comment is unexpected. It refers to his standing with Maecenas.

32-9:   when Horace gets to the Esquiline, for the morning *salutatio*, he is waylaid by a succession
of messengers and petitioners waiting to catch him there.

32f.   **black Esquiline:** for Maecenas's palace on the Esquiline see *Sat.* 2.3.308N. The
establishment of Maecenas's Gardens (*Horti Maecenatis*) had recently transformed the site
of a cemetery for common people (Hor. *Sat.* 1.8.6-16, Varro *Ling.* 5.25). Gloomy
associations still remain. The main part of the cemetery was in the Campus Esquilinus,
outside the Servian *agger* and the *Porta Esquilina*, not on the hill proper where the *Horti*

were located (Platner-Ashby s.v. *Horti Maecenatis*, Grimal, 143-5, R.C. Häuber, *Kölner Jahrbuch für Vor- und Frühgeschichte* 23 ([1990], 11-107). A gruesome account of modern excavations of this burial ground can be found in Hopkins, 208-10.

34   **surge up**: it is hard to say what metaphor is suggested. It could be a wave crashing and swelling up (K-H), or a pack of scavenging dogs, cf. Juv. 10.218f., *circumsilet ... morborum omne genus.*

[*per caput*: *per* in the sense of *super*, cf. Livy 1.48.7.]

34-38:   the three utterances give examples of the type of thing said to him by people waiting to catch him. It is far less likely that they form part of Horace's own thoughts.

35   **meet him**: Roscius asks Horace to assist him with some official business, the nature of which is unclear. It could be support in court (Schol. ad loc.) but there is also evidence that the *Puteal Libonis* was a place where money lenders transacted business (Cic. *Sest.* 18, Hor. *Epist.* 1.19.8, Pers. 4.49, Platner-Ashby s.v. *Puteal Libonis*, J. Andreau, 'L'espace de la vie financière à Rome', in *L'Urbs*, 162 [*feneratores*]).

the Well: it was the custom to mark spots struck by lightning with a sort of stone well-head. This one was named after a Scribonius Libo who had been given the task of enclosing the spot.

the second hour: cf. Cic. *Quinct.* 25, [Naevius] *ipse suos necessarios ... corrogat, ut ad tabulam Sextiam sibi adsint hora secunda postridie.* In Rome legal and other business began too early for someone like Horace who liked to stay at home until the fourth hour (about 10 a.m. at the equinox, cf. *Sat.* 2.7.33N), cf. *Sat.* 1.6.121ff., *ad quartam iaceo*, *Epist.* 1.17.6f., *si te grata quies et primam somnus in horam delectat.*

35-7:   [*orabat, orabant*: the imperfect tense was used in messages or letters. The time when the message was originated was past in relation to the time when it was received. E.g., Ter. *Eun.* 532f., *Thais maximo te orabat opere ut cras redires.*]

36-7   **Quintus**: Horace is addressed by his *praenomen* (cf. *Sat.* 2.5.32N, where the explanation may be diffferent). *Praenomina* were not normally used for close friends in either Cicero or Catullus, but here the reason may be the intimacy of the *collegium*, the 'closed circle' required by J.N. Adams, *CQ* 28 (1978), 145-66, at 165. J.G.F. Powell, *CQ* 34 (1984), 238-9 admits perplexity.

treasury officials: senior civil servants, often *equites*, see *Sat.* 2.5.56N. Horace is asked to attend a meeting of their guild. After his return from Greece to Rome, following the battle of Philippi (in 42 B.C.), Horace had purchased the post of *scriba quaestorius* ([Suet.] *Vit. Hor.* 1.6-7 Klingner), which he has begun to treat as a sinecure (Fraenkel 1957, 15). It seems that though Horace is no longer involved in the performance of day-to-day duties, the *scribae* wish to preserve their association with him. Hence the message stresses the extraordinary nature of the business to be discussed. We do not know if and when he resigned this post. Reckford 1959, 200, suggests that he did so after he became Maecenas's client, Fraenkel 1957, 15, that it was following the gift of the estate, but Brink (on *Epist.* 2.2.51-2) reads this passage as showing him still in office, and Armstrong 1986, 263ff. points out that the post was purchased for life.

38-9   **Maecenas**: the satire can be dated to late 31-early 30 B.C. Octavian had not yet returned to Italy after the battle of Actium, and Maecenas had been put in charge (Dio Cass. 51.3.5-6) with permission to use a duplicate of Octavian's own signet ring (Pliny *HN* 37.4.10). Maecenas's prominent public role leads to pressure on Horace, who perhaps acted as his private secretary, to use his influence.

39:   a virtuosic line, comprising six verbs.

[*dixeris*: perfect iussive subjunctive, equivalent to the protasis of a condition, cf. *Sat.* 2.7.32, Juv. 3.78.]

40-58: this section appears to be a digression, but puts an apologetic defence of the friendship with Maecenas, now long-standing, now recognised by the gift of the estate, right in the middle of the satire. Under the guise of disarmingly explaining that the nature of his friendship with Maecenas has been misunderstood and that it 'really' gives him no access to secrets of state, Horace lets us see the pleasure he takes in their private and easy intimacy as well as the unavoidable unpopularity it generates, see, in general, DuQuesnay, 24-7. In contrast to *Sat.* 1.6.45ff., where Horace is chosen as a friend for his qualities as a man and a poet and the possibility of a friendship based on mutual interest (cf. Cic. *Amic.* 15), Horace here depicts himself performing the traditional duties of a client, see N. Horsfall, *Ancient Society* (Macquarie) 13.3 (1983), 161-66. The passage should be compared with Ennius *Ann.* 268-286Sk (where the characteristics of the great man's friend, including absolute discretion, are listed straightforwardly. This is possibly a self-portrait of Ennius himself, see O. Skutsch, *Studia Enniana* [London, 1968], 92ff., S.M. Goldberg, *TAPhA*119 [1989], 247-61 at 260: 'Nor is Ennius' companion just an after-hours friend... We are far from casual conversation.', E.S. Gruen, *Studies in Greek Culture and Roman Policy* [Leiden, 1990], 110ff.).

40-2 **The seventh**: Horace refers back to *Sat.* 1.6.54-62, esp. 61f., *iubesque*/*esse in amicorum numero*. There he tells us that Virgil and Varius had suggested a meeting to Maecenas. Nine months later he was invited to become one of the great man's formal circle of friends. The dating cannot be pin-pointed definitely (see Nisbet 1984, 8f., 198 n.26). Seven consular years earlier, by inclusive reckoning, would put the beginning of the friendship early in 37 B.C., when Horace was 27. Then, soon after, in spring 37, Horace accompanied his patron on the journey to Brundisium (*Sat.* 1.5, Broughton *MRR* II 396-8), where Octavian was due to meet Antony. However, this journey may have taken place a year earlier (Rudd 1966, 280-1, n.1, Pelling on Plut. *Ant.* 35). 'Closer to the eighth' means nearer to the end of the seventh year. G.B. Conte, *Memoria dei poeti e sistema letterario* (Turin, 1974), 79 n.4, has noticed the echo of an epic introductory formula, cf. Hom. *Od.* 2.89f., 'Already three years have passed — and a fourth will soon be gone — since ...'

42-3 **when making a journey**: clients were expected to keep their patrons company on shorter or longer journeys within Italy (*Sat.* 1.6.101-3, *Epist.* 1.7.75ff., *Epist.* 1.17.52ff., advice to the client not to complain!) or abroad on official business or military campaigns, see further N. Horsfall, 'Poets and Patron', *Publ. of the Macquarie Ancient History Association* 3 (1981), 1-24, at 2f. Here there may be an allusion to the journey to Brundisium (*Sat.* 1.5).
carriage: a *raeda* was a four-wheeled Celtic travelling wagon, drawn by four horses, and used for long distance travel, cf. *Sat.* 1.5.86, Cic. *Att.*17.1, Balsdon, 213, 'In nature something like a char-à-banc, it might be very smartly ornamented in metal and could be adapted for sleeping.'

43 **entrust small-talk**: 'entrust' is ironic in conjunction with the unimportant topics. The metaphor of safe-keeping continues in *deponuntur* below at 46.

44f.: the expression imitates familiar casualness.
Chicken: a nickname.
the Thracian: Thracians were a kind of gladiator, armed like a Thracian with a curved scimitar, two grieves and a small square shield (see M. Grant, *Gladiators*[2] [London, 1971], 56). Horace is being asked whether he thinks these two gladiators make a good match (*compositio*), the sort of question much discussed at the time. Cicero, however, upbraids Caelius for writing to him from Rome of day-to-day news like *gladiatorum compositiones* (Cic. *Fam.* 2.8.1, Ville, 363) instead of political analysis.
Syrus: a slave name. Thracians could be paired with *murmillones* (Cic. *Phil.* 7.17), identified by their helmets, with the image of a sea-fish for the crest.

45   **are nippy** (lit. 'bite'): this vivid metaphorical use (unusual with this verb in Latin) probably belongs to vulgar speech, cf. Petron. *Sat.* 42.2, *aqua dentes habet*, Hofmann[3] §138.

46   **leaky ear:** Horace suggests that the reason Maecenas doesn't discuss more important matters with him is that he cannot be trusted, cf. *Odes* 1.27.18, *depone tutis auribus*. But this is a smoke-screen as Horace, of course, did observe the client's obligation to preserve confidentiality, cf. *Epist.* 1.18.37f., 67ff., J. Griffin 'Augustus and the Poets: "Caesar qui cogere posset" ', in F. Millar and E. Segal (edd.), *Caesar Augustus. Seven Aspects* (Oxford, 1984), 189-218, at 195f. There may be a reminiscence of a comparison in Terence, *Eun.* 105, *plenus rimarum sum, hac atque illac perfluo* (Fantham, 67), though the subject there is selective rather than comprehensive unreliability.

48   **our friend:** instead of saying 'I', Horace, with assumed humility, speaks of himself in the third person, cf. Plaut. *Rud.* 1245. In a similar colloquial usage, found in comedy, *noster* is used for members of the same household, Plaut. *Amph.* 399, Ruckdeschel, 135, Hofmann[3] §128.

      envy: springing from the same motive as at *Sat.* 1.6.45-52, his friendship with Maecenas, his elevation beyond his status as 'freedman's son'. Here, however, it seems more a cause of pride than concern.

48-9: Horace implies that Maecenas chooses his company for pleasure, especially when he is relaxing (cf. *Sat.* 2.1.71ff., Lucilius is the companion of Scipio's and Laelius's leisure). But these are also occasions on which their being together would be conspicuous.
      [*spectaverat/luserat:* the pluperfect is regular in generalising clauses of repeated action, Woodcock §194. The conditional sentence is paratactic, cf. 38.]

48   **games:** either public shows in the Circus or plays in the theatre. It may be that this point is evidence for Horace's social status (see *Sat.* 2.7.53N), as the knights had sat with the senators in the first fourteen rows of the theatre since 67 B.C. (*Lex Roscia Theatralis*, cf. *Epod.* 4.15f., *Epist.* 1.1.62, E. Rawson, '*Discrimina ordinum*: The *Lex Iulia Theatralis*', *PBSR* 55 [1987], 83-113 = 1991, 508-45, L.R. Taylor, *AJPh* [1925], 163, *TAPhA* [1968], 478. Similar *de facto* arrangements for seating in the Circus may already have existed, Balsdon, 260f., J. Humphrey, *Roman Circuses: Arenas for Chariot Racing* [London, 1986], 77, Hopkins, 17 n.25.)

49   **played:** Maecenas was a keen ball-player, cf. *Sat.* 1.5.48-9, Balsdon, 166.
      Campus: the Campus Martius (Field of Mars), an open meadow on flat land in the bend of the Tiber which young Romans used for athletic and military exercises, cf. *Sat.* 1.6.126, *fugio Campum lusumque trigonem*, Cic. *Fat.* 34, *nec quod in campum descenderim id fuisse causae cur pila luderem*.
      lucky devil (lit. 'Fortune's son'): cf. Petron. *Sat.* 43.7, *plane Fortunae filius*, Otto, 144f. Cf. *Sat.* 1.6.52-4, where Horace denies that his friendship with Maecenas was a matter of chance. Calling him 'lucky' may imply that he is unworthy, cf. Pliny *HN* 2.22, Fortuna is *indignorumque fautrix*, cited by Rudd 1966, 41. Success was ideally owed to a conjunction of worth and fortune, Virg. *Aen.* 12.435-6.

50   **Rostra:** the platform from which the speakers addressed the people. It was named after the beaks of the enemy ships with which it was decorated (after Antium, Livy 8.14.12). After 42 B.C. it had been rebuilt on the NW side of the Forum. A remark made by a speaker travels from the heart of the city to the cross-roads (modern piazzas) in the residential districts.

51   **seeks my opinion:** 'consults' me, as if an oracle or 'voice' of the gods, cf. 52.

52   **gods:** those on high, beyond the reach of ordinary men. The designation involves both flattery and envy, cf. *Epist.* 1.19.43 (*Iovis auribus*).

53   **Dacians:** a Balkan people who lived north of the Danube and threatened the province of Macedonia with savage raids. After having been disappointed with the results of an

embassy to Octavian in 35-4 B.C., they transferred their support to Antony. In 30 or 29 M. Licinius Crassus was sent to Macedonia to deal with these and other barbarian tribes who continued to give trouble, Dio Cass. 51.23-6 with Reinhold ad loc., Virg. *G.* 2.497, Hor. *Odes* 3.6.13ff., *RE* XIII.1 270ff., *The Cambridge Ancient History* X (1934), 116-8.

54   **a joker:** the word *derisor* is rare, and the few instances diverge in meaning. Here it seems to be that he takes nothing seriously, especially his questioner, cf. *Epist.* 1.19.43. The famous ironist Socrates is *derisor omnium* at Sen. *Ben.* 5.6.6.

    drive me mad: usually *ago*, cf. *Sat.* 2.3.135. The strengthened form, *exagito*, here found for the first time in Latin, probably belongs to everyday speech, see *CIL* VI.29471, Sil. 2.296, Juv. 6.29.

55f.:   Horace is questioned about another current topic, land allocation. In the winter 31-30 B.C. troops disbanded after the battle of Actium raised disturbances when they were returned to Italy without having been paid off. Early in 30 B.C. Octavian was forced to come suddenly to Brundisium to organise allocation of land to his veterans, Dio Cass. 51.3-4, *Mon. Anc.* 3.3, 16, 15.3, Suet. *Aug.* 17.3, L.J. Keppie, *Colonisation and Veteran Settlement in Italy, 47-14 B.C.* (London, 1983), 73ff.

    Sicily: *Triquetra* means 'three-cornered' (cf. Greek *Trinakria*). The metrically more convenient designation is first found in Lucr. 1.717, cf. Sil. 5.489, Quint. 1.6.30.

58   **mortal:** mock solemn.

59-76: amidst the distractions of city life Horace longs for the freedom and peace of the country, in particular the simple and relaxed meals he shares with his friends and neighbours, discussing things that really matter. Cf. the elder Cato's dinners with his country neighbours, Cic. *Sen.* 46, Plut. *Cat. Mai.* 25. At 67ff. the wishes merge into description. The dinner party is idealised in several respects: its 'socially egalitarian setting' (D'Arms in Murray 1990, 318f.), the simplicity and unimportance of the food, and the undisguisedly academic nature of the philosophical talk, cf. Plut. *Mor.* 613A-C (on the suitability of philosophical talk at a dinner party), 614A, 'the height of sagacity is to talk philosophy without seeming to do so'.

59   **occupations:** the demands made on his time, as adumbrated in 32ff.

    [*perditur*: the passive of *perdo* is not found in classical Latin, except at Lucr. 2.831, where *disperditur* also falls under suspicion. The argument for retention is the emphasis that comes from the unusual form at the beginning of the line (K-H). Otherwise read Müller's *deperit* (not found of wasting time, Gow ad loc.) or Postgate's *disperit* (cf. Catull. 14.11, with *labores*).]

    with many a prayer: i.e. of this sort, the following. The three prayers beginning with the emphatic 'o' correspond to the three 'if' clauses in the opening paragraph, forming a link and a contrast, Lejay, 515. Also note the anaphora of 'when', expressing yearning.

60   **country estate:** for this meaning of *rus* see Cic. *Rosc. Am.* 133, Hor. *Epod.* 2.3, Stat. *Silv.* 4.5.1.

61-2 **books ...:** the picture is of the mode of life called *otium* ('leisure', e.g. Cic. *Tusc.* 5.105, *quid est enim dulcius otio litterato?*), see Balsdon, 136-44, J.-M. André, *L'otium dans la vie morale et intellectuelle romaine* (Paris, 1966). For Horace the country provides an opportunity for reading or writing (cf. *Sat.* 2.3.9-15, *Epist.* 1.18.109f.) as well as the sleep which was a traditional attraction of country life (Virg. *G.* 2.470, Hor. *Epod.* 2.28, *Epist.* 1.14.35, 2.2.78).

    drink in ... forgetfulness: as if drinking from the fountain of Lethe, cf. *Epod.* 14.1-4, Virg. *Aen.* 6.715, *longa oblivia potant*, Val. Flacc. 4.536, *longae ducentem oblivia poenae.* On the other hand, because of the ablatives (of means?) *somno, inertibus horis* K-H suggest that *ducere* = *adducere* ('induce', 'bring on'). The neuter plural *oblivia* is usual in hexameter poets for *oblivio* (Lucr. 3.828, 1066 etc.).

pleasant: cf. 96. For the Epicurean feeling, cf. Lucr. 2.3, 19, 31. The urbane *iucundus* is excluded from high epic, see Ross, 76ff.

sollicitae: cf. 79.

63   **bean:** our broad bean, a food of the poor, *Sat.* 2.3.182, Martial 10.48.16. Horace is making fun of the tradition that Pythagoreans were forbidden to eat them (Cic. *Div.* 1.62 with Pease, A. Delatte, *Serta Leodiensia* [1930], 33-57, M. Marcovich, *Philologus* 108 [1964], 29-39, W. Burkert, *Lore and Science in Ancient Pythagoreanism* [Camb. Mass., 1972], 183ff.). It was thought that souls of the dead might inhabit beans, as there were resemblances between the bean plant and the human body. The humble food is elevated by the philosophical associations, as the whole dinner becomes a philosophical symposium.

Pythagoras: see *Sat.* 2.4.3N.

64   **greens:** Horace's simple country meal is similar to Ofellus's *standard* fare (*Sat.* 2.2.116f.), vegetables flavoured with bacon, which precluded the need for additional oil (see *Sat.* 2.3.125), Hollis on Ov. *Met.* 8.648, Kenney on *Moretum* 55-8, Martial 5.78.10, Stat. *Silv.* 4.9.34. The diminutive *holuscula* underlines the frugality, cf. Cic. *Att.* 6.1.13, Juv. 11.79, 3.167 (*cenula*), Hanssen, 143.

Here the 'golden line' is humorously inappropriate to the subject matter, cf. 103-4N.

65   **nights and feasts of the gods:** because free from care (ps.-Acro).

[*deum*: the archaising genitive, cf. *Sat.* 2.2.104.]

66f.   **before my own Household God:** not to be dismissed as a cliché, in spite of *Epod.* 2.63-6, *videre ... vernas ... circum renidentes Lares.* Cf. Treggiari 1979, 65, 'these words [the household gods] have a high emotional content .... The shrine of the *lares* means a settled home ... '

homeborn slaves: born and trained in the household (Balsdon, 106f.). They had a reputation for forwardness, (Sen. *de provid.* 1.6, *vernularum licentia*), but could also be useful, Hor. *Epist.* 2.2.6, *verna ministeriis ad nutus aptus eriles*, Nepos. *Att.* 13.4 with Horsfall's note. The slaves were fed from the left-overs, Petron. *Sat.* 67.2.

after making a food-offering: to the Penates (*Sat.* 2.3.176N), in the old country fashion, cf. Hor. *Odes* 3.23.19f., Prop. 3.7.45, Ov. *Fast.* 2.633, *libate dapes.* However, the expression *libatis dapibus* is ambiguous and some commentators take it as 'after we had tasted the feast', cf. Virg. *Aen.* 5.91, Ov. *Am.* 1.4.33-4, *Ars Am.* 1.577.

67ff.   **Just as each one pleases:** see *Sat.* 2.2.123N. The contrast with city conventions is drawn more explicitly here. At a formal drinking-party the president of the feast (*magister bibendi*, see Catull. 27.3 with Fordyce, Hor. *Odes* 1.4.18) prescribed in what proportions the wine and water were to be mixed, and how many cups were to be drunk (the 'laws'), cf. *Odes* 3.19.11-17, Cic. *Verr.* II 5.28. The implication, as at Pl. *Symp.* 176a-e (each is to drink as much as he wishes, and there is to be no compulsion), a passsage which was surely in Horace's mind, is that not all symposiarchs were as sensitive to the principles of decorum as Plutarch's (*Mor.* 620E-F). Horace's guests are capable of regulating their own drinking, an indication of their wisdom.

[*prout*: like *quoad* (*Sat.* 2.3.91) scanned as a monosyllable. It is extremely rare in poetry.]

unequal: varying not in size, but in strength, depending on the amount of water added.

takes: OLD s.v. *capio* 3. Others interpret as 'holds', cf. *Sat.* 1.1.46, Plaut. *Curc.* 110.

70   **grows mellow** (lit. 'becomes damp'): *uvesco* is a rare verb. Its metaphorical meaning (found only here) is derived from that of the adjectives *udus* and *uvidus,* see N-H on *Odes* 1.7.22.

more happily: expresses not just his preference, but also the positive idea of enjoyment promoted by the easy atmosphere. Cf. Pl. *Symp.* 176e, 'for pleasure'.

71   **And so conversation arises:** after-dinner conversation (*sermo* = Greek *leskhê*, the *vox propria*) is enhanced by wine, see Pl. *Symp.* 176a-b, Thill, 147. The talk matches that

prescribed in Varro's satire on the conduct of dinner parties, Varro *Sat. Men.* 337-8B (*Nescis quid vesper serus vehat*): the talk should be beneficial and give pleasure: 'this will happen if we talk about those things which relate to common experience in life about which there is no time to talk when engaged in law or on business'. For the value placed on talk at dinner parties see *Epist.* 1.5.11, Cic. *Fin.* 2.25, Cic. *Sen.* 46, (the Sabine Cato, who delights in talk at city dinner parties) *etiam in Sabinis ... conviviumque vicinorum quotidie compleo; quod ad multam noctem, quam maxime possumus, vario sermone producimus.*

other people's villas: gossip about buying and selling as well as building and renovation (cf. *Sat.* 2.3.308) typifies urban conversation at a time when there was a 'vast amount of luxurious building', see E. Rawson, in M. I. Finley (ed.) *Studies in Roman Property* (Cambridge, 1976), 85-102, at 101-2, Varro, *Rust.* 1.13, *nunc contra villam urbanam ... certant.*

72   **Lepos:** the name means 'Charm' or 'Grace' and seems to be typical for such mime-actors, cf. Suet. *Vesp.* 19.2 (*Favor*). According to ps.-Acro he was a highly-thought of dancer liked by Octavian. The passage indicates the popularity that pantomime gained under Augustus, see Brink on *Epist.* 2.2.124, Balsdon, 274-6.

73   **we discuss:** cf. *Sat.* 1.4.137f., *haec ego mecum/compressis agito labris.* The topics Horace instances are well-known problems of Hellenistic moral philosophy, but the themes of friendship and wealth are also chosen for their relevance to this satire. For a similar summary of ethical questions see *Epist.* 1.18.97-103, in a context reminiscent of *Sat.* 2.6. There, however, Lollius is urged to study philosophy, and here we have a gathering of unsophisticated country neighbours. The context's allusions to Plato's *Symposium* do nothing to attenuate the reader's perception of paradox, which Horace risks arousing by his technical style. For the view that the fable makes this conversation seem natural, see Brink 1965, 7.

74   **virtue:** moral excellence in the technical philosophical sense. But is goodness *by itself* enough to ensure the happy life? This, the Stoic position, is debated in relation to the views of the other schools in Cic. *Tusc. Disp.* 5.

happy: happiness was generally acknowledged as the main goal of life (Arist. *Eth. Nic.* 1095*a*14-*b*14). Where philosophers disagreed was over what it is and how it is achieved. It is unlikely that a philosopher would allow wealth alone to be constitutive of happiness though some held that external goods such as position, health etc. mattered (e.g. Arist. *Eth. Nic.* 1099*a*31-*b*8). Wealth is in the last position in the Academic (4th-3rd cent. B.C.) Crantor's rank order of goods, Sextus *Adv. Math.* 11.51-8, cf. Sen. *de vita beata* 21-6. *Beatus* primarily refers here to spiritual felicity (cf. *Sat.* 2.4.95), though the conjunction with *divitiis* hints at the subordinate sense 'wealthy'. Horace often plays on these two meanings, e.g. *Odes* 2.2.18 with N-H, 2.18.14, 4.9.45ff. (explicitly), Lyne 1989, 5, cf. *Epist.* 1.6.46f., *ergo/si res sola potest facere et servare beatum.*

75   **friendships:** friendship was much discussed in ancient ethics. The seminal treatment is Arist. *Eth. Nic.* Books 8 and 9, then Cic. *Amic.* esp. 26-28, see J.G.F. Powell, *Cicero: Laelius, on Friendship* (Warminster, 1990), Introduction §2. For Horace see W.S. Maguiness, *Hermathena* 51 (1938), 29-48, 52 (1938), 27-46, R.S. Kilpatrick, *The Poetry of Friendship Horace Epistles I* (Edmonton, 1986). An important treatment of friendship in Roman society is Brunt, 1965.

self-interest or rectitude: the question contrasts the opposed theories of the Epicureans and Stoics. Epicurus, while attaching great importance to friendship, had based his theory of it on utilitarianism, cf. Diog. Laert. 10.120, Cic. *Fin.*1.65-70, 2.82, J.M. Rist, *Epicurus An Introduction* (Cambridge, 1972), 127ff., A.A. Long, *Hellenistic Philosophy* (London, 1974), 71f. The Stoics more idealistically maintained that friendship depends on and is produced by virtue (SVF III 625, Cic. *Amic.* 20).

6   **nature of goodness:** it was precisely on the question of the 'highest good' (*summum bonum*) that the philosophical schools of antiquity differed most clearly from each other (Cic. *Fin.* 1.39), a fact exploited by the Sceptics, see the doxography at Cic. *Ac. Pr.* 2.129ff. This is the only place where Horace uses the formula *summum bonum*, cf. Juv. 5.2.

[*eius*: cf. *Sat.* 2.1.70. The genitive singular of the pronoun *is* was avoided by the Augustan poets (Axelson, 70f.; avoidance is already discernible in Ennius's *Annals*), though Lucretius had used it frequently (W. S. Maguiness, 'The Language of Lucretius', in D. R. Dudley [ed.], *Lucretius* [London, 1965], 69-93, at 79 and n.20). Here the prosaic, Lucretian style is appropriate to the subject matter.]

7f.   **Cervius:** a genuine name (Schulze, 243). The country neighbour is portrayed as another Ofellus, both being spokesman for the traditional moral values which survive in the countryside (Ramage, 84).

prattles: *garrire* is used of inconsequential talk or gossip, sometimes with a pejorative nuance (*Sat.* 1.9.13). The word itself belongs to everyday conversation (comedy, satire, Cic. *Att.* 12.1.2, 6.2.10).

old wives' tales: the story takes the place of the reading which provided entertainment at urban dinner parties (e.g. Nep. *Att.* 14.1), but such fables were thought appropriate for women and children, Quint. 1.9.2, Väterlein, 21f. Horace's introduction apologetically acknowledges the tale's triviality (note the diminutive *fabellas*) but the interjected qualification (*ex re*, 'to the point') reminds us that fables and myths can convey important truths, Plato *Rep.* 350 e2f., *Gorgias* 527a5, Apul. *Met.* 4.27, West 1974, 70: 'And those who call this a simple tale have been taken in.' Cf. Gellius *NA* 2.29.1, 'Aesop ... has justly been regarded as a wise man, since he taught what it was salutary to call to mind and to recommend, not in an austere and dictatorial manner, as is the way of philosophers ... '

8f.   [*nam*: the postponement of *nam* and other particles is a neoteric mannerism which begins in Latin in Catullus in imitation of Hellenistic usage, Fordyce on Catull. 23.7, Ross, 67-9, Hor. *Sat.* 2.3.20, 41, 302, *Epist.* 2.1.186, Virg. *Aen.* 1.444, 10.585, Austin on Virg. *Aen.* 1.333 (*et*), 4.33 (*nec*).]

praises: cf. *Sat.* 2.7.22N, *Sat.* 1.1.9ff. The 'praise' is that of *mempsimoiria*, envy of another's circumstances, a favourite theme of popular morality. So the concern with ethics drops to the level appropriate to satire.

Arellius: assumed to be a local wealthy landowner.

troubles: cf. 62, 66N, *Odes* 3.1.48, *divitias operosiores*. Epicurus fr. 478, 479 Us.: 'For many wealth does not bring about the end of their troubles but a change to worse evils', cf. Sen. *Ep.* 17.11.

79-117:   it is interesting to compare the fable with the other extant versions, Aesop 314 Hausrath-Hunger (West 1974, 67), Babrius 108 Perry 1965, Phaedrus *Fabulae Novae* 9 (OCT). The Babrian version is later than Horace, but their similarity raises the question of whether they are linked through an earlier source (K-H). The oppositions which inform the fable (country vs. city, peace of mind vs. anxiety) are, less straightforwardly, the themes of the whole satire, and the contrasting meals, which symbolise the two opposed ways of life, are thematically linked to the occasion, Horace's country *cena*. The town-mouse's parasitical existence (cf. Plaut. *Capt.* 77, parasites compared to mice, *quasi mures semper edimus alienum cibum*, Diog. Laert. 6.40 [mice as parasites of Diogenes], Braund in Braund 1989, 42) also brings in the theme of dependence vs. independence. Cf. Rudd 1966, 246, 'In form the fable is ... two *cenae*, within a *cena*', 251f., Witke, 71ff., West 1974, passim, Langford, 186ff. The character of Cervius is not reflected in the linguistic style of the tale.

79   **Once upon a time:** *olim* begins a traditional tale or adage, Hor. *Sat.* 2.3.253, *Epist.* 1.1.73, Plaut. *Stich.* 539, see also Langford, 203 n.87. West 1974, 70 points out the informal effect of beginning the tale at the beginning of the sixth foot.

80   **they say:** another signal of the traditional tale or myth, cf. *Sat.* 2.3.169ff.N (Serviu
Oppidius), *Odes* 1.7.23, 1.16.13, 3.5.41 (Regulus).
a country mouse entertained a town mouse: the juxtaposition of *rusticus urbanu*
brings to prominence right at the beginning the dominant city/country oposition with whic
the wealth/poverty contrast is aligned.

80-1: the repetitive word patterning has an ambiguous effect. Some take it as the redundancy c
familiar language (K-H, Lejay, Witke, 72n.), but others as poetic sophistication producing
mock-heroic tone, L-H-S II 707[1], West 1974, 150 n.5, Langford, 182.

82   **rough:** the description gradually becomes more apt to countryman than mouse. It is har
to translate all the senses of *asper*: his hard life (Phaedr. 3.7.12, *in silvis asperam vita*
trahens, Virg. *Aen.* 5.730, *aspera cultu*) affects his appearance (unkempt) and his character
(austere).
careful: like the wise, but sometimes ungenerous, *paterfamilias*, Cic. *Quinct.* 11
paterfamilias et prudens et attentus, Hor. *Epist.* 2.1.172, *ut patris attenti*, Ter. *Ad.* 954,
nimium ad rem in senecta attenti sumus, cf. Hor. *Epist.* 1.7.91, *durus ... nimisque attentus*.
[*quaesitis:* dative. The same word is used for the ant's stores at *Sat.* 1.1.38.]

82-3   **relax his tight disposition:** like Ofellus (*Sat.* 2.2.118ff.), he is generous to his guests. I
the Augustan period *artus* ('tight') begins to take over the metaphorical meanings o
angustus ('narrow', 'restricted', 'straitened', cf. *Odes* 3.2.1, *angustam ... pauperiem*). Th
juxtaposition of *artum* with *solveret* brings out the contrast in their literal meanings, Wes
1974, 71.
[*hospitiis:* translated as dative, but it could well be ablative, 'in hospitality'.]

84   [*invidit avenae: invideo* ('begrudge') with the gen. sing. is a unique usage. Quint. 9.3.17
explains the construction as 'Greek', on the model of *phthoneô tini tinos*, but E. Löfsted
Syntactica II (Lund, 1933) 416 sees also the influence of the independent use of th
partitive genitive.]
chickpea: West 1974, 71 shows how it is only in Horace's version that the dietetic detai
shifts from representing what a real mouse might eat to echo as well that of th
anthropomorphic model, the poor farmer. The chickpea (in human terms a food of th
poor, cf. *Sat.* 1.6.115, *Sat.* 2.3.182, *Ars P.* 249) becomes a delicacy.
oat: *avena* is the wild-oat, a weed that infests grain-crops, see Mynors on Virg. *G.*1.154.

85   **bacon:** the *pièce de résistance*, see 64N.

86   **variety:** by imitating a city practice (the subject of Ofellus's criticism, cf. *Sat.* 2.2.71ff.), h
hopes to overcome a city malaise (*fastidia*, *Sat.* 2.2.14).

88   **father of the house:** a periphrasis for 'host', cf. *Sat.* 2.8.7, rather pompous for a mouse.

89   [*esset:* imp. subj. of *edo* (old form), cf. Virg. *G.* 1.151.]
emmer wheat and darnel: to be taken together. Emmer wheat was the grain grown fo
breadmaking and darnel was a rye-grass found as a weed in grain-crops (Mynors on Virg
G. 1.154). After the harvest it was difficult to separate the darnel seeds from the goo
grain. So just as the poor man's bread contained unwholesome darnel seed, the countr
mouse has to eat the mixture.
feast: the poetic singular *daps* probably has an ironically elevated tone here, in keeping
with the pervasive mock-heroic stylistic elements deployed in the fable, cf. Catull. 64.304
79. *Daps* and *dapes* (67, 108) are not used in any other of the *Satires* (cf. Axelson, 106f.).

90ff.   **the townsman said:** the country mouse has brought out his hoarded luxuries, but all th
town mouse can see is poverty. The town mouse's words hint at wider contexts. Just as a
Horace's dinner party, after dinner conversation has turned to the question of 'the happ
life'. In his invitation to come to town the town mouse subscribes to a pseudo-Epicurea
doctrine which justifies his parasitic life of pleasure, and he tries to convert his friend fron
what he sees simply as endurance of a harsh environment (*patientem* hints at *karteria*

['patient endurance'], SVF III 264, for Stoics the virtue that belongs to poverty). See Bond 1985, 84 and West 1974, 74f.

2   **civilisation:** life in the country was often regarded as exile from human civilisation. In Plato's *Phaedrus* (230d) Socrates is not interested in the country because it has nothing to teach him, cf. Cic. *Off.* 3.112, *criminabatur etiam* [M. Pomponius L. Manlium] *quod Titum filium, ... ab hominibus relegasset et ruri habitare iussisset,* cf. *Rosc. Am.* 20, 44, 74. Hence the countryman can be presented as antisocial, cf. Menander *Dyskolos* (Ramage, 67ff.).

wild woods: 'Romans were ... prone to admire well-cultivated land, and to regard mountainous areas as backward and inhospitable', J.G.F. Powell, *Cicero: Laelius, on Friendships* (Warminster, 1990), 110, see J.C. Davies, *G&R* 18 (1971), 152-165.

2   [*vis tu:* cf. *Sat.* 1.9.69, Sulp. ap. Cic. *Fam.* 4.5.4, *visne tu te, Servi, cohibere* ... (a sententious context). This is a regular formula for exhortation or dissuasion, Hofmann[3] §50.]

3   **step out on the road** (lit. 'pluck the road'): the expression is poetically high-flown, cf. Virg. *Aen.* 6.629, *carpe viam* with Austin, Lejay on *Sat.* 1.5.94f., *longum/carpentes iter,* where it is first attested in Latin. Lejay ad loc. explains the concept as progressive accomplishment ('step by step'), not necessarily implying speed.

3-7   **since earthly creatures ...:** the banal moralising is dressed up with poetic expressions: the archaic and poetic word for 'death' (*letum,* 95) belongs to the vocabulary of the *Odes,* Ruckdeschel, 42-3, West 1974, 75; the tmesis of *quocirca,* found only here, has the flavour of older epic, Ennius or Lucretius; *aevi brevis* 'short-lived', cf. *Epist.* 2.1.144, stands for a poetic compound (*aevum* is poetical, Ruckdeschel, 37-8); the pathetic epanalepsis of *vive* may be unparalleled in the *Satires*; it belongs to epic, particularly neoteric epic, cf. Catull. 64.61f., Fordyce, 275, Williams 1968, 705.

The complex of ideas, i.e., the impartiality of death, enjoying the moment, the shortness of life, belongs to the symposiastic context (Alc. 38.1ff. Lobel-Page, Theogn. 973ff., Eur. *Alcestis* 782ff., Hor. *Odes* 1.4, Petron. *Sat.* 34.6-10, 72.2, etc.) and is quite banal, cf. Lucr. 3.912ff. However, the structural correspondence of the mouse's little harangue with the philosophical discussion at Horace's dinner party encourages us to see in it hints of a 'fashionable Pseudo-Epicurean' doctrine (West 1974, 74, Bond 1985, 84, Epicur. fr. 491 Us., Sen. *Ep.* 15.9, *stulta vita ingrata est et trepida: tota in futurum fertur*).

95   **for big or small:** impartiality of death, cf. Hor. *Odes* 1.28.15f., *Odes.* 1.4.13f. (with K-H), 2.18.32ff., *Epist.* 2.2.178f. (*grandia cum parvis*). West 1974, 75 comments on the witty incongruity of philosophy expounded by a mouse in such ambivalent terms.

no escape: another commonplace, cf. Catull. 5.3-6.

my good fellow: 'the philosopher's button-holer' (West 1974, 75), see *Sat.* 2.2.1N.

96   **while you may:** a catch-phrase in these contexts, cf. Ter. *Haut.* 345, *fruare dum licet,* Hor. *Odes* 4.12.26, *nigrorumque memor, dum licet, ignium,* etc.

live a happy life: for the connotations see 74N, 2.4.95.

among pleasant things: cf. 62, in opposition to the hardship of 91. Like *beatus, iucundus* is ambiguous, implying Epicurean pleasure (Lucr. 2.31) or anticipating the luxuries the mouse enjoys, even the 'nice' food (Cic. *Tusc.* 5.97-100), esp. 101ff. Far from being a true follower of Epicurus, he is actually a *philêdonos,* a devotee of the ordinary life of pleasure (Arist. *Eth. Nic.* 1095[b]14-22, Hor. *Odes* 1.1.19-22, *Epist.* 1.6.66).

live mindful: echoed by Persius 5.153, *vive memor leti, fugit hora.*

97   **brief your life-span:** another sententious commonplace, cf. Plaut. *Most.* 725, Sall. *Jug.* 1.1, Hor. *Odes* 2.16.17, *brevi ... aevo* with N-H, *Epist.* 2.1.144, *memorem brevis aevi,* Otto, 375.

97-105:   the description of the journey and arrival (which has a general similarity to Virg. *Aen.*
6.629-38) parodies epic style (Leich, 26f., Cèbe 1966, 304 n.6, West 1974, 76), reading
burlesque when applied to the mice. The epic diction is also undercut by some metric
informality, e.g., the stop at the end of the fifth foot in 98 and the elision in the fifth foot i
102.

97   **These words:** *haec ubi dicta* is an epic formula, (cf. Lucil. 18W, Virg. *Aen.* 1.81 etc.)
usually found in Virgil at the beginning of a line, not after the bucolic diaeresis (word-en
after the fourth dactyl, e.g., 95, 99, 100, 115, cf. Nilsson, 136-8 and table xix).

98   **bounds:** the historic present of narrative. The verb suits the mouse but as West 1974, 7
points out, epic heroes also frequently leap, e.g. Hom. *Il.* 13.140.

99   **the pair carry on to the end of their purposed journey:** cf. Virg. *Aen.* 6.384, *ergo ite*
inceptum peragunt ('they carry on to the end of the journey they had begun'), *Aen.* 8.90
There may be an echo of Ennius in this phrase, Leich, 26f., cf. Norden ad *Aen.* 6.384
Horace perhaps burlesques the epic nocturnal journey of a pair of heroes, e.g. Diomed
and Odysseus in Hom. *Il.* 10, Nisus and Euryalus in Virg. *Aen.* 9 (West 1974, 76).

100   **creep up to:** *repere* and its compounds are properly used of animals. *Subrepere* (which
occurs only here in Horace and is not frequent until after the Augustan period) has bee
chosen for its suitability to the mice, but one also wonders if there is as well a hint o
military attack by night, cf. Luc. 2.506, *mediis subrepit vinea muris.*
[*nocturni*: the adjective used adverbially belongs to poetic style, *Ars P.* 269.]

100f.   **And now ... , when ...:** the inverted temporal clause, a favourite epic construction. Here i
begins after the bucolic diaeresis (cf. 97N), whereas in Virgil it usually begins with the line
Cf. *Sat.* 1.5.20f., *iamque dies aderat, nil cum ... sentimus, Sat.* 1.5.9-10, *iam nox inducere*
terris/umbras, cf. Virg. *Aen.* 3.521-2, *iamque rubescat stellis Aurora fugatis/cum ...*
videmus.

101f.   **plant their footsteps:** mock heroic in tone, cf. Virg. *Aen.* 6.159 (with Norden ad loc), *G*
3.195, used literally of gnats and fleas at Lucr. 3. 388-90. West, 76, thinks 'of th
scuttering of mouse paws'.

102f.   **with rich scarlet:** *coccum* from Greek *kokkos,* cf. English cochineal, first attested here, bu
frequent in Imperial authors (cf. Lyne on *Ciris* 31). The dye was obtained from an insec
(*Coccus ilicis*) which fed on the scarlet-oak, but was thought in ancient times to be a berry
Plin. *HN* 22.3, J. André, *Etude sur les termes de couleur dans la langue latine* (Paris,
1949), 116-7. By using a term new at the time Horace hints that the wealthy owners of the
house are up with the latest exotic fashion (for the association of scarlet and wealth, se
Lucret. 2.35-6, cf. Hor. *Sat.* 2.4.84).
blazed on top of ivory couches: the poetic colour contrast was inherited by the neoterics
from the Hellenistic poets (Kroll on Catull. 61.9, Lyne 1978, 29-30, Catull. 64.48-9 etc.).
canderet: for an explanation of the subjunctive, see 3N. *Candere* usually refers to a
dazzling white, cf. Catull. 64.45, *candet ebur soliis* ('ivory gleams on the thrones'), but here
it means 'to shine', 'be brilliant', cf. Enn. *Trag.* 243, 250, 301J, Cic. *Arat. Progn.* fr.II, André
1949 (cited above), 31-33. Couches inlaid with ivory are another sign of wealth, *Odes*
2.18.1.

103-4:   'Two ["golden lines"] in succession enhance the grandiosity of town mouse's scene of
operations' (Wilkinson 1985, 216). Strictly speaking 103 (aBCAb) is not a 'golden' line,
but the point remains. Note also 105, cf. West 1974, 77.

104   **many ... great:** the repetition of the adjectives conveys an atmosphere of grandeur and
heroic proportions (*magnus* is the traditional heroic epithet). West 1974, 77, compares
Hom. *Il.* 16.776, *keito megas megalôsti, Od.* 24.30 (Achilles), Virg. *Aen.* 10.842, *ingentem*
atque ingenti vulnere victum. Cf. *Sat.* 2.2.39.
dishes: properly a serving dish, *ferculum* came to be used of a 'course'.

105   **baskets:** *canistra* is from Greek *kanastra*. This was a flat round basket, often mentioned
for use in sacrifices or sacrificial feasts, e.g., Tib 1.10.27, Virg. *Aen.* 8.180, commonly used
for serving food, cf. Cic. *Att.* 6.1.13, *in felicatis lancibus et splendidissimis canistris
holusculis nos soles pascere*, Ov. *Met.* 8.675 (Baucis and Philemon).

     piled up: it is usually the tables which are 'piled up' with food for the dinner, Plaut. *Men.*
101, *ita mensas exstruit*, Lucil. 470f.W, Cic. *Pis.* 67, *exstructa mensa non conchyliis aut
piscibus sed multa carne subrancida*. A hint of this usage remains: the tables have been
cleared but the serving dishes left ready for the mice (Lejay ad loc.).

     aside: at a distance, not necessarily far off, cf. *Epist.* 1.7.32.

106ff.:   compare with 83ff.

106   **crimson:** cf. *Sat.* 2.4.84, 2.8.11N.

107   **tucked-up:** the host runs about like a servant, cf. Hor. *Sat.* 2.8.10N, 70, 1.8.23f., Prop.
4.3.62 (*popa*).

     scurries: the frequentative *cursitare* conveys both his activity as server and his gait as
mouse, cf. *Odes* 4.11.9f. (slaves preparing a feast).

108   [*nec non*: connects the two clauses.]

     the duties of a homeborn slave, first licking: *praelambens*, more vivid and more mousy
than *praegustans* (cf. Livy 40.59.8, *oleas quoque praegustasse mures*), may have been
invented for this context. *Verniliter* is also rare, making it difficult to decide on its
meaning. There are two main lines of interpretation:

1) *verniliter* means 'in cheeky slave fashion' and refers to the pilfering habits of slaves, e.g.
Lucil. 629W, *iucundasque puer qui lamberet ore placentas*, Juv. 9.5, cf. *Sat.* 2.4.79.
Against this it has been argued that such behaviour does not suit the urbane host (Rudd
1966, 305 n.4). It may be, however, that the town mouse fails to live up to his unusual role
as host, and that, in contrast to the self-denial of his more upright friend (89) and his own
earlier fastidiousness (87), he cannot restrain his natural impulses (K-H ad loc.), see R.G.
Mayer, *PCPhS* 31 (1985), 33-46 at 38.

2) *verniliter* means 'like a faithful slave' (cf. Caecil. *com.* 131) and refers to the practice of
pretasting food to guard against poisoning. Whether this practice was already well-
established in Rome, or just now becoming fashionable (West 1974, 72), we cannot say.
Augustus did have a *praegustator* (*CIL* VI.9005) who died in A.D. 43 and Pliny *HN* 21.12
reports Antony making use of *praegustatores* at the court of Cleopatra. There is no clear
contemporary occurrence of *praegustare* with this special meaning (though McKeown on
Ov. *Am.* 1.4.33-4 sees a hint of it there).

Orelli ad loc. (followed by Rudd 1966, 246) suggested a compromise which saves the
mouse's manners: he tastes the food beforehand in order to check its quality.

[*ipse*: Lambinus's *ipse* is attractive because it removes the difficulty of explaining what
distinction would be emphasised by 'these very duties'.]

111   **plays the happy guest:** 'plays' not in simulation but in the sense 'fulfils the role', 'shows
himself completely', cf. Cic. *Fam.* 8.17.1, *mirificum civem agis*.

111-15:   the *dénouement* is precipitated by the noise of the double doors being opened and
swinging shut — an impersonal, apocalyptic event beyond the mice's understanding (see
West 1974, 77f. on the aptness of Horace's conception of the catastrophe, Rudd 1966, 246,
on the excellence of this as an ending). Cf *Sat.* 1.2.127ff. (the unexpected return of the
husband), 'nor do I fear that ... the door be broken down, the dog bark, the house re-echo all
round with an almighty din'.

113f.   **They ran:** at this dramatic moment the historic infinitive *currere* (correlated with the
intensifying *trepidare*) begins the sentence, focusing attention on the action, cf. *Sat.* 2.8.35.

114f.   **lofty house:** implies a grand dwelling, cf. *Epod.* 9.3, *sub alta ... domo*, Virg. *G.* 2.461,
foribus domus alta superbis, Hom. *Il.* 6.503, 22.440, *domos hypsêlos* (of Priam's palace).

Molossian hounds: large and fierce. Used as watch-dogs for the house, as here and Aristoph. *Thesm.* 416 (to stop lovers getting in!), or as shepherd-dogs (Arist. *HA* 9.1 [608ᵃ30], Hor. *Epod.* 6.5). They took their name from the Molossians in Epirus in N-W Greece. On the need for watch-dogs in Rome see Courtney on Juv. 6.415.

115-7:   as often, the fable ends with direct speech, cf. *Sat.* 2.3.151ff.N, cf. Aesop: 'You can keep your high living and all these courses. I prefer to live frugally but in freedom and security' (West's translation, 1974, 67). The mouse's last words, authentically Epicurean, are a reply to the town mouse's 'philosophy' at 90ff. They also draw the moral for the whole fable, and point to wider connections with Horace's meditation on his own way of life (see Brink 1965, 13). The poem ends with the end of the fable, without a return to the dinner-party, or the poet's own voice, (Wili, 115), but a sense of closure comes from the element of reflection, the key thematic words *tutus* and *tenuis*, and the 'vigorous colloquialism' of the farewell itself (West 1974, 78).

117   **keep me happy:** to be remembered is the declaration at *Sat.* 1.6.128ff., *haec est vita ... his me consolor, victurum suavius...* Cf. *Odes* 3.29.14ff., *mundaeque parvo sub lare pauperum /cenae ... sollicitam explicuere frontem.* To what extent does the mouse's moral now apply to Horace himself? Cf. Epicurus fr. 207 Us., 'It would be better for you to lie without fear on a bed of straw than be full of anxiety with a golden bed and luxurious table.'
simple: a simple diet symbolises the simple life, the important theme that connects art and life in Horace's construction of himself in his work overall, cf. *Odes* 2.16.13, West 1974, 78, H.J. Mette, *MH* 18 (1961), 136-9, Cody, 107f.
vetch: bitter vetch, *Vicia Ervilia*, a lentil-like legume grown as fodder, Cato *Agr.* 27, Virg. *Ecl.* 3.100, Columella, *Rust.* 2.10.35, André², 38.

Satire Seven

Inventive and amusing, full of lively vignettes and linguistic variety, 2.7 is one of Horace's best satires. The dramatic fiction is of a realistically imagined confrontation between master and slave, but, since the slave attacks his master with his own (borrowed) weapons, the poem can also be read as an ironic examination of the poet's role as moralist, or even, in Evans's words 'our most fully developed Horatian satire on satire itself' (312). In its form it repeats *Sat.* 2.3 in miniature, with the difference that the embedded Stoic lecture is throughout directed at, as well as addressed to, Horace himself. The material and the techniques are also familiar, though never just simply repeated; rather it is a matter of pointed allusion to earlier positions, or the conscious recapitulation of themes in one of Horace's final satires.

The main speaker is Horace's slave Davus, who, posing as *liber amicus,* seizes the opportunity to berate his master presented by the Saturnalian festival, a time when distinctions between master and slave were temporarily elided (see Evans, 310ff., Bernstein, 455ff.). As the satire progresses the initial role reversal of master and slave is seen to complement the main theme of Davus's argument — his demonstration that masters are no better than slaves, or, in this case, since he insists on the comparison, Horace than his slave, Davus. So the general theme is enriched by the counterpoint of legal and moral slavery.

Davus is characterized as a typical slave, loquacious and insolent, and he himself amusingly subscribes to the view of slaves held by the slave-owning class, that they are gluttonous, thieving, sexually coarse and lazy, and kept in line only by the threat of punishment (see C. Stace, 'The Slaves of Plautus', *G&R* 15 [1968], 64-77, Bradley, 26ff.). The relationship between Horace and his slave is reminiscent of the master/slave relationship in comedy, partly because in direct speech hey both use colloquial language familiar to us from comedy (e.g. *ausculto*, 1, 'I listen'; *narra*, 5, speak', 'tell me'; *furcifer*, 2, 'crook'. In this way too, the roles are reversed, since Davus also speaks like Horace, the author of the *Satires*.

Throughout the satire we are reminded of the realities of the slave's position. The relationship between master and slave was maintained by fear (cf. 2, 44), the slave being the possession of a master (3), who could inflict any punishment he chose (Bradley, 119ff.). The satire abounds in references, overt or covert, to slave punishments (22, 31, 47, 66, 71, 105, 118). In short, the slave lacks all rights of self-determination. This, Davus sets out to show, is true also of the 'fool'. The 'fool' is a slave in that being under the sway of feelings and bodily urges, he too is subject to a master and likely to be punished. Thus the ethical doctrine is refracted through the vulgar perspective of the slave who knows what it is to be a slave. Nonetheless we can still discern the moralising import of the argument. Freedom is autonomy, self-control and self-determination: 'autonomy meant freedom not only from the command of others, but also from bodily desires and emotions; freedom from the bodily desires entailed "self-control", the mastery by the rational self of those bodily desires and emotions which threatened to enslave it'. (R. Just, 'Freedom, Slavery and the Female Psyche', in P.A. Cartledge and F.D. Harvey (edd.), *Crux: essays in Greek history presented to G.E.M. de Ste Croix* [London, 1985], 180).

Davus's main target is Horace, but direct criticism of his master does not begin until 22ff., where, under Horace's urging to get to the point, he exposes the inconsistency he sees between Horace's behaviour and the moral ideals he espouses (all familiar from earlier satires). Hinting in passing that Horace's friendship with Maecenas is really subservience (29-42), Davus comes to his main point: if Horace does not have control over his own life, he should not think himself better than his slave. At 46 he begins a more formal harangue, drawing on Stoic doctrine he has picked up from a fellow-slave, Crispinus's door-keeper. Now he tries to prove that in their subservience to their irrational desires for pleasure (sex, art and food) master and slave are no different. Unlike the criticisms raised in 22ff. and 112ff., which do cohere with traits of the *persona* that Horace has constructed in the *Satires*, the accusations of *luxuria* in 46ff. do not match the Horace we know (but see the end of *Sat.* 2.3). For this reason critics have been reluctant to take them as directed at Horace himself.

What sharpens the dilemma is that just as the criticisms become generic and second-hand (the reader recognises typical Stoic doctrine filtered through the door-keeper) Davus begins the more direct and seemingly personal contrast of himself with his master. Some find an escape in the reference to Horace as a knight (see 54N). If it could be shown that Horace was not a knight, we would have external support for regarding the whole list of faults as purely hypothetical. In any case, Davus's vivid depiction of Horace the adulterer turns out to have a more indirect application (see 72N). Similar problems arise with Horace the comic lover (89ff., cf. *Sat.* 1.4.111-14, his father's teachings deter him from both adultery and debased love of a call-girl) and the glutton (103ff.).

Our aim in underlining these contradictions is not to pin down the real Horace but to interpret the gap between the poet as moralist and the moralist as man. The *persona* who speaks the philosophical sermons and exposes the faults of others must have aspirations to good living in order for his perspective to be convincing (a test Davus fails). But here, in an infinite regression of ironic mirrors, Horace lets this mask slip and shows that the real man might be different, simultaneously revealing that this is just another version of 'Horace', as much a fiction as the other. On the one hand, the gap between the preacher and what he preaches, admittedly exaggerated, shows the difficulty of living life according to a consistent set of principles. On the other, as we protest against Davus that our Horace is not like that, we are put in the position of defending the satiric victim in general against doctrinaire moralising.

Davus's thesis on the enslaving passions of love, fear, and greed was held by most ancient ethical systems; what was peculiar to the Stoics was their paradoxical formulation of it. So the main theme of the satire is the Stoic dogma that 'every fool is a slave', i.e. that a man ruled by his passions does not have control over his own life (see Cicero *Paradoxa Stoicorum* 5, Lejay, 541-2, A. Erskine, *The Hellenistic Stoa. Political Thought and Action* [London, 1990], 43-63). This theme emerges at 46ff., attributed to a Stoic source, but it has been anticipated in the introductory section on inconsistency and discontent by a series of allusions to the freedom/slavery antithesis (e.g. 4, 12, 20, 31, 32ff., 38; Rudd 1966, 190). The technique of indirect approach is already familiar from the 'diatribe' satires of Book 1 (1-3, see also *Sat.* 2.3). We are not only misled as to the topic (inconsistency) but also as to the philosophical framework (see 6-20N). Inconsistency is the initial topic of *Sat.* 1.3 (see Fraenkel 1957, 86 and n.4, Rudd 1966, 188ff.); here it is treated as a matter of relevance to Horace himself, foreshadowing its importance in *Epistles* Book 1 (McGann 1969, 12f.; Macleod, on *Ep.*1.1).

In several ways *Sat.* 2.7 recalls *Sat.* 2.3. Both satires are dialogues set at the time of the Saturnalia. In each an associate of Horace tries to enlighten him with second-hand Stoic doctrine, the 'sermon' making up the bulk of the satire. Both conclude with lively passages of direct speech in which the interlocutor makes a personal attack on Horace. However, in contrast to the looser construction of *Sat.* 2.3, *Sat.* 2.7 has an allegorical coherence of character, theme and setting. Equally significant is the juxtaposition with *Sat.* 2.6. Horace and his life are central to both but the satirical caricature drawn here turns upside down the charming self-portrait of the preceding poem.

1   **I've been listening:** listening to what? The poet does not make the initial situation clear and various explanations have been offered (see Palmer ad loc.). Two recent suggestions, that take into account the role reversal of master and slave, are attractive: according to Bond 1978, 85 Davus is repaying Horace 'for some of the verbal punishment which he has had to endure throughout his lifetime as a slave', while for Evans, 309-10, 'Davus, having listened to Horace sermonise for a long period ... now has his chance to play satirist and proceeds to deliver his own diatribe', cf. Juv. 1.1, *semper ego auditor tantum, numquamne reponam*? These interpretations are not incompatible, seeing that people like Davus (and Mulvius) cannot tell the difference between abuse or reprimand and satire. For the opening see Lucian, *Icaromenippus* 1, 'For a long time I have been following you about listening ... '

2   **Is that Davus?:** Horace affects not to know his own slave as well as *he* turns out to know him. Davus's name is important for his characterisation: he is a *servus callidus*, the typical slave of comedy, cf. Menander (in eight plays), Plaut. *Amph.* 365, Ter. *An.* 194, Hor. *Sat.* 1.10.40, 2.5.91, *Ars P.* 237. In comedy slaves could be portrayed as knowing better than their masters, Donatus on Ter. *Eun.* 57ff., cf. *Sat.* 2.3.265.

3   **a bought slave:** the technical term *mancipium*, 'usually confined to cases in which the slave is regarded as a chattel' (Buckland, 8), is in strong contrast with 'friend', the word through which Davus claims the equality only allowed at the time of the Saturnalia.
     honest fellow: the Latin adjective *frugi* (its opposite is *nequam*, 100) is the usual term of praise for a slave, Ter. *Ad.* 959, Cic. *De Or.* 2.248.

4   **too good to live:** cf. *vitalis* ('long-lived') *Sat.* 2.1.61N. Behind this lies a proverbial idea that what is good does not survive long, see Claud. Quadr. fr. 9P, Ov. *Am.* 2.6.39, Martial 6.29, Sen. *Controv.* 1.1.22, Otto, 375. Davus may be parodying the description of the slave-dealer who had to specify faults when he put a slave up for sale, cf. *Epist.* 2.2.16 with Brink's note.
     December's freedom: the setting is the Saturnalia (cf. *Sat.* 2.3.4-5), a festival celebrated publicly on 17 December and privately, in the late Republic, for seven days, with much feasting, drinking and merriment, see Scullard, 205-7, Balsdon, 124f. It was a time of freedom from normal restraints, especially for slaves, who temporarily became the equals of their masters. 'During the Saturnalia slaves are given every license' (Macrob. *Sat.* 1.7.26,

cf. Pliny *Ep.* 2.17.24, D'Arms in Slater 1991, 176). Here the freedom is that of speech, the satirist's prerogative, cf. *Sat.* 1.4.5, 103, 132 (A.K. Michels, *CPh* 39 [1944], 173-77; N. Rudd, *Mnemosyne* 10 [1957], 319-38, at 325ff.).

6-20: Davus's first speech is chiastic in structure (see Rudd 1966, 189). First a generalisation divides the world into two kinds of people, those who stick to a vice they are decided on, and those who swing between good principles and bad behaviour. The two kinds are illustrated by examples: Priscus (8ff.) is inconsistent, Volanerius (15ff.) intent on gambling. A *sententia* or maxim (18-19) draws the conclusion that consistency, even in vice, is preferable, bringing home the point by a proverbial example (20). Davus uses Horace's favourite technique of opposing pairs of individuals to put his master in a bad light (cf. *Sat.* 1.2.23-30, Introduction §4). Davus's philosophical orientation is not yet revealed as Stoic, nor is the wise man's consistency (*aequabilitas*) positively adduced, see Cic. *Tusc.* 4.55, Fraenkel 1957, 86 n.4. Here the contrast is the Peripatetic one between the deliberately self-indulgent man (*akolastos*) and the one who is deficient in self-restraint (*akratês*), see Arist. *Eth. Nic.* 1146^{b}22ff.: 'the one is led on in accordance with his own choice, thinking that he ought always to pursue the present pleasure; while the other does not think so, yet pursues it.' (Transl. Ross) People deficient in self-restraint are capable of knowing and choosing the good (*Eth. Nic.* 1148^{a}1-10) but can be overcome by desires or passions. Aristotle tends to restrict the dispositions of self-restraint and temperance to bodily desires and pleasures, a point Davus does not well illustrate with his examples, though the main topics of his lecture (46ff.), sex and food, fit better.

6 **Some people ... the majority:** Davus's introductory formula immediately strikes the sententious note of the diatribe-style. For *pars hominum* see Lucil. 186-7W, Hor. *Sat.* 1.1.61, *Epist.* 1.1.77.

7ff. **their chosen course:** with an ironic reference to *propositum* as a philosophical term: 'it implies the deliberate adoption of certain principles of life and the deliberate choice in each action of what is in accordance with those principles' (F.H. Colson *CQ* 20 [1926], 101-2 on *Odes* 3.3.1).

waver (lit. 'swim'): or 'are at sea', cf. Varro, *Ling.* 8.74, Sen. *Ep.* 35.4, *mutatio voluntatis indicat animum natare.* The nautical metaphor may be continued in *capessens* ('holding the right course', cf. Virg. *Aen.* 4.346, 5.703) and *obnoxia,* though the latter also brings in the idea of slavish subservience, cf. Plaut. *Truc.* 835, Livy 23.12.9.

right ... wrong: for the neuters of the moralising discourse see *Sat.* 2.2.6N.

8f. **Priscus:** unknown and very likely unreal; his name, meaning 'old-fashioned', is belied by his behaviour. Presumably because of the past tense *vixit,* Rudd 1966, 138-9 classes him among those known to be dead.

noticed: in a critical way, with the eye of censure, cf. *Sat.* 1.6.14.

sporting three rings: see 53N. He swings between the opposite extremes of too much and too little. At this period one ring was normal, and three would have been considered excessive (Isid. *Orig.* 19.32.4 records contemporary criticism of the immensely wealthy Crassus for wearing more than one).

10 **change his stripe:** in the context of the other examples this probably means no more than that he simply changed his dress; a change of stripe could indicate a change of aim in life but whether multiple changes were allowed under Augustus is doubtful. For example, Ovid (*Tr.* 4.10.29-30, 35-6) changed from the broad to the narrow stripe when he decided to give up public life. The width of the stripe of the tunic was an indication of status: it was narrow for knights, wider for senators (cf. *Sat.* 1.5.36, 1.6.25, 28) and young men of equestrian status wishing to enter the senate through the quaestorship (see L.M. Wilson, *The Clothing of the Ancient Romans* [Baltimore, 1938], 63).

13   **a man of learning at Athens:** the contrast is between two antithetical styles of life, that of
the dissolute lover and that of the philosopher (cf. Prop. 3.21.1-2 with Fedeli's notes). Hor.
Epist. 2.2.81ff. illuminates the contrast implied here between a fast life in the capital of the
world and philosophical retirement. Some MSS read *doctor* ('a teacher'); Lejay (551)
argues in support of this reading that if Priscus had set himself up as a moral authority the
criticism would be more forceful, but it was hardly normal for a Roman to teach in Athens,
while many members of the Roman élite went there to study, see Rawson 1985, 10-11.

14   **all the Vertumni:** either hyperbole (cf. Catull. 3.1-2) or as if referring to the god's multiple
manifestations. Priscus owes his characteristic mutability to the god of change, but, since it
does him no good, it must be a result of the god's displeasure. Vertumnus, Etruscan in
origin, presides over change or metamorphosis, see Prop. 4.2, Ov. *Met.* 14.623ff.
Propertius derives the god's name from his versatility, associating it with *vertere* ('to turn').
Vertumnis ... natus iniquis ('born with the Vertumni against him') is modelled on the
proverbial formula *dis iratis natus* ('born under angry gods'), cf. *Sat.* 1.5.97-8, 2.3.8, Otto
110, Ruckdeschel, 163. (The phrase *dis iniquis* is found in inscriptions, e.g., CIL
XIV.2055.10, VI.10192, cf. Virg. *Aen.* 5.809.)

15   **Volanerius, the play-boy:** Volanerius appears to be the *scurra* who has come down in the
world (cf. *Epist.* 1.18.21). Like Maenius in *Epist.*1.15.26ff., he has wasted his fortune in
high-living and now scrapes by in a moral and social underworld in which amusement and
pleasure are the main business of life. The *scurra* in Horace has the characteristics of the
Greek parasite — buffoonery, excessively cruel and irresponsible wit, flattery and poverty
(see Maenius in *Epist.* 1.15.26ff., *Sat.* 1.3.21ff., and the distinction at *Epist.* 1.18.1-4
between the friend and the unfaithful *scurra*), cf. Cic. *Quinct.* 55, Lejay, 551ff., P.E.
Corbett, *Eranos* 16 (1968), 118f., *The Scurra* (Edinburgh, 1986), 58-69, Wiseman 1987,
276. Volanerius himself is unknown. The name, which is rare, may be of Etruscan origin
(Schulze, 148 n.1).

           gout: Horace uses a medical term (from Greek *cheiragra*) which means 'pain or gout in the
hands'. The words *podagra* and *cheragra* do not receive the proper meaning of 'gout' (due
to over-indulgence in food and drink) until the first century A.D. (W.G. Spencer, *Celsus De
Medicina* I [London and Cambridge, Mass., 1950], 463-5). The implication is that
Volanerius's 'gout' is an appropriate punishment for his vice, in which he nevertheless
persists after becoming incapacitated. In Seneca's *Apolocyntosis*, the emperor Claudius,
also addicted to gambling, is made to play in the underworld with a dice-box with no
bottom (12, 15).

17   **by the day:** because he could not afford the upkeep of a slave.
           dice-box: a Greek word is used, in keeping with the Greek origin of such games.
Theoretically gambling was illegal, *Odes* 3.24.58, Balsdon, 154, Griffin, 13-14.

19f.   **comes out ahead of him:** or 'is better than'. The incontinent person, in whom Horace is
meant to recognise himself, suffers more from pangs of conscience, but is curable because
he can be persuaded to change (see 23ff.). To say that Volanerius's sort of consistency is
'better' is philosophical nonsense, as Horace is quick to point out ('rot'), cf. Stahl, 46. But it
was a view raised, if not endorsed, at Arist. *Eth. Nic.* 1146*31ff., 'a man who by conviction
acts badly or pursues pleasurable things or deliberately chooses them would be thought to
be better than a man who does any of these things not through judgement but through
incontinence'. (Trans. Apostle) Cf. Arist. *Eth. Nic.* 1150ᵇ31ff.
           slogs: *laborat* combines the ideas of working and being in distress, cf. Lucr. 3.733, 5.1430
etc., Hor. *Sat.* 1.4.26.
           with the rope now taut, now slack: the exact reference of the image is obscure
(commentators prefer the idea of the animal on a tow rope pulling a barge, *Sat.* 1.5.18), but
the meaning seems to be: you will still suffer even under the antithetical circumstances,

because you cannot achieve an even tenor (cf. the naval term 'take an even strain'), cf. *Epist.* 1.10.48, Pers. 5.118, Sen. *Dial.* 10.16.3, 'the man who is not yet free drags a loose chain.' Bond 1978, 86 seeks to add point by interpreting the image according to Stoic theories of tension in the soul. The right tension is a concomitant of virtue, the relaxed soul falls into chaos.

21   **Won't you tell me:** similar moves herald a change in direction at about this point in the satire at *Sat.* 1.2.23 and 1.3.19-20. The technique of indirect approach is already familiar from the 'diatribe' satires of Book 1 (1-3, see also *Sat.* 2.3). The snatch of dialogue is 'realistic', that is, it uses colloquialisms and expressions familiar to us from Roman Comedy.
[**hodie:** with intensifying rather than temporal force is frequent in Plautus and Terence, but is not found elsewhere in Horace, see Ruckdeschel, 73, Austin on Virg. *Aen.* 2.670.]

22   **you crook:** cf. 66, 91-4. *Furcifer* (lit. 'bearer of the fork'), also found only here in Horace, is a term of abuse frequent in comedy, especially for slaves, see Ruckdeschel, 66. It refers to the slave's punishment by which a forked frame was put on the man's neck and his arms were fastened to the projecting ends.
At you, I say again: *inquam* adds emphasis to the personal pronoun 'you', cf. Plaut. *Men.* 651, 653, Cic. *Quinct.* 37, *TLL* VII.1 1784.63, and implies that 'him' in 19 was meant to be taken as a reference to Horace. It is a technique of the diatribe-style to bring home the general point by switching to the second person, cf. *Sat.* 1.1.69.

22-7:   the criticism of Horace, that he knows what is right but will not or cannot reform, is more pointed than an accusation of *mempsimoiria* or wanting what one does not have, which is what *laudas* seems to be about to introduce. In ancient moralising inconsistency was linked to discontent with one's lot, manifested as envy of the lives of others. It is inconsistent to yearn after another way of life but not be willing to change, cf. Hor. *Odes* 1.1.17f., *Epist.* 1.1, 1.7.78ff., and above all *Sat.* 1.1.1-19 (with Lucr. 3.1066-75, Fraenkel 1957, 90ff., Rudd 1966, 20ff., M. Dyson, *CQ* 30 [1980], 133-39). Davus shows that Horace fails to live up to the ethical teachings of his own satires, though, as he says at *Sat.* 1.1.19, 'it is possible to be happy'. As the paragraph proceeds his instability is shown to be the consequence of a lack of independence (*autarkeia*).

23   **of the people of old:** as in *Sat.* 2.2 (esp. 89ff.) and 2.6.

24   **if some god:** as at *Sat.* 1.1.15, Cic. *Sen.* 83. Horace's own use of a device of diatribe-style is turned against him.

25   **what's right:** *rectum* ('virtue', 'the good') is a term of ethical discussion, see 7, 25, 112, cf. Cic. *Nat. D.* 1.36, Hor. *Sat.* 2.6.75.

27   **pluck the sole of your foot out of the mire:** proverbial, see Barsby on Plaut. *Bacch.* 384, Otto, 201f.

28   **At Rome:** this is pointedly directed at *Sat.* 2.6.60 (cf. *Epist.* 1.8.12, *Romae Tibur amem ventosus, Tibure Romam,* Lucr. 3.1066-75). The city/country antithesis is reflected in the chiastic word order.

30   **your carefree greens:** in an ethical context simplicity of diet symbolises an inner freedom based on contentment with little, cf. N-H on *Odes* 2.16.13. The poet has his earlier satires in mind (*Sat.* 1.6.110ff., 2.1.74, 2.2.117, 2.6.60ff., cf. *Epist.* 1.5.2). At *Epist.* 1.15.42ff., *tuta et parvula laudo ... ,* Horace admits this sort of inconsistency directly, comparing himself to the *scurra* Maenius.

31   **under duress** (lit. 'in chains'): like a prisoner or slave, see Plaut. *Men.* 77ff. (a parasite), Rudd 1966, 190.
hug yourself: cf. *Sat.* 1.2.54, *te ... amas* is reflexive, see *OLD* s.v. *amo* 10a.

32   **boozing somewhere:** the verb used (*potare*) implies drinking to excess, at the symposium following a dinner party, see *Sat.* 2.8.3, *Odes* 1.20.1 with N-H, *Odes* 2.11.17.

32f. **Should Maecenas invite:** here *iubeo* has primarily its weakened sense of 'ask', 'bid', 'invite', (cf. *Sat.* 1.6.61, *Epist.* 1.7.14, *OLD* s.v. 7), but Davus also hints at a stronger meaning ('command'), alluding to Horace's dependence on Maecenas, symbolised by his standing as a regular guest, cf. *Sat.* 1.6.47, *convictor*. In a letter to Maecenas, Augustus asked him to let Horace move from Maecenas's table to his own, [Suet.] *Vit. Hor.* 2.3-8 Klingner, Fraenkel 1957, 18. Now Davus glances at those dinners with Maecenas which Horace omitted to mention in *Sat.* 2.6.

at lighting-up time: the time indicated is very late. 'After the ninth hour' was the usual time for dining in summer, i.e. about 3.45 p.m. (Cic. *Fam.* 9.26.1, *Anth. Pal.* 11.44 [Philodemus], Hor. *Epist.*1.7.71). The tenth hour of *Auct. ad Her.* 4.64 may be for winter, when the hours were shorter (E.J. Bickerman, *Chronology of the Ancient World* [London, 1968, revised 1980], 13ff., Balsdon, 17f.) or for busy people (Mart. 7.51.11). Maecenas dines late because he is busy, cf. *Epist.* 1.5.3, *supremo sole*, in an invitation to a lawyer. According to Davus the lateness of the invitation goes to prove Horace's subservience to Maecenas. Palmer ad loc. sees modesty in it: Horace is making no claims for his standing with Maecenas, if he says that Maecenas only thinks of him at the last minute. Similarly, unlike Maecenas (*Sat.* 2.8.21ff.), he is not of sufficient standing to bring his own guests, parasites whom he leaves in the lurch.

34 **quickly** (lit. 'more quickly'): the comparative adverb is frequent in orders in comedy and colloquial speech, cf. 117, Plaut. *Mostell.* 679, Ter. *Haut.* 832, Hor. *Odes* 2.11.18, with N-H.

bring (lit. 'Is no-one bringing?'): the MSS divide between present and future tense. The stylistic context, comic-realistic, with a question functioning as an order, supports the present (Hofmann[3] §67).

35 **you blether:** the vivid, onomatopoeic verb *blatero* (not found elsewhere in Classical Latin) sounds a vulgar, disrespectful note.

are off: *fugis* is clearly preferable to *furis* ('you rave'), as it gives an additional and essential part of the story — Horace's hasty departure.

36 **Mulvius:** unknown. Mulvius and the others are 'parasites', interested in scrounging a meal, and not above criticising Horace behind his back. Note the difference from the solitary meal described at *Sat.* 1.6.114ff., for having *scurrae* must be a sign of living a certain style of life, Plaut. *Mostell.* 22.

38 **my nose leans back at the smell** (lit. 'I lean back my nose at the smell of cooking'): a collocation of words that recalls Greek comic compound epithets for parasites, e.g. Eup. fr. 173K, 'frying-pan-sniffer', *Com. Adesp.* fr. 1042K, 'close-watcher of cooking smells', Juv. 5.162, *captum ... nidore.*

[*supinor:* is reflexive, with the accusative which follows the active verb retained, cf. *Ars P.* 302, *purgor bilem.*]

39 **greedy-guts** (lit. 'a frequenter of low eating-houses'): the word *popino* is insulting both in its meaning and form, cf. Varro *Sat. Men.* 308B, *nebulo, Sat.* 1.1.104, 1.2.12, Suet. *Gram.* 15 (insults cast by Pompeius Lenaeus against the historian Sallust in a 'very bitter satire', see E. Fraenkel, *Eranos* 53 [1955], 78).

40 **Why should you:** the contrast is strongly emphasised by the personal pronouns.

41f. **cloak your vice in fine words:** Horace is accused of being a glutton and Maecenas's parasite, while claiming to be his 'friend'. The metaphor of disguise is picked up by the literal disguise at 55.

42 **a bigger fool:** the Stoic terminology (as at *Sat.* 2.3.43N, 158-9) anticipates the mention of Crispinus and the lecture proper. For the Stoic the 'fool' is the opposite of the 'wise man'. The fool is a slave, the wise man is free (83), cf. Cic. *Fin.* 3.60, *Parad.* 35, 'If slavery is, as it is, the obedience of a broken and abject soul, lacking the power to make its decisions, who could then deny that all who are fickle, greedy, in short, all who are without virtue, are slaves?' But as the Stoics did not allow degrees of moral goodness or its opposite (*Sat.* 1.3.120ff., Rist, 81ff.), Davus here, as elsewhere (40, 47, 96), shows the incompleteness of his indoctrination (Lejay, 540).

43   **five hundred drachmas**: the price is expressed in Greek values as in comedy, cf. 89. The Roman equivalent is 2,000 sesterces, 'a typical price for an ordinary slave of poor quality', M.I. Finley (ed.), *Slavery in Classical Antiquity* (Cambridge, 1960), 9-10. See also R. Duncan-Jones, *The Economy of the Roman Empire* (London, 1974), 348-50.

43f.   **keep your hand and bile in check**: in spite of having allowed Davus to begin, Horace expresses impatience at 21-2, and here the violent anger and threats of punishment which he displays at the end of the satire are anticipated. The fault he thus implicitly admits, as part of the *mise en scène* (Lejay, 553), incontinence with respect to temper, is less disgraceful than those he is accused of (see Arist. *Eth. Nic.* 1149^{b}24-5). There was a large philosophical literature on anger in the ancient world, see Cic. *QFr.* 1.1.37, Seneca *De Ira*.

45   **Crispinus's doorkeeper**: see *Sat.* 1.1.120, 1.3.139, 1.4.14, Oltramare, 129-37. There is piquancy in Davus's choice of authority, seeing that Crispinus, a Stoic philosopher and poet, and thus a kind of double of the satiric *persona* of Horace, had already been criticised (in Book 1) for verbosity and lack of judgement. But, unlike Damasippus, Davus cannot quote the philosopher himself; the doctrine, to which he attributes some importance (on the solemn *edo* see *Sat.* 2.7.51N), comes somewhat garbled through the mouth of his fellow-slave.

46-71:   the lecture on slavery begins. Underlying it is the Stoic paradox that 'all fools are slaves', *SVF* I 219, 222, 226 (Zeno), Diog. Laert. 7.121 = *SVF* III 355. However, the Stoic paradox is not argued for its own sake, but for the opportunity it gives Davus to prove his master a slave. The first topic is the contrast between an affair with a *matrona* and sex with a *meretrix* (both equally culpable according to the Stoic doctrine of the 'equality of sins', *Sat.* 1.3.96, Cic. *Parad.* 20, 22). The slave can get what he wants without danger or emotional disturbance, while the higher-class adulterer disguises himself as a slave, running the risk of being punished like a slave and of losing his wealth and social standing, as well as his peace of mind. The material is reminiscent of *Sat.* 1.2.28ff., a diatribe against love for married women, where similar arguments are deployed, the difference being that there the satirist claims to prefer and practice the casual liaison with the *meretrix*. For subjection to a woman as a type of slavery see Cic. *Parad.* 36 and on the elegiac 'slavery of love' (*servitium amoris*) F.O. Copley, *TAPhA* 78 (1947), 285-300, R.O.A.M. Lyne, *CQ* N.S.29 (1979), 117-130.

46   **You are captivated**: the chiastic word order enacts the contrast, Cody, 119 n.4, cf. *Sat.* 1.2.27. 'You' is the general and exemplificatory second-person singular of the diatribe-style, but, as with the name Davus ('take me, a slave'), there is an ambiguity. Davus intends 'you' to refer to his master in a more specific way than is usual in the diatribe, Stahl, 47, Taylor 1925 (cited at 53ff.N), 163, 'Horace certainly intends the reader to consider that he is the person addressed throughout.'

47   **deserves crucifixion**: crucifixion was a punishment inflicted only on slaves (*Sat.* 1.3.82). The reference to servile corporal punishment is a vivid way of defining the moral slavery of the lover, but the harping on such punishments belongs to the slave's characterisation.
fault: *pecco* possibly has its erotic sense (*Sat.* 1.2.62-3, *Odes* 1.27.17, 1.33.9, Adams, 202) as well as the technical Stoic sense of 'sin', 'transgress' (Lejay, 546).

47-50   **When irresistible nature ...**: in contrast to the treatment of the same topic in *Sat.* 1.2, obscene words are avoided (Adams, 221, 225. Indeed, according to Adams, 36ff., 221, *cauda* ['tail'] may be a euphemism.). All the same, the description of Davus's sexual activity is graphic (cf. Cic. *Fam.* 9.22.1, *totus est sermo verbis tectus, re impudentior*): for *intendo* of an erection, *Sat.* 1.5.83f., Adams, 46; visibility see *Sat.* 1.2.84-5; for the metaphor of 'beating', Adams, 145ff.; buttocks, Lucr. 4.1270, Adams, 194; the horse-riding position, Adams, 165f. The last was a position in which (it was thought) the woman serviced the man, an act of perversity and immodesty, women being passive by nature (Sen. *Ep.* 95.21).

51f. **with reputation intact:** cf. 67N. Davus defines himself as free in contrast to the lover, whom he cynically deflates with the word 'piss'. Those who practised the 'life of love' flaunted their lack of concern for their reputation (cf. Griffin, 5f., 34, 39-41).

worried: for *sollicitum* of the lover see *Sat.* 2.3.253N. Jealousy and fear of the wealthy rival (a stock figure of Latin love poetry, Hor. *Epod.* 15.13, Prop. 1.8.3 with Fedeli) constitute emotional slavery.

piss in the same place: cf. Catull. 67.30, Pers. 6.73, Mart. 11.46.2. Urination is a 'crude metaphor' for ejaculation, Adams, 142.

53ff. **thrown off your signs of rank:** there is a problem of interpretation here. Historians argue, on the basis of this and other evidence, that Horace was, or could have been, a knight and a member of the panel of jurors, see L.R. Taylor, *AJP* 46 (1925), 161-70, *TAPhA* 99 (1968), 469-86, Armstrong 1986, Wiseman 1971, 70-74, C. Nicolet, *L'ordre équestre à l'époque républicaine* I (Paris, 1966), 441-56, II (Paris, 1974), 914-5. On the other hand, literary scholars regard the case as not proved (Fraenkel 1957, 14-5 is silent; Rudd 1966, 278 n.2 thinks it 'probable' that Horace was a knight). Lejay (550) argues that 46-71 do not refer to Horace. He regards the second person singular as indefinite, the fictitious interlocutor typical of the diatribe-style: Horace was neither a knight nor an adulterer (cf. Coffey, 89). Certain readings of the context (see 72-4N) show persuasively that Horace could have been a knight though not an adulterer (Taylor 1925, 163, Armstrong 1986, 258-9), but we should not ignore the methodological paradox of the relation of biographical 'truth' and fiction in a literary work.

knight's ring: in the late Republic 'knights' by rank (*equites equo publico*) and senators wore a plain gold ring on the fourth finger of their left hand. As a sign of rank it was generally associated with the equestrian order (cf. Ov. *Am.* 3.8.15, Pliny *HN.* 33.8ff., Suet. *Iul.* 33, Juv. 11.43, 129; M.I. Henderson, *JRS* 53 [1963], 61-72).

Roman dress: the distinctive white toga.

juror: i.e. a man of moral probity.

Dama: cf. *Sat.* 2.5.18, *spurco Damae*. Dama is a typical slave name, often found in Latin legal works for a hypothetical slave, cf. *Sat.* 1.6.38, 2.5.18, 101, Pers. 5.76.

55 **a cloak:** originally soldier's garb (Cic. *Phil.* 2.76), the *lacerna* was a dark-coloured mantle with a hood, cf. Pers. 1.54, Juv. 8.144f. A little later wearing of the *lacerna* became so prevalent that Augustus forbade its use in the forum (Suet. *Aug.* 40).

perfumed head: spruced up with unguents for the occasion, cf. *Epod.* 5.57ff., *senem ... adulterum ... nardo perunctum*, *Odes* 3.24.20.

56 **are you not what you're disguised as?:** the condition of slavery that Horace assumes as a disguise is shown to be a spiritual slavery to the passions of fear and lust, cf. 66. See Cic. *Tusc.* 4.11-12 where, in Stoic theory, fear and lust (*metus* and *libido*) are opposed passions, both springing from false belief about the future (also Hor. *Epist.* 1.6.10, 1.18.98-9).

58-67: the adulterer's surrender to love and its consequences is compared to the free man's selling himself into the worst sort of slavery. The comparison depends both on the condition of *infamia* (ill repute due to moral turpitude) and the extremity of the punishments that could be inflicted.

59 **sell yourself as a gladiator:** Roman citizens, impelled by financial ruin (cf. *Epist.* 1.18.36) might sell themselves to the owner of a troupe of gladiators. Becoming a gladiator entailed the swearing of an oath to accept the sort of corporal punishment meted out to slaves.

Horace's wording alludes to the terms of the contract quoted at Petron. *Sat.* 117.5, *uri, vinciri, verberari ferroque necari* ('to be burnt [i.e. branded?], bound, flogged and killed with the sword', cf. Sen. *Apoc.* 9.3, *Ep.* 37.1). For more information on the oath see Ville, 247-8, 251.

[*uri*: there is doubt here over whether to take *virgis* with *uri* and therefore *uri* as 'scorched' or 'scourged' (*OLD* s.v. *uro* 10, cf. Kenney on Lucr. 3.1019, Hor. *Epod.* 4.3, *Epist.* 1.16.47) or with *necari*. The closeness of the wording to the gladiators' oath suggests that *uri* here has the same meaning. For 'burning' as a punishment see *Epist.* 1.15.36f., Plaut. *Asin.* 548, Lucr. 3.1017, Tib. 1.5.5f., Juv. 14.22. Reluctant gladiators were sometimes driven to fight with whips and hot irons, Sen. *Ep.* 7.5. C.P. Jones, *JRS* 77 (1987), 139-59 argues that there is not good evidence for penal branding, as opposed to tattooing, in Rome.]

shut up in a foul chest: this is probably an allusion to a famous incident of the 'adultery mime' in which the lover was hidden in the chest to avoid discovery by the husband (like Falstaff in the laundry basket in Shakespeare's *The Merry Wives of Windsor*), cf. Juv. 6.41-4, R.W. Reynolds, *CQ* 40 (1946), 77-84, J.C. McKeown, *PCPhS* N.S. 25 (1979), 71-84. Cf. the allusion to comedy at 89-91.

61ff. **have lawful power**: cf. *Sat.* 1.2.37-46. In the Republic, if a husband caught his wife in the act of adultery, he could kill her (without legal consequences, *sine iudicio impune*) and probably her lover as well, see Cato in Aulus Gellius *NA* 10.23.5. This right, which does not seems to have been much exercised, was withdrawn by the *Lex Iulia de adulteriis* of 18 B.C. See P.E. Corbett, *The Roman Law of Marriage* (Oxford 1930, reprinted 1969), 127ff., J.F. Gardner, *Women in Roman Law and Society* (London and Sydney, 1986), 129-30, S. Treggiari, *Roman Marriage* (Oxford, 1991), 270-85, 293. Valerius Maximus (6.1.13) gives examples of beatings, castration and sexual assault inflicted on adulterers.

63-7 **or lie on top as she sins**: for *superne* in this physical sense ('from above') see Lucr. 6.434, Livy 1.25.12. I adopt Shackleton Bailey's punctuation of this controversial passage and K-H's explanation of the connection of *illa tamen* etc. to the previous sentence. The comparison is between the adulterer and his mistress (not the *matrona* and the *meretrix*) in order to show that he is the guiltier party. If 65 does not explain the woman's behaviour, it is also difficult with what follows (though see D. Wiesen, *Mnemosyne* 34 [1981], 87-95). Shackleton Bailey (1982, 84f.) supports the emendation *peccatque pudice* ('and she sins with modesty') by reference to Prop. 2.23.22, a passage which stresses the disadvantages of an affair with a married woman who is bent on concealment. See also Rudd 1966, 299 n.47, R. Verdière, *Eos* 53 (1962), 111-124, at 116ff.

66f. **in the stocks** (lit. 'under the fork'): the slave's punishment symbolises the condition of slavery. See 22N, 47N.

a raging master: cf. 93N. There *dominus* ('master') is clearly figurative, but in this context there is an ambiguity between the literal and metaphorical, the physical and moral slavery. Rudd 1966, 299 n.47 argues that here too it has a figurative sense, '*Dominus furens* exactly suits lust as an irrational master', cf. Cic. *Parad.* 33, 40, 41, *Sen.* 47.

your whole substance: cf. *Sat.* 1.2.61-2, *bonam deperdere famam,/rem patris oblimare.*

reputation: the adulterer who surrrenders to his passion becomes *infamis*, the argument used by Horace's father to deter him at *Sat.* 1.4.114.

70 **What wild beast**: the example is proverbial, cf. *Epist.* 1.16.50f. The adulterer is stupider than the beast which can learn from experience to avoid danger.

72-4 **"I'm not an adulterer"**: cf. Cic. *Parad.* 34. Like the popular preacher Davus anticipates Horace's denial of the fact and brings in a new Stoic argument. The previous section had stressed the dangers of adultery (see also *Sat.* 1.2.37-46). But, according to the Stoic viewpoint, one should not take credit for abstaining from wrong-doing through fear of the consequences. For example, at *Epist.* 1.16.46-56 the slave who holds back from committing a crime through fear of punishment cannot be called *good*. So, if it is such fear that inhibits him, Horace is still no better than a slave. This is consistent with the Stoic view of morality as a matter of intention, the wicked desire being as wrong as the deed i might provoke. Hence the Stoics' emphasis on the elimination of irrational passions, cf. Cic. *Fin.* 3.32, 'the passions of fear, grief and lust are sins, even without an ensuing result', *Parad.* 20, L.R. Taylor, *AJP* 46 (1925), 163 n.13.

by god (lit. 'by Hercules'): there are only two instances of this oath in Horace, the other being at *Epist.* 1.15.39 (Maenius the *scurra*). It emphasises the negative and adds a touch of everyday speech, Hofmann[3] §39.

74   **nature ... run wild:** for the image of the passions as a horse (also at 93-4) see Varro, *Sat. Men.* 177B, Hor. *Epist.* 1.2.62-3, *Odes* 4.15.10, *evaganti frena licentiae*, Sen. *Ep.* 23.4, Lucian *Cyn.* 18. For the thought commentators cite the Stoic Cleanthes ap. Stob. *Floril.* 6.19 Mein. (Pearson 95), 'Whoever longs to do something wicked, but holds back from it, will do it if he gets the opportunity.'

76   **an act of manumission:** slaves were freed by formal or informal acts of manumission. Here the reference is to the formal ceremony of manumission known as *manumissio vindicta*. In this, master and slave went before a qualified magistrate. There, a third party (sometimes a lictor) took the role of *assertor libertatis* to claim free status for the slave, touching him with a rod (*festuca*). The master did not oppose the claim and the slave was declared free by the magistrate. See Plaut. *Mil.* 961, Pers. 5.75-8,88,125,175, Gaius *Inst.* 4.16-17, Buckland, 441f., 451ff., S. Treggiari, *Roman Freedmen during the Late Republic* (Oxford, 1969), 20ff. In late sources the word *vindicta* denotes the rod, but its original meaning is unsure, cf. Plaut. *Curc.* 212, Ogilvie on Livy 2.5.10, *OLD* s.v. *vindicta* 1b. Arr. *Epict. Diss.* 2.1.26ff. builds an extensive moral illustration on the manumission ceremony (see also 4.1.7).

77   **wretched fear:** the man who lives irrationally, swayed by his emotions, is no different from the slave in constant fear of his master, cf. Cic. *Parad.* 40 (note the swing from ambition to fear), Hor. *Epist.* 1.16.65-6. Cicero (*Tusc.* 4.19) defines *formido* as 'constant fear'.

78-80 **'deputy':** again Davus draws his argument from the realities of the slave's position. From the *peculium,* the fund slaves were allowed to hold as if it were their own property, a slave could buy another slave to work for him. But since, strictly speaking, both slaves were owned by the same master, they were also 'co-slaves' (Cic. *Parad.* 37 also alludes to the metaphorical Stoic sense, cf. Sen. *Ep.* 47.1). For *vicarii* see Plaut. *Asin.* 433-4, Cic. *Verr.* 1.93, 3.86, Mart. 2.18.7, Paul. *Dig.* 9.4.19, Buckland, 239ff., A.M. Duff, *Freedmen in the Early Roman Empire*[2] (Cambridge, 1958), 53-4.

81   **give me orders:** see *Sat.* 2.3.189N.
           [*alii:* the MSS divide between singular and plural. If we read the plural there is a reference to the passions which master Horace. The singular suits the puppet image better, and the *dominus* of 66 and 93.]

82   **wooden puppet:** the comparison belongs to the philosophical tradition. In Plato *Leg.* 644d-645c there is an extended development of the puppet image (called a myth), according to which man is torn between the rival attractions of pleasure and fear (or pain), but is still attached to the golden cord of reason. Persius (5.128-9) refers to 'cords', imitating Horace. This application of the image is not found again until the Stoic Marcus Aurelius, who used it frequently (7.3, 2.2, 3.16, 6.16 etc.), see Lejay, 546-7, H.O. Schröder, 'Marionetten. Ein Beitrag zur Polemik des Karneades', *RhM* 126 (1983), 1-24. In other philosophical discussions of puppets what is of interest is their apparent automatism (M.C. Nussbaum, *HSPh* 80 [1976], 111-59, at 146ff.). This may add point to the comparison: to all intents and purposes Horace moves himself, but those in the know can detect the action of the manipulator.

83   **Who, then, is free?**: for the Stoic device of the rhetorical question and answer see *Sat.* 2.3.158ff.

83-8:   **The wise man:** for other descriptions of the Stoic sage see *Sat.* 1.3.124-33, *Epist.* 1.1.106-8 with Macleod's note, Cic. *Fin.* 3.75, *Tusc.* 4.38, *Parad.* passim, *Mur.* 61ff. (tested against real life), Sen. *Ep.* 57.3 with Summers's note, Lejay, 541-2. Describing the Stoic wise man (*sapiens*) was a challenging (Cic. *Tusc.* 4.36 says paradoxical or 'extravagant') way of discussing the ideal of virtue, e.g. *Tusc.* 5.28ff., 'men equipped with and distinguished by all the virtues are wise as well as good ... And if the noble distinction of this title of "wise", most worthy of Pythagoras, Socrates and Plato, so delights them, let them constrain the soul to despise the things which dazzle them, strength, health, beauty, riches, distinctions, wealth, and count as nothing the things that are their opposites: they will be able in clearest accents to claim that they are terrified neither by the assault of fortune nor the opinion of the mob nor by pain or poverty, and that they regard all things as resting with themselves, nor is there anything beyond their control which they reckon as good.'
dominion: the wise man is his own master. The solemn *imperiosus* gives the line an unusual five-syllable ending.

84   **makes fearful:** see the passage quoted above and the Stoicising version of Eur. *Bacch.* 492-8 at *Epist.* 1.16.73ff. The wise man does not fear these 'evils' because he has learnt to judge them correctly as things that cannot damage his virtue, cf. Cic. *Tusc.* 1.100f. (death), Hor. *Epist.* 1.10.39-40 (poverty), Arr. *Epict. Diss.* 4.1.60, 69-70. The lightness of the dactylic line playfully echoes the wise man's unconcern.

85   **stand up to:** as if a slave 'answering back' his master, cf. 103, Plaut. *Men.* 620-1, Ruckdeschel, 22.

86   **complete in himself:** self-contained. The ideal of self-sufficiency (*autarkeia*), the condition of inner freedom, was inherited by the Stoics from the Cynics (see *Sat.* 2.2, Diogenes ap. Diog. Laert. 6.66, Rist 1969, 5-10, 58ff.), cf. Cic. *Parad.* 17 (the self-sufficient man compared to one dependent on fortune), 'he must be perfectly happy, who is completely self-dependent, who locates all his goods in himself', Arr. *Epict. Diss.* 4.1 passim.
sphere: Davus's picture of the Stoic sage as 'rounded' or 'spherical' is a striking extension of the Stoic teachings on the nature of the cosmos and the divine. The idea that 'god' was spherical can be traced in pre-Socratic philosophy, in Xenophanes (Diels-Kranz I 21B 23-6) and Parmenides (DK I 28B 8, 29-42) as well as Empedocles (DK I 31B 17,15-20; 27; 27a; 28; 29; 35). Like the Stoic cosmos, the Stoic god had the shape of a sphere, the perfect form (Pl. *Ti.* 33b, cf. *Symp.* 189e), cf. *SVF* II 1009, Cic. *Nat. D.* 1.18, 2.45-9 with Pease's notes. Marcus Aurelius uses the sphere as an image of the wise man (12.3, 8.41). He also regards the soul (*psyche*) as spherical (11.12). Seneca (*Ep.* 113.22) satirically raises the idea of spherical virtues.

86f.   **polished surface:** in Horace's use of the image the philosophical idea of perfection is less important than the sphere's smoothness. Troubles slide off the wise man like 'water off a duck's back'.
nothing from outside: there is a reference to 'externals', a technical term of Stoicism, though not confined to it, cf. *SVF* III 96, Cic. *Tusc.* 5.25f., *Off.* 1.66, 3.21, Arr. *Epict. Diss.* 1.1.9 etc. The question of how far happiness depended on external circumstances was much debated in ancient ethics. For the Stoics true happiness came from virtue which was not affected by 'externals'.

88   **Fortune:** cf. *Sat.* 2.2.126. Here Fortune is equivalent to the Greek *Tyche,* the goddess of chance, symbolising the incalculable, the way things turn out (see M.P. Nilsson, *Greek*

Piety [Trans. H. J. Rose, Oxford, 1948], 86, Dover, 138ff.). The wise man cannot be conquered by Fortune, cf. *SVF* I 449,21f., Cic. *Parad.* 34, Hor. *Odes* 3.29.49ff., *Epist.*1.1.68-9 with Macleod's note. Commentators cite a well-known saying of Epicurus (ap. Diog. Laert. 10.144), to which Cicero refers twice (*Fin.* 1.63, *Tusc.* 5.26), 'Fortune but seldom interferes with the wise man'. Horace's image is stronger, since *ruit* suggests a violent attack (cf. *Odes* 1.19.9), the result of which is the maiming of Fortune herself (*manca* ['half-strength'] means literally 'with a weak or crippled hand'.).

89f. **A woman asks you for five talents:** the style changes suddenly, to point the contrast of the real with the ideal. A vignette in the style of New Comedy illustrates the lover's slavery, cf. Cic. *Parad.* 36, Hor. *Sat.* 2.3.259-64N, Pers. 5.165-6, Arr. *Epict. Diss.* 4.1.20. The locked-out lover (*exclusus amator*, cf. *Sat.* 2.3.259f.) in love elegy often exemplifies the thought that love is slavery, e.g. Tib. 1.1.55-6, Ov. *Am.* 1.2.17f., F.O. Copley, *TAPhA* 78 (1947), 285ff. Here the treatment meted out to the lover is particularly humiliating (note the violence suggested by *repulsum*) but he does the woman's bidding even so.

five talents: the talent is a Greek monetary unit, in keeping with the Greek setting of New Comedy. Five talents is an outrageous sum, given that five *minae* represents a reasonable gift in comedy (Plaut. *Truc.* 739) and 1 talent = 60 minae, cf. Plaut. *Mostell.* 973.

93 **a relentless master:** cf. 66N. Lust is imagined as a charioteer (see Rudd 1966, 193), an inversion of Plato *Phaedrus* 246aff., where reason drives the chariot. There may be an allusion to a well-known anecdote about Sophocles in old age: when asked about his love-life he said he had escaped from sexual desire as if he were a slave escaping 'from a mad and savage master' (Pl. *Resp.* 329b-c, Cic. *Sen.* 47, put into the mouth of the Elder Cato).

95-101: the point of this paragraph is that, in spite of what Horace might consider his own superior taste, the master and slave are committing the same fault (becoming too involved) and should receive equal blame, cf. Cic. *Parad.* 37, 'when I see you gazing and marvelling and uttering cries of admiration, I judge you to be the slave of every kind of foolishness' For the desirable *athaumastia* ('absence of wonder'), cf. *SVF* I 239,17ff. (Zeno), Hor. *Epist.* 1.6, Sen. *Ep.* 8.5, Arr. *Epict. Diss.* 1.29.3. Excessive enthusiasm (note *torpes*) is irrational, or 'foolish', cf. *Epist.* 1.1.47. In Cicero's fifth *Stoic Paradox*, as here, the section on the folly of those who take an excessive delight (note *mirare*) in works of art and luxurious surroundings (37) follows immediately upon the section on subservience to a woman (36). Sall. *Cat.* 11.6 sets admiration of works of art beside sex and drink (*amare potare*) as signs of decadence. In general on art and corruption see Griffin, 7-8.

95 **Pausias:** Pausias was a fourth-century B.C. artist from Sicyon (see Pliny *HN* 35.124, A. Griffin, *Sikyon* [Oxford, 1982], 147-57), known for the refinement of his technique. His paintings were often small, of flowers or boys. Artistic depiction of gladiators, on the other hand (here we should be thinking of something like an advertising poster, cf. Pliny *HN* 35.52, under Nero), appealed to the same low taste as the shows themselves (Cic. *Fam.* 7.1.2-3, Hor. *Epist.* 2.1.182-6, Petron. *Sat.* 29.9, 45, 52.3, N. Horsfall, *G&R* 36 [1989], 70-89, at 84-5, Ville, 449-50). M.J. McGann (*CR* 6 [1956], 97-9) suggests that there is a veiled transition to the new topic: a reference to Pausias could be taken to continue the theme of enslavement to sensuality, since his name was associated with licentiousness (but see Coffey, 232 n.94). In the same way, Davus may be shown to attempt to mask a passion for the subject of *his* painting by an interest in its technique.

you lunatic: cf. *Sat.* 2.2.33. Note that at *Sat.* 2.3.20ff. Damasippus's connoisseurship may be termed an 'illness', cf. [Hippocr.] *Ep.* 17, p.376L, Cic. *Verr.* 2.4.1, Hor. *Epist.* 1.6.17-8, Sen. *Ep.* 115.8, *nos circa tabulas et statuas insanimus*.

96f. **with straining knees** (lit. 'with tensed calf'): most commentators take this phrase with the verb *miror* ('I admire'), on the grounds that it adds colour to the verb and makes a better contrast with *torpes* ('you swoon'). It describes Davus's attitude as he stretches to see over the crowd (K-H); the result is that he abandons his errand to gaze (a dawdler, 100) and gets into trouble (see Rudd 1966, 193-4).

Fulvius: the name of a free man (Ville, 242 n.33).

Rutuba: this may be a nick-name. *Rutuba* means 'confusion' at Var. *Sat. Men.* 488B, see Rudd 1966, 293 n.18.

Pacideianus: Lucilius (172-5W) described a gladiatorial combat between two champions, Aeserninus and Pacideianus, a popular episode, to judge by Cicero's references (*QFr.* 3.4.2, *Opt. Gen.* 17, *Tusc.* 4.48, here quoting the menaces uttered by Pacideianus). It is not clear whether this is the same person, quoted, as it were, from Lucilius (Fraenkel 1931, 130 n.1, Rudd 1966, 140), or a later gladiator, who had taken, as a *nom de guerre*, the name of his famous predecessor (K-H for chronological reasons; for the practice Friedländer IV, 257-63). The names would have been indicated in the painting, as they often were in depictions of gladiators, whether in mosaics, wall-paintings, or even on glass cups (cf. Petron. *Sat.* 52.3, 45.11, lamps), for gladiators were popular heroes, rather like football or tennis stars today (cf. *Sat.* 2.6.44, Ville, 334-9).

99   as if they were really fighting: Davus praises the paintings he likes for their naturalistic representation, naively claiming an interest in artistic technique, when what attracts him is the subject matter. This sort of comment is mocked at Petron. *Sat.* 52, though it remains true that realism of representation was an important criterion in the appreciation of art in antiquity.

100   their weapons, real heroes: the collocation of the two words *arma* ('weapons') and *viri* ('men', 'heroes') sounds like parody of an epic formula, e.g. Virg. *Aen.* 1.1, 2.668, 9.777. See A. Bloch, *MH* 27 (1970), 206-11.

a rogue and a dawdler: *nequam* ('rogue') is the standard word of blame for the slave, the opposite of *frugi* (3N), cf. Plaut. *Cas.* 257, 741, *Poen.* 1030. Being a keen spectator of games or an enthusiast for pictures are among the recognised defects of a slave (others are lying, thieving, and running away) in Venuleius *Dig.* 21.1.65, cf. Hor. *Epist.* 2.2.14-16.

102-11: now master and slave are compared on the point of gluttony — the contrast lying in the kinds of food available to each, and the means at his disposal with which to acquire it. The slave is beaten, while for the master excessive indulgence brings its own punishment, ill-health.

102   [*Nili:* 'of no value', 'worthless'. *Nil* or *nihil esse* means 'to be a nonentity', whereas the context requires an expression of moral blame.]

104   Subservience to the belly: cf. 38. The semi-personification of the belly (cf. *Epist.* 1.15.32) occurs in comedy and in vituperative and moral contexts, cf. Lucil. 70W, Sall. *Cat.* 1.1, 2.8, Cic. *Cael.* 44, Ruckdeschel, 65. The 'good slave' at Plaut. *Men.* 970 has to make a calculation of 'back against gullet, legs against belly'.

more ruinous: the slave's punishment — a beating — is immediate and obvious, but Davus argues that the master is also punished for his gluttony. Since the master is not free to indulge himself without unpleasant consequences, there is really no difference between master and slave.

107   turn to gall: for the thought see *Sat.* 2.2.75. The verb *inamaresco* is found only here in Latin.

108f.   baffled feet: 'made fools of' (Wickham). Either the unsteady feet of the drunkard, because drink distorts or deceives bodily movement, or more permanently damaged by gout (Lejay ad loc.).

the unsound body: cf. *Sat.* 2.2.77-8, *corpus onustum/hesternis vitiis.*

109-11: a parallel argument to 104ff., showing the absurdity of applying different standards. If the slave's small transgression is punishable, the free man, a glutton on a far grander scale, should not be judged guiltless.

body-scraper: a common household item of no particular value used by athletes and bathers to clean excessive oil and dirt from the skin before washing, see Gardiner, 84, 88, figs. 45, 59, 60, Petron. *Sat.* 91.1.

to do his gullet's bidding: see 104N, *Sat.* 2.2.40N.

111-18: as at *Sat.* 2.3.321ff. from here on the criticism is more pointedly directed at Horace himself. Davus exposes Horace's lack of inner integrity and peace of mind.

112ff. **you can't endure your own company:** in the influential passage of Lucretius Book 3 already noted (1066-75, see 22N), discontent shows itself in restlessness and inconsistency of behaviour, e.g. Lucr. 3.1068-70, 'In this way each man keeps trying to escape from himself: yet against his will he is stuck to the self, which we know he cannot in fact escape, and hates himself, because in his sickness he does not know the cause of his illness.' Here Davus gives a similar explanation for Horace's lack of steadiness — the desire to escape himself. This section is connected thematically with the introductory section (21ff.), which also seems to criticise 'real' traits of Horace's character (Lejay, 555), cf. *Odes* 2.16.19-20 with N-H.

112 **free time:** for the importance to Horace of *otium*, cf. *Sat.* 2.6.59ff.

113 **like a runaway or truant:** both are terms for slaves who absent themselves without leave from their master. A *fugitivus* has no intention of returning, Ulpian *Dig.* 2. 1.1.17. The comparison links the topic of discontent to the slavery theme.

114 **cheat anxiety:** *fallere curam* may be a poetic metaphor, especially in the light of the following line. The more usual expressions are *curis levare* or *solvere* ('free from cares') (*TLL* IV 1473.69 and 78). With the thought compare Lucr. 3.1066 (the restless man seeks oblivion in sleep).

wine ... sleep: cf. *Sat.* 2.3.3, *vini somnique benignus*, 2.6.60ff.

115 **black companion:** the style rises with the figurative expression. 'Black' suggests thoughts of death (fear of death is the context in Lucretius), cf. Lucr. 2.47ff., *curae sequaces*, Hor. *Odes* 2.16.21-22, 3.1.40. Like Lucretius, Horace associates *cura* ('worry', 'anxiety') with desire and fear (*Epist.* 1.2.51, 1.18.98ff.) and treats it as the state opposite to that of inner peace and freedom, M. Hauser, *Der römische Begriff cura* (Diss. Basel, Winterthur, 1954), 77 and 81. *Comes* is also Lucretian, 2.580, 3.290, 5.1129f., 6.1159.

116 **a stone:** as if to drive away a troublesome dog, cf. Plaut. *Mostell.* 266.

arrows: the weapons of a god (cf. Apollo at *Odes* 1.12.24 or an epic hero). The threats rise in scale from the comic to the tragic (Scarpat ad loc., citing Sen. *Herc. Oet.* 1278, *unde fulmen mihi?*).

[*'unde mihi lapidem?'*: cf. *Sat.* 2.5.102N.]

117 **mad:** Horace's 'frightful temper' was brought in as evidence of his madness at *Sat.* 2.3.323. See also, as a sign of madness, throwing stones at one's slaves, *Sat.* 2.3.128N.

or versifying: see *Sat.* 2.3.321-2N.

118 **ninth labourer:** Davus is brought back to the reality of his position as slave by the threat of punishment, cf. Plaut. *Mostell.* 18-9, 'You will increase the total [of slaves] in the country, the kind that works in iron', i.e. wears iron fetters, Ter. *Phorm.* 247-50, Petron. *Sat.* 69.3, Sen. *Dial.* 3.29.1, Juv. 8.179f. For an urban slave's view of life in the country see *Epist.* 1.14.19ff.

my Sabine farm: the reference makes yet another link between this satire and the previous one. Here possession of the country estate confirms Horace in his role of master. Note the poem's abrupt ending.

Satire Eight

The subject of this final satire is a dinner party given by Nasidienus Rufus. Two aspects of the dinner receive particular attention, the food provided, and the social interaction between host and guests. As in *Sat.* 2.2 and 2.4, food is not simply described for its own sake, but shown to represent, and set in a critical light, a way of life, or a character (see Introduction §6). As the narrator Fundanius sees it, Nasidienus's character is largely defined by the food he serves and the way he serves it. In the social interaction, Nasidienus and his hanger-on Nomentanus, and Maecenas's two *scurrae,* Vibidius and Servilius Balatro, play the leading roles. Maecenas, the guest of honour, is no more than named (16, 22), and, though the whole performance is for his benefit, we are told nothing of his reactions. Fundanius, a comic poet (*Sat.* 1.10.42), is one of the three 'literary' guests, all friends of Horace and Maecenas. If Nasidienus invited them to provide intellectual tone, his expectations do not seem to have been fulfilled. Nevertheless, the presence of this group links this satire to those in Book 1 in which Horace depicts his relationship with Maecenas and his poetic friendships (1.5, 1.6, 1.10, see O'Connor, 32).

In this satire Horace dramatises the gourmet's obsessions and prescriptions mocked in *Sat.* 2.4. For the dialogue setting and some of the incidents he draws on the tradition begun by Plato's *Symposium*, but diverges from it in the satiric treatment of the host, the attention paid to the food and the absence of general topics of conversation. The topic of the dinner party is Lucilian (e.g. Book 20, Granius's dinner party, Cic. *Brut.*160, see *Sat.* 2.8.11N, Fiske, 165, 408-415). We also find it as a topic and a structural framework in Varro's *Menippean Satires*, and, in later satire, Juvenal 5, Petronius *Satyricon* (Trimalchio's dinner) and Lucian's *Symposium*. Of Menippus's *Symposium* nothing is known. Maecenas himself wrote a *Symposium* in which Virgil, Horace and other contemporaries appeared (Servius on Virg. *Aen.* 8.310). Meal-descriptions in letter-form are another genre of food-writing that fill in the background to the form and subject of the satire, e.g. the letters of Lynkeus and Hippolochos describing sumptuous banquets (from the Hellenistic period, quoted in Ath. 4.128A-130D). Closer to Horace's time, Cicero's letters attest general interest in the dinner party both as a social event and symbol of a way of life, Cic. *Fam.* 9.26, *Att.* 9.13.6 (Fraenkel 1931, 136 n.2).

While the literary background is important for the textual dimension of the satire, we should not forget that it purports to represent contemporary life and manners. As we shall see, understanding of this satire is hampered by our lack of knowledge of the nuances of Roman manners and social conventions, but we can safely assume that then, as now, gossip about dinner parties was a way of building and reinforcing the cohesion of self-defining social circles, just as failing the test as host or guest results in exclusion from them. Here we need to reckon with the double standards that operated: on the one hand, dinner parties were based on an ideal of equality, friendship and free speech between people of all ranks (cf. D'Arms in Murray, 1990), but on the other, the normal hierarchies of status were preserved, as, for example, in the seating arrangements.

The identity of Nasidienus Rufus is a puzzle. As Roos argues, he could have been a real person (the name is found on an inscription of the first century A.D., *CIL* XIII.8270). Or the name may be genuine but not that of a known contemporary. In this case Nasidienus would be a type of the *parvenu* (Rudd 1966, 222), whose name perhaps suggested unsophisticated Italian origins, and had comic overtones, i.e. 'red nose'. Lambinus (see Palmer, 368-9) advanced the theory that the name was a pseudonym for Q. Salvidienus Rufus (on whom see Wiseman 1971, 258), a friend of Octavian and Agrippa in 44, but disgraced and put to death by Octavian in 40 B.C., after a conspiracy to induce his troops in Gallia Narbonensis to desert to Antony was betrayed. His rise to great heights from lowly origins (Vell. Pat. 2.76.4, Suet. *Aug.* 66) would fit, but there would seem to be no point in reviving one so long dead to put him in a totally different social and political context.

If Nasidienus is a fictitious character, it follows that the events of the dinner party are also invented. No real obstacle to this is presented by the participation of living people and the fact that the satire reads like an account of something that had happened (but see Coffey, 89). Maecenas and the poets play a very small part in the action, and one of the leading players, Nomentanus, may well be a figure from literature, or at least not still be living. If Nasidienus were a named living person, this satire would be the only one to ridicule such a person at length.

The point of the satire is also debated. Is it just a *divertissement*, a comedy of manners, or does it have a moral message? Rudd 1966, 216ff. has demonstrated that Nasidienus's fault is not meanness but vulgar affectation, stupidity, social ambition and vanity. In spite of his boring culinary disquisitions he is ignorant of the 'art of dining well' (cf. Cic. *Fin.* 2.25, where Cicero comments that the 'principal dish' of a good dinner is 'good conversation', cf. Lucil. 203-5W). Nasidienus is allowed to hang himself with his own rope, with a little help from Maecenas's *scurrae*. Maecenas and the poets represent the the society to which Nasidienus aspires, but from which he is disqualified by his vulgarity and lack of *savoir faire* (see the treatment of the unnamed social climber in *Sat.* 1.9). To a certain extent Nasidienus is on the right track when he tries to impress Maecenas by luxuriousness of food and drink (Maecenas perhaps produced a famous wine [Pliny *HN* 14.67], and experimented with eating donkey foals [Pliny *HN* 8.170], Griffin, 13ff.), but he badly misjudges the situation in thinking that is all that is required. Fundanius has no doubt that he deserved the guests' barely concealed mockery and their insulting departure, but the question arises whether there may not also be criticism directed at the guests' behaviour and a suggestion that their vengeance is misplaced (see Baker). To modern eyes Nasidienus can appear pathetic in his eagerness to please and Balatro's rudeness to him embarrassing (Wilkinson 1968, 5-6, Balsdon, 35).

In relation to this question two aspects of the satire deserve particular notice, the role of Horace and the ending of the satire. The satire ends abruptly, without any closing conversation between Horace and Fundanius, and Fundanius breaks off his account at the moment of the guests' departure. They are said to have 'escaped'. When? Some think it was before the end of the dinner proper, others at the end of the dinner, when they could decently take their leave (see 93-5). In any case they have taken their 'revenge', which consists in not eating any more of the carefully prepared dishes. Thus they deny Nasidienus the satisfaction of playing through to the end his role as host, and this is the most wounding punishment they could have inflicted. Clearing Maecenas and his friends of the hasty departure's rudeness only removes some of our discomfit with the satire.

Horace's own role in the poem may give a clue to his purpose, but, as is usual with an ironist, the picture is not clear-cut. He was absent from a dinner that we might well expect him to have attended (Lejay, 583). This may be intended to absolve him of rudeness to his host and to allow him to put in a critical perspective the description of the events as well as the events themselves. Does he implicitly criticise Fundanius's attitude and expose it as lacking in urbanity (Baker, 225ff.)? Here it is difficult to disentangle the poet/character's moral stance from his literary technique. Ironic distance is typical of the representation of Horace's *persona* in this book, but there is no uniformity in his attitude to his interlocutors. Here he may have literary reasons for interposing another author, the comic poet Fundanius, who shapes the events he describes as a comedy (M. Schmidt, *PhW* 57 [1937], 1071-2) or a farce. In his last satire Horace steps aside almost completely in favour of another writer. We could take this as a compliment to Fundanius and a lesson about the inter-connections between satire and comedy, and between satire as conversation and satire as created from other literary texts (see O'Connor, 24, 32ff.).

If *Sat.* 2.7 is the summarising 'diatribe' satire, *Sat.* 2.8 is the last of the entertainments. Not written explicitly as an epilogue, it still rehearses some of the main topics of the book, linking the food and hospitality theme to the autobiographical relationship with Maecenas theme and portraying yet another failed search for the 'happy life'. The tight symmetrical structure of the book (see Introduction §7) removes the need for a formal epilogue, which is also absent from the *Epodes* and *Odes* Book 4.

The structure of 2.8 follows the pattern of the other dialogue satires in this book. The introductory conversation between Horace and Fundanius (1-19) leads into Fundanius's narrative account of the events of the evening. There is no concluding conversation, however, and the satire ends abruptly with the end of the narrative. Horace intervenes once more, towards the end (79-80), to express his reaction to the comedy (*ludos*) that Fundanius has described. The central narrative is framed by Horace's two interventions (18-19, 79-80), with the first and last sections of almost equal length.

1-19: Horace meets Fundanius, and asks him to describe the dinner party he was at the day before, at Nasidienus's. He replies with details of the food, wine and service, setting the scene for the rest of the account. Such an introduction is part of the symposium tradition, cf. Plato *Symp.*173-4, Lucian *Symp.* 1.

1   **How did you like:** the direct question with *ut* belongs to familiar speech (cf. Hor. *Epist.* 1.3.12), and the verb *iuvare* is particularly appropriate for the enjoyment of food, cf. *Sat.* 2.2.22, *Epod.* 2.49, *non me Lucrina iuverint conchylia.* There is already a hint that food will be more important than philosophy. For the question see Petron. *Sat.* 65.8, 'and he inquired how he had been entertained'.
    rich Nasidienus's: as well as wealth and good fortune *beatus* can imply happiness (see N-H on *Odes* 1.4.14, Lyne 1989, 5-6). This ambiguity (see *Sat.* 2.6.74N), is an important clue for us in establishing our attitude towards Nasidienus (Reinelt, 52ff.). The ironic complicity between Horace and Fundanius shows us that some amusement is bound to come at Nasidienus's expense. *Nasidieni* is scanned 'Nasidjeni'.

2   **they told me** (lit. 'you were said to be'): supply *es* with *dictus*. Cf. *Sat.* 2.5.54. Ellipse of the second person of *esse* in the perfect tense is not as common as that of the third. It may be colloquial (Ruckdeschel, 155). The four occurrences in Virgil's *Aeneid* are in direct speech (1.237, 5.192, 687, 10.827).

3   **carousing ... from midday:** another scene-setting detail. Smart parties which began early were called *convivia tempestiva*, Cic. *Sen.* 46. Their length gave scope for greater luxuriousness, Cic. *Att.* 9.13.6, *cenas ... quam lautas, quam tempestivas, Fam.* 9.16. 8. Contrast Horace's praise of the 'short dinner' in the country, *Epist.* 1.14.35. For the regular dinner time see *Sat.* 2.7.33N.

4   **I never enjoyed myself:** see *Sat.* 2.2.120N. The apparent meaning is that Fundanius enjoyed the food, but later we realise it was the comic spectacle of Nasidienus's discomfiture.
    [**Da:** cf. Virg. *Ecl.* 1.18 (*sed tamen iste deus qui sit, da, Tityre, nobis*), *redde, Sat.* 2.8.80, and *accipe* ('listen'), *Sat.* 2.2.70, 2.3.46 etc. It is not easy to define the tone of *da*. Ruckdeschel, 78 thought it colloquial, Pinotti on Ov. *Rem. Am.* 796 a poetical usage. Perhaps it is a slightly grander or more mannered way of eliciting information (like what you say to an oracle [*OLD* s.v. *do* 27b]). *Da* could only have replaced *dic* through a scribe's reminiscence of the *Eclogue* passage, whereas *dic* could be a gloss on, or subconscious normalisation of, *da.*]

4-5   **if it's not troublesome:** a polite formula (cf. Cic. *Att.*13.31.1, 13.42.1, cf. Lucil. 1118W, Hor. *Epist.* 1.2.5, Hofmann[3] §125). Such phrases occur in the conversations which begin philosophical dialogues, e.g. Cic. *Nat. D.* 1.17, *Ac. Post.* 1.14, *Sen.* 6. Fraenkel 1957, 137 saw a specific parodic allusion to Pl. *Ti.* 17b, 'if it's not troublesome, recapitulate it from the beginning', since Horace's 'first' may pick up Plato's 'from the beginning'. For the whole question see Petron. *Sat.* 66.1, 'Trimalchio said, "What did you have at the dinner"?'

angry belly: is more elevated than the 'barking stomach' of *Sat.* 2.2.18. There may be epic parody here, hinted at by 'Tell me ... first' (see Hom. *Il.* 1.6, Virg. *Aen.* 1.753, *a prima dic, hospes, origine*) and the idea of the appeasement of wrath (Rudd 1966, 220 n.45).

6-9: the *gustatio* (see *Sat.* 2.4.12ff.N). Wine was not served until after this course.

6 **Lucanian boar**: see *Sat.* 2.2.42N, 2.3.234. Boar as part of the *gustatio* indicates a particularly elaborate and luxurious meal, cf. the menu of the pontifical dinner at Macrob. *Sat.* 3.13.12.

gentle Southerly: the wind was warm enough to flavour the meat but not so hot that it would go off quickly, see *Sat.* 2.2.41N. Throughout the dinner Nasidienus seeks to heighten his guests' appreciation of the dishes by revealing their secrets (cf. 43-4) but his comments have the opposite effect (92-3). Trimalchio (e.g. Petron. *Sat.* 40.7) makes similar comments.

7 **father of the feast**: an idiosyncratic circumlocution for 'host', cf. *Sat.* 2.6.88, *pater domus*. *Pater* may hint at his pride in what he is offering and the concern he shows for the meal's success, cf. 58-9. Throughout the satire Horace uses a variety of expressions for the host (see M.A. Gosling, 'By any other name ... Horace, *Sermones* 2.8 and Juvenal 5', *LCM* 11.7 [1986], 101-3 for an analysis of their significance). *Erus* and *dominus* are standard (cf. Varro, *Sat. Men.* 339, *dominus ... convivii*, Cic. *Vatin.* 31, *ipse epuli dominus*), while *parochus* (36) is jocular, and *convivator* (73) occurs first in Horace.

7-8: vegetables were normally served in the *gustatio*, either as appetisers or as an aid to digestion. According to Plut. *Quaest. Conv.* 733F-4A this 'cold course' was originally served after the main meal, cf. *Sat.* 2.2.43, where the full stomach is said to prefer such sharp-flavoured vegetables, and 2.4.58-60.

baby turnips: see *Sat.* 2.2.43N. Andrews, 151 (cited at 9N) suggests *rapulum* may be lamb's lettuce.

lettuce: usually mentioned for its digestive properties. See *Sat.* 2.4.58f.N.

9 **parsnip**: *siser* was a plant cultivated for its piquant root, see *Mor.* 73, Cels. 2.24.2 (*siser* is mentioned with lettuce among vegetables 'most suited to the stomach'), Pliny *HN* 20.34, 'it excites the stomach', André[2], 17-18, n.28. It was particularly liked by the emperor Tiberius, who had a supply sent from Gelduba, on the Rhine (Pliny *HN* 19.90). A.C. Andrews, *CPh* 53 (1958), 145-52 argues for the identification with the parsnip rather than the skirret.

fish-pickle paste ... lees of Coan wine: for the serving of these condiments see *Sat.* 2.4.73N. Here they are mentioned for their pungency, as an aid to digestion, Curtis, 29.

10 **with tunic girt-up high**: see 70, *Sat.* 2.6.107, *ut succinctus ... hospes.* The tunic is tucked up to allow freedom of movement, but 'high' suggests another reason, to show off the attractions of a beautiful boy, cf. Juv. 5.56, Courtney on Juv. 11.146, Sen. *Dial.* 10.12.5, 'how carefully they gird up the tunics of their fancy-boys'. The guests are meant to notice the slaves as they bustle around. On waiters and their tasks see D'Arms in Slater 1991, 171ff.

11ff.: great care is taken to do things properly. Here, as elsewhere, there is a correspondence with Catius's instructions (*Sat.* 2.4.81ff., cf. Petron. *Sat.* 34.3).

11 **rubbed down the maple table**: Horace adapts a line from Lucilius, *purpureo tersit tunc latas gausape mensas* (598W, Book 20). The dinner described by Lucilius was probably that given by Granius (see introduction). The Lucilian allusion may mark this as a 'Lucilian' satire (cf. *Sat.* 1.5), but we do not know if any more pointed connections were being made between the two contexts. Horace changes Lucilius's 'broad tables' to 'the maple table'. Maple was not the most highly esteemed veneering wood (Martial 14.90), but, according to Pliny *HN* 16.66-8, it was not far behind citrus-wood (Rudd 1966, 216,

Meiggs, 291-2). It is unlikely that we are meant to think badly of Nasidienus for having a maple table.

coarse crimson cloth: *gausape* (the word is of foreign origin) was a shaggy woollen cloth used for making blankets (Augustus mentioned his in his will [ap. *Gramm. Lat.* 1.104]) and cloaks. The rich colour is the telling detail; it may be incongruous to use this sort of cloth to wipe tables.

12f.   [*iaceret ... posset*: the subjunctives reflect the instructions of the host, as attributed reasons.]

13-17:   commentators explain that there is an element of tasteless display in the pomp and ceremony of the serving of the wines, and in Nasidienus's offering a variety of wines. Wine was served at this point in the meal, whereas in the old days it had only been served with the dessert (Serv. on Virg. *Aen.* 1. 723).

13f.   **Attic maiden:** in sacrificial processions at Athens, the 'basket-bearers' (*kanêphoroi*) carried on their heads the baskets of offerings. This was one of the most prestigious functions in the procession. The comparison underlines the solemnity of the slave's entrance (cf. *Sat.* 1.3.10-11, Cic. *Off.* 1.131).

14   **Hydaspes:** the slave is named after a landmark in his country of origin (the river in the Punjab now called the Behat). A slave from so far East would have been a luxury. In the dining rooms of the rich prestige was attached to wine waiters, who were expected to be pretty boys, young, long-haired and sexually attractive, see Cic. *Fin.* 2.23, D'Arms in Slater 1991, 173.

15   **Caecuban:** the best Roman wine, from a single vineyard in southern Latium (Pliny *HN* 14.67). Horace elsewhere refers to it as appropriate for special celebrations, e.g. *Epod.* 9.1, 36, *Odes* 1.37.5.

Alcon bearing Chian: a slave with a Greek name brings in the Greek wine. For the celebrated Chian see *Sat.* 2.3.115, *Epod.* 9.34, Pliny *HN* 14.73, Ath. 1.32F.

without sea-water: it was common to mix sea-water with ordinary Greek wines (Plaut. *Rud.* 588, Pliny *HN* 14.73, Galen 10.833K, Ath. 1.33E), but Nasidienus's Chian has *not* had this treatment. The sea-water was a preservative (N-H on *Odes* 1.20.2, 2.5.20), and Nasidienus's Chian is too good to need it. (Columella states that the best wines need no preservative [12.19.2], see also Galen loc. cit.) The phrase could also be translated as 'unmanly', 'emasculate', its probable meaning at Persius 6.39, where it occurs in the same position in the line. (*Maris* comes from *mas, maris* [m.] 'male' or *mare, maris* [n.] 'the sea'.) Housman (*Classical Papers* II 861ff.) argued for the primary meaning 'emasculate' on the grounds that Alcon needs an epithet to balance *fuscus* with *Hydaspes*. Horace must have been aware of the pun.

16f.:   commentators take Nasidienus's offer of a variety of wines as ostentation (cf. Pliny *HN* 14.96-7, Caesar served four different wines together [Falernian, Chian, Lesbian and Mamertine] for the first time at one of his public banquets). Petronius's parvenu host Trimalchio also offers additional wines, *Sat.* 48.1, 'If you don't like the wine, I will change it.' It may show rather a pathetic and misjudged eagerness to please, e.g. Plut. *Quaest. Conv.* 708C, says it is not good form to make enquiries about the tastes and preferences of a prospective guest.

Alban ... or Falernian: the next two best Italic wines after Caecuban, especially before Pliny's day, Pliny *HN* 14. 61-4, Ath. 1.33A. At Juv. 5.33 the host keeps the Alban to himself. Alban, also mentioned at *Odes* 4.11.2, is 'sweet and excellent', second only to Falernian, at Dion. Hal. *Ant. Rom.* 1.66.3. Griffin, 66f. comments interestingly on Horace's knowledge of wines.

pleases you more: this kind of comparison (*magis*) occurs frequently in the talk of food experts, cf. 49, *Sat.* 2.2.29, *Epist.* 1.15.22f., Stat. *Silv.* 4.6.9-10.

18-19:   Horace's comment (*divitias miseras*) could be a reaction to all he has heard so far, or to the last lines in particular. Maecenas's name, casually inserted in Nasidienus's quoted words, prompts Horace to further enquiry about the other guests. This leads into the next section — the guests and the seating arrangements — further conventional symposiastic topics, Luc. *Symp.* 5, cf. Plato *Symp.* 173e, Lucil. 815W.

18   **The sorrows of the rich!:** the translation is that of Shackleton Bailey 1982, 85-6. Horace's ironic comment, which unpacks the ambiguous *beati* (1N) by denying that Nasidienus is happy as well as rich (Reinelt, 54), has been variously interpreted. Shackleton Bailey connects it with Balatro's mocking commiseration in 65ff.: the rich man is made unhappy by worry over which of the excellent wines he has at his disposal might best please his distinguished guest. For another view, taking *miser* as at *Sat.* 2.2.66, see Rudd 1966, 217-8. A *miseri* at Stat. *Silv.* 4.6.8, introducing a passage on futile gastronomic discussion may be a clue. All these views assume that the adjective applied to *divitias* reflects Nasidienus's condition. Bentley, on the other hand, took the phrase as 'poor wealth', i.e. unhappy in having Nasidienus as an owner.
     [**quis:** = *quibus. Quis cenantibus* is abl. abs.]

19   **Fundanius:** a contemporary writer of 'New Comedy', comedy in the style of Menander, cf. *Sat.* 1.10.40-2. The fact that the dinner is narrated by a comic playwright turns it into a comic performance. Fundanius's name neatly precedes his listing of the other guests.
     had a wonderful time: a colloquial expression, which picks up what Fundanius said in 4, adding a note of irony, cf. Catull. 23.5, 27, Cic. *Nat. D.* 1.114, *deum ... 'mihi pulchre est' et 'ego beatus sum' cogitantem*, Ruckdeschel, 115.

20-41:   now that interest has been aroused, Fundanius gives the guests' names and the seating-plan, cf. Cic. *Fam.* 9.26.1, *et quidem supra me Atticus, infra Verrius, familiares tui*, Lucian *Symp.* 6ff., 38. Characterisation of the least important guests shades into descriptions of their behaviour early in the first course. Nomentanus acts for the host, interpreting the meal to the other guests. Vibidius and Balatro, under Maecenas's protection, indulge themselves in the wine, to the host's dismay.

20-3:   Horace cleverly matches the order of the names to the seating order, from 'top' to 'bottom'. Each of the three couches arranged around the table had three places, to make nine in all (Gell. *NA* 13.11.2). Fundanius is first on the 'top' couch, Maecenas last on the middle couch, in the place of honour. The host's normal place was in the adjacent position on the next couch, the first on the 'bottom', but Nasidienus has put Nomentanus here instead, so that he can explain the food to Maecenas. The seating plan displays the status of the guests and the relationships between them, see Plut. *Quaest. Conv.* 616A-B.

20-1:   placed together are the three poets, as guests something of a challenge for Nasidienus (Baker, 220-1). Viscus Thurinus and Varius were literary friends of Horace and Maecenas. Two brothers Visci are mentioned at *Sat.* 1.10.81-6, with Varius and others, as the sort of critics and readers Horace sets store by. The social climber at *Sat.* 1.9.22-3 claims, 'If I know myself well, you will not think more of Viscus as a friend, or Varius.'

20   **Viscus of Thurii:** called *Thurinus* to distinguish him from his brother? Which of the two was the critic addressed in Gallus's epigram to the critics (8) is not known, see R.D. Anderson, P.J. Parsons and R.G.M. Nisbet, *JRS* 69 (1979), 125-155, esp. 143-7.

21   **Varius:** the poet L. Varius Rufus was an influential member of Maecenas's circle, to which he introduced Horace (*Sat.* 1.6.55). At *Sat.* 1.10.43f. his epic poetry is praised, but he also wrote elegiac poetry and a famous tragedy, *Thyestes*. Very little of his work is extant. After Virgil's death, as his literary executor, he disobeyed his instructions to burn the *Aeneid*. With Virgil, he is named as one of Horace's dearest friends (*Sat.* 1.5.40ff.) and most valued critics (at *Sat.* 1.10.81). See further N-H's introduction to *Odes* 1.6, E. Bickel, *SO* 28 (1950), 17-43, W. Wimmel *ANRW* II 30.3 (1983), 1562-1621.

21-2   **Servilius Balatro**: Servilius is scanned 'Serviljus'. The word *balatro* meaning 'jester', 'buffoon' (perhaps as one of a professional class) is attested at Varro, *Rust.* 2.5.1, Hor. *Sat.* 1.2.2. Here it seems to be used as a nickname. He has a certain wit (65ff., 83).

Vibidius: unknown. His main interest is in drinking (33f., 81-2).

extras (lit. 'shadows'): *umbrae* was the Latin term for uninvited guests brought as friends by invited ones (see Plut. *Quaest. Conv.* 707AB). E.g. at *Epist.* 1.5.28 Torquatus has to reply to Horace's invitation specifying how many (within defined limits) extras he will be bringing. Maecenas has brought a couple of *scurrae*, or parasites, whose main function was to amuse their patron (see *Sat.* 2.1.22, 2.7.15N). To have professional entertainers, or parasites, present was in the tradition of the symposium, cf. Xen. *Symp.* 1.11ff., Lucian *Symp.* 17-19, Balsdon, 48.

23   **Nomentanus ... Hogg**: Nasidienus's parasites, see Wiseman 1987, 276 on their different status from Maecenas's. The bottom table was conventionally their place, cf. the description of *imi derisor lecti* at *Epist.* 1.18.10-14. Nomentanus tries to console Nasidienus after the accident (60), as well as taking a leading role in looking after the guests. It is not clear if this Nomentanus should be distinguished (as he often is, presumably so that the names may all refer to living people) from the Nomentanus consistently characterised elsewhere in the *Satires* as a spendthrift (see 2.1.22N). For Rudd 1966, 143, whatever his origin he has become a type figure. Cf. Maenius *Epist.* 1.15.26 (a Lucilian character).

Hogg: his name, Porcius, which belongs to a Roman *gens* (cf. the famous Porcii Catones), and was derived from *porcus* (Varro, *Rust.* 2.1.10), can be taken as a reference to his gluttony. This is his only appearance in the satire.

the master (lit. 'himself'): colloquial for 'the master of the house', Petron. *Sat.* 29.8, Juv. 5.114.

24   **funny trick**: his gluttony was designed to make people laugh, thus combining the two sides of the parasite. Cf. Ath. 7.298E.

[*ridiculus absorbere*: the adjective with an adverbial infinitive is a special feature of Horace's style, e.g. Hor. *Ars P.* 204, L-H-S II 350f., see Wickham I, App. 2, Woodcock §26.]

25   **Nomentanus was there for this**: cf. *Sat.* 2.6.42ff. Why does Nasidienus give Nomentanus this prominent role? It seems that he is afraid that the guests may miss the more *recherché* dishes, and has instructed his hanger-on to draw them to their attention. In this Nomentanus acts as the flattering parasite, echoing his patron (see *Epist.* 1.18.12-14). In the composition of the satire this gives a further touch to the characterisation of Nasidienus (the guests *must* be told), but adds variety by diverting the focus of attention from him for a little while.

26-30:   the details of this passage are disputed, but it seems clear that the dishes are strange in some way, either due to the mode of preparation or to the choice of ingredients.

26   **the rest of the crowd**: an ironic reference to all the other guests, including Maecenas, in contrast to the knowing Nomentanus.

28   **from any familiar to us**: the taste had been changed in the cooking, a favourite Roman practice, cf. Apicius 4.12.4, (*patina de apua sine apua*) *ad mensam nemo agnoscet quid manducet* and B. Flower, 19ff. on 'the Roman passion for disguise of food, both in appearance and taste', Rudd 1966, 218-9. For a different explanation see Shackleton Bailey 1982, 87-8.

29f.   **loin**: fillets from the flank or loin were the choicest part of the boar (Mart. 10.45.4, Juv. 5.136), but the word *ilia* is not found elsewhere of fish. Some have taken it as 'roe', e.g. *TLL* VII.1 325.57ff.

flounder: the *passer* was a flat-fish like turbot and sole (Pliny *HN* 9.72).

turbot: see *Sat*. 2.2.42N.

had not tasted: *ingustata* is a word coined by Horace (cf. Greek *ageustos*), meaning either 'which I had never tasted before' or 'which I had not yet tasted (on this occasion)'.

31f. **After this he told me:** Nomentanus is showing off expert knowledge. Apples belong to the dessert, a later stage in the dinner. They could be mentioned without being on the table at this point, but K-H infer from this line that the guests stayed to the end of the meal, see 93N.

honey-apples: a type of apple, said to be quick-ripening and to have a honey taste, probably to be identified as the early ripening 'summer-apple', the Greek *melimelon*, Diosc. 1.115, Varro *Rust*. 1.59.1, Pliny *HN* 15.51. Nomentanus shows off his knowledge by referring to a type.

moon is less than full: this is taken variously as the new moon and the waning moon. Behind this precept is a large body of superstition about the moon's effect on vegetation, often connected with the idea that growth of plants was nourished by dew, thought to be moisture sent down by the moon, Virg. *G*. 3.337, Pease on Cic. *Div*. 2.33, *Nat. D*. 2.50. It was therefore considered important to time agricultural operations according to moist or dry phases of the moon, e.g. fruit for storing should be picked when the moon is waning in order that it contain as little moisture as possible, cf. Varro, *Rust*. 1.37.1, Pliny *HN* 15.59, 62, Columella, *Rust*. 12.19.3 (grapes). On the other hand, 'apples are said to "shrump up" [wither] in Devonshire if picked when the moon is waning', T. Harley, *Moon Lore* (London, 1885), 197-80, cf. D. Kuijper, *Mnemosyne* 19 (1966), 38-41, arguing that the moisture and warmth needed for the apples to ripen are provided in the early phases of the moon. *Ad lunam* usually means 'by moonlight', cf. Virg. *Aen*. 4 523, and we could take it this way here if we think Horace is poking fun. Otherwise, the *ad* in *ad lunam* means 'at the time of', cf. *ad ver*, Cato *Agr*. 105.2.

33 [*audieris*: fut. perf. see *Sat*. 2.4.27N.]

34 **drink him bankrupt:** Palmer's translation. *Damnose* is found only here in Classical Latin.
we'll die unavenged: cf. 93, 'taking our revenge'. The declaration of war is humorously couched in parodic quotation of an epic or tragic catch-phrase, possibly from Ennius (Norden on Virg. *Aen*. 6.370 n.1), and later used by Virgil *Aen*. 2.670 (Aeneas), 4.659 (Dido) etc. The epic language reminds us of the 'wars' which could break out at parties, cf. *Odes* 1.27.1-8.

35f. **larger cups:** were normally brought in when the symposium was well advanced, so that more wine could be drunk, Eur. *Ion* 1178ff., Plato *Symp*.223c, Hor. *Epodes* 9.33, Petron. *Sat*. 65.8, Fraenkel 1957, 73 and n.1. At a formal symposium wine was mixed according to prescribed proportions and healths were drunk (*Odes* 3.19.11). The *scurrae* show disrespect for the host by overriding his arrangements, and wishing to start serious drinking before the main course is over, in order to put an end to the talk about food.
Pallor then transformed: Nasidienus's reaction is depicted in epic style, cf. Hom. *Il*. 7.479, *Od*. 11.43, Virg. *Aen*. 4.449, Juv. 1.43. He takes seriously the jocular threat, which he sees as a danger to his careful planning, rather than to his purse (Rudd 1966, 219).
caterer: *parochus* was the technical name for the person responsible for providing the essential supplies for travellers on official business (cf. *Sat*. 1.5.46, Cic. *Att*. 5.16.3, and, another joke, *Att*. 13.2a.2). It suggests that the guests see him only in this light.

37-8: there is no reason to question these motives attributed to Nasidienus, as commentators have done in the past.

37 **slander:** wine proverbially loosens the tongue, cf. *Sat*. 1.4.86-9.

39: an unusually short spondaic line expresses the effort put into drinking, the scale of the words illustrating the size of the cups and the draughts (Nilsson, 81f.). Epic parody?, cf. Virg. *Aen*. 9.165, *indulgent vino et vertunt crateras aenos*.

Allifanian cups: from Allifae (Castello d'Alife) on the border of Samnium and Campania. According to Salmon, 71, 126n. the ware manufactured there was 'pottery of a very common sort'. Perhaps such cups were known to be large. Cf. Cic. *Pis.* 67. [*Allifanis*: dative of the neuter.]

40-1: the guests on the bottom couch, Nomentanus and Porcius, are on either side of the host and would not dare to offend him by going against his wishes (cf. *Epist.* 1.18.11, *sic nutum divitis horret*).

flagons: *lagoena*, cf. 81, a word borrowed from Greek. See *Sat.* 2.3.273N.

42-53: the *pièce de résistance* is served. Nasidienus describes it proudly, and at length. The hints already given about his personal supervision of the preparations are confirmed. Note his desire to be regarded as a culinary expert, when he gives recipe for the sauce (cf. *Sat.* 2.4.63ff.), pointing out that he has used the best of everything, and indicating his own innovation, as well as that of one of his fellows. Nasidienus's quoted speech brings him centre stage and sets the scene for the accident, an unanticipated climax that destroys the effect he has carefully prepared.

42-4: in a luxurious meal fish was the most expensive item, *Sat.* 2.2.34N, 2.4.37-9, 76-7, Juv. 5.80-106. Nasidienus has not committed the crime of serving it in a dish that is too small or that of taking no thought for the sauce. His practice conforms to Catius's precepts.

moray eel: *muraena helena*, a marine eel, purplish-brown mottled with yellow markings, sometimes confused with the lamprey, cf. Pliny *HN* 9.169 (the best came from the Straits of Messina), Juv. 5.99 (the mean host is served the *murena*), Archestratus ap. Ath. 7. 313A, *RE* XVI.I 652ff., D'Arcy Thompson 1947, 162ff., André[2], 100. At the end of the Republic they were, with the mullet, the most fashionable fish for luxurious banquets. Apicius gives a variety of sauces for them boiled or grilled (10.2.1-6). These creatures were popular not only for eating but also as pets kept in fish-ponds (Pliny *HN* 9.170-2).

pregnant: i.e. containing the roe. Pliny, *HN* 9.76, says it may spawn in any month, and, in fact, it dies after spawning. It is important for the gourmet to know the time when and conditions under which the flesh is best, 6-7, *Sat.* 2.4.30, 45. [*futura*: this use of the future participle to add a hypothetical clause is not found before Horace, cf. *Odes* 2.3.4, L-H-S II 390.]

45-6 **oil**: cf. *Sat.* 2.4.69N, the first pressing gives the best oil (Columella, *Rust.* 12.52.11). Note the elaborate periphrasis, as at 49f., here perhaps standing for the Greek compound *ômotribes* (Rudd 1986, 175).

46 **fish-sauce**: recipes for *garum* may be found in *Geoponica* 20.46 (see Flower, 21-3). Used in Roman cooking as we would use salt, it consisted of the liquid strained off from fish offal saturated in salt and left to ferment, and added an 'exquisite taste to food' (Pliny *HN* 31.88), Curtis, 6ff. Pliny *HN* 31.93-4 confirms that the best is from Spanish mackerel, but Horace is the earliest author to mention Spanish *garum* specifically, cf. Strabo 3.2.6, Curtis, 58f. It was similar to the fermented fish-sauces extensively used in South-East Asian cookery, e.g. the Vietnamese 'nuoc-nam', see Curtis, 19ff., T.H. Corcoran, *CJ* 58 (1963), 204-10.

47 **this side of the sea**: i.e. not imported from Greece, in contrast to the Chian.

49 **white pepper**: *Sat.* 2.4.74N. At this period pepper was still a luxury, J. Innes Miller, *The Spice Trade of the Roman Empire* (Oxford, 1969), 80ff.

49f. **vinegar ... through spoiling**: cf. *Sat.* 2.2.58, *mutatum ... vinum*, Macrob. *Sat.* 7.6.12, *acetum culpatum vinum est*. Vinegar was made by allowing wine to ferment. **Methymnean**: the adjective identifies Nasidienus's vinegar as the best, since Lesbian is often mentioned with Chian as a favourite Greek import, cf. *Odes* 1.17.21.

51-2 **I first taught**: cf. the claim to have introduced a new practice at *Sat.* 2.4.74N. For *monstro* used of transmitting technical knowledge see *Ars P.* 74, Lucr. 5.1106, Mynors on Virg. *G.*

1.19. Comparison with sauces in Apicius shows that a sauce's individuality came from the choice of herbs, but Nasidienus's innovation hardly deserves the status of an 'invention' and now the self-important didactic manner is out of place. The whole speech displays the gourmet host's obsessive desire to produce something unique to his own table.

rocket: a pungently flavoured salad herb, *Moret.* 84, Pliny *HN* 19.154, 20.126-7, Apicius 6.2.6, 7.14.3, 9.10.7, André², 202 n.62.

bitter elecampane: *Sat.* 2.2.44N.

Curtillus: unknown.

unwashed: so that their flavour is not diluted.

53   **ut melius:** 'as (being) better', that is the practice of adding them unwashed. [*quod=id quod.*]

fish-brine: the commercial product is meant, *Sat.* 2.4.65N.

54-78:   the accident occurs before the guests have had a chance to taste the dish. Nasidienus breaks down completely. The incident is used to display aspects of his character. He takes it as a real tragedy, and is impervious to the irony in Balatro's commiserations. Nomentanus consoles his friend with some banal remarks on Fortune, while the other guests laugh or mock. Something similar occurs in Petronius *Sat.* 53-5, a mishap (an acrobat's fall), followed by Trimalchio's epigram on Fortune. Petronius need not be imitating Horace (Smith on Petron. *Sat.* 54.1), but see J. Révay, *CPh* 17 (1922), 202-12, M.T. Rodriguez, *Atti dell. Acc. Pel. dei Pericolanti* 57 (1981), 267-80.

54   **tapestries:** luxurious furnishings, probably wall-hangings rather than a canopy (Marquardt I, 310ff.), cf. *Odes* 3.29.15, Virg. *Aen.* 1.697, Val. Max. 9.1.5, *Attalicis aulaeis contectus parietes.* See also G.M.A. Richter, *Furniture of the Greeks and Romans* (London, 1966), fig. 601 (the Ikarios relief).

54-6:   the style has general epic colouring, and the simile is epic, with the dust recalling that of battle-scenes, cf. Hom. *Il.* 11.151f., Enn. *Ann.* 264Sk., Virg. *Aen.* 11.876f.

57   **worse:** i.e. a structural collapse.

58f.   **Rufus:** it is odd that Nasidienus, if fictitious, has the same *cognomen* as Varius.

as if his son ...: Nasidienus's folly is shown in his lack of a true sense of values. There may also be some connection with his description as *cenae pater* (7) in that the dinner is cut off before it has reached fulfilment. There is a touch of poetic pathos in the word *immaturus*.

60   **in philosophical vein:** *sapiens* is ironic in that Nomentanus's wisdom is banal, as his flattery adept.

61-3:   Nomentanus knows what to say. His consolation elevates the accident to a sphere of general significance, thus confirming Nasidienus's own estimate of its importance.

Alas: *heu* occurs only here in the *Satires*. He pretends to sympathise with Nasidienus's feelings, but mocks them by exaggeration.

Fortune: 'cruel' fortune is found elsewhere in poetry only at *Ciris* 313 (see Lyne ad loc.), Petron. *Sat.* 114.8.

sport: Fortune's sport is often alluded to, cf. *Odes* 3.29.49f., *Fortuna saevo laeta negotio et/ludum insolentem ludere pertinax,* N-H on *Odes* 2.1.3, Juv. 3.40, Petron. *Sat.* 55.3.

64   **turns up his nose at everything** (lit. 'hung everything from his nose'): a comic expression invented by Horace, cf. *Sat.* 1.6.5 (Maecenas does not), Pers. 1.118 (Horace), Lilja 1972, 212. Balatro is the kind of *scurra* who is always witty at others' expense, cf. *Sat.* 1.4.34-5.

65-74:   Balatro expresses ironic commiseration for Nasidienus's troubles. He begins and ends with some general moralising, which, like Nomentanus's, offers a universal interpretation of the accident. In the central section he pretends to show understanding of the host's worries and desire to ensure that everything is done well, cf. Hor. *Epist.* 1.5.21ff., Juv. 14.59-67 with Courtney, Sen. *Dial.* 10.12.5. See also Catius's instructions on cleanliness at *Sat.* 2.4.78ff., and, for a description of what is to be avoided, Cic. *Pis.* 67, Rudd 1966, 220.

66   **fame**: reputation as an elegant host, e.g. Sen. loc.cit. (at 65-74N), *ex his elegantiae lautitiaeque fama captatur.*

67   [*tene ... torquerier*: for the exclamatory acc. and inf., see *Sat.* 2.4.83N.]

67ff.: Balatro dares to say to Nasidienus's face what other parasites boast of behind their patron's back, e.g. Ter. *Phorm.* 339ff., 'You contribute nothing, but come to dinner washed and scented after a bath without a care in the world while he is harrassed by worry and expense. Everything is done for your pleasure while he can only grin and bear it, you're the one who smiles, takes first seat and first drink.' (Trans. Radice) See Sen. *Dial.* loc.cit. (at 65-74N).

67   **grandly**: or 'splendidly' implies brilliance and sumptuousness. *Laute* (not used elsewhere in Horace) belongs to familiar speech, Nep. *Chabr.* 3.2, cf. Pers. 6.23 (*lautus*).
       tormented: cf. Juv. 14.64, *ergo miser trepidas.*

70   **be girt-up and coiffed correctly**: i.e. in the latest fashion, see Sen. loc.cit. (at 65-74N) and the description of elaborate hairdos and intricately arranged tunics at Philo, *On the Contemplative Life* 50-3 (II 479 Mang.) — a description of luxurious banquets.

72   **stable-boy**: *agaso* is the usual term for a groom (Enn. *Ann.* 427Sk). Is 'stable-boy' meant literally or is it a term of abuse? Cf. Pers. 5.76, also ambiguous. The parallels at Juv. 5.52, where a groom waits on the poor client, and Lucian *Symp.* 15, show that such slaves could be brought in as waiters. The clumsy waiter may be a dinner-party topos, cf. Petron. *Sat.* 52.4-6.

73-4   **the host's genius ...:** a maxim, with carefully balanced word order underlining the paradox, cf. Lucr. 3.55-6, where Kenney quotes Eur. fr. 237N^2, 'it is trouble that makes it possible to achieve reputation'. For a military application see Livy 28.12.2 (Hannibal), 'it is unclear whether he was more wonderful in adversity or good fortune'. A *mot* of Aemilius Paulus claimed that the general and the host required the same spirit (Plut. *Aem.* 28.5, see also Plut. *Quaest. Conv.* 615F). Nasidienus does not discern the mocking flattery in the comparison to a general, for he thinks Balatro takes him as seriously as he takes himself.
       host: *convivator* is rare and found first here. Balatro plays up to Nasidienus' self-importance by using an official-sounding term.

75-6   **May the gods...:** Nasidienus's thanks show his naivety. In what he says we recognise a common expression of thanks, more elaborately phrased, e.g. Plaut. *Stich.* 469, *bene atque amice dicis. Di dent quae velis!*, *Mil.* 1038 etc.
       [*preceris*: the subjunctive is regular in such expressions, see W. M. Lindsay, *Syntax of Plautus* (Oxford, 1907, reprinted 1936), 66f.]
       [*ita*: introduces a paratactic remark which gives the reason for the preceding wish, cf. Plaut. *Men.* 596, *Di illum omnes perdant, ita mihi/hunc hodie corrumpit diem.*]

77   **slippers**: this shows that he intends to leave the table, for the slippers were removed on reclining for the meal, cf. Hor. *Epist.* 1.13.15, Plaut. *Truc.* 363f., *cedo soleas mihi, properate, auferte mensam*, 367, 479, Gell. *NA* 13.22.5. Again see Richter (cited at 54N), fig. 601. It was not done to wear them in public, Petron. *Sat.* 27.2.
       [*videres*: potential subjunctive, see Woodcock §121]

77-8:   as was noticed by the ancient commentators, the alliteration of 's' 'paints' the sounds of the whispering. On sibilants see Wilkinson 1985, 13-15.

79-80:   the 'interval' caused by Nasidienus's retreat provides a natural opportunity for Horace's question.
       watch no other shows: with the reference to laughter in the following line, this comment shows that we are meant to recognise the events described as a 'comedy', an entertainment, cf. Plaut. *Cas.* 760, *neque (credo) usquam ludos tam festivos fieri quam hic.*
       [*deinceps*: spondaic.]

80-95: in the final scene Vibidius and Balatro continue to make their presence felt. In Nasidienus's absence Vibidius complains about a break in the supply of wine, and Balatro feeds the other guests' laughter. Nasidienus returns, followed by a series of new dishes, but unable to endure his commentary upon them, the guests eat nothing more, and leave abruptly.

80-82: note the contrast with 13-17.

82 cups: i.e. 'drinks', cf. *Sat.* 2.6.69-70.

83 [*fictis rerum*: cf. *vanis rerum*, *Sat.* 2.2.25, *Ars P.* 49, *abdita rerum*. *Fictis* is dative, a rare use with *rideo*, cf. Pers. 3.86.]

with the Buffoon egging us on: *secundo* is either a metaphor from wind driving a ship (Hor. *Epist.* 2.2.201), or modelled on such phrases as *Iunone secunda*, Virg. *Aen.* 4.45. In either case there is a hint of epic style.

84f. Nasidienus, you ...: the apostrophe is another epic touch, the mock solemnity marking the drama of the moment, e.g. Hom. *Il.* 4.127, Rudd 1966, 220.

[*mutatae frontis*: the use of the genitive of description with *redis* is an extension of its common use with *sum*, cf. *Sat.* 1.4.17-18. The genitive of description is used of external characteristics in poetry and post-Augustan prose, Woodcock §85.III.]

to set bad luck right: this has a proverbial ring (Otto, 38), cf. Ter. *Ad.* 741, *illud quod cecidit forte, id arte ut corrigas* (a comparison of life to a game of dice).

86 trencher: *mazonomos* is the Latin transcription of a Greek word for a wooden trencher, originally used for serving barley-cakes (Pollux 6.87), but by the Romans to serve fowl (Varro, *Rust.* 3.4.3).

87ff.: the pedantic detail of the description of the dishes is an echo of Nasidienus's commentary upon them, cf. 6ff, 92-3.

87 male crane: *grus* is commonly feminine, as *anser* (88) is masculine. We are to imagine Nasidienus pointing out the birds' sex as of gastronomic significance. At this time stork was more popular than crane, but crane returned to favour later. Hence Nasidienus may be setting a trend, see *So:* 2.2.49N, Varro, *Rust.* 3.2.14, Hor. *Epod.* 2.35, Stat. *Silv.* 4.6.8-9, Apicius 6.2.1-6, André[2], 120-1.

88 white goose: the colour of goose defines it as the best domesticated kind, Columella, *Rust.* 8.14.3, 'take care to choose geese of white colour', Stat. *Silv.* 4.6.9-10, 'which goose ...'

liver: geese force-fed on figs to produce *paté de foie gras*, a luxury highly prized by the Romans, Ath. 9.384C, Pliny *HN* 10.52, Juv. 5.114, André[2], 129f.

89 hare's wings: thought to be the best part, see *Sat.* 2.4.44.

90f. [*edit*: the old optative used as subjunctive, cf. *Epod.* 3.3, where it has archaic, legal tone.]

90-1: blackbirds: as in southern Europe today (E. Romer, *The Tuscan Year* [London, 1984], 120, blackbirds and thrushes), a variety of songbirds were eaten in antiquity, cf. *Sat.* 2.3.245 (nightingales), Varro, *Rust.* 3.5.1, 14, Ath. 2.65D-E (with other birds), André[2], 125.

with burnt breast: this must mean 'crisped' not 'spoilt', to avoid a contradiction with 'delicious things'.

wood-pigeons: cf. André[2], 121, Apicius 6.4.1-4.

without the rump: if we take *suavis res* ('delicious things') at face value, the implication is that Nasidienus did not prize the rump, though others did, Sen. *Ep.* 47.6, Martial 3.60.7, Gell. *NA* 15.8.2.

delicious things: an ironic echo of Nasidienus's 'more delicious'.

92f. origins and natures: cf. *Sat.* 2.4.35-6, 45-6. The terms *causas* and *naturas* suggest scientific-philosophic research, e.g. Lucr. 1.949f., 4.500 etc., Virg. *G.* 2.490. Stat. *Silv.* 4.6.8-11 mocks similar gastronomic investigations in a list of indirect questions (introduced by 'how', 'which', 'why', 'where?') typical of the scientific-philosophic didactic approach, e.g., Virg. *Aen.* 1.742ff., Hor. *Epist.* 1.12.16-24. Again Nasidienus's fault is to have imported the lecture into the dining room in his anxiety to have his culinary triumphs recognised.

-5   **fled:** it is usually assumed that the guests left in a rush, but some critics argue that we should not suppose that they left rudely while the meal was still in progress but that they stayed to see but not to taste the rest of the meal (K-H ad loc., Shackleton Bailey 1982, 88, Rudd 1986, 137 n.7). The abrupt ending has been criticised by Rudd 1966, 222 as 'structurally the weakest in the book', but Shackleton Bailey loc. cit. justifies it as characteristic of narrative satire, cf. Seneca's *Apocolocyntosis*. Farce also ended without a resolution, Cic. *Cael.* 65, *mimi ergo exitus, non fabulae; in quo cum clausula non invenitur, fugit aliquis e manibus, dein scabilla concrepant, aulaea tollitur.* The poem ends with the end of Fundanius's account, without a return to the opening conversation, and so without an opportunity for an authorial summing-up. This open ending is the main reason for the satire's moral ambivalence.

5   **Canidia:** the witch of *Epodes* 5 and 17, and *Sat.* 1.8, mentioned as a poisoner at *Sat.* 2.1.48N. Her name appears here unexpectedly as a kind of satiric signature (cf. the hits at Crispinus and Fabius at *Sat.* 1.1.120, 2.134), making a structural link with Book I (*Sat.* 1.8, Fraenkel 1957, 148) and the last *Epode* (R.W. Carrubba, *The Epodes of Horace A Study in Poetic Arrangement* [The Hague/Paris, 1969], 42-3). Important too is the jocular connection between Canidia and bad food, established in an *Epode* addressed to Maecenas (3.7-8); Fundanius is repeating an in-joke (Baker, 231).

breathed poison: snake breath was regarded as so foul as to be poisonous, Columella, *Rust.* 8.5.18.

African snakes: particularly fierce, cf. *Odes* 3.10.18.

Index

CLASSICAL TEXTS

Editorial Advisor: Professor M.M. Willcock (London)

Published volumes